The Cult of We

The Cult of We

WEWORK, ADAM NEUMANN, AND THE GREAT STARTUP DELUSION

Eliot Brown AND Maureen Farrell

CROWN
NEW YORK

Published in the United States by CROWN, an imprint of Random House, a division of Penguin Random House LLC, New York.

CROWN and the CROWN colophon are registered trademarks of Penguin Random House LLC.

Hardback ISBN 978-0-593-23711-3
International Edition ISBN 978-0-593-23975-9
Ebook ISBN 978-0-593-23712-0

PRINTED IN CANADA ON ACID-FREE PAPER

crownpublishing.com

2 4 6 8 9 7 5 3 1

First Edition

For Dad, Mom, and Nick
—Eliot

For Jason, Cecilia, and Annabel
—Maureen

Built into the speculative episode is the euphoria, the mass escape from reality, that excludes any serious contemplation of the true nature of what is taking place.

—JOHN KENNETH GALBRAITH, *A Short History of Financial Euphoria*

CONTENTS

Authors' Note   xi

PROLOGUE: The Summit   3

PART I

CHAPTER 1:   The Hustler   13
CHAPTER 2:   Greenhorns   20
CHAPTER 3:   Famous Energy   27
CHAPTER 4:   Physical Facebook   32
CHAPTER 5:   Manufacturing Community   38

PART II

CHAPTER 6:   The Cult of the Founder   51
CHAPTER 7:   Activate the Space   63
CHAPTER 8:   Me Over We   71
CHAPTER 9:   Mutual Fund FOMO   77
CHAPTER 10: Bubbling Over   90
CHAPTER 11: Catnip for Millennials   105
CHAPTER 12: Banking Bros   117
CHAPTER 13: Taking Over the World   125

PART III

CHAPTER 14: Friends in High Places 137

CHAPTER 15: It's Tricky 150

CHAPTER 16: One Billion Dollars per Minute 157

CHAPTER 17: Neumann & Son 166

CHAPTER 18: Crazy Train 171

CHAPTER 19: Revenue, Multiple, Valuation 180

CHAPTER 20: Community-Adjusted Profit 192

CHAPTER 21: Adam's ARK 201

CHAPTER 22: The $3 Trillion Triangle 207

CHAPTER 23: Summer Camp 217

CHAPTER 24: Shoes Off, Souls Inside 224

CHAPTER 25: Flying High 234

CHAPTER 26: Both Mark and Sheryl 250

CHAPTER 27: Broken Fortitude 260

PART IV

CHAPTER 28: Diseconomies of Scale 273

CHAPTER 29: Guitar House 283

CHAPTER 30: The Plunge Before the Plunge 293

CHAPTER 31: To the Energy of We 305

CHAPTER 32: Twenty to One 314

CHAPTER 33: WeWTF: The S-1 Sh*t Show 324

CHAPTER 34: A Setting Son 330

CHAPTER 35: Paranoia 336

CHAPTER 36: The Fall of Adam 346

CHAPTER 37: DeNeumannization 362

CHAPTER 38: Bread of Shame 369

Epilogue 383

Acknowledgments 399

Notes 403

Index 433

THE IMPLOSION OF WEWORK IN SEPTEMBER 2019 WAS AN AS-
tounding moment in business. Nearly $40 billion in value on
paper vanished, virtually overnight, as the investment world woke
up to the reality that America's most valuable startup wasn't a tech
company but simply a real estate company—one that was losing
more than $1.6 billion a year. Its charismatic, hard-partying CEO,
once lionized as the archetype of the modern-day "visionary"
startup founder, suddenly became a target for criticism, particularly
for his self-enrichment. In the wake of the company's sudden unraveling, investors lost money, and employees lost their jobs; the
CEO left rich.

As reporters covering the saga for *The Wall Street Journal,* we had
seats at the forefront of this downfall, chronicling the company as it
buckled, and unearthing new details that became part of the story
of its collapse. Still, despite an extensive reporting effort at the time,
we were left with countless key questions unanswered.

At the story's heart was a simple mystery. *How did this happen?*
Why did some of the world's top investors and bankers fall under
the spell of this company? How did capitalism contort to view
something so inherently simple—a company leasing real estate—as
a disruptive tech startup valued higher than Fortune 500 companies
like FedEx and Target? Was the WeWork story an outlier, or was it

simply the most vivid example of a cultural rot that had formed within twenty-first-century entrepreneurial and investment culture?

In these pages, we attempt to answer these questions. While much was clear in public view—WeWork's CEO, Adam Neumann, raised too much money, set expectations too high, partied too hard, and, ultimately, flew far too close to the sun—a more complex tale lay in the underlying infrastructure that enabled the office subleasing company's rise and fall. WeWork's money trail led to the country's top banks, to a Middle Eastern monarchy eager to transform its economy, to mutual funds hungry to get a piece of the Silicon Valley action. The trail led to an eccentric and insecure Tokyo tycoon who yearned to be taken seriously by the American technology elite. There was a whole system thirsting to believe in the vision of a messianic and charismatic founder and the profits he could seemingly deliver. It's a story about the toxic brew of confirmation bias, fuzzy math, and hubris. It's a story about what people will do when they are allowed to spend other people's money with minimal oversight.

Our portrait of the WeWork saga draws on interviews with more than three hundred individuals who have shared their time, knowledge, experiences, and materials. It includes interviews with former and current WeWork executives, staff, and board members; SoftBank staff; bankers, advisers, investors, landlords, rivals, friends and family members of the Neumanns; SoftBank CEO Masayoshi Son; and numerous others. The vast majority of these people spoke on the condition that we would not reveal their identities as sources, with many citing nondisclosure agreements they signed with WeWork or other parties involved.

Neumann declined to sit for an interview for this book. Still, he was presented with the facts about him we intended to include, and through a representative, he provided feedback on a portion of those facts, which informed our writing.

Throughout the book, we refer to people by their surnames on second reference. To avoid confusion over Adam and Rebekah

Neumann when they are mentioned in close proximity, we refer to her as Rebekah.

While many of these interviews were conducted in 2020, after WeWork's fall, this book is also the product of years of reporting for *The Wall Street Journal.* Eliot Brown covered WeWork first as a real estate reporter and then as a venture capital and startup reporter based in San Francisco, following the company as it came to embody the age of monstrous startups with enormous losses. Maureen Farrell watched its swift and unusual rise while covering IPOs and capital markets for the *Journal* in New York.

After Brown first met Adam Neumann in 2013, the company made Neumann available for a handful of meetings, and it also made other senior executives available for numerous on-the-record interviews over the years. The book's endnotes detail the information obtained from those interviews, as well as facts drawn from others who agreed to speak on the record for this book.

Throughout the book, we've carefully reconstructed scenes and incorporated dialogue. A reader should not assume that a person quoted in a scene has spoken to us. We also have drawn on an extensive array of internal documents at WeWork, including board minutes, investor slide shows, financial presentations, contracts, tape and video recordings, emails, and photographs.

Every detail and conversation in this book has also been subjected to fact-checking, and throughout we have followed a cardinal rule we've learned as *Wall Street Journal* reporters: "no surprises." The key people in this book have been made aware—and given an opportunity to comment on—the revelations contained in these pages.

We owe a huge debt of gratitude to our sources, who in many cases have given us hours upon hours of their time, painstakingly walking us through their memories of these events. Without them, telling this story—which we believe is a vital parable of the twenty-first-century economy—would not have been possible.

—*Eliot Brown and Maureen Farrell*

The Cult of We

The Summit

THE CROWD FILLING THE MICROSOFT THEATER IN DOWN-
town Los Angeles buzzed with anticipation. Technicians in
the control room readied cameras and then unleashed a kaleidoscopic array of spotlights that lit up the theater—the same one used
for the Emmys. The roughly five thousand attendees began to rise
from their seats, cheering and clapping their hands to the beat of a
pulsating pop song.

Adam Neumann emerged.

Wearing a light blue button-down shirt with sleeves rolled up,
black pants, and white sneakers, the high-octane thirty-nine-year-
old jumped up and down with his hands outstretched, beckoning
people to continue clapping. The crowd erupted. Some of the
eight cameras that sprang into action put his face up on a giant
screen behind him. If strangers had stumbled into the auditorium,
they could be forgiven for mistaking Neumann for a talent show
contestant, or perhaps a televangelist. He walked toward center
stage pumping his fist.

It was January 8, 2019, and most of the youthful crowd was the
staff of WeWork, the massive office space startup Neumann had co-
founded nine years earlier. Neumann, six feet five with a mop of
shoulder-length dark brown hair, had summoned most of the company's employees from around the world for a three-day confab

called Global Summit. New recruits and veteran executives alike were tasked with soaking up a cascade of presentations extolling the company's virtues and its extraordinary growth. How WeWork was about people taking part in "something greater than themselves," as the company's Israel-born co-founder often preached. How We-Work rental office space was about "making a life, not just a living." How they were *making the world a better place.*

In standard parlance, it was a corporate retreat. But Neumann didn't like to do things like other companies, even other startups. WeWork needed to be *more.* Everything had to be extreme—startup culture turned up to 11. This was a company that boasted free beer on tap in its offices and piped booming pop music into its avant-garde bathroom stalls. The Los Angeles summit was just one of two epic getaways held each year—the other being a music-fest-like event called Summer Camp. Five months earlier, WeWork had flown its global staff to the U.K., busing them to a giant field an hour and a half outside London for a long weekend of inspirational corporatespeak, capture the flag, and late-night dance parties.

The company wasn't cutting any corners with its Los Angeles fete either. A day earlier, WeWork employees converged on Los Angeles International Airport, most of them traveling from the company's New York headquarters. A caravan of coach buses shuttled the staffers east from LAX to downtown, where they filled thousands of rooms across nineteen separate hotels. To WeWork employees, it felt as if they occupied the whole downtown; you couldn't walk outside without seeing someone wearing WeWork swag or a summit-sanctioned yoga class in an outdoor plaza.

The week ahead would bring a trip to Universal Studios, the entirety of which WeWork rented for a night, including the rides. Booze flowed freely, and a band played at a central square. Inebriated staffers soared around Hogwarts Castle on one of the Harry Potter rides.

Through the days, dull presentations on WeWork's finances were broken up with lighter fare. Ashton Kutcher judged a mini awards show for promising small startups; a blizzard of confetti fell on the winner. Celebrities like P. Diddy and Jaden Smith popped by to watch or speak on panels. A Red Hot Chili Peppers concert served as the coda to one day of programming. Neumann's wife, Rebekah, interviewed the lead singer, Anthony Kiedis, onstage. Their conversation hit on topics that included spirituality, addiction, pain, soul mates, and breast milk. During the show, Neumann danced in the front row and got into a tussle with security guards concerned with overcrowding.

It all cost roughly $10 million.

At other companies, the event and its price tag might have been seen as an extravagance. The CEO's judgment and fiscal responsibility might have been questioned. But WeWork wasn't concerned. After nearly a decade in business, the company wasn't profitable—or anywhere close. It was losing more than $3,000 a minute, on average, and had lost more than $1.6 billion the prior year. But Uber, Airbnb, and the mattress website Casper were all unprofitable. Losses were par for the course for buzzy Silicon Valley companies.

Startups didn't always grow and spend like this. But a decade-long deluge of money into Silicon Valley had established new cultural norms. Excess was in. For investors, it was the cost of doing business. The world was changing; entrepreneurs with giant vision needed room to grow and express themselves, they said. Rapid expansion was the goal, and these companies had plenty of that. They were building the future of the economy, and surely that future would bring profits.

Or so they hoped.

FAWNED OVER BY A STAR-STUDDED ROSTER OF INVESTORS, NEU-mann had managed to collect more than $10 billion over nine years, one of the largest investment hauls ever for a U.S. startup. Finance giants like Fidelity, T. Rowe Price, and Wellington were investors. Jack Ma, the founder of Alibaba; Steve Cohen, the hedge fund giant; Harvard University—they all had bet on Neumann. Wall Street was even more enamored: the CEOs of both JPMorgan and Goldman Sachs lavished him with attention. And Masayoshi Son, chairman of the Tokyo-based SoftBank Group and the most prolific tech investor in the entire world, had taken a particular shine to him, anointing Neumann the planet's next great tech CEO. Admirers compared Neumann to Jeff Bezos or Steve Jobs—a business titan who could see around corners and would chart a revolutionary course.

The fund-raising conveyor belt had provided Neumann with the money not only for extravagant parties but also for constant, rapid expansion. By the beginning of 2019, WeWork had grown enormous, with 425 locations in twenty-seven countries around the globe. Its work spaces, with their instantly recognizable bluish glass-walled offices and common areas that looked like Brooklyn coffee shops, were rented to more than 400,000 people. Amazon, Facebook, and Microsoft were snapping up space from WeWork to house their own employees. Neumann's obsession was doubling revenue every single year, a breakneck pace of growth that was far faster than the software companies to which Neumann liked to compare WeWork. It was faster than Uber. Faster than Airbnb. Even faster than Amazon nearly a decade after its founding. WeWork was going to grow bigger than all of them, he believed.

His own lifestyle mirrored his rising brand. A few weeks earlier, he'd taken the company's private jet to Kauai, where he hit the waves with the surf legend Laird Hamilton. Neumann now pegged his personal net worth at $10 billion. He had seven homes, and a trail of support staff followed him everywhere, including a hairdresser and a stylist who had flown from New York to Los Angeles especially for the summit. He even stayed in a different hotel from the rest of the staff, holding court in Beverly Hills at the Peninsula hotel. Late the night before, he and aides huddled over beers in the hotel's stodgy birch-paneled bar, finalizing some details around a deal for a new chunk of funding. They weren't dwelling on We-

Work's growing red ink. The company's fortunes were on the rise. Weren't they?

AFTER GREETING HIS STAFF IN THE MICROSOFT THEATER—THE thousands present and roughly four thousand others watching from New York and offices around the world—Neumann told them he had an announcement. He paced back and forth on the stage, just as he did in private. Neumann would rarely sit still during a meeting.

As of early that morning, he declared to the room, WeWork had completed a deal for a new investment from SoftBank. The deal, which gave WeWork $1 billion in new cash, valued the company at $47 *billion,* he said, his voice rising.

That, he said, now yelling, "makes us the second-highest-valued private company on the planet." As he finished the sentence, he thrust his left index finger in the air, holding it up as the crowd cheered again.

Neumann was obsessed with valuation—the worth of a company, as determined by its investors. He was adamant the $47 billion figure be at the top of the press release sent out that day. To him, valuation was a crucial marker—a testament to everything he'd built. The figure meant that WeWork was now second to just Uber among U.S. startups (contrary to Neumann's declaration, it was also behind at least two Chinese startups and some older companies that had remained private). But it was worth more than scores of Fortune 500 companies like FedEx. It was worth more than Ford. A decade earlier, Neumann had been a struggling baby clothes salesman. Now he'd built a company worth the equivalent of United Airlines—times two.

The announcement was just the start. Neumann spoke for ninety minutes, meandering onstage and walking up and down in the aisles in the crowd, shaking hands with employees as a spotlight and cameras followed him. Often talking slowly for emphasis, he told the story of WeWork—of how it formed, where it was going, and how it was different.

"The technology companies, and social media," he said, "made us promises of a better future, of a more connected future; the truth couldn't be further.

"We're disconnected."

WeWork was the answer.

WeWork was "a community, a company, a family," he said.

Its focus—caring about the community over the self—was going to drive WeWork further upward, he told the audience. It would become the model for other companies around the world to follow. It would be the basis for WeWork's nascent expansion into other areas, too. He'd always seen WeWork as far more than just offices; it was a "community company" designed to bring people together, to erase boundaries between work and outside life. Now he wanted to make that loftier goal explicit. He was changing the company's name.

"Moving forward: The. We. Company," he said, pausing between each word for effect. WeWork would still exist, he said, but as a division of the We Company, which would have a far more expansive vision. The company's mission, he said, was to "elevate the world's consciousness."

The work had begun in earnest. WeWork had started an elementary school overseen by Rebekah Neumann. Elsewhere, the company was creating dorm-like apartments for adults. In another endeavor, WeWork now ran its own coding academies to train people for tech jobs. The We Company would expand from here. The future appeared bigger, brighter, and unstoppable.

As he continued, Neumann mused of WeWork's continued expansion—of its valuation climbing ever upward. Next year, he said, it would be $100 billion.

"That valuation we're going to get—do you know what we're going to do with that money? Elevate. The. World's. Consciousness."

Neumann made clear WeWork would be keeping up its blistering pace of growth, doubling revenue annually.

"Why am I not willing to grow less than 100 percent? Because we have a mission to complete," he said.

As the crowd sat in rapt attention, Neumann expounded on the company's future. It would expand throughout Africa; it would start its own TV show; it would hire military veterans en masse. The company was going to be even more devoted to helping the environment, and to doing the *right* thing in business. "If you do the right thing, you make the most money," he said.

Left unsaid in all of it—what the mostly young, mostly idealistic employees didn't grasp—was that $1 billion wasn't going to get them very far. WeWork wasn't close to making any money—any profit—at all. The massive growth that Neumann was talking about came at an extraordinary cost, putting the company deep in the red. To keep the machine running, WeWork would need billions upon billions of dollars to roll in again and again as the company grew.

But for nine years, Neumann's funders—from venture capitalists in Silicon Valley to the Japanese conglomerate SoftBank—cared more about the growth than the losses. Their bet was that more funding would continue coming from somewhere. Someone else would believe in WeWork just as much as they did. The risk would be passed on to others.

Surely it wouldn't be that hard.

PART I

CHAPTER I

The Hustler

ADAM NEUMANN BELIEVED HE WOULD BE THE MAN TO RE-invent baby clothes.

It was 2006, and he was twenty-seven years old. Neumann was already running his own fledgling business that aspired to mass-produce pants and onesies with built-in knee pads for crawling babies. He named it Krawlers. Despite his sincere belief in the brilliance of his concept, Neumann was still hunting for ways to get the business moving, let alone to turn a profit. He flew to China to meet with suppliers. He pushed his product on baby retailers.

Neumann had arrived in New York from Israel in the fall of 2001, landing in a city reeling from the 9/11 terrorist attacks. Yet, in times of boom and bust alike, New York always beckoned dreamers like Neumann. His reason for the move, he told his friends, was simple. He wanted to get rich. New York was "where opportunity happens."

He moved in with his younger sister, Adi, and lost no time making connections. Adi, a model who appeared on the covers of magazines including international editions of *Elle, Vogue,* and *Cosmopolitan,* brought in plenty of money to support a flashy lifestyle. The two shared an apartment, which doubled as Adam's office, on the fifteenth floor of a building in Tribeca that attracted a gregarious crowd. Twentysomethings flitted in and out of one another's apartments or socialized on the roof.

While Neumann had flirted with modeling himself—he had a distinctive look, lanky with long, flowing dark brown hair and a face marked by high, rounded cheekbones—he opted to pursue dreams of another sort.

Neumann had launched Krawlers while a student at Baruch, a public college in Manhattan known for its business program. The budding entrepreneur had tested out a string of business ideas, including a collapsible high heel, before eventually landing on padded infant clothes. Friends say he got the idea by seeing a similar product in Israel. He took to Krawlers with his trademark intensity, dropping out of Baruch to work on it full-time. He talked about how big the company would become—how they'd be selling millions of dollars of Krawlers clothes a year. He borrowed money from his sister, raised more from a wealthy hedge fund manager she was dating, and invested $100,000 he'd received from his grandmother.

Neumann knew little about children. He was young and single, and his time was dominated by working, drinking with friends, chain-smoking cigarettes, and churning through dates with different women. And the business logic of Krawlers had obvious holes: typically babies crawl for only a period of months.

Yet Neumann proved to be a gifted salesman, particularly when face-to-face with a potential buyer.

At trade shows where many of the clothes were sold, Neumann was a magnet for the small-business owners. His dramatic appearance, his booming voice with its emollient accent, and his vibrant energy stood out amid rows of infant clothing purveyors—so much so that a small crowd often huddled around him. He conjured a world in which a baby couldn't be happy without built-in kneepads. He'd walk potential buyers through the experience of being a parent and having children crawl. Your child will love you more because of these clothes, he'd tell them, with a smile. The company's slogan became "Just because they don't tell you, doesn't mean they don't hurt."

At a trade show in Manhattan's Javits Center around 2006, Daniel Rozengurtel spotted Neumann's head above a swarm of people at the Krawlers booth. Rozengurtel and his wife had started an e-commerce website called Spiffy Baby. It didn't take long for Neumann to convince the couple, who had recently had a baby, that the kneepad-lined clothes were something they'd need for their child—as would their customers. Within a single conversation, Neumann struck Rozengurtel as amazing. He put in an order.

On a good day, Neumann sold thousands of dollars of baby clothes at a time. He bounced off the walls with energy and ideas, constantly hustling and calling prospective investors and retailers. He struggled to sit still for long periods; he constantly paced around his office as he talked on the phone. He loved the negotiating, the banter, and the sport of it all. He would even haggle with bewildered department store salespeople.

Neumann wasn't rich yet, but he was having fun and learning the ropes of deal making. And his twenties in New York, in all their kinetic glory, were stable—at least when compared with what came before them.

NEUMANN WAS BORN IN APRIL 1979 IN THE SOUTHERN ISRAELI city of Be'er Sheva' to a pair of medical students at Ben-Gurion University. He and his sister relocated each time his parents switched hospitals as part of their training. His parents divorced when Adam was seven, and he and Adi went with their mother, Avivit, to the United States, where she secured an oncology fellowship in Indianapolis. Neumann's childhood, by his own account, was "shitty." A bright child, he suffered from severe dyslexia, making reading difficult. His mother, who would go on to be one of Israel's top oncologists, was often exhausted from her work ministering to cancer patients. She would often scream at him, he later confided to friends. She had a habit of spending well beyond her means, which would periodically leave the family short on money.

After two years in Indianapolis, Neumann and his family returned to Israel, where his father had remained. The siblings lived with Avivit. She lined up a job at a hospital in western Israel, as well as a part-time gig on a kibbutz—one of numerous socialist-inspired communities scattered throughout the country, remnants of a utopian movement started decades earlier. Because of her work as a doctor there, the Neumanns got housing within the kibbutz's gates.

The kibbutz, Nir Am, had roughly six hundred residents and sat ten miles inland from the Mediterranean Sea, just on the northern edge of the Negev Desert. The ethos of the kibbutz movement was one of sharing and egalitarianism. For decades after its founding in 1943, Nir Am residents supported the kibbutz by picking grapefruits and potatoes in the fields or working in the on-site cutlery factory, a low-tech maker of forks, knives, and spoons. Salaries were equal. Cars were shared—with driving hours controlled by a sign-up sheet. In Nir Am's brutalist concrete dining hall, families would join together to eat meals of cereal, chicken, or falafel.

Neumann, then eleven, struggled to make friends. The children in Nir Am had grown up in the community and knew one another like siblings. Neumann and his mom and sister, on the other hand, were outsiders: they were simply renting space there. But Neumann eventually endeared himself to the others. He was loud and fun and invited peers over to his room, where he showed off American trinkets, like his Nintendo video-game system. Outside, they'd play basketball, or sometimes with a baseball Neumann brought from America. As years passed, his friends became the center of his community; he slept in the house designated for teenagers, where he had a sizable room of his own.

Neumann's time in Nir Am coincided with sweeping changes in the kibbutz structure. Throughout Israel, the idealistic dreams of the kibbutz had begun to falter. These communities were designed to be self-sustaining, but decades into their existence they relied heavily on government subsidies. The vision wasn't working, and as finances deteriorated, Nir Am began to change—to introduce capitalistic reforms to the troubled socialist structures. More residents took jobs outside the kibbutz, while all residents began to pay for meals and air-conditioning; food waste and electricity use plunged. (Later the cafeteria would shut down and be converted into a co-working space.)

Neumann loved the sense of community at Nir Am and the close bonds he made, but the economic egalitarian spirit didn't rub off on him. He told friends he wanted to leave and make *millions* of dollars. He would later carp about the inherent unfairness of kibbutz life. Slackers and hard workers received the same pay, he'd say.

IN ISRAEL, MILITARY SERVICE IS COMPULSORY, A RITE OF PASSAGE during which men and women, usually serving in their late teens and early twenties, often forge lifelong friendships and vast peer networks. Neumann, aiming high, scored a spot in the naval academy, an elite placement within the Israel Defense Forces, second in prestige only to fighter pilot training. The position required seven years of service rather than the mandatory three. The navy screened cadets with rigorous tests, seeking candidates who could combine physical agility with problem solving.

Neumann, athletic and sharp, completed the initial training—a stage where attrition is high. Still, his leadership showed itself more on days off, when he would corral friends for windsurfing expeditions on the Sea of Galilee. As he moved into the next phase of his naval training—serving on boats and helping coordinate operations on land—he made it clear to friends that the rigid, rule-bound hierarchy of the military wasn't for him.

One evening, Neumann and several junior officers attended a party on a rented cruise ship near the naval base. Neumann was supposed to be on his assigned navy ship, watching over it while it was docked for the night, he told others. A missile boat isn't like a car in a parking lot: one can't just roll up the windows, lock the door, and leave it alone. Yet, while downing drinks with a fellow cadet on the cruise ship, Neumann boasted about how he'd snuck off to join the party boat, leaving his post unattended.

While his classmates went on to serve as officers for many more years, Neumann would not. Several officers who served with him say he got a medical exemption, claiming an ailment they suspected was exaggerated in order to avoid years of seafaring. Instead, he stayed in the port in Haifa, occasionally teasing his colleagues when they returned from a few days at sea. They weren't amused.

Rather than serving the full seven years, he ended his service after five—bored and frustrated by military service. By the summer of 2001, he was eager to leave the country. His sister—then a celebrity in Israel—brought him onto a segment on the Guy Pines show, a gossipy talk show that was a hit there. Wearing a white tank top and wraparound sunglasses, Neumann, twenty-two, outlined his own plans while sitting next to his sister. "We're moving to New York," he told the interviewer, before gleefully recounting a time he visited Adi on a prior trip to the city and met Matt Damon at a club.

NEW YORK PROVED TO HAVE THE GLITZ NEUMANN IMAGINED— the bars and the clubs and the beautiful people.

But business wasn't turning out as he'd hoped.

As he tried to get Krawlers going, it became clear that thousands of dollars in sales here and there weren't going to build the baby clothes empire he'd imagined. While he didn't have to answer to any boss but himself, building a business was hard. Neumann's dyslexia weighed him down. Reading was difficult, as was using a computer: he had to ask others to send emails, or he would send typo-ridden messages himself. Finances, meanwhile, were shaky, and the company was subsidized by his sister and others. Red ink was in great supply. In 2006, Neumann wrote to his clothes designer, Ranee Kamens, that the company had lost $45,000 in the past year. Returns piled up, and Krawlers had to give customers credits for the following season—a sign of defective or low-quality products.

"Spring season was not a good season for us," he wrote.

Kamens, too, was struggling to get paid. She left Krawlers by the fall, but had yet to be paid for her work from the prior spring. She wrote an email requesting that compensation, and Neumann responded that he'd take care of it.

Two weeks later, Kamens sent him another message, noting, "My birthday is the 19th. It would be a great present if we c/d be settled by then."

She didn't hear from him.

Neumann realized Krawlers wasn't headed where he wanted it to go. It was hard to see how he'd be the millionaire he'd boasted he'd become while at Nir Am.

"It's not going to be a one billion dollar business," he told Roy Ramon, a good friend he first met in the navy.

He needed a bigger idea.

CHAPTER 2

Greenhorns

ADAM NEUMANN WAS HALF-NAKED WHEN HE FIRST ENCOUN-tered his future co-founder.

Miguel McKelvey was headed to a colleague's Tribeca apartment, where there was a midday party on the roof. It was summer 2005, around the same time that Neumann was sketching out his ambitious plans for Krawlers. McKelvey, a mild-mannered architect in his early thirties, was in an elevator at 95 Worth Street when a tall man in shorts, but no shirt or shoes stepped in. Bursting with energy, the man launched into conversation with others in the elevator, speaking with some accent.

When the elevator stopped to let a rider off, the shirtless figure with long wavy hair held the door open to prolong his conversation; the other passengers all waited awkwardly while he kept talking. The strange interaction left an impression on McKelvey, who stood even taller than Neumann, at six feet eight. He's breaking all social norms, all at once, he thought.

Soon, on the rooftop, the two chatted. It turned out that McKelvey's colleague—Gil Haklay—lived with Neumann. McKelvey was intrigued by the extroverted man he'd just met; Adam was just the type of person he gravitated toward. As he later explained to an interviewer, "I like to be *next* to the center of attention." They would keep in touch.

.   .   .

Mᴄᴋᴇʟᴠᴇʏ ᴡᴀs sᴏᴍᴇᴛʜɪɴɢ ᴏғ ᴛʜᴇ ɪɴᴠᴇʀsᴇ ᴏғ ɴᴇᴜᴍᴀɴɴ. ʜᴇ had moved to New York the prior year and hadn't met many people outside his small architecture firm. He wasn't big into drinking or social gatherings.

When he talked, he tended to avoid eye contact, looking down at the floor with his hands dangling from his pockets. He spoke with a dull monotone and peppered his slowly articulated sentences with "like."

One thing he did have in common with Neumann was an off-beat childhood. McKelvey, too, was raised on a tiny commune of sorts, a collection of five women who were close friends and decided to raise children together as a single unit in Eugene, Oregon, largely without fathers in their lives. McKelvey considered himself to have five siblings—four sisters and one brother—all from mothers other than his own. Later, as he became aware of the unusual circumstances of his childhood, he'd make up stories about the whereabouts of his dad. The family was poor; they drove beat-up cars and shopped with food stamps.

McKelvey had also dabbled in entrepreneurial endeavors. After college, he started a business with a friend in Japan that connected Japanese locals with Americans who could teach them English. But he'd longed to be an architect—he studied architecture at the University of Oregon—and just before he turned thirty, he moved to New York to take a job at a small firm that designed some of the first American Apparel retail stores and personally worked on their rapid build-out all over the United States.

After the chance meeting on the Tribeca rooftop, McKelvey occasionally saw Neumann through Haklay. One day in 2006, Neumann called the architect asking for help finding and designing his new office. Krawlers, by then, had merged with another baby clothes business called Egg Baby, and Neumann was looking for an affordable space. McKelvey suggested he look in Brooklyn, where rents were cheaper. Neumann took him up on it, moving his company to Dumbo, a tiny cobblestone-filled neighborhood of aging former warehouses that had an artistic if fast-gentrifying vibe. Neumann's new office was at 68 Jay Street, the same building where McKelvey worked.

IN DUMBO, NEUMANN WAS RESTLESS. HE KEPT TRYING TO WRING a profit out of baby clothes, but success eluded him. He began spending more of his time brainstorming the next business that might make him rich. He batted around ideas with anyone who'd listen. He talked about them with friends, with friends of friends, with a bartender at the local dive, ReBar. What were good industries to get into? Where were people making money? Food service, gyms, real estate, women's wear—it really didn't matter.

McKelvey became one of these sounding boards, and the two often went for long strolls around the neighborhood. One idea, Neumann told McKelvey, came to his attention thanks to a classmate at Baruch whose son, Cheni Yerushalmi, ran an office space provider in Manhattan and the Bronx called Sunshine Suites. Yerushalmi showed Neumann his business, which catered in part to small technology companies, renting them turnkey offices and desks by the month. It was a simple and not terribly exciting idea, but as Yerushalmi made clear to Neumann, it was highly lucrative. Demand was strong, and small companies were in great supply.

His interest sufficiently piqued, Neumann suggested to McKelvey that perhaps the two of them could do their own version—in Dumbo. Neumann set to work on Josh Guttman, the landlord at 68 Jay. Guttman and his family had bought up a series of aging industrial buildings in the area years earlier, and they now owned a sizable portfolio of properties throughout Brooklyn. The extroverted Neumann cultivated a rapport with Guttman and his son, Jack, floating the idea of converting Guttman's building into a co-working space. It was a brash move for a struggling entrepreneur with zero experience in real estate—one who was sometimes late with his own rent payments. But as McKelvey would say later, Neumann held "an endless faith in his ability to convince people to do things he wants them to do."

Jack Guttman was no exception. He agreed to hear a full pitch from Neumann and McKelvey about what they would do with an empty floor of a nearby building.

McKelvey was left to figure out the details. He worked through the night to create proposed floor plans, a business plan, and a website. He dubbed the proposal Green Desk, hoping to evoke an eco-conscious ethos.

When they walked into the meeting with Guttman, they explained that Brooklyn was full of entrepreneurs with tiny companies that had no need for the ten- or twenty-person offices with multiyear leases that Guttman's buildings offered.

Instead, Neumann and McKelvey proposed a Sunshine Suites–like business where they'd divide each floor of a Guttman building into tiny two- or three-person offices and a cluster of desks built around a shared open space with conference rooms and coffee. Everything would be plug and play; Green Desk would supply the furniture, the internet, the printers, while tenants would rent by the month. From a business standpoint it had some smart elements: tenants would pay more per desk than they would in a standard office, given the convenience and flexibility, while the Guttmans would be able to fit far more separate tenants in a given floor because the desks and offices were packed close together. Neumann and McKelvey estimated that this model could bring in $75 to $80 a square foot a year compared with the roughly $20 a square foot that was the Guttmans' norm.

The Guttmans bit. They offered Neumann and McKelvey a floor of one of their buildings at 155 Water Street—a onetime pipe factory that had become a den of low-cost artist lofts until the Guttmans cleared it out. Quickly they hashed out a deal. The Guttmans would throw in some money for renovations. Neumann and

McKelvey—as well as Haklay, their mutual friend—would design the space and run it and find tenants. The three entrepreneurs would own half of the company, and the Guttmans the other half.

They set out to work. It soon became clear that McKelvey, who left his architecture job, would be bearing the brunt of the labor. Neumann continued working on baby clothes and other potential ventures, while Haklay, too, kept his job as an architect.

As they plotted out plans for the old brick building that ran up against the Manhattan Bridge, they had little doubt they could fill it. Light streamed in from the large windows onto its wood floors, and one could look out over the rest of the charming neighborhood.

McKelvey's main idea for the design was to give the space more light and flourish than a standard office. Rather than use standard cubicle dividers or drywall between all the offices, he put glass dividers between them, with sunlight running straight through to the exposed-brick walls. Ironically, it was a key differentiator from Sunshine Suites, which McKelvey found claustrophobic and uninviting without natural light. (Still, they borrowed other elements from the business: Green Desk had its tenants sign a rental contract nearly identical to the one created by Sunshine Suites.)

The resulting space was hardly the Ritz. The common areas were mostly just coffee machines and some Ikea tables, and the new cubicles looked cheap. Its main selling point—that it was eco-friendly—didn't seem to run too deep. Beyond noting that the offices used clean energy, the sustainability section of Green Desk's website advertised recycling facilities in the building and paperless billing.

The plan was to spend near nothing on marketing. They posted on Craigslist and a local blog, and the spartan website boasted of "turnkey carbon neutral office space." Monthly rent of $300 to $2,500, depending on desks and business needs, would include "high-speed internet access, a VoIP phone and a connection to an

MP3 music server with thousands of songs" plus faxing and fresh organic coffee.

Before they'd converted the space, McKelvey gave tours to prospective renters, showing them potential "offices" based on tape markings and sketches, and started signing people up right on the spot. Somehow, the threadbare effort worked. Within weeks of launch in May 2008, freelancers, nonprofits, and small businesses began to file into the fifth floor at 155 Water Street.

As they watched the desks fill up, Neumann and McKelvey hosted a "networking" event for their renters. It was really just a low-key party, but they observed the group mingle and forge connections.

Neumann wanted to pitch the "community" aspect of the business early on, but McKelvey was wary. He had a reverence for that word—a vestige of his mothers' idealism around what they sought to create in Oregon. He told Neumann to hold off. "We really have to do it before we talk about it," McKelvey would later say. Otherwise, "people would see that as fake."

The Guttmans loved the office subleasing model and wanted more. They expanded to another floor, and then another, and another. MTV took over a still unrenovated floor to film a TV show for several months. The popular news website *Gothamist* took one of the larger offices. Quickly, 155 Water was filled with roughly 350 tenants. They expanded into another Guttman building, 68 Jay, back where the entrepreneurs had their original offices. (Neumann kept his Krawlers office there.)

And, miraculously, Green Desk continued to flourish even as the economy began to crater around the entrepreneurs. The subprime mortgage crisis sparked a historic crash in the country's financial system, and New York was at its epicenter. Every sector of the economy seemed to be hit. Yet somehow, small businesses still wanted office space in Brooklyn. Perhaps it was the flexibility; perhaps it was former bankers starting something themselves. Whether smart or lucky, Neumann and McKelvey had clearly stumbled on a product for which there was untapped demand, and one that could make money. It was clear that if Neumann stuck with the Guttmans, he could get rich—eventually bringing in the millions he'd dreamed of.

But Neumann was feeling a familiar sensation—restlessness. He talked to McKelvey about rushing into Manhattan, San Francisco, and elsewhere. Neumann had dreams of something giant, on the scale of hundreds of millions of dollars in value or more. It was the start of a movement; they wanted to go huge.

Neumann and McKelvey talked to the Guttmans about the idea, but the family wasn't interested in expanding to other landlords' buildings. The Guttmans had their buildings in Brooklyn, and they wanted to fill them, ideally at higher rents than before. That was real estate.

The partnership had hit its ceiling.

By mid-2009, Neumann and McKelvey had struck a deal with the Guttmans, who would buy the trio out. Neumann, McKelvey, and Haklay would be paid about $500,000 each. As quickly as it began, the entrepreneurs' experience with Green Desk was over— just a year and a half from initial incorporation to its sale.

Haklay took the money and went his own way, eventually returning to Israel, where he'd been raised.

Neumann, meanwhile, asked McKelvey to keep his money safe for him. "Put it somewhere else because I know I'll spend it if I have access to it."

The nest egg, Neumann declared, would go toward their next venture. He and McKelvey were just getting started.

CHAPTER 3

Famous Energy

T HE REDBRICK BUILDING AT 95 WORTH STREET WAS A CATA-
lyst for more than just Green Desk.

In the few years Adam Neumann lived there in the middle
of the 2000s, the building was heaving with twenty- and
thirtysomethings—redolent of a college dorm. Neumann made
friends throughout the building, inviting them to his apartment or
hanging out with them on the roof. One such neighbor turned
friend was Andy Finkelstein, a self-assured talent agent who was
around Neumann's age. He, too, was a highly social creature and a
locus for connections. The two became close.

One day around early 2008, Finkelstein told Neumann he
should meet his friend Rebekah Paltrow, who had just moved back
to New York from Los Angeles. The suggestion came just as Neumann was starting Green Desk. Thus far, Neumann had steered
clear of settling down into a relationship, but Finkelstein had a feeling the two might hit it off. Not only was Paltrow a close friend
from his Cornell days, but other qualities—she had a wealthy family; her first cousin was Gwyneth Paltrow—might appeal to Neumann, who liked proximity to fame.

A dinner date was set. Tall and thin with long, sleek dark hair
and a regal bearing, Paltrow was immediately captivating to Neumann. She had a wide smile and teeth that could light up her face.

Over the meal, Paltrow, whose intonation betrayed hints of her Long Island upbringing, spent much of the meal questioning Neumann's values: Why was he on this planet? Was he just trying to make money with his baby clothes business, or was he doing something greater for the universe? She mocked him and grilled him, throwing the typically cocky Neumann off balance. Within minutes of meeting him, Paltrow said, "You, my friend, are full of shit," Neumann later recalled.

To Paltrow, by the end of the night, it seemed as though her destiny was not only to date Neumann but also to guide him. She wanted to teach him and channel his ambition and charisma into something far greater than Green Desk, let alone Krawlers. As she later recounted in an interview, "I just knew he was going to be the man who would hopefully help save the world. The second I met him."

THE YOUNGEST OF FOUR CHILDREN, PALTROW WAS BORN IN 1978 in Great Neck, a tony enclave on Long Island's North Shore that was the basis for *The Great Gatsby*'s West Egg.

Her family's wealth stood out even in a neighborhood where money was flaunted. Many of the girls in Paltrow's class—but not Rebi, as she was known until her early twenties—wore the same $10,000 Cartier watch known as the Panthère. Gwyneth Paltrow would tell a magazine reporter in 2016 about her cousin's upbringing: "Her mother Evelyn has amazing taste: every linen perfect. They had a lot of help and every comfort." Adam Neumann would later say he thought Paltrow had "the perfect childhood."

The money mainly came from her mother's side. After escaping Hungary during the Holocaust, Evelyn's father co-founded one of the largest private label lingerie companies in the United States and the Philippines, where a street in Manila was later named after him. Rebekah's father, Bobby, added to their fortune via the junk-mail business. He became an investor, and then an executive, at a third-generation direct-mail company—one that seemed to print money when times were good. Paltrow told an interviewer that her father had instilled a deep work ethic in her. "There was no being a dilettante in my house. You had to rise up and deliver."

Around age eleven, Paltrow's family was turned upside down by the death of her older brother from cancer. Grieving, her parents uprooted their family, moving north of the city to Bedford.

She started seventh grade at Horace Mann, a private school in the Bronx attended by the offspring of some of New York's wealthiest families. Her house in Bedford would ultimately become the site of memorable parties as she entered her teens. By high school, friends would pop champagne in her giant hot tub; clothes were optional. When she turned eighteen, she amazed her friends by inviting them to a party at a restaurant in Manhattan, attended by her cousin Gwyneth and Gwyneth's then boyfriend, Brad Pitt.

When Paltrow arrived at Cornell, a member of her family's domestic staff helped replace some of the furniture in her freshman dorm room with Paltrow's own. She often joined her family on short vacations to St. Barts and ski trips to Aspen, bringing friends and her boyfriend, Brian Hallisay, who later became an actor. Her close circle of female friends—many she knew since high school—came from similarly affluent backgrounds, and all looked like models, a college classmate recalls. "They were all like the cast of [MTV's] *The Hills* before that was a thing," she said.

Paltrow spoke often of spirituality—taking Buddhism classes and yoga and pushing friends to think about the animals they were killing with their meat-based diets. Her sanctimoniousness and privileged background provoked eye rolls from many classmates.

After graduation in 1999, following a few pit stops, she moved to Los Angeles in the early years of the 2000s. While she briefly flirted with a banking job in New York for a few months, Paltrow decided to pursue acting, attempting to follow in her cousin Gwyneth's footsteps. She told friends she had "famous energy." She spent her days studying acting and meditating from a house where she lived in the Hollywood Hills, a house with sweeping views of the city.

In L.A., Paltrow's desire for spiritualism and proximity to fame led her to the Kabbalah Centre. The center had become a trendy locus for many of Hollywood's top directors, financiers, and actors who wanted to mix their pursuit of enlightenment with a bit of clubby socializing. While it had roots in Jewish texts, the Kabbalah Centre was known for a broad, trans-religious mysticism that counted Madonna among its disciples. Critics, including many in the broader Jewish religious community, derided it as a profiteering New Age celebrity cult.

Paltrow became a regular at the center. She frequented Wednesday night dinners hosted by the actor couple Ashton Kutcher and Demi Moore, where they'd study texts with one of the center's spiritual leaders.

Kutcher had become a friend, as had the fellow 1990s-era actors James Van Der Beek and Lucy Liu.

By the time she headed back to New York around 2007, Paltrow had little on her IMDb profile to show for her time in L.A. Although she studied under some of the top acting coaches, she rarely auditioned for parts and hadn't landed much besides a small role on *Punk'd*—Kutcher's reality TV show. By the time she met Neumann, she was talking about directing independent films or becoming a theater actor.

The pair dived into a romance, but Paltrow quickly laid down the law. If they were to continue dating, she insisted that Neumann— who was raised Jewish but was not observant—get in touch with his spirituality. She brought him to the Kabbalah Centre in New York, where he embraced the mysticism and quickly warmed to the high-profile networking opportunity.

Paltrow soon introduced Neumann to Kutcher, who, flush with money from eight seasons starring in the Fox sitcom *That '70s Show,* was beginning to dabble in startup investing. The actor and the entrepreneur quickly became friends, talking endlessly about new business ideas. When Kutcher and Moore were in town filming a movie, months before their wedding, the two couples spent hours drinking and partying with a small group in a suite at the Trump International Hotel.

In October 2008, the actors attended Paltrow and Neumann's nuptials in Manhattan—a small ceremony in an indoor garden event space owned by the designer Donna Karan, another friend of Paltrow's from Kabbalah. Paltrow's cousin Gwyneth attended, as did Van Der Beek and Liu.

The couple, who had become engaged months after meeting each other the prior year, would build a life together.

CHAPTER 4

Physical Facebook

B Y THE FALL OF 2009, ADAM NEUMANN WAS CERTAIN OF ONE thing. His next venture would be something far more expansive than just another Green Desk—far more than just a provider of desks.

His success in Dumbo didn't just show that there was demand for communal office space. Neumann and McKelvey also saw it as an indication of a broader generational shift. The millennial generation entering the workforce, they believed, was hungry for social interaction at work. The traditional model of isolated offices was inherently antisocial. There was no reason that work couldn't—or shouldn't—resemble the fun of a college dorm, or even the atmosphere of a club.

So for their venture, they reckoned that office space would be an anchor—a way to create a whole ecosystem of other companies and services dominated by young people with the same aesthetic and social inclinations. Even hipster millennials needed space to work.

Naming the company took months. They'd host brainstorming sessions with friends at Adam and Rebekah Neumann's East Village apartment, but nothing panned out. None of their ideas evoked a *big* brand. One of those nights, the talent agent Andy Finkelstein— who had introduced Rebekah to Neumann and remained invested in their relationship and ventures—blurted out, "We Work." The center of the business could be "We," the collective pronoun, which could then be tacked onto all manner of ancillary businesses: We-Live. WeSleep. WeEat.

Neumann called McKelvey the next day with the name. He was sold.

Neumann quickly registered a series of internet domains, snatching up WeWorld.biz, WeWorld.info, and we-are-1.info.

As they sought a location to bring their broader entrepreneurial visions to life, Neumann and McKelvey had the kind of nomadic work life for which they were trying to offer a solution. The two met in their apartments or on the fly—Neumann was spending less time in Dumbo, ceding the baby clothes business to his colleagues—and sketched out a vision for communal housing and upscale hostels. They imagined getting into lending and even sailing. Work was changing. Like Ron Livingston's nihilistic cubicle dweller in *Office Space,* white-collar workers were craving something more. Boundaries between work and play were vanishing, Neumann and McKelvey observed. They pointed to tech companies like Google, which lured employees with free food and on-site gyms. Employees were entertained with scooters in the hallways and beach volleyball. Work shouldn't be some negative distraction from the rest of life; it should be integral to a happy life, they believed.

At the heart of their work-play vision was the idea that their offices would create tight-knit communities. Later, the two would call it a "physical social network" and a "physical Facebook." Neumann loved to tell others how the "iPhone was all about I." We-Work, he said, would be about *We.* Companies would work together—and thrive together—turning to one another for services, deals, and partying. They would all be separate businesses, but feel part of the same WeWork family.

They'd seen how much their tenants at Green Desk coveted the community. For a few hundred dollars a month, they'd give people not only a work space but also a chance to be part of something "bigger than themselves," they'd say. Although neither of them were millennials (Neumann and McKelvey were both born early enough to be considered Gen X), they thought twentysomethings would gravitate to this more than the handful of other co-working companies that had sprouted up in the city in the past couple of years.

Neumann's time at the Kabbalah Centre provided further inspiration. He had become a regular, taking classes and attending services. Friends saw him weave ideals and phrases he learned into the WeWork rhetoric. "With Kabbalah, it's not about *I—me—mine,*" reads a book by one of the directors of the Kabbalah Centre. "It's about our relationship with others and the world." WeWork, too, was going to be about sharing and improving life for others. And it would be about helping small businesses grow; Neumann would later call it a "capitalist kibbutz."

Neumann, since joining Rebekah's orbit, was now constantly surrounded by a stream of people with access to vast sums of money: new friends, her family, her family's friends, their Kabbalah network. Suddenly Neumann had a deep reservoir of people to whom he could pitch his ideas and from whom he could seek advice and investments.

NEUMANN AND MCKELVEY WEREN'T THINKING SMALL. EVEN BEfore the company got off the ground, Neumann would talk with friends about how it was going to become a $500 million company or a $1 billion company. Friends found the vision intoxicating.

Grandiose rhetoric aside, the planned rollout looked a lot like an improved Green Desk. The concept was that WeWork would rent space in a building, then slice up that space into small offices and desks, which entrepreneurs and small businesses would rent from WeWork.

But rather than partner with a landlord—splitting profits as they had in Dumbo—the two realized it would be easier to just lease the space they needed like any other business in need of an office. This meant more risk—if no tenants ever came, they would still have to pay the rent—but huge potential profits, because the landlord wouldn't collect anything above the agreed rent.

First, they would need a building. Neumann had been able to sweet-talk his last landlord into handing over space, but beyond the Guttmans he and McKelvey knew few in the real estate world. As they hunted for vacant space, landlord after landlord raised similar concerns. They boiled down to this: Why would a landlord hand over his building for five years to two kids with an unproven concept?

In the end, though, one landlord did. A friend introduced Neumann and McKelvey to Abraham Talassazan, who owned a sprinkling of office buildings in Manhattan. In 2007, Talassazan had paid $21 million for a slender six-story redbrick building at 154 Grand Street. It was a third-rate aging office block in Manhattan's Nolita neighborhood, a nebulous intersection at the edges of Little Italy, Chinatown, and SoHo that lacked the character of any of the three, but the area was turning increasingly upscale.

Neumann and McKelvey met Talassazan at a good time. By mid-2009 his building was in trouble. Prior tenants were largely cleared out, and despite months of effort he could find few new takers. Talassazan was forking over monthly payments to cover his loan on the property and maintenance, with no income coming in.

The crippling economic fallout of the Great Recession was hitting landlords like Talassazan hard. They had enjoyed years of booming success in Manhattan as an expanding economy pushed up rents and quickly filled empty spaces. But by late 2008, banks, law firms, and marketing agencies that had been hunting for additional floors and whole buildings suddenly switched direction. Giant buildings were put up for sublease as the same law firms and banks raced to shrink quickly. Planned skyscrapers were halted; rents plummeted. Numerous building owners would soon default on their debts and lose multibillion-dollar portfolios of towers to lenders.

So when Talassazan met Neumann and McKelvey, he wasn't immediately dismissive. The entrepreneurs, dressed in jeans and T-shirts, walked the building's six stories of rickety stairs and run-down wood floors, but full of windows and light. They liked what they saw.

Neumann gave Talassazan and his staff the WeWork pitch. The office world was going to be changing: young New Yorkers were going to want office space like this, Neumann told them. He confidently referred to the building as merely their future "first" Manhattan location.

With few other options, Talassazan decided to proceed.

Meanwhile, Neumann and McKelvey kept hunting for more locations. It was an audacious move, given that they barely had enough money to finish the first building, let alone start a new one. As the quixotic duo toured one building, a skeptical landlord suggested they talk to someone else who seemed to share their mix of ambition and naïveté, a man named Joel Schreiber.

IN HIS LATE TWENTIES, SCHREIBER HAD A BOYISH FACE AND RE-served personality. He typically dressed in dark suits and was taciturn, sometimes speaking up only to elaborate on his successful real estate investments. He liked to describe himself as a trend spotter: he had made some investments in the Williamsburg neighborhood of Brooklyn before values soared. (Years later he would rack up an impressive number of lawsuits from former partners and others in real estate who alleged he owed them money or didn't make payments.)

Schreiber met Neumann and McKelvey by happenstance while they were touring a building in the Bronx. As Neumann told him about his ideas for WeWork, the normally subdued real estate investor became animated. Schreiber's mind raced with ideas about where the business could go.

Within a day of meeting Neumann, Schreiber offered to invest in his company. Despite having zero paying customers at that point, Neumann and McKelvey threw out a giant number, saying it would be valued at $45 million. Schreiber didn't negotiate: he agreed to invest $15 million for one-third of the company, far more than the two entrepreneurs had ever seen.

McKelvey, who was about to become a father for the first time, was astounded and awed by the brashness and persuasive powers of his partner. He and Neumann were ecstatic. With little more than a pitch and no offices in use yet, they had created a company worth $45 million.

MEANWHILE, THE 154 GRAND NEGOTIATION WITH TALASSAZAN and his team proved bruising, dragging on for months. In the end, both Neumann and McKelvey had to personally sign for the lease. It's a rare move for companies leasing large spaces; Bank of America's CEO doesn't have to pay if the bank breaks a lease. It meant WeWork couldn't fail: if the company collapsed, the two entrepreneurs would be on the hook, owing $51,000 per month to the landlord, for the full five-year term. Eternally confident in their plan, the two entrepreneurs pushed ahead.

By December 2009, everything had come together. Having started the year in a small-scale business in Brooklyn amid a crumbling economy, the duo now had a vision, a name, a building in Manhattan, and an investor who pledged them millions. They signed the lease.

CHAPTER 5

Manufacturing Community

Lisa Skye awoke to a predawn email on February 1, 2010—one of the first of many from her new boss. "Good morning," the email began. "Let's build the largest networking community on the planet."

The thirty-three-year-old had met Adam Neumann only five days earlier. She was working as a loan officer at a mortgage company and bumped into him at a networking event. Always eager to meet people and a bit tired of her job, she stayed long after the event ended, striking a quick rapport with Neumann. As they chatted, Neumann persuaded her to join his new business. Five days later, it was her first day at WeWork, as the company's very first "community manager." Her mandate, Neumann explained, was to help get the company's first space at 154 Grand open to the public within three weeks. The desks needed to be full as quickly as possible, and she would have to find people to rent them.

For weeks, Neumann, McKelvey, and their friends had been scurrying to ready a small corner of the building, built in 1891, for its debut. Kyle O'Keefe-Sally, McKelvey's "brother" with whom he grew up in Oregon, was sleeping in the dust-covered space so he could put in even more hours. They cleaned the brick walls by blasting them with baking soda at high pressure; they laid Ethernet cables themselves and installed glass partitions. On top of all that,

McKelvey and his wife would have their first child—a son—a few days after the space opened.

As others assembled desks, Skye started seeking out tenants, whom WeWork had decided to call "members." Once again the recruitment effort leaned heavily on Craigslist, but her sales strategies also extended to coffee runs. At a nearby Starbucks, she often struck up conversations with customers she spotted hunched over laptops.

"Hi, do you come in often?" she'd say, before launching into the pitch. "Offices are just $650 a month."

Those first WeWork offices were a bit of a hot mess. The elevator in 154 Grand was painfully slow and often out of service. The stairs were uneven. The space was a far cry from the curated, lounge-like rooms that would come later. The communal area was just a cramped kitchen with coffee. There was no tech support. (Soon after, WeWork brought in an IT person: a sixteen-year-old tech whiz—Joseph Fasone—who was sometimes in class when the internet went down, which it did sporadically.)

Despite these blemishes, Skye watched with amazement as the offices filled. She quickly rented the first seventeen offices, and then month after month the space kept growing. McKelvey and Neumann renovated the rest of the building, floor by floor, and offices were snapped up just as fast. There were lawyers, graphic designers, a filmmaker, a green roof designer, a filtered water bottle startup. Many of their members had spent years bouncing between coffee shops, buying an occasional latte in exchange for Wi-Fi. WeWork finally gave them something worth paying for.

Part of the appeal was the aesthetic. McKelvey had improved on the design from the Green Desk days, creating offices with walls that seemed sturdier and less cheap. Even without bountiful communal space, it looked cutting edge. Rows of offices were laid atop diagonal wood floorboards, each office separated from the other by a glass wall with a thick black aluminum frame. Light streamed in from the windows, through the glass, and passersby could see into every office and conference room, each adorned with Ikea light fixtures. It felt more like a hip coffee shop than a sterile corporate cubicle farm. With sliding doors that could easily be kept open, members felt a sense of connection and camaraderie. Neighbors up and down the halls would introduce themselves and chat. Neumann, believing engagement among members would be key to WeWork's growth, would himself lead occasional happy hours with members standing in a circle, introducing themselves.

These first members had the sense that they were at the vanguard of something new and different. As the economy was beginning to thaw after the multiyear freeze of the financial crisis, work was shifting, breaking further away from suits, fluorescent lights, and gridded white ceiling tile. A backlash against corporate America was brewing—one that would later manifest itself in the form of Occupy Wall Street. People wanted something new—something that felt more organic and wholesome. Tiny startups began to sate this hunger.

WeWork arrived at this particularly fortuitous moment in a changing New York. Big shifts were happening in all segments of society, from food to design to geography. Changes citywide emanated from Brooklyn, which had become more brand than borough, with hipster subcultures nurtured in its artsy neighborhoods. Coffee shops throughout the city and country were adopting Brooklyn-like features: white subway tile and exposed brick replaced drywall. Words like "artisanal" and "craft" became ubiquitous in product descriptions. Food trucks—offering Korean burritos or cupcakes—popped up everywhere.

WeWork's offices—which would later add 1990s arcade games and craft beer on tap—appealed firmly to those craving this urban landscape tinged with hipster chic, hitting on what would turn out to be a geyser of demand.

Abe Safdie had worked for a large corporate law firm before the crisis but was now on his own, working out of his apartment; his girlfriend aired frustrations that he never left home.

On a walk through Nolita with his girlfriend, he saw an eye-catching sign on the side of 154 Grand offering office space. It had an illustration of someone smashing a computer on a desk. He walked in for a tour to find that the office had barely opened and most of the floors were still empty, coated with dust. Safdie loved what he saw and picked out a one-person office on the spot.

The initial impetus for Safdie wasn't camaraderie or socializing, but he quickly warmed to WeWork's culture, striking up conversations with his neighbors. Every once in a while, those neighbors would be tiny startups with legal questions. While he ran a comfortable business practice facilitating mergers and acquisitions for mid-sized companies, suddenly he found he was giving a lot of casual legal advice. Entrepreneurs with offhand questions morphed into new clients, and Safdie quickly became proficient in advising on venture capital investments, which he found more enjoyable than corporate mergers. He put up a sign next to the communal printer, saying he could provide legal services for small companies. What had started as an unintentional side hustle quickly became his main gig.

Safdie sensed something was changing about the city; in the wake of the financial crisis, there was a new zeitgeist. It was all around him at WeWork, he thought, and he wanted to dive in deep. Later, he would move to two other WeWork buildings, before WeWork itself hired him as the company's general counsel.

THE DIVISION OF LABOR BETWEEN NEUMANN AND MCKELVEY quickly became clear. McKelvey would focus on the operations, making sure that offices opened, that members paid their fees, that glass got delivered.

Meanwhile, Neumann was the dealmaker in chief, hunting for new offices and new investors. Unlike with Green Desk, his full boundless energy went to WeWork. Skye watched as the CEO paced back and forth on empty floors of 154 Grand, barking into the phone to potential landlords and investors. (Rebekah Neumann was largely focused on her acting career; she was known to tell friends as they toured the first office that she chose the coffee, and that it was the "secret" to the business's success.)

Hungry for expansion, in late 2010, Neumann found David Zar, a young real estate investor who was hunting for a tenant to fill some empty floors in a building near the Empire State Building, recently vacated by Chase Bank. Over a bottle of whiskey, they struck a deal for WeWork's second location. WeWork's investor, Joel Schreiber, signed the guarantee for the lease.

The expansion, though, was costly, and by 2011, only a year after WeWork had opened, the company already faced a cash crunch. McKelvey, who was managing the company's finances in addition to his other roles, was forced to call Schreiber regularly to ask for his promised payments. The investor, who had put in less than the full $15 million, kept delaying without a clear reason, giving the duo misgivings. At one point to cover payroll and other expenses, they turned to Rebekah, who gave them a loan of $150,000, but at a fairly high interest rate.

Neumann, nervous about finances, turned to a friend he'd met through the Kabbalah Centre, Steven Langman, a successful private equity investor and something of a mentor to Neumann. Langman told him it was time to move on from Schreiber and to look for other wealthy investors. He suggested Samuel Ben-Avraham, a well-known investor in New York's fashion industry, and another contact from the center. Neumann had already discussed starting a co-working space aimed at the fashion sector with him. Ben-Avraham stepped in—at a discounted valuation to Schreiber of about $35 million—and supplied the needed cash for a stake in the business. That was soon followed by another chunk of money from a fellow Kabbalah Centre member, Marc Schimmel, a real estate investor and ex-boyfriend of Madonna's.

These new names, better known than Schreiber, lent an aura of respectability and glitz to the business—one that was used to attract more potential landlords and funders.

As the company swelled in size, Neumann and McKelvey went to lengths to stretch their cash as far as they could. The company would buy used networking equipment on eBay, then send it across the Hudson River to New Jersey, to avoid the e-commerce sales tax that it would face in New York. Danny Orenstein, the company's first head of development, watched Neumann drilling down on expenses. He wanted to know how much they paid for all the various components of wood floor installation and how WeWork could do it cheaper. Rather than buying professional-quality furnishings, Orenstein and colleagues found themselves shuttling to Ikea in Zipcars, stuffing them full with tabletops and light fixtures. Sometimes they'd just take all of one type of tabletop in stock, and come back later to do the same once Ikea had restocked. On some Zipcar runs for supplies, the cars were so fully packed that the vehicles' underbellies would scrape the pavement on bumpy roads.

Neumann prized speed. The pace of expansion would impress future investors and bring in new revenue to cover costs. He took to setting opening dates for floors that staff thought were arbitrary and unrealistic. Then he cranked up the pressure by advertising an opening date to new members that staff figured was impossible to hit. But they had to, and they did.

Offices at David Zar's building filled quickly, so Neumann stepped on the gas, expanding further. In 2011, WeWork added a third building, in the club-filled Meatpacking District. And then a fourth, a giant location at 175 Varick Street near Tribeca.

The aggressive schedule required for this rate of expansion meant constant long hours. Every time a new floor was scheduled to open—often in order to hit Neumann's compressed timetables—much of the company's staff toiled late into the next morning, assembling desks, installing toilets, and finishing what the contractors hadn't. Neumann largely avoided the all-night sessions, though McKelvey often stayed late doing manual labor himself.

Bolstered by frequent pep talks from Neumann, the staff felt they were part of something important—something that would facilitate a new, kinder, and more compassionate concept of work for a young generation. They watched with glee as their members—often tiny startups—made their way in the world, thanks in part to the connections their founders had made at WeWork.

As their breakneck expansion yielded results, Neumann became more certain of WeWork's future glory. After Ben-Avraham's and Schimmel's investments, they had a comfortable amount of cash to pay their bills, and the overall financials of the business model bolstered their optimism. In 2011, WeWork brought in $7.4 million of revenue and spent only slightly more than that, giving the business a loss of just $50,000—a good sign for an expanding business that still had new offices under way. Revenue was up fivefold from 2010, when they'd generated just $1.5 million. As 2012 approached, the company looked as if it was going to be profitable already.

All of the promises and dreams Neumann and McKelvey had been pitching and building were *actually coming true.* People were coming. They were working. They were building a community. The company kept finding good buildings. And floors were opening by—or near—the arbitrary dates Neumann set. On top of it all, there were now waiting lists to get into their spaces—virtually unheard of in real estate.

Emboldened, Neumann began to prepare to expand WeWork nationally, planning initial offices in San Francisco and Los Angeles. Other cities would follow soon after.

One night he was talking with Orenstein and asked him whether his then girlfriend was okay with his constantly working late. Orenstein responded that it didn't seem there was much other choice.

She should know, Neumann responded, that she is dating someone who is the equivalent of "one of the founding members of Google."

As WEWORK RAMPED UP ITS GROWTH, REBEKAH NEUMANN FOcused her attention on the nebulous task of "branding"—both for the company and for her and Adam. She tapped her Hollywood and Kabbalah Centre connections to sprinkle a bit of New York's Page Six socialite crowd into WeWork's image.

Early on, she had turned to Mandie Erickson, a high-profile publicist she met at the Centre, to help plan a June 2010 magazine launch party hosted by WeWork. The pair lined up the musician Pete Doherty and John Lennon's son Sean for the night's entertainment. While Doherty never made it to the party—he was detained at JFK thanks to a warrant out for his arrest—the line for entry wrapped around the block.

Rebekah hadn't let go of her acting dreams, however. She considered bringing the musician Patti Smith's autobiography *Just Kids* to the screen—she planned to play Patti Smith—but ultimately decided on funding and producing a short film. *Awake* was a fifteen-minute short centered on a twentysomething woman struggling with addiction and suicidal ideation.

They were able to secure big names for the tiny project, including the actress Rosario Dawson and once again Sean Lennon. The film's director, Hunter Richards, and others involved were surprised that Dawson would actually play a supporting role and that Rebekah would be the lead. The film's crew found her performance—and the end product—cringeworthy, and the film didn't get a spot at the Sundance Film Festival or any of the desired acclaim that Neumann had outlined when she was starting the project.

Rebekah didn't give up. She devoted part of the WeWork space at 175 Varick Street to companies and people in the film industry, and she tried to launch an arm of the company dedicated to producing films, but despite her shuttling to L.A. for many pitch meetings, it fizzled before getting off the ground.

As stardom seemed less and less likely, though, she turned her focus to growing her husband's main business. She dived further into branding, coming up with a number of the defining taglines for the company. She was credited with coining "Do What You

Love," which WeWork put everywhere, emblazoning the slogan in white cursive font on black T-shirts and black flags that would hang outside WeWork locations. Another, "Make a Life, Not Just a Living," was often repeated internally to sum up the ethos of what WeWork was trying to build.

At the same time, she was spending a great deal of time at home. The Neumann family was expanding: she had the first of what would eventually be five children during Adam's time as CEO.

When she next bumped into Richards, she told him she was done making movies.

"I'm sick of Hollywood," she said. "I'm producing babies now."

REBEKAH NEUMANN'S DALLIANCE IN THE FILM INDUSTRY MIGHT not have brought her fame, but it did open doors. Adam Neumann became friends with Richards, a handsome, charismatic film buff who often stayed in the couple's apartment. The two men spent nights downing bottles of Don Julio 1942 tequila—which retailed for more than $125 apiece—at the Waverly Inn, the scene-y West Village spot owned by *Vanity Fair*'s editor, Graydon Carter. Richards, in turn, introduced Neumann to Sean Parker, the Facebook founder Mark Zuckerberg's mentor and early investor who was played by Justin Timberlake in the 2010 movie *The Social Network*.

Neumann *loved* the movie. While many critics dwelled on the withering portrait of a narcissistic Zuckerberg and the cutthroat tactics he and Parker used to build Facebook—Neumann came away with a different impression. He seemed fixated on how the movie had glorified the two founders. The Parker character's most memorable line—"A million dollars isn't cool. You know what's cool? A billion dollars"—gave Zuckerberg a model for how to maximize the power of his then nascent social media business. It was a line that surely resonated with Neumann. He was enamored of the real-life Parker, who founded Napster at nineteen and was the first president of Facebook.

He and Richards—and sometimes Rebekah—frequently stopped by Parker's capacious six-thousand-square-foot, eight-story, $20 million town house on a tree-lined block in the West Village. Parker and his friends called it the "Bacchus House." It was the home of constant, round-the-clock parties that attracted a stream of well-heeled tech investors as well as celebrities. Neumann soaked up the scene of fantastic wealth and debauchery from the tech entrepreneurs and investors. He seemed awed by the excess.

As Neumann rubbed shoulders with these wealthy Silicon Valley exiles in New York, he began to talk more about how WeWork shared all sorts of the tech companies' qualities. To Parker, he compared WeWork to Facebook, saying it was about connecting people, "but it's in the third dimension." Parker and many of his investor friends were skeptical. They liked Neumann but didn't take him seriously as a businessman, much less a tech entrepreneur of their ilk.

IT WASN'T JUST PARKER AND HIS FRIENDS WHO OFFERED A TASTE of Silicon Valley success. By 2012, tech and startups began to saturate Neumann's circles.

When he and McKelvey were first brainstorming WeWork, they figured it would appeal to one-, two-, and ten-person businesses of all stripes, from fashion labels to law firms to graphic design companies, that wanted a new, communal way of working.

But as the company grew, they noticed that tech startups were snapping up many of WeWork's two- and four-person offices as soon as they became available.

New York City was becoming a locus for tech. Companies like Google were gobbling far more additional office space than most big banks in Manhattan, and tech happy hours and events held at WeWork offices proved a successful way to lure new members. On the other side of the country, San Francisco was a boomtown, bouncing back from the financial crisis far faster than New York thanks to a surge of job growth and hot new companies. The idea laid out in *The Social Network*—that some ambitious young adults could become rich and successful through internet businesses—had entered the mainstream.

The startups in WeWork's offices were often funded by venture capitalists—the moneyed and intrepid investors who back fledgling companies that they believe have potential for breakthrough and explosive growth. The VCs provide the money for getting off the ground—the rent, among other things—and they take a big piece of the upside, if and when the investments turn into winners.

It was a model doing particularly well at the time. Companies like Instagram were selling for astounding amounts; Facebook bought the photo-sharing app for $715 million after it raised just $57 million of investment.

As Neumann and his staff looked around, they saw parallels between the company they'd built and the startup culture embodied by its renters. WeWork staff eschewed the stilted corporate image of suits and ties, preferring T-shirts and jeans. Like seemingly every other startup in San Francisco, Neumann and WeWork staff viewed their work as "mission driven"—the hours spent at the office were for the greater good. Adopting the vernacular of the tech world, WeWork added "innovation" to the mission statement on its website.

Neumann and the staff closest to him—at the time a mix of friends and family—saw opportunity everywhere they looked. The only trick would be raising money to keep growing WeWork quickly—a lot of money.

Venture capital would be their answer, too.

PART II

CHAPTER 6

The Cult of the Founder

I N LATE 2011, MICHAEL EISENBERG WAS LEAVING AN EVENT AT the InterContinental hotel in Tel Aviv for dinner with his wife when his phone buzzed with a New York number.

The voice on the other end of the call introduced himself as Adam Neumann.

Eisenberg wasn't entirely surprised to hear from Neumann. Eisenberg worked for a prominent Silicon Valley–based venture capital firm called Benchmark. In conversations the investor was having with peers from the Israeli-tech expat community in New York, Neumann's name kept popping up. Everyone insisted he meet the promising entrepreneur.

Neumann was calling for advice. He was trying to build an on-line social network for WeWork members and figured the investor could help. He, conversely, had heard Eisenberg's name in startup circles; the investor was a known quantity among techies in New York.

Eisenberg, eight years older than Neumann, had a booming voice and a full head of hair; he had lived the geographic inverse of the entrepreneur on the other end of the line. Born in Manhattan, he grew up in the United States and graduated from Yeshiva University before immigrating in his twenties to Israel—a place he had long wanted to live.

He started his career with a stint in political consulting but eventually found himself unemployed. Like many smart men in their twenties, Eisenberg saw an open door in investment banking and began advising tech firms as Israel's tech sector was growing, a gig that led him to become a venture capitalist. His job was hunting for entrepreneurs. The holy grail was finding that once-in-a-generation founder before anyone else: the person with both a propulsive business idea and an X factor, an innate sense of how to sell the vision to others.

For the next two hours, Eisenberg mostly listened, enraptured by the fast-talking man in New York. His battery draining, he plugged his phone into an outlet in the lobby wall, straining to stay tethered to the conversation.

Without even laying eyes on Neumann, Eisenberg was enamored. He would be in New York in a couple of weeks; they needed to meet in person.

He counseled Neumann to sit tight. Don't take any investment from anyone else, he said.

IF SILICON VALLEY WERE A ROCKET, VENTURE CAPITAL WOULD BE its fuel.

The small, clubby corner of the financial system was the source of crucial early funding for almost every major tech company in the country, including Amazon, Apple, Facebook, Google, Microsoft, and Oracle. Based out of low-slung offices on a mundane suburban strip up the hill from Stanford University, these tiny, overwhelmingly male firms made bets on the digital future, pushing money into businesses ranging from food delivery to videoconferencing—and sometimes much more far-fetched ideas like $700 cold-pressed juice machines—well before they had shown they can make a profit.

The modern venture capital industry started after World War II, when investors were concerned that the post-Depression financial system was far too risk averse and that American innovation would suffer as a result. Early venture capitalists quickly gravitated to investments in new technology like mainframe computers, realizing their potential for outsized profits compared with other industries. As semiconductor and computer companies began to sprout on former apricot groves and flower fields in the low-lying area south of San Francisco, the financiers followed suit and set up their own offices in the burgeoning Silicon Valley.

The theory behind the sector was a simple one. There were plenty of entrepreneurs with good ideas and experience, but the traditional routes to starting a business—using bank loans or tapping home equity—weren't conducive to innovation. Banks don't like writing loans to high-risk companies, and lots of big inventions need years' worth of cash to fund research and development before they can start selling anything.

So venture capitalists—wielding money raised from wealthy individuals, endowments, and retirement funds—bought stakes in companies, giving them money to endure long periods of losses while the entrepreneurs refined their product and business plan. The endgame was to get a company up and running, then sell it to a bigger company or take it public through an initial public offering—an IPO—where VCs could sell their shares.

Because most of these companies were likely to fail, VCs were constantly on the hunt for new business ideas. Just one company in ten might find success, but that one would rake in enough profit to pay for all the misses. The rare breakout hit minted millionaires, or made millionaires even richer. One early investor in Apple, for instance, wrote a $57,000 check in 1978 that turned into nearly $22 million two years later when the company went public.

By the 1990s, VC firms were delivering huge returns to their investors—sometimes more than 50 percent a year—as the internet and personal computing exploded. Investors in VC funds were surpassing the returns they would have gotten by putting money in stock-trading mutual funds. It was out of this boom that Benchmark, where Michael Eisenberg worked, was founded in 1995 by four men, all of them steeped in the tech and investing worlds. Their ambition was to become the go-to VC firm in Silicon Valley. They raised some outside money and set out to find nascent companies.

It wasn't long before they found a hit that would bring them a lifetime of riches and fame. In early 1997, Bruce Dunlevie, one of Benchmark's founders, introduced Pierre Omidyar to the other partners. Omidyar, an entrepreneur who was almost thirty, was building an online flea market, one with a buggy website and a sizable community of collectors reselling Beanie Babies. Still, the partners at Benchmark saw promise and invested $6.7 million. Two years later, eBay had become one of the hottest stocks in the nation, and Benchmark's investment was worth more than $5 *billion*. It was one of the most profitable venture capital investments of all time, and Benchmark was immediately elevated to the elite ranks of the VC universe.

By 2001, though, the dot-com boom had turned into the dot-com bust. Companies buzzing with promise folded practically overnight; office vacancies soared, rents plunged, highways went from congested to empty. Fortunes vanished, and investors racked up huge losses as the sector turned toxic. The economy's spotlight moved back to New York and Wall Street as the VCs and tech companies that survived licked their wounds.

It started a years-long funding drought. The fire hose of money almost entirely turned off, and the number of startups shrank. But by the time Adam Neumann started WeWork in 2010, the Bay Area was buzzing again. Wall Street had seen its own rather significant self-inflicted bust in the subprime mortgage crisis, and the economy was far sunnier on the West Coast. Facebook was booming and was on track to return an astounding profit to its early VC backers; the same could be said of the VC-funded Groupon and Twitter. And the advent of Apple's iPhone in 2007 would unleash a whole new category of company: smartphone apps.

In the wake of the financial crisis, money managers—desperate to park their funds somewhere more lucrative than low-interest-rate government bonds—were no longer enticed by housing and banking. Instead, they followed the scent west, boosting shares of publicly traded tech companies like Google and Amazon while flooding venture capital firms with new investment. In 2011, VC firms raised $24 billion from investors, nearly double their haul of 2009.

This outpouring of money resulted in a burst of startups that would go on to reshape the Silicon Valley landscape and become household names in Americans' daily lives. Between 2009 and 2012, VCs wrote early checks to startups like Uber, Airbnb, Pinterest, Instagram, Snapchat, and Square. Suddenly you couldn't walk into a coffee shop in Silicon Valley without hearing talk of the next industry ripe to be "disrupted" by a startup.

Amid all the optimism, there was a noticeable change in venture capital strategy that would set apart this generation of startups from their prerecession forebearers. In past eras, venture capitalists saw their job as first sniffing out brilliant ideas and innovative companies and only then finding top-notch talent to place at the helm. Founders frequently stood aside as their companies grew up, ceding the day-to-day leadership to a professional CEO handpicked by the VCs.

By 2010, the herd had begun to question the traditional wisdom, influenced by a few data points that were impossible to ignore.

Amazon was booming, having been led since its inception by Jeff Bezos, who had transformed the company from the plucky bookselling firm started in his garage to the world's dominant e-commerce company. Mark Zuckerberg stayed firmly in control of Facebook, by far the most successful new tech company started in the twenty-first century. Then there was Apple's co-founder Steve Jobs, who had a cultlike following in the Valley and was in the midst of making Apple the country's most valuable corporation.

What these startups-turned-juggernauts had in common was not lost on venture capitalists: driven founders with a gift for salesmanship.

It didn't take long for a handful of influential new venture capital firms—Peter Thiel's Founders Fund and Andreessen Horowitz—to begin openly marketing themselves as "founder-friendly." They lavished praise on CEOs who had started their companies and promised the founders a long leash, saying they had a better chance of thriving than companies who brought in mercenary chief executives. This approach won over many founders who loved the idea of being able to stay in control.

The herd followed suit, and worshipping at the altar of the founder quickly became Silicon Valley's new religion. Some called it the cult of the founder. VCs were obsessed: they wanted well-spoken entrepreneurs with a strong vision, someone who could not only come up with an innovative idea but also, crucially, sell it to others and lure more funding and followers. Founders Fund even wrote on its website that "entrepreneurs who make it have a near-messianic attitude."

Money flowed to those like Brian Chesky, the magnetic cofounder and CEO of Airbnb, who had impressed his first funders at Y Combinator not with his idea—they thought people wouldn't cede their homes to strangers—but with the creativity he exhibited in a side project, a cereal called Obama O's. It flowed to Alex Karp, the quirky CEO of the data analysis firm Palantir, who wasn't a data analyst—he holds a PhD in social theory—but was a fantastic storyteller.

Distinctive sartorial choices, like the Steve Jobsian black turtlenecks, were a plus. A little bit of crazy never hurt. Founders needed to inspire.

WHEN BENCHMARK'S MICHAEL EISENBERG FINALLY ENCOUNtered Adam Neumann in the flesh, a few weeks after their marathon phone call from Tel Aviv in late 2011, the lanky entrepreneur did not disappoint.

Neumann whisked the venture capitalist around WeWork's offices in the Meatpacking District, its third location. The physical social network Neumann had described on the phone to Eisenberg now took shape before his eyes. The energy was palpable, the lobby blaring music and the coffee stations packed with twentysomethings dressed in jeans and sneakers. It all seemed so different from any office Eisenberg had ever seen; it was like a trendy bar or coffee shop, full of ideas and conversations bouncing around the room, one where customers had a visceral connection to the place and to one another. As Neumann introduced Eisenberg to members, the investor sensed they all loved being there.

Most impressive of all to Eisenberg was Neumann himself. He looked like the lead singer in a rock band, swaggering through the light-filled rooms. He pointed out design decisions that had fostered the vibrant community. But the room seemed to bend to Neumann. When he spoke to anyone, locking eyes and smiling broadly, they were enraptured. He amplified the energy of the space. Neumann, Eisenberg told others, was one of the best salesmen he'd ever met, and he'd met a lot.

Back in Israel, Eisenberg called into Benchmark's Monday morning partner meetings and on multiple different weeks, he implored his colleagues to check out this company. He couldn't quite describe why WeWork was so amazing, but the persistence of Eisenberg's pitch eventually wore Bruce Dunlevie down.

Later, Dunlevie spotted a day where his calendar was free, and booked a red-eye flight to New York.

Dunlevie was riding into the sunset of his venture capital career when he hopped aboard the plane. One of the four original partners at Benchmark, the mild-mannered investor was known for being an early backer of Palm, creator of the 1990s hit PalmPilot handheld device. Before that, he had been quarterback of his high school football team and gone on to get an MBA at Stanford. Slim, tall, and balding, Dunlevie was far more intellectual than a standard VC. He read books voraciously and avoided publicity—the opposite of many of the modern-day VCs who spend endless hours consuming and dispensing ideas on Twitter. He also had a reputation for being the resident bull in a firm full of optimists. When eBay's stock soared 40 percent in a single day in 1998, for instance, Dunlevie's partners wondered if that was the peak. He cautioned his partners that "it goes up from here" and that anyone selling was leaving money on the table. He was right: eBay's share price would be nearly ten times higher within the next year.

In New York, Neumann eagerly awaited the investor's arrival. Even though his dyslexia made even rudimentary computer use a challenge, Neumann was obsessed with the tech world—the corner of the financial universe behind what were now some of the world's largest businesses—and he was learning about its power brokers.

And now Benchmark, one of the most respected venture capital firms in the country, was validating his faith in WeWork's future. The firm had backed eBay, Instagram, and Uber, and now, Neumann told others, it was interested in *him*.

The tour had to go perfectly. The floors he would show to Dunlevie needed to be packed with people. He asked some employees to curate playlists.

Dunlevie spent hours with Neumann. At first, he found the entrepreneur to be evasive on hard questions—a bullshitter. But as the day went on, Neumann opened up more. As he pried more details of the finances out of Neumann, Dunlevie was impressed. With just a few million dollars and virtually no advertising, Neumann had already opened numerous buildings, filled them, and even started waiting lists. Those buildings were taking in far more than they cost to run, and the company was on track to turn a profit in 2012, unlike the money-losing startups Benchmark usually backed.

And like Eisenberg, Dunlevie was mesmerized by the devotion of those subtenants to the company—to the idea. The spaces were as full of energy as Neumann himself. With the reserved Dunlevie in tow, Neumann knocked on office doors—barging in even if the members were on phone calls—and asked for a minute of their time. They gushed about the friends they'd made.

Like Facebook and other social networks, Dunlevie realized, WeWork was taking off in part because it had a dorm-room-like energy. All of these twentysomethings wanted to interact with one another—to hook up with one another.

Soon after, Neumann boasted to his staff that Dunlevie told him he was "selling sex." Neumann loved it.

Dunlevie discussed the potential investment with his partners, who soon invited Neumann and Miguel McKelvey to California. The partners saw a lot to like, and some red flags, too. They were wowed by Neumann. He was a storyteller. He projected a tremendous confidence about what the future would hold; his confidence was contagious.

And they were mesmerized by the strong finances; WeWork's profit margins at its buildings, before other expenses, looked like some software companies'. The company also hit on trends that Benchmark had been looking to capitalize on. America's urban revival of the decade was still in its early days, and the firm wanted to tap into the burst of well-educated young people opting to live in city centers.

The downside, though, was potentially very significant: the company looked like a real estate business. Typically, venture capitalists don't invest in real estate, because it can't *scale* like a software company. The whole allure of software companies is that once they spend money to build their products, they can sell more and more software to new users at very low costs—sometimes just the price of sending a file. Profits grow exponentially.

Real estate, on the other hand, is more linear. Each time a landlord finds a new tenant, the owner needs to build new office space to fit the tenant. Even giant real estate companies see relatively few benefits of scale: buying in bulk could decrease costs somewhat, but landlords still have to pay for space to house the tenants. Ten buildings have the same profit margins as one building. This is why real estate companies raise less money than tech companies, and do so from non-software investors.

Neumann insisted WeWork wasn't a real estate company. After all, WeWork was making a lot more on individual locations than landlords would. Members were coming for the community, not just a desk, he said. Dunlevie, meanwhile, saw WeWork more like a services startup. Just as companies pay monthly fees for outsourced services like accounting, here they were paying for outsourced offices and work culture.

With Dunlevie a strong advocate, the Benchmark partners made their bet. Neumann would find a way to make WeWork giant. He was a winner, full stop, and they knew they'd be kicking themselves in a few years if they turned him down.

As Dunlevie said later, the thinking was, "Let's give him some money and he'll figure it out."

WHEN DUNLEVIE CALLED NEUMANN AND MCKELVEY WITH AN offer, Neumann wasn't impressed. The valuation—in the tens of millions of dollars—was too low. Valuation is a gauge of how hot and in demand the company is and how big its backers think it may be years in the future. The higher the valuation, the bigger the check a VC firm needs to write for the same-sized slice of the company. The bigger the check, the more money the company has available to plow into expansion.

McKelvey didn't have the same valuation lust as Neumann and was ready to be happy with whatever Benchmark was offering—aware of the power of their brand in tech circles. In the four years since he and Neumann had sweet-talked the Guttmans into letting them use his building for Green Desk, the co-founder had retreated into a more supporting role. He oversaw design and development, and at times marketing. He didn't want the responsibility of running the show: he'd later tell colleagues he liked starting projects but not following through on them. Neumann, who had initially consulted McKelvey on all sorts of matters, had found new executives and mentors to turn to instead. WeWork was clearly Neumann's show, and McKelvey recognized that would be increasingly true in the future.

Seeing the potential for tension in their asymmetric partnership, McKelvey approached Neumann to renegotiate their financial agreement with each other. The entity they controlled, We Holdings LLC, had a nearly even split between the two founders, as well a small stake for some friends and family. But he offered to cede a large chunk of future profits to Neumann, so long as he was guaranteed a certain amount up front—giving him some protection if Neumann overreached in the future. And if the company ever made it huge—being worth hundreds of millions of dollars— Neumann's stake in the LLC would jump to roughly 85 percent and McKelvey's would dip to 15 percent. McKelvey was pleased that he was richer than he ever imagined, and the renegotiated deal gave Neumann some license to reach high.

After Dunlevie made the offer, the entrepreneurs and the VC haggled on the phone. Neumann thought WeWork should be valued well over $100 million, he told Dunlevie. After a few minutes of back-and-forth, they met in the middle: Benchmark offered to invest $15 million in a deal that valued WeWork at just over $100 million. It was a hefty valuation for a young startup at the time, particularly one helmed by an inexperienced baby clothes salesman and based outside Silicon Valley. Together with another $2 million coming from Neumann's friend and mentor Steven Langman and his private equity group, Rhône, WeWork would get $17 million of new money to expand. Neumann and McKelvey, meanwhile, would get more than $500,000 for themselves—a sum the new investors figured would give Neumann some reward for what he'd built and a decent chunk of spending money to enjoy himself.

Neumann had interest from others, though none with the cachet of Benchmark. It was a tantalizing prospect to join the Benchmark portfolio, an elite club of Silicon Valley tech startups. A hundred million dollars meant that Benchmark saw big things in WeWork.

Neumann was getting the recognition—and the first taste of riches—that he had always craved. He took the deal.

CHAPTER 7

Activate the Space

Benchmark's imprimatur—and the $15 million that accompanied it—imbued WeWork with a new swagger. The stamp of approval from the vaunted Silicon Valley moneymen infused the company with a sense of invincibility and the aura of a booming Silicon Valley–style startup. Employees at WeWork believed the concept of the workplace was about to be revolutionized, and WeWork was leading the way.

Adam Neumann's lofty rhetoric was turning into reality.

He called much of WeWork's staff—numbering a few dozen—into his office one by one to give them stock options. Tech startups often grant employees shares that will be worth something only if the company succeeds. As each employee looked on, Neumann took out a scrap of paper and started to scribble numbers. Here is what your stock will be worth *when* WeWork is worth $500 million, he would say. And here it is at $1 billion. And here it is at $5 billion. Employees stared wide-eyed, seeing their stock grant swell from, say, $10,000 to $100,000 and then *half a million dollars.*

The implication was clear. It wasn't a question of "if." WeWork was bound for great heights, and everyone was going to get rich.

Through the rest of 2012 and into 2013, those ambitions were reflected in the company's expansion. It plotted locations in Chicago, Portland, and overseas to London. Real estate staff began boasting to skeptical landlords that the VCs behind eBay and Instagram were now backing them. Neumann leaned into his tech aspirations: to emerging tech startups, he pushed WeWork Labs, an open-floor-plan option where everyone worked without dividers. Modernist couches began sprouting up in WeWork lounges, an upgrade from the low-cost Ikea furniture of the early days. And to make good on his promise of a physical social network, Neumann hired software engineers to make an app on which members could connect with one another, find business partners, and make friends. He pushed a health insurance option for members, allowing tiny companies housed within WeWork's walls to offer their employees some of the benefits typically reserved for bigger companies.

WeWork was no longer one of those tiny companies. Since 2010, it had expanded to four locations in Manhattan, another in Los Angeles, and two locations in San Francisco. Neumann was now courting some of the biggest landlords in New York. He brought in local officials and reporters to show off the swelling business. And he sought out new investors, knowing he'd need far more than Benchmark's money to realize his vision of turning WeWork into a multibillion-dollar company.

With the parade of potential partners coming and going, Neumann perfected his sales pitch.

The tour was key. Guided by some of his deputies who had worked in the startup scene, Neumann obsessed over details, telling staff to "activate the space"—to show that WeWork was bursting with life and energy, that it was dramatically different from the sterile, boring offices of the past.

With this refrain in mind, Neumann's staff would instruct employees to be in the office at the time of the scheduled tour—sometimes at 9:00 or even 8:30 in the morning, frustratingly early for the twentysomethings. If a floor on the tour had empty desks, staffers would be asked to pick up their laptops and relocate to fill them so that the floor would appear to be packed with industrious

WeWork members no matter the hour. WeWork managers fussed over the playlist: the volume had to be fun but not distracting.

The cherry on top was the serendipitous event. When an employee running the front desk got the order to "activate the space," it meant a mad dash to throw an impromptu party with pizza, ice cream, or margaritas. The manager then sent an email to members and WeWork employees to gather in the common area for the free goods—without mentioning that investors were in tow. As the jeans-clad workers mingled over ice cream sundaes or drinks, Neumann whisked his guests by the commotion, sometimes remarking something like "events like this are always happening here." He'd then continue walking them through the glassy hallways, past the beer on tap and the arcade games.

From there, Neumann would lead them to his office, where he explained the business and the inevitability of its rapid growth. His guests were often suit-wearing landlords or investors, some old enough to be his parents. Sitting across from the towering, long-haired, smiling man in jeans and a T-shirt, they were taken aback by Neumann's panache. Spending an hour or two with Neumann was incomparable to any typical real estate meeting. Even before noon, he offered shots from the tall brown Don Julio 1942 tequila bottle he kept behind his desk. He dropped the names of actors like Ashton Kutcher or mayors like Rahm Emanuel of Chicago. Other times Rebekah and his two young daughters would pop in during a meeting—hugging him or running around his office. He was a fun family man—warm, brimming with hope and positivity—but he also had an air of brilliant business savvy to his pitch. To the landlords and investors, he seemed to *get* young people. It was a time when the word "millennial" was just beginning to invade the lexicon and businesses were scrambling to decode that generation.

Neumann gushed to his guests about the "We generation," his shorthand for millennials, who he said were looking for something fulfilling—more than just a job and a desk. Smartphones and digital social networks had fostered an era of loneliness in which people stared at screens and didn't have meaningful interactions; WeWork would be the solution.

Increasingly, he would talk about WeWork as a tech company. He pointed out the similarities between WeWork and highly regarded startups like Uber and Airbnb, saying that WeWork was all about sharing space. WeWork, he told some potential investors, was also just a "platform" like Facebook or LinkedIn—one on which the company could layer services like accounting and software products, finding ways to generate further revenue from rent-paying members down the road.

To the press, he boasted of the communal aspects of WeWork. He implored reporters not to portray WeWork as a real estate company. One public relations firm hired by WeWork in 2013 was instructed to not pitch to real estate reporters but to hunt for others, like tech reporters, to cover the company. When stories referred to WeWork as a "real estate company" or "real estate startup," WeWork PR representatives were instructed to call reporters and ask them to change the description.

In reality, WeWork's tech was hardly cutting edge. The company was struggling to put together a basic billing system, let alone build a killer app. But investors didn't dwell on these details. The pitch was too compelling.

Part of the appeal was the conviction with which Neumann declared that the business would maintain its growth rate. When a location opens up in a new city like Portland, he'd say, it will be full within weeks. It was something he inherently couldn't *know,* but he said it with such confidence that it left no room for doubt.

"By 2020," he'd say, "40 percent of the entire workforce in the U.S. will be small businesses, entrepreneurs, and freelancers. They all need a solution."

He glossed over details. The stats he tossed around actually referred to how corporations were shifting to rely on long-term freelance arrangements instead of full-time staffers, which would likely have little effect on co-working demand. But guests usually were too entranced to ask tough questions.

Neumann conducted countless meetings and walkthroughs like this throughout 2012 and 2013. Like the star of a hit Broadway play, he mastered the performance, with the curtains rising day after day for a newly enraptured audience.

The pitch made Neumann a hit with some of the biggest landlords in the city. Still starving in a postrecession New York, where few tenants were expanding and banks were still shrinking, big property owners started buzzing to one another about Neumann, the energetic character who was signing shockingly large leases for such a young company. He became friendly with Mort Zuckerman, chairman of the office landlord giant Boston Properties and owner of the New York *Daily News;* he hung out at Zuckerman's house in the Hamptons and discussed a possible investment in the business. He chatted with the leaders of firms like Forest City Ratner and Rudin Management. To these titans of New York real estate, Neumann would explain how he wasn't competing; he was appealing to a demographic that ordinarily worked out of their homes or coffee shops, a group far too dispersed for landlords to attract on their own. Like Benchmark, they were amazed at how his early spaces garnered healthy profit margins: as he told them, each location was spitting out profit margins of more than 30 percent. That meant that for every $10 WeWork spent in a month on rent and staff salaries for an office, that office was taking in more than $13 from members—a figure that didn't include all the money WeWork spent on expansion and headquarters staff.

They were all impressed by WeWork's growth rate, too. The company took in $19 million of revenue in 2012 and was on track to pass $30 million by the end of 2013. Neumann hungered to grow even faster in the future. After all, it was a good way to push We-

Work's valuation even higher; investors loved fast growth and placed a premium on companies that were expanding rapidly.

Of course, a rapid pace of growth would require that much more investment. WeWork, after posting a tiny profit in 2012, was back in the red and losing money as it plowed cash into expansion. Benchmark had provided a start, but its style wasn't to fund a company for years with ever-larger funding rounds. If WeWork was going to keep climbing upward, it would need more investors with far more money, all believing in the company's exponential trajectory. Anything less, and WeWork would be an airplane in a stall.

By the spring of 2013, wework's rising ambitions brought it to a new headquarters. It signed a large lease for more than 120,000 square feet at 222 Broadway, where its own offices would sit alongside space rented by members. The boxy lower Manhattan building was where Oliver Stone's film *Wall Street*—the 1980s critique of corporate avarice—was filmed. (Neumann's office was down the hall from where Gordon Gekko proclaimed that "greed is good.")

Growing bigger meant the company was burning through the Benchmark cash. Neumann had left the task of additional fund-raising until perilously late in the process. By this time, WeWork had one or two months of cash—at most—left in its accounts. Fund-raising is always a high-wire act for money-losing startups, and Neumann was habitually late to lots of things, so this wasn't terribly out of character. Still, senior employees worried that the entire company could unravel if for any reason Neumann couldn't pull it off.

Neumann, seemingly nonplussed, began to focus on finding investors for WeWork's second round of funding. In venture-capital-speak, it is known as the Series B, following Benchmark's Series A funding round. Successful startups typically take on a few rounds and then go public, once they are on a path to profit.

To the delight of the WeWork team, Goldman Sachs was interested. While the bank is better known for running IPOs than investing in startups, it had a division that invested clients' money in early-stage startups. After pitching WeWork to the bank, Neumann and his staff hopped onto a conference call, where the Goldman team said they were interested in investing at a roughly $200 million valuation.

It was a giant number: more than double the valuation that Benchmark had given WeWork six months prior. Neumann and McKelvey's joint entity still held a huge percentage of shares—more than half—so the deal would give them paper wealth they couldn't have imagined just three or four years earlier. It was a very lofty valuation for any young company, let alone one with just a few offices open, and the Goldman name alone would open other doors.

Neumann, though, wanted more. After mulling the offer, he hopped on another call with the bank.

"No," he told the Goldman team.

An awkward silence followed. Neumann didn't negotiate; he just told them it was too low. He thanked them for their offer and ended the call.

Neumann's subordinates and his advisers were jolted and concerned. WeWork now risked running out of cash simply because Neumann wasn't content with a mere $200 million company.

It didn't take long for Neumann to round up the needed money. Another Silicon Valley VC firm, DAG Ventures, had taken a look months earlier. The firm was known for betting on software companies, and it frequently invested in promising startups already backed by Benchmark.

The firm liked WeWork's progress and loved Neumann's drive. DAG came back with an offer: they were prepared to lead a $40 million investment at a $460 million valuation. Neumann quickly found others to join in with smaller checks, because he'd been courting numerous other investors who could add credibility. Joining in the round were the investment bank Jefferies, the large New

York landlord Rudin Management, and Joey Low, a well-liked investor based in Israel who had friends in the New York real estate scene.

By May 2013, it had all come together—just weeks after the Goldman Sachs offer.

WeWork executives exhaled. Neumann's gamble had paid off. *What couldn't this guy do?*

CHAPTER 8

Me Over We

As WEWORK GREW, ONE PHRASE ADAM NEUMANN LIKED TO employ was "we over me." He used it to capture the ethos of the "We generation" he described to funders. He used it to justify endless workdays for staff, meetings that would bleed into the early morning, weekends devoted to opening up the next WeWork location. In company meetings, he'd say to staff that they were creating WeWork *together*. It was their company, and sometimes that meant making personal sacrifices for the greater good.

But as he preached a gospel of egalitarianism, Neumann was quietly cutting favorable deals for himself.

When a company like WeWork raises tens of millions of dollars in a big Series B round, the money is usually crucial for expansion— for transforming a company from a tiny startup to a legitimate challenger to larger rivals. With its $40 million, WeWork was by no means short of places to spend money. Beyond its desire to open new offices around the globe, it needed new staff—bodies to lighten the load of a growth-focused team that was used to endless workweeks with little vacation, and more people to build the cutting-edge technology Neumann promised.

But not all of the $40 million WeWork raised went to expansion. A large chunk went into Neumann's bank account.

The company lent nearly a quarter of its recent fund-raising haul—$9 million—to We Holdings LLC, the entity Neumann created with McKelvey that held their shares in WeWork. Neumann expected that he'd repay the loan as WeWork's valuation rose.

In hindsight, it was a harbinger of many similar cash withdrawals to come. Neumann and McKelvey had taken out over $500,000 when Benchmark invested in 2012 but Neumann had committed to taking no salary as a concession. Now he was taking out a far larger amount just to fund his own lifestyle.

This act was antithetical to the standard startup playbook. Historically, founders led scrappy lives while the company was in its early years. Only once a company gets big enough and sells or completes an IPO—listing on a stock exchange—should the founder be able to take money out, the thinking went. The idea was that all investors and employees would get rich at the same time. If founders got rich first, it could diminish their drive.

But Neumann wasn't interested in roughing it. His board of directors was easy to sway, consisting only of himself, the founder-friendly Bruce Dunlevie of Benchmark, and Steven Langman, his friend who ran a private equity firm. For a company now valued at $460 million, $9 million perhaps seemed like a nominal sum. After all, the business was going well, and the valuation was on a course to keep rising.

It was clear to the directors, as well as anyone who knew Neumann well, that he was overextended, unable to control his spending in his personal life. He appeared eager to keep Rebekah happy and give her the comfortable life she expected for their expanding family. Perhaps the millions might ease Neumann's anxieties, the thinking went.

Indeed, Neumann and his wife had been living large. He had long felt destined for wealth and fame. But now, as WeWork's success with investors grew, Neumann's head grew with it.

Many of their friends were wealthier than the Neumanns. Around the time that WeWork was getting off the ground, they upgraded from a modest condo in the East Village to a sprawling five-thousand-square-foot loft they rented in Tribeca. Neumann persuaded the landlord to fork over some money for renovations. They had the floors painted jet black, a stark contrast to the electric-orange furniture they brought in. Its walls lined with expensive art, the apartment garnered a feature in *New York,* for which the designer Laser Rosenberg told the magazine that "Adam's company, WeWork, handled the building of the kitchen."

But with the infusion of cash from the loan, the Neumanns kicked their spending up a few notches. Travel became more extravagant. Neumann began taking private planes, sometimes borrowing the jet of his new friend and investor Mort Zuckerman. A WeWork staffer started whisking Neumann around in an SUV.

Shortly after they completed work on their Tribeca condo, the couple decided to buy an 1840s brick town house near Sean Parker's party house in the West Village. They paid $10.5 million for the house, with a mortgage of $8.4 million, and plotted a lengthy renovation that called for a lavish roof deck filled with trees and a "stroller parking garage."

BEYOND BORROWING FROM THE COMPANY, NEUMANN FOUND other ways to make some money for himself off WeWork: its buildings.

Around the time Benchmark came into the company, Neumann got a chance to personally invest in the building that held one of WeWork's early locations in Manhattan, 175 Varick Street. He rounded up a group of friends and WeWork investors to pay roughly $1 million for a small stake in the building. Despite some misgivings, the WeWork board—Langman and Dunlevie—permitted it to go through, given the small check.

It wasn't a very savory financial structure. The deal meant that WeWork—using investors' money—was paying rent to a building personally owned, in part, by Neumann. Among other potential pitfalls, the arrangement would make any future negotiations awkward, given that Neumann was on both sides, potentially giving him an incentive to let WeWork pay a higher rent than it normally would have.

The stake quickly turned a big profit. The building's owner decided to sell a little more than a year later, and Neumann was also manager on the property and thus entitled to an outsized share of the earnings. He turned a roughly $1 million investment into more than $3 million—a huge windfall.

Seeing the ease with which money poured in through this structure, Neumann wanted to do it again. He zeroed in on a building in Chicago where WeWork was eyeing its first location in the area. A local developer there, Jeff Shapack, was trying to buy and renovate a building in a former meat-packing district west of downtown, a neighborhood marked by cobblestone streets and a young population. Neumann agreed that WeWork would be his tenant, if he could also buy a stake in the building with Shapack. Neumann would again have been on both sides: tenant, using the money of Benchmark and other investors to sign the deal, and landlord, using his own funds.

This time, his investors slammed the brakes. Michael Eisenberg persuaded Neumann to drop it; the structure was a bad look, he said. If WeWork was serious about becoming a giant business, the conflicts could scare off future investors and raise all sorts of knotty questions. What if WeWork needed to renegotiate a lease? Would Neumann's company negotiate with an entity partially owned by Neumann?

But because the deal was well under way, the board said that WeWork would buy the stake instead of Neumann. After that, they told Neumann, WeWork shouldn't be using its money to buy real estate.

IN MID-AUGUST 2013, A SEAPLANE CIRCLED OVER RAQUETTE LAKE, a picturesque vacation spot in the Adirondack Mountains. It skidded onto the surface and slowed to a stop, bobbing in the water. Adam Neumann stepped out.

WeWork was throwing a summer-camp-themed party 275 miles north of New York City, and all its staff and members were invited. Its staff attended for free, and members paid nominal sums to join. New West Coast members were even given subsidized plane flights. With more VC money in hand, WeWork wanted to show members and staffers alike that WeWork was the complete opposite of a sterile corporate firm.

The startup took over an entire summer camp—one owned by the family of Mark Lapidus, the company's head of real estate and a first cousin of Rebekah Neumann's. Hundreds of attendees waited on Manhattan street corners, where they were picked up by a caravan of green charter buses. The drive was nearly five hours, but the free-flowing booze helped the time pass.

Once they made it through the mountains to sprawling Raquette Lake, the passengers traded the bus for a boat, which ferried them across the lake to cabins. The property was packed with everything a twelve-year-old at sleepaway camp could dream of. For three days, the attendees could rotate among archery, high ropes courses, rock climbing, swimming, canoeing, motorboating, and softball. Throughout the weekend, there were pie-eating contests and giant team games, all doused with alcohol. Neumann lorded around the camp and cut to the head of the line where attendees waited for boats to take them waterskiing and elsewhere on the lake.

At night, the camp turned into a music festival, complete with lasers and smoke machines. Eight bands were brought in. It was a mix of indie rock—Ra Ra Riot was the headliner—and EDM like White Panda. The crowd danced with glow-stick headbands.

When Ra Ra Riot played a set, Neumann had them deviate from their act to play Journey's "Don't Stop Believin'." The CEO sang onstage alongside the band.

Neumann's VIP treatment—even in a campground—marked a

contrast to his co-founder. Miguel McKelvey didn't fly in by plane, instead opting to take the bus along with the employees. Around that time, Neumann stopped informing McKelvey of certain key decisions, including some that took place during private discussions with WeWork's directors. McKelvey would often be surprised to learn that Neumann had met with board members for dinner ahead of official meetings.

If there was any discord below the surface, it wasn't apparent to the hard-partying WeWork faithful who had gathered upstate. On one of the nights, Neumann got up on the band stage to speak and address everyone.

"Thank you. Thank you for being part of something that actually has a meaning," he said, clutching a microphone, his face taken over by a big smile. "The thing that all of us know is, if you want to succeed in this world, you have to build something that has intention . . . ," he said, looking out over the crowd below.

"Every one of us is here because it has a meaning—because we want to do something that actually makes the world a better place," he yelled.

His voice continuing to rise, quickening in pace, he added: "And we want to make money doing it!"

Cheers erupted.

CHAPTER 9

Mutual Fund FOMO

I N FEBRUARY 2014, ADAM NEUMANN ONCE AGAIN HAD A REASON to smile. On the first of the month, WeWork had opened buildings in three new cities—Boston, Washington, D.C., and Seattle, adding to its existing outposts in New York, Los Angeles, and San Francisco. The company's coffers were growing. Neumann had raised money yet again, this time at an even more stunning valuation. WeWork was now officially a unicorn—Silicon Valley's term for startups that were worth more than $1 billion.

To attain this new designation, Neumann had accepted money from a new source: JPMorgan Chase. The bank's asset management division, essentially a private equity group within the bank, invests billions of dollars on behalf of outside investors. Larry Unrein, a longtime private equity executive who oversaw investments at AT&T's retirement fund before switching to JPMorgan, had been looking to invest in WeWork, but his earlier proposals hadn't gained traction with others at the bank. By the time WeWork wanted to do its Series C, its track record was convincing enough to give Unrein the green light. The bank led a $150 million investment into the company, valuing it at $1.5 billion. It was a huge slug of money—more than twice what WeWork had raised in its four-year history.

Staff were elated by their boss's adept ability to win over deep-pocketed investors at giant valuations. Thanks to his magic touch, they were all getting rich. For employees holding stock options—which generally varied from thousands to hundreds of thousands of dollars when they were issued—their stock was now worth over *ten times* more than when Benchmark invested two years earlier, at least on paper. Just four years old, WeWork was already the billion-dollar company Neumann had envisioned when he was opening the first building.

Still, he wasn't close to being done. Airbnb would soon nab a *$10 billion* valuation, and Neumann saw himself in that stratosphere. More and more, he was portraying WeWork as a tech company. WeWork was part of the sharing economy; it needed offices just as Uber and Airbnb needed cars and apartments, he told investors. Its tech was cutting edge, he'd say. The entrepreneur who could barely use a MacBook managed to pepper references to technology effortlessly into his pitch.

WeWork was offering "space as a service"—a play on the "software as a service" business model that was taking off in Silicon Valley. The company was "powered by technology at every layer," according to slide presentations. In these pitches, WeWork neatly displayed data within screenshots of iPhones and MacBooks, as though they were essential tools for using the office space.

Armed with the teched-up marketing mystique and with a financial system hungry for startups, Neumann embarked on one of the more shocking feats of valuation growth in startup history, just months after receiving JPMorgan's $1.5 billion valuation. In a mere sixteen months, WeWork's valuation ballooned to $5 billion and then again to $10 billion, despite little change in the trajectory of the business.

Enabling it all was a surprising new player pouring money into Silicon Valley startups: mutual funds.

.   .   .

It was early 2015, and gavin baker was frustrated. baker, one of the star portfolio managers at the giant mutual fund manager Fidelity Investments, had just heard from a banker that his biggest rival fund manager, Henry Ellenbogen, had recently invested in a shared office space company he'd never heard of: WeWork. Ellenbogen's firm, T. Rowe Price, had valued it at $5 billion.

The deal marked the end of a swift Series D fund-raising round put together by Neumann. Armed with his tech-saturated slide deck, Neumann had sold Ellenbogen on his idea that WeWork was a bet on the sharing economy—not some humdrum real estate concern. Ellenbogen was so impressed by the rapid growth that he boasted to *The Wall Street Journal* that anyone who saw WeWork's finances would "compare it to a brand or tech company—maybe Chipotle or Uber." Uber had become red hot, with its valuation soaring to $41 billion by the end of 2014, making it the most valuable private, venture-backed startup in the United States.

Baker, energetic and competitive, had long been frustrated that Fidelity wasn't competing for all the same deals as T. Rowe. He fired off an email to Fidelity's private markets team, asking them why he hadn't seen the company's pitch or met the CEO. Fidelity, he believed, needed to be out there on the same field as its competitors, scooping up the hottest startups in Silicon Valley as they hunted for new investments. He didn't want to miss companies like this again.

Had baker and ellenbogen—two highly respected mutual fund managers—clawed their way up the ladder at Fidelity and T. Rowe Price just a few decades earlier, they wouldn't have been wading into the world of startups. Instead, they would have been focused on picking stocks—finding the best companies that trade on the Nasdaq or New York Stock Exchange, where the financials were filed openly for all the world to see.

Since the 1920s, mutual funds had given investors a low-cost way to trade in and out of a basket of stocks. The funds gave Americans the chance to stow away their money while letting professionals make the bets. Fidelity's founder, Edward Johnson II, compared his portfolio managers to violin virtuosos—stock pickers who were empowered to bet as they saw fit, each playing his own song. For decades, these virtuosos were custodians of Americans' wealth as households entrusted their retirement savings and extra cash to mutual fund managers like Fidelity, T. Rowe Price, and Vanguard.

But by the 1990s, mutual fund managers were regularly outperformed by broader stock market indexes like the S&P 500 and the Nasdaq. Championed by Vanguard's founder, Jack Bogle, index funds made many question the supposed genius of mutual fund stock pickers. Rather than pay modestly higher fees to the mutual funds, investors were becoming inclined to pay tiny fees for baskets of stocks that simply tracked an index of publicly traded companies. "Active managers" like Baker and Ellenbogen were losing ground—and assets under management—to these passive funds.

And there were fewer actual stocks to pick. In 1997, the number of U.S.-listed companies peaked at 9,113. By the time Baker and Ellenbogen started managing their institutions' well-known funds in 2009 and 2010, as private capital became more plentiful and executives sought to avoid the added reporting pressures from the public markets, that number had dropped by a third, to fewer than 6,000.

Around this time, Ellenbogen made a move that would help usher in a new era for mutual funds. He oversaw a 2009 investment in Twitter when it was still a private company, well before its 2013 IPO. The Twitter stake wound up being a bonanza for Ellenbogen. By 2015, it had returned more than ten times T. Rowe's investment; by 2017, it was twenty times.

Typically, investments in still-private companies like Twitter were strictly the domain of venture capital firms. Traditionally, VC firms would fund startups for the first few years until the company went public and then hand off the baton to the much larger mutual funds, which in turn would buy into companies like Amazon and Google in their IPOs. Then the VCs would typically sell their stakes and pass the bag onto the new investors.

But Ellenbogen's eye-popping returns on Twitter attracted attention in the stodgy mutual fund community. Then came Facebook's 2012 IPO. When the social-networking company went public, it was already valued at $104 billion, making it the largest valuation ever for an American company at IPO. It had grown into a far larger enterprise than anyone was used to seeing in a private company.

It was a big contrast to even the late 1990s. Amazon, for example, was valued at just $440 million when it went public in 1997, allowing public market investors who got in early to eventually get a more than thousandfold return on their money. With Facebook, the beneficiaries of this early success were the private market investors, because the public market investors had less room for growth, given its already hulking size by the time it listed on the Nasdaq.

The mutual funds were tired of missing out. They had spent years losing dollars to index funds. One good way to beat the stock market, they reasoned, was to buy companies that aren't on the stock market. The private investment market, after all, wasn't just about buying and selling through a broker. It was governed by relationships, and CEOs could pick and choose which investors they wanted. Deals were a negotiation over price and terms, not just placing a buy order for some shares.

So numerous mutual funds opened their spigots to startups. They would commit only small slivers of their funds to the space, they said. But even slivers of the *trillions* of dollars they oversaw meant geysers of money suddenly rushing into technology companies—or any company that could pass itself off as one. By 2015, mutual funds had $8 billion of investments in venture-capital-backed private companies, up from $16 million two decades earlier.

It was a tiny crumb of the mutual funds' total investments but a huge chunk in the context of the venture capital industry, which raised around $38 billion a year.

The effect of this influx of investment cash from mutual funds was to push already lofty startup valuations even higher. It was a move layered with risk. Mutual fund managers who typically invested in public stocks had learned their trade through number crunching, deep financial analysis, and a conservative long-term approach. They of course could be won over by a charismatic public market CEO, but that executive would still have to disclose reams of financials every single quarter. A CEO could sell a dream to public investors, but he could just as easily be unmasked by the numbers he was forced to report.

The private markets, by contrast, had no real guidelines on what metrics had to be reported or what disclosures needed to be made. Absent outright fraud, which the SEC and the Department of Justice had license to target, the arbiters were largely the investors themselves. And they were all fighting to get into the same buzzy companies. It was a dynamic ripe for clouding judgment.

Further, investors in private markets couldn't buy and sell stock in an instant, as the public markets could. Not only would that trap a mutual fund in a bad investment, but it also made it hard to determine the *true* valuation of a company. Investors had to make an educated guess as to how a company would trade once it went public in the future, and that's how they valued the company.

In this world, certain founders shone. With fewer disclosures required, private companies could lean heavily on showing revenue growth—something all investors wanted—and offer little detail on the spending that fueled the growth. A CEO was largely selling the company's "story," painting a picture of how the world was changing in his or her favor, be it the obsolescence of car ownership or the appeal of a hotel room based in a home. Revenue would keep growing, CEOs would say, and profits were sure to follow.

Further adding to the chaos was the relative scarcity of startups looking for big sums. Giant mutual funds like Fidelity were hoping to spend billions, so they certainly didn't want to waste time parceling it out in bundles of $10 million. Given that relatively few companies could absorb $200 million at a time, startups that could take large checks were that much more appealing to mutual funds.

Baker, having watched Ellenbogen's success and widespread acclaim in this new game, saw the importance of finding the next Twitter or Facebook. Wooing tech founders became a key part of his job. "What matters the most in venture capital and private investing is whether you're invited to play," Baker would later tell *The Wall Street Journal*.

Getting in the door was the most important part.

On a friday afternoon in the spring of 2015, baker finally got his chance to look at WeWork.

The banker who first informed Baker about WeWork was helping Neumann's company raise another round of funding. After Baker expressed interest, he set up a meeting with the CEO. Neumann arrived at a conference room on the eleventh floor of Fidelity's headquarters in Boston's Financial District. When Baker came in, Neumann told him he needed to get something off his chest. Others at Fidelity, Neumann said, had actually looked at WeWork earlier, for the same round that T. Rowe looked—something Baker didn't know at the time. Neumann explained he'd had a terrible experience with the Fidelity employees he met. They didn't understand WeWork's business at all, or even *try* to understand it, Neumann told him. And they were very low energy.

Bespectacled and bearded, Baker prided himself on his ability to connect with entrepreneurs more easily than the stereotypical suit-wearing fund manager. An excitable extrovert nearing forty, he could get along well with big-vision founders. As he liked to tell the entrepreneurs, investing was an accidental career path. As an undergraduate at Dartmouth College, he imagined he'd be a ski instructor or a mountain-climbing guide.

Baker, chagrined by his initial miss on the WeWork investment, set about winning over Neumann. He asked Neumann to give the institution another chance. Neumann calmed down. "The energy is so different than the first time," he told Baker. "The energy with you is so good."

Neumann began walking Baker through the story of WeWork. As Neumann spoke, Baker fired off an email to other fund managers inside Fidelity. Within fifteen minutes, Neumann was surrounded by nearly a dozen of Baker's colleagues, including Will Danoff, who ran one of Fidelity's largest and most successful funds, and Andy Boyd, who oversaw Fidelity's private capital efforts. By the end of the meeting, Baker and Danoff had promised to meet Neumann again the following Friday to tour one of WeWork's Boston locations.

On that tour, Baker, Danoff, and numerous other Fidelity employees blitzed through the WeWork office. The floors were packed and buzzing with activity, as planned. The Fidelity team was hooked on Neumann's every word. He told them how he could redesign Fidelity's offices to make them more productive and enticing to young workers—how they, too, could have a community as vibrant as WeWork.

By the end of the meeting, Danoff and Baker were convinced it could be a promising investment. They'd do further work, they told Neumann, but they gave him strong signals that Fidelity would be on board.

Not everyone in the firm was bullish. When Andy Boyd, who ran the private markets group, evaluated WeWork in 2014, he and an analyst on his team couldn't make the math work at a $5 billion valuation. With their opinions unchanged this time around, the analyst even filed a memo detailing her many concerns with the company. Its revenue was tied to physical space—it looked like a real estate company, not a tech company, so the valuation was far too high. Even with high occupancy rates and minimal spending on marketing, each building could generate only a limited amount of revenue, unlike, say, a piece of software.

But in 2015, when Neumann charmed Danoff and Baker, the two well-regarded investors looked more kindly on WeWork's numbers. The firm saw some of the risks, but numerous top investors were already in the company, and the numbers looked great; existing locations were generating far more money than they cost to run. What's more, WeWork's revenue was soaring, and its profit projections were eye-popping. WeWork was projected to go from $73 million of revenue in 2014 to *$2.8 billion* in 2018. Given how strong its margins were at its buildings, WeWork expected more than $1 billion in *profit* in 2018.

In the end, the views of Baker and Danoff won out. Internal misgivings by Boyd and the analyst were drowned out by the possibility for a home run—based on the story Neumann was pushing. Plenty of other companies like Uber were exploding in valuation because other investors had believed in their extraordinary potential. For the two fund managers, this was their chance to be part of something huge. If Neumann was right and WeWork was due to turn into a $100 billion company, it would make them and Fidelity look good. And if he was wrong, it wasn't a ton of money to lose. It was a gamble worth taking, they thought.

The investment went through.

Baker put in about $10 million from his fund, while Danoff's far-larger fund committed over $200 million—both small numbers for the two managers, but a big check for WeWork. After rounding up other investors to bring the investment haul to more than $400 million, WeWork announced the deal on June 24, 2015. Just six months after the T. Rowe Price deal had valued WeWork at $5 billion, Fidelity's investment valued WeWork at $10 billion. The company was vaulted into a whole new category.

Suddenly WeWork was the seventh most valuable startup in the country. Now it would be mentioned in the same breath as Airbnb, Uber, and Snapchat; it was worth more than the $9 billion blood-testing company Theranos and more than all but a handful of publicly traded office landlords. Even the nation's largest publicly traded office owner, Boston Properties, was now within reach, at $20 billion. WeWork was by far the most valuable startup in New York City.

Neumann himself was now worth around $3 billion on paper.

BEYOND ALL THE NEW MONEY COMING INTO THE COMPANY, THE fund-raising rounds were extraordinary wins for Neumann in another arena. Both deals enhanced his standing within the company and swelled his personal bank account balance.

Seeing the massive demand from the mutual funds, Neumann added a condition to the deals. He wanted to sell some of his own shares too, and he wanted to sell them at the valuation at which the funds were investing. He wanted tens of millions of dollars from each of them.

T. Rowe Price asked Neumann why he would need so much money. It was an unusual move, after all: Travis Kalanick at Uber had made a point of telling investors and employees that to demonstrate his commitment to the company, he hadn't sold a single share. But Neumann explained that it was just a small slice of his overall holdings—a few percentage points—and that millions of these dollars were earmarked for charity. (Neumann was uncharacteristically quiet about charitable causes he funded: he liked to stay anonymous and rarely disclosed whom he had donated to. Recipients included groups tied to sick children and the Kabbalah Centre. At other times, he would simply give money away to help others, paying for top doctors when a colleague or friend was in need of a procedure.) And the rest of the money would pay for a few luxuries here and there, like private jet travel. He was tall, he told them, and commercial flights were uncomfortable.

Neumann's board members and prior investors were concerned, but they let the sales go through. The main entity controlled by Neumann, We Holdings, and another earmarked for his charity sold $120 million between the T. Rowe Price and Fidelity deals. That was on top of $14 million withdrawn in the funding round led by JPMorgan.

The mutual fund deals also enabled Neumann to seize more control. Until T. Rowe Price came along, Neumann had controlled more than 50 percent of the shares in the company, keeping him firmly in the pilot's seat. But given that T. Rowe Price was buying a decent chunk of the company, its investment could have upset that balance. Neumann then mandated that all shares from existing investors carried ten times as many votes as a standard share. Existing investors like Benchmark didn't find this problematic, because their votes increased, too.

When Fidelity entered the scene, Neumann wanted to change the terms again. He devised yet another structure with the help of his new chief legal officer, Jen Berrent, a brusque and driven attorney in her early forties who had worked with WeWork while a partner at a corporate law firm. Neumann's votes—and those of a few other early investors—would be in a separate class that got ten votes per share. This time, most everyone else, including Benchmark and Fidelity, would get one vote, not ten. As Berrent devised it, the structure would let Neumann stay in command of the company for years to come. He had a stake of around 30 percent, but even if he sold it off so that he had only around 5 percent of the shares, he would still be in full control.

Neumann was strategic about pushing this new structure through the board, which needed to approve it. After explaining to Fidelity that the mutual fund would have to abide by this new structure if it wanted to invest, he sprang it on the board. The new investors, he told the directors, had already agreed to the change, and now the rest of the board needed to agree, too.

Bruce Dunlevie of Benchmark was surprised, and not happy.

Neumann didn't need such control, he told him. It could even come back to hurt him. Dunlevie tried to paint a dark picture for Neumann of what could come if he spurned any guardrails.

"Absolute power corrupts absolutely," he told him, parroting British historian John Dalberg-Acton's famous quote.

Neumann responded by pointing out what he saw as Benchmark's hypocrisy. Benchmark backed both Snapchat and Uber, two companies in which the CEOs had enhanced voting power that gave them a firm grip on their companies. Amid the influx of money from mutual funds and others, the balance of power had shifted in Silicon Valley. Founders who looked and acted the part—decisive leadership, expansive vision—had plenty of sway over investors eager to place bets on the next Steve Jobs. Mark Zuckerberg had secured his control over Facebook by selling shares to Russian investors years before the IPO, in exchange for the ability to vote those shares. He also had shares with ten times the votes of a standard share. Travis Kalanick of Uber and Evan Spiegel of Snapchat struck similar arrangements. Neumann was trying to build a company the size of Google, and Google's founders had voting control. Why shouldn't he get it, too?

Dunlevie relented. He wouldn't vote against the structure, he told Neumann. Making him rework the terms could be a bad look for the new investors, and other CEOs of hot startups indeed had similar setups. As Neumann had hoped, the board then signed off on the move, surrendering their own power as they gave him full founder control. It would prove to be a turning point with vast implications for WeWork's future. A teenager had been given a sports car with a full tank of gas.

On a weeknight in April 2015, as he was preparing to finalize the deal with Fidelity, Neumann held an impromptu celebration in his office.

It was around 9:00 p.m., and only a handful of employees were still working at WeWork's headquarters at 222 Broadway in lower Manhattan. Neumann pulled several of his close friends and associates into his own office and called them over to his bar cart. As they downed shots of tequila and blasted hip-hop, the small gathering became increasingly boisterous. One executive started dancing on a table with the speakers held over his head.

Miguel McKelvey stepped outside Neumann's office so that he and another colleague could converse and actually hear each other. Through the glass that separated Neumann's office from dozens of desks, they watched Neumann, holding a large bottle of tequila, pull his arm back as he readied to throw it. McKelvey sidled out of the way. Moments later, Neumann released the bottle, sending it crashing through one of three panes of glass, spraying shards into the common office space. McKelvey avoided injury.

Another employee followed suit. The bottle hit the middle panel two-thirds of the way up, immediately shattering it. The blue-tinted glass cascaded to the floor. A third bottle followed, and the entire glass wall that separated Neumann's office from his employees was in shards on the floor. The room cheered.

At that moment, a member of WeWork's cleaning staff walked by. Chris Hill, Rebekah Neumann's brother-in-law and a senior executive, ran out and told her not to worry. They'd clean it up themselves.

By the morning, there were three new panels of plexiglass in place, and the shards had been cleaned from the floor. There was not a trace of the previous night's debauchery, except that one member of the tech team had to ask why his computer monitor was cracked.

Neumann was entering a new era. There was more money to throw around, and there were plenty of people to clean up after him.

CHAPTER 10

Bubbling Over

MARK DIXON WAS DUMBFOUNDED.

The fifty-five-year-old CEO of Regus couldn't make sense of the company he kept reading about in the press. Its valuation was so high, yet its business was so simple. Businesses renting office space, with coffee and beer on tap? Surely there must have been more to the story than just what was presented. What am I missing? he thought.

Dixon was hardly a bystander. Regus was the world's dominant provider of serviced office space. The company leased space from landlords, then renovated it into smaller offices that were subleased at a premium to other companies. Since launching in 1989, Dixon had grown the company's footprint to an enormous forty million square feet, a space equivalent to that of thirteen Empire State Buildings, spread across 104 countries. It was profitable, growing briskly. The stock market valued Regus at well over $2.5 billion.

WeWork was a fraction of its size; Regus had about fourteen times more people paying for desks than the startup darling did at the end of 2014 and had been around for two decades longer. And yet WeWork was worth four times *more* than Regus.

Why?

. . .

Dixon, a likable, glass-half-full businessman with sandy hair and nascent jowls, had risen from working-class roots in Britain to become a global CEO with a sprawling Monaco estate and multiple vineyards. At sixteen, he had dropped out of school and started a sandwich delivery business. From his tiny bicycle-based enterprise, he graduated to hot dogs. From there he recognized there was money in bread and became a sizable manufacturer of buns. He sold that business and made a turn far away from the culinary: he saw potential riches in the world of leasing office space.

Venturing into continental Europe, in 1989 he opened a business center in Brussels, renting out offices to small businesses. He would lease a space, renovate, and arrange for services like providing phones, while the short-term subtenants paid a premium to take advantage of the plug-and-play space. It was simply real estate arbitrage. Dixon was leasing at a low price, spending some money to spruce up the space and make the property inviting, and then finding tenants to sublease at a significantly higher price.

He wasn't the first entrepreneur to come up with the idea. Indeed, these enterprises proved strangely magnetic to optimistic and charismatic entrepreneurs who built them up in booms and saw them crumble in downturns.

The sector's most notable pioneer was a flamboyant Southern California attorney named Paul Fegen, who rapidly created a giant collection of office space centers for small law firms in the 1970s. Fegen used his swelling riches to throw a constant stream of giant parties; one had fourteen hundred invitees and featured a Hollywood stylist cutting Fegen's lengthy beard for guests to watch. For another he rented out a roller disco; attendees included *Wheel of Fortune*'s Vanna White. His rapid expansion proved wobbly, though. During a real estate bust, his company plunged into bankruptcy in 1982. Fegen later became a magician, showcasing his card tricks on *America's Got Talent*.

A decade or so later, an ambitious Dixon saw appeal in the same business model, and with a combination of skill and timing he was soon proved right. Demand was high, and he was able to self-fund expansion for years, spreading the Regus name across Europe. In the late 1990s, he made a big push into the United States as the dot-com boom from Silicon Valley led to a global surge in demand from tech startups and others. Large corporations began to warm to the concept, flooding Regus with new clients as they turned to the provider for satellite offices. The company nearly doubled in size and revenue annually, year after year. An affable salesman, Dixon won over landlords and investors with his pitch: that Regus was at the forefront of a change in how everyone would work.

The overall industry was growing, too. Numerous U.S. opera-tors had popped up, filling their offices with dot-com companies and others paying healthy rents. But Dixon had a particular hunger to keep growing, said Frank Cottle, who built up his own network of serviced offices, which was later acquired by Regus. "If Mark needed to chop down a tree and all he had was a hammer, he'd beat on it until it fell down," Cottle said.

Dixon preached to anyone who would listen how the old model of companies signing long-term leases was on the way out. Small companies had too little staff to worry about office management; big companies liked the flexibility of short-term leases. The Silicon Valley magazine *Fast Company* declared Regus the "office of the future" in a lengthy feature; British papers were constantly profiling Dixon and Regus. "If we get it right, we have an opportunity to change the world," Dixon once said.

When he took Regus public on the London Stock Exchange in 2000, investors were thrilled with its rapid growth and gave the company a huge valuation of more than $2 billion. It was a rather lofty mark—four times that of the company's annual revenue. Dixon told investors, just as Adam Neumann would for WeWork a generation later, that it should be worth ten times its revenue—closer to dot-com companies. Still, even with his disappointment at the stock market's valuation, Dixon was sitting pretty. He was ranked the tenth-richest person in Britain.

Then came the dot-com bust.

Regus's startup tenants vanished en masse, while large companies recoiled from their relatively expensive Regus space, returning to standard buildings with long-term leases. Given Regus's rapid growth, the company largely signed leases at or near peak rents, meaning it continued to face enormous monthly bills even though its revenues plunged. Dixon had always claimed that Regus's business was recession-proof, but now his ambition and optimism were met with a near-ruinous reality check. Losses surged. The U.S. division filed for Chapter 11 bankruptcy protection, and Regus's main U.S. competitor, HQ Global Workplaces, did the same; Regus's stock plunged more than 98 percent from its peak, to nearly zero.

If Regus was the office of the future, the future would be a long way off.

Dixon escaped insolvency. Damaged but not broken, he restructured leases and rebuilt the company. This time he pursued more modest growth, having learned the hard way that doubling every year was far too fast for a sustainable business, especially one that takes in money from subleases that can quickly vanish. He inserted more favorable clauses into his deals with landlords. When the 2008 recession came, Regus fared much better than in the prior downturn, showing how the office arbitrage business could actually work in a recession as long as growth was modest and sustainable.

By the time WeWork was rounding up its money from mutual funds in 2014, Regus was enjoying years of profits amid modest growth. It had become truly enormous in size, with more than 300,000 desks for rent around the world and more than $2.5 billion in annual revenue.

Its dominance over the market made WeWork's rise from nowhere that much more confusing. By every metric, WeWork was far more valuable but far smaller. At a valuation of $10 billion, the company was worth roughly $300,000 per member (or "occupied desk," as Regus called it), while the same calculation for Regus came out to roughly $10,000 per member. And most astonishingly, WeWork's valuation was more than *fifty times* its revenue for 2015, a nosebleed number for even a booming, profitable software company. Regus was valued at less than two times its revenue.

Suddenly everyone was asking Dixon about WeWork. Analysts asked about it on earnings calls, investors queried Dixon on how WeWork was worth so much, and everyone wanted to know why it was getting heaps of praise in the press.

A grumpy Dixon sought to investigate. From afar, the company's business model looked exactly like Regus's: leasing office space long term and subletting it short term. But surely WeWork must have been doing something different to merit its colossal valuation—something that tech investors understood but that wasn't obvious to an outsider? Representatives from Regus toured WeWork spaces and even rented one so they could analyze the business from the inside, hunting for some special sauce that explained the difference.

Eventually, Dixon and his team came to a simple and sober conclusion: WeWork had a nearly identical business model. In terms of making money—revenue, income, costs—there was no special sauce to be found. They couldn't find any clear differentiator beyond hype and the "community"-obsessed marketing.

The truth was a bit more complex.

WeWork was doing a lot of things that Regus wasn't. WeWork tapped into millennial culture openly, in a naked effort to attract members who had never before dreamed of office space. While Regus was heavily based in suburbs, WeWork was coasting on the urban renaissance. WeWork's architecture was both inviting and efficient—it was able to pack far more desks into the same amount of space—so the "energy" that Neumann gushed about to investors felt real. Regus's offices, on the other hand, were known to be sterile—many felt soulless—and vacancy was higher than at WeWork. Whatever WeWork's faults, its design wasn't sterile.

A problem for WeWork, though, was that these advantages didn't lead to profits. The energy and aesthetic of WeWork didn't result in noticeably higher rents; instead, WeWork's rents were comparable to Regus's. While Facebook and LinkedIn benefited from a "network effect" where the bigger they got, the better they could serve targeted high-priced ads or charge more to recruiters, there was no real corollary for WeWork. As WeWork got bigger, so too did its costs—it still had to build desks—while average rents tended to be flat or even go down. Members rarely used the company's app—the magic elixir that was meant to supercharge We-Work's physical social network. Not only did it fail to create the sense of a WeWork-wide community Neumann said it would, but it offered few opportunities for WeWork to make money selling any other services or software.

And while WeWork had more density, it was heavy on staff—people paid to slice fruit for the fruit water, refill the free coffee, organize events, and answer members' questions. Regus, meanwhile, charged for coffee and made good money on it. It also made a killing charging high prices for IT services and phone lines. Its model didn't engender much loyalty or enthusiasm from its tenants, but it allowed Regus to churn out healthy profits. In essence, it was an office company comfortable with calling itself an office company. It didn't advertise its community; at the end of the day, its clients were there to rent its desks.

More frustrating for Dixon still, WeWork was growing at basically the same pace of Regus during the dot-com boom, but it was bleeding red ink as it did so, burning through far more cash than Regus ever did. Regus largely self-funded its own expansion, turning to private investors only for one large funding round of $100 million. WeWork raised four times that in a single round in 2015. Years later, WeWork would release financials that showed that its individual locations open for at least eighteen months had the same profit margins as those of Regus—bringing in about 20 percent more than they cost to run, not accounting for other costs of running the corporation—corroborating Dixon's conviction that We-Work was no different.

But for WeWork's investors, Regus wasn't on their minds. Instead, mutual fund managers and VCs were amazed by WeWork's growth rate; for these investors, who typically put money in software companies, it was a rare find to come across a company able to keep doubling in size each year. The problem was that this was circular logic. If WeWork didn't continue to raise more money at giant valuations, it would never have been able to keep up the pace. Instead, its business would have looked a lot like Regus's—but for millennials.

After carping to friends and staff about how the numbers didn't add up, Dixon decided to act. If the market wanted buzzy, glass-wall-filled workstations, so be it. In January 2015, he bought a small Dutch company called Spaces. Its offices made it look like something of a WeWork clone, filled with glass dividers, large common spaces, and a jeans-and-backpacks feel. Regus began quickly rolling out new Spaces locations across the world, steering money away from its core of sterile Regus offices.

Asked on an investor call about WeWork, Dixon was now able to say more confidently just how similar the two companies were.

"They've done very well with their PR and their marketing, and they're sort of talking about the business as if it's a technology business," he said. "But it's exactly what we do."

Like a tall flute of champagne, modern capitalism has long been full of bubbles that rise to the surface and pop.

In seventeenth-century Holland, the bubble was multicolored tulip bulbs, the prices of which surged so much that some nice homes cost the same as one exotic bulb. In 1840s England, it was railroads: so many people piled into an overbuilding frenzy that railroad investment was more than 7 percent of all of the country's GDP. Bubbles caused a surge of brand-new, completely empty skyscrapers to be built in 1929; they caused Beanie Babies to sell for $5,000 apiece; they led the 1998 internet company Kozmo.com to think it made economic sense to hand deliver candy bars and magazines to college students' doors in less than an hour without a delivery fee.

Simply put, bubbles are the result of a herd of people who collectively start paying more for something than its intrinsic value. They are, at their core, a very human creation—a stampede of investors who are following the scent of a compelling narrative. Gluts of capital combine with a fear of missing out. The result is mania. The rising price feeds on itself, and investors convince one another the world has changed—that high prices are here to stay.

Those participating are often intelligent—even aware of the madness. Yet conformity has a powerful pull. In the 1950s, the psychologist Solomon Asch showed subjects two cards—one with a line and another with three lines. He'd ask, which of the three lines was the same length as the one line? When a subject was answering with only one or two peers who answered the same question, the subject almost always answered right. But when the subject was with a group of others—a group that had been secretly instructed to select the wrong answer—the subject often went along with the group's irrational choice.

In bubbles, the herd and its collective psychology prevail over the individual. Euphoria wins out over skepticism. *Beanie Babies won't be just a fad. Housing prices will never fall again.* Still more investors clamor to get in on the rising riches, pushing prices up further.

It wasn't just wework.

By 2015, the U.S. startup world was a bubble zooming to the surface. The same venture capital and mutual fund machine that had agreed to label WeWork a $10 billion tech enterprise rather than a modest-sized real estate firm was showering money across a legion of young Silicon Valley companies. These startups pledged to disrupt everything from mattresses to coffee, inflating valuations as red ink piled up.

That monsoon of money trickled through everyday life in San Francisco, the new capital of Silicon Valley startups. The city quickly became a terrarium of money-losing startups that turned former jewelry and rug storage spots into buzzy offices with Ping-Pong tables and macchiato stations. Employees at VC-funded HR software companies (Zenefits) would line up for lunch at VC-backed salad purveyors (Sweetgreen) and stop for coffee at VC-backed coffee shops (Philz), wearing VC-backed wool sneakers (Allbirds). They'd get rides for well below their cost from unprofitable ride-hail companies (Uber) or park their cars below cost with unprofitable on-demand valets (Luxe). They'd purchase homes through unprofitable startup brokerages (Compass) and store belongings with unprofitable self-storage companies (Clutter). Discounts abounded: a massive wealth transfer was going on from venture capital funds spilling over with money to consumers who got below-cost products. One particularly enterprising bargain seeker—a former startup entrepreneur named Ben Yu—ate dinner for free for one hundred days thanks to startup freebies, got thousands of dollars from a car rental startup, and received a free three-month membership on a jet-share startup. The bubble had grown into a biosphere; the walls were nowhere to be seen.

At a basic level, what was happening was the amount of money chasing companies had grown far faster than the number of good ideas. The success of Facebook and the lack of other options turned Silicon Valley into a magnet for money managers looking to park their funds. Everyone from Fidelity to pension funds to celebrities like Jared Leto, Kobe Bryant, and the members of Linkin Park were stuffing money into startups.

Prices had nowhere to go but up. Unicorn startups valued at over $1 billion went from numbering just a handful to a stampede. One new unicorn was minted every week or so, on average; there were more than ninety by year-end. The millennial-focused insurance company Oscar Health. The tortoiseshell glasses vendor Warby Parker. The neighborhood-focused website Nextdoor.

Rising valuations gave the illusion of success. In reality, little had changed beyond investor demand, and many companies that saw their valuations rocket into the hundreds of millions or billions hadn't shown that their basic business model could even be profitable—a rather elementary requirement for a viable business outside Silicon Valley. Instead, these companies poured investors' money into revenue growth, which they accomplished by selling goods under cost.

Uber's valuation soared above all others, past $50 billion. As millions changed their transportation habits and began summoning chauffeured cars via the app, the company could make a very legitimate claim that it was a truly disruptive technology. But in Silicon Valley at the time, this was by no means enough: Why be satisfied with simply overhauling a sizable chunk of urban transportation? Investors ignored the fact that the company was losing money on every ride and focused instead on the hope that Uber was going to completely replace personal car ownership. It would be the go-to courier for everything from packages to laundry, rivaling FedEx and Amazon. It would decrease congestion (it increased it), make its *own* self-driving car technology (it's lagging), and spit out profits (it hasn't).

Those who missed out on pumping money into Uber were desperate to find the next one. A whole breed of startups were branded the Uber of *X*—on-demand services that arrive within minutes after the touch of an app. There were at least three on-demand car valets, an Uber for laundry called Washio, even an Uber for cookies called Doughbies. Consumers could suddenly request home cleaners with an app, or summon a company to box up and ship a package within minutes—for a nominal fee. The only problem: none of these made any economic sense. They almost all failed, despite gobbling up millions from their investors.

In a world awash in cash, many VCs and mutual funds were aware of the bubbly environment; some would even talk privately about how valuations had gotten out of control. But they persisted because everyone seemed to be playing the same game; highly valued startups kept raising more money at even higher valuations. Crucially, investors were betting that when all these startups eventually went public some years down the road, the stock markets would be just as excited about these companies as the VCs and mutual funds. As long as the public markets were playing the game, too, everything would work out. Then they'd all be able to sell their stock at huge valuations.

The media could have applied the brakes to the runaway train of optimism. But in 2015, Silicon Valley was by and large lionized in the press, treated with a certain deference rather than the skepticism later applied to Facebook and Amazon, once their extraordinary size and influence became more apparent.

The startup-focused press in particular was more cheerleader than watchdog.

The digital publication *TechCrunch* amplified narratives about how startups would disrupt *X* industry and reshape the world. *Fast Company,* the magazine that had declared Regus the "office of the future" two decades earlier, was a bastion of hagiographic profiles of founders and their startups. It declared companies like the glasses seller Warby Parker and the beauty products shipper Birchbox as some of the most innovative companies. In these outlets, big old companies with sluggish bureaucracy and bad customer service were the villains; young idealistic disrupters who created slickly designed apps were the heroes. A high valuation was a badge of honor.

A certain coziness existed between many startup reporters and their subjects. At least ten *TechCrunch* reporters and editors would go on to work at venture capital firms. (The publication's founders came from venture capital backgrounds.) *Forbes* and *Fortune* churned out optimistic covers of their own, featuring entrepreneurs like the Theranos blood-testing company CEO, Elizabeth Holmes. *Forbes* magazine would write two big features on Adam Neumann, with one highlighting how "heat-mapping technology" had helped We-

Work "make the most of every millimeter" and how its scale had created price advantages.

With little skepticism from the media and elsewhere, tech investors began to pile money into an emerging class of companies that weren't tech companies but acted the part. These companies rode the wave of the tech boom, using the same tropes that other start-ups used to earn a rush of investor cash. They ran witty subway ads in millennial-friendly sans serif fonts, displacing the prior generation of ads from plastic surgeons, dermatologists like Dr. Zizmor, and vocational schools. Companies have long sought to imitate and borrow lingo from the tech world. In the electronics boom of the late 1950s and the 1960s, countless old-line companies added "tronics" to their name to get more attention. In the dot-com bubble, the famed editor Tina Brown said her much-hyped new magazine *Talk* proclaimed itself a "cultural search engine."

In this boom, the imitation-meat company Beyond Meat wasn't a veggie burger maker but a "platform" like Facebook or YouTube—that made plant-based meat. The fast casual grilled cheese chain The Melt thought gizmos like an online ordering system entitled it to tech-like valuations, rather than grilled cheese valuations. The discount razor maker Harry's boasted about its "subscription" revenue from repeat razor buyers, a term common in software companies, and raised hundreds of millions of dollars in venture capital. The mattress company Casper was the poster child of a successful tech startup, gushed about in the tech press for revolutionizing the mattress industry with its comfortable foam mattresses delivered in a box to a customer's door. At its heart, Casper was less of a mattress maker and more of a marketing company—one that attracted eyeballs to its website and then contracted factories to make foam mattresses similar to the mattresses they'd make for Casper's competitors.

WeWork was a by-product of the same mass delusion that raised the valuations of "tech" companies higher and higher. Investors saw a physical social network with amazing growth rather than a collection of people paying market rents for office space that had losses growing just as fast as revenue. When Neumann told them We-Work was like Uber and Airbnb, the investors focused on the few parallels between those businesses rather than numerous fundamental differences, including how Airbnb and Uber are *asset light* and don't have costly fifteen-year leases for their homes and cars.

These investors were considered the smart money—the ones investing on behalf of wealthy families or endowments or pensions who had their pick of advisers. But in a world awash in cash, these investors feared missing out on the next big, highly lucrative idea. More often than not, the risks were brushed aside, the downsides minimized.

As the buzz around WeWork continued to build among the VC and startup set, some onlookers far from the Silicon Valley echo chamber began to grow more skeptical.

Brandon Shorenstein was one of them. The twenty-nine-year-old scion of one of the West Coast's great real estate dynasties had been charmed by Neumann when they met in 2012. After a tour of WeWork's space in lower Manhattan, he was impressed with the vibe of the offices and Neumann's ability to fill his locations.

Trim with curly brown hair, Shorenstein worked at Shorenstein Properties, a giant landlord that had at various times owned some of the marquee towers in San Francisco. By mid-2015, he was an executive vice president and an influential voice within the company run, at the time, by his father.

Neumann told Shorenstein he liked the prestige of the firm and wanted to work with him. Shorenstein saw it as a good experiment, and months later they struck a deal in Chicago, with We-Work signing a lease to take all of the office space in a relatively small building Shorenstein was buying in the city's Fulton Market neighborhood.

But as WeWork grew, Shorenstein became suspicious. The first red flag came during the negotiations for the Chicago building—

when Neumann said that he personally would be taking a stake in the building, too. It was the same deal in which Neumann was going to buy a personal stake before ceding it to WeWork; Shorenstein was buying the building with the local developer Jeff Shapack. The potential conflicts of interest were so apparent that Shorenstein was amazed Neumann would even consider such a move.

Shorenstein watched as other well-known landlords embraced the company and the idea of co-working. One large office owner after another kept signing deals with WeWork. Shorenstein, though, wondered why investors were treating it like a tech company. It was so clearly just a real estate company, he thought. What on earth were these seasoned investors seeing?

He'd looked at a few other deals with Neumann, but nothing came of them. Later, in 2015, his phone rang while he was at an investor conference in New York. He was busy, but it rang again. And again. And again. When Shorenstein looked at his phone screen, he saw numerous missed calls from Neumann.

Neumann was calling Shorenstein from Los Angeles, where he and his CFO at the time, Michael Gross—a former hotel executive with blond hair and sparkling white teeth—were looking at office buildings. Neumann and Gross were in the city's Arts District, where pour-over coffee shops were sprinkled in between decaying old factories. The two, with a handful of other WeWork employees, rolled up in a black SUV that reeked of marijuana to meet a young office space leasing broker who was waiting to take them on a tour of a former Ford factory that built the Model T. Neumann insisted the broker down two tequila shots before commencing the tour. It was before noon, but the broker assented.

When the group stepped inside, Neumann loved the boxy five-story structure and its big old factory windows. He then started running around its cavernous empty spaces. He saw the signs that said Shorenstein, and a lightbulb went off. He *knew* Brandon Shorenstein. He rushed off, leaving those behind puzzled. As the broker waited, he repeatedly dialed Shorenstein. When they finally connected, Neumann yelled that he was in Shorenstein's building.

"Oh my God, this is amazing," Neumann shouted into his phone. "I'm going to lease the whole thing."

Taken aback by the rowdy person on the other end of the line, Shorenstein said they should talk the next day.

Neumann came back to the broker and his staff, looking pleased with himself. He proclaimed his news: he'd be taking over the *whole* building. Then he walked over to a giant marketing poster on a stand that displayed the building's features. "You won't be needing this anymore," he announced. He picked it up, raised it high, and tugged both sides down on top of his head, so as to break it in two.

The poster board proved a tougher adversary than expected. He pulled for a few more moments, with no luck; it just flexed. Then he pushed it onto the ground, folding it with his foot and a hand. It bent in half, awkwardly. From there he rejoined Gross in the SUV, and they raced off.

Shorenstein didn't hear back from Neumann. But he did hear from his own broker, getting a full rundown of Neumann's behavior. It was all too much for him: the antics, the insane valuation. What was it that made WeWork and Neumann so successful? He wouldn't do more deals with them, he decided. He wanted to stay far, far away. Neumann was crazy, and WeWork was a bubble, he thought. It wasn't going to end well.

CHAPTER 11

Catnip for Millennials

WEWORK'S GROWTH WAS SHOWING NO SIGNS OF SLOWING, and by 2015 Adam Neumann needed more bodies and more people he could trust to run things.

Thus far, the company had mostly been a family affair. The ranks of WeWork leadership were filled by people close to the Neumanns: friends, family, friends of friends. Rebekah Neumann's brother-in-law Chris Hill—whose family suffered a large financial loss with Bernie Madoff—ran operations. Neumann's friend from the navy Ariel Tiger ran finance until 2014. Neumann's childhood friend Zvika Shachar did odd jobs for Neumann. Rebekah's cousin Mark Lapidus ran real estate. And Rebekah Neumann had taken over the brand and marketing departments the previous year. Even his recently hired CFO, Michael Gross—who had previously been the CEO of a boutique hotel company—had been a childhood friend of Rebekah's cousins.

To keep up its exponential growth, WeWork needed to make some changes. By this point, WeWork had planted flags in Seattle, Austin, Tel Aviv, and Amsterdam. Once upon a time, a location opening was a big deal for which the whole company rushed to get the space in shape. Now, a few years later, multiple offices could open on the same day. The plan was to be everywhere around the world within a few years.

To make the rapidly growing machine run better, Neumann started to bring in professionals. He lured executives from Uber to help fill desks with paying customers. He wooed a seasoned operator from Time Warner Cable, Artie Minson, to be his COO. If WeWork was going to keep expanding, he needed a deeper bench.

Dave Fano, a fast-talking architect with a shaved head and a sunny personality, was one key recruit. Fano was one of three partners at Case Design, a hive of brainy architecture talent in New York that had consulted with WeWork on some of its architectural software. Fano and his two co-founders, Steve Sanderson and Federico Negro, had become experts in "building information modeling," or software that sought to further digitize architecture and construction, industries in which different firms still worked in silos, passing paper plans to one another rather than all using the same software.

Roni Bahar, an energetic self-starter who oversaw the design and development of new offices at WeWork, saw potential in Case early on and shoveled more and more work its way as the WeWork wheels kept turning faster. The firm built software for WeWork to better plan projects and timelines, helping turn WeWork into a machine that could quickly spit out plans for new offices. Bahar commissioned Case to make a Google Earth–like interactive map that Neumann could show to investors, integrated with buildings in every city, with projections of how many members and how much revenue WeWork could get from cities around the world. It showed the potential of diving deeper with the Case team, which Bahar wanted to acquire. Neumann loved it and began to court Fano to join WeWork and run its real estate and design teams.

At first Fano was reluctant. Despite all the parties, Neumann could be callous with his employees: he was parsimonious with salaries and benefits and required staff to work late hours. Case, on the other hand, offered unlimited time off. Employees could work from anywhere; no one even signed an employment contract. Fano's staff was intellectual, with a penchant for putting on headphones and disappearing into a project for days. The Case team often grew exasperated at the lack of rigor among the young, hard-partying WeWork employees who were constantly devising new, contradictory directions for the Case team to follow.

Neumann, though, was determined to lure Fano. One day in 2015, he told Fano to be at Teterboro Airport west of Manhattan the next morning. They were going to take a private jet to California to look at some properties. Meet me on the plane, he said.

After waking up and trudging to Teterboro to arrive at 6:00 a.m., Fano found himself on a plane that, despite the early hour, soon began to feel like a rowdy party as passengers downed tequila and smoked pot. After stopping in Los Angeles for a day of meetings before heading north, Neumann whisked Fano on a helicopter from San Francisco to a conference in Napa wine country.

During the trip, Neumann started to captivate Fano with his visions for WeWork and for Fano's own career trajectory. He made it seem inevitable that WeWork would soon have a million members, even when it only had close to thirty thousand. It was going to transform more physical real estate than any other company in the coming years, he said. Fano began to get excited about Neumann's promise to give him a top seat at a company that was going to bring enormous change to design and construction. He could bring a whole industry into the modern age. Architects were always held back by their clients, the people actually funding the work. Here was a chance to help run the business of a client with ambitions to grow at an unprecedented scale.

There was also the fact that WeWork's projects now accounted for almost a third of Case's revenue. If he demurred, Fano knew that WeWork could very well move its business to another firm, leaving a sizable dent in their growing company.

Shortly after Fano returned from California, he discussed the deal with his partners, who agreed to take it. Despite some resistance from Case staff, the architecture firm was swallowed by WeWork, and employees moved into its headquarters.

. . .

THE WEWORK THAT FANO AND CASE ENTERED HAD LONG SINCE shed the scrappiness of a twelve-person operation. There were no more late-night sessions during which the whole staff had to install toilets and assemble Ikea desks. Instead, the company's ranks were packed with a few hundred young idealists eager to change the world through office space.

As a workplace, it appeared to be an urban twentysomething's dream: it offered a mix of parties and socializing and hard work that felt rewarding. The office culture was different from a bank or corporate advertising agency. The company's annual Summer Camp featured ever-larger games of capture the flag and concerts: the Chainsmokers played in 2015 in exchange for WeWork stock. Parties were frequent at the office, too, and throughout the year. New office headquarters? A party. Halloween? Another party. Weekend of corporate development and meetings? Huge party.

It helped, too, that their boss was the embodiment of cool, fun, and success all at once. Neumann would sometimes skateboard to the office. When a snowstorm hit during one of WeWork's annual all-hands summits, Neumann snowboarded from his apartment to a building where the staff was waiting in lower Manhattan, towed by Roni Bahar, who attached a rope to the back of his Jeep. Neumann showed off a video of his commute to a cheering crowd.

The company's culture played well on social media. WeWork staff would post pictures on Instagram of the inspirational slogans scrawled on T-shirts, printed on mugs, and spelled out in neon signs at WeWork offices. "Hustle Harder." "Embrace the Hustle." "Do What You Love." "Thank God It's Monday." "Can't Stop Won't Stop." Staffers posted endless pictures of well-designed new offices, along with photos of tequila shots and prosecco flutes. Friends would comment, "So jealous!!" and "Are they hiring?"

Carl Pierre was just twenty-five years old when he was hired by WeWork to run its nascent Washington, D.C., operation. He'd just sold a startup and was hooked immediately by WeWork's lofty rhetoric: he wanted to improve the way people work. He had no desire to spend his days at a faceless corporation; he and his peers yearned to hear that they were changing the world—doing more than just taking a paycheck.

Further sweetening the pot for Pierre was that WeWork *looked* like a millennial stereotype. Good design was in vogue, and WeWork's aesthetic was eminently Instagrammable. Mid-centurymodern couches sat by windows where light streamed in; jugs of fruit water glistened with curated colorful medleys of honeydew, cucumbers, and lemons.

"It was like catnip for millennials," Pierre said. "We wanted it so badly."

The "We generation," Neumann told staff and investors, didn't have boundaries between work and play. Office life and home life were more fluid now. Fun happened at the office. People were constantly working. Workaholic tendencies were seen as a virtue; they were integral to the distinct culture of WeWork. Neumann frequently brought his spiritual adviser—a teacher from the Kabbalah Centre named Eitan Yardeni—into the office. In his talks to the entire company and weekly meetings with top aides, Yardeni would preach the gospel of hard work while also dispensing life advice.

Still, even though Neumann had four children of his own by then, the WeWork lifestyle was challenging for older employees and parents. While all-nighters were less common than in WeWork's first years, employees on even the lowest rung were expected to work twelve-hour days or more when necessary. Meetings would stretch late into the night; sometimes Neumann would have his deputies stay until 1:00 or 2:00 a.m. On Monday evenings, the entire company would stay for a ritual staff meeting called TGIM, often until 9:00 or 10:00. Beer was served, and sometimes metal trays full of tequila shots in plastic shot glasses were passed around like hors d'oeuvres at a wedding.

At the time, few considered the party-like atmosphere to be

problematic. In 2014, after WeWork's new head of human resources got so drunk at a staff party she had to be rushed to the hospital, the incident didn't seem to spark much concern internally.

A small subset of its staff, though, were wary. One former manager recalled being told to "drink the Kool-Aid," in a positive way. He was confused: Did these millennials not know about the 1970s cult and ensuing mass suicide that had inspired the term?

WEWORK WAS HARDLY THE ONLY ORGANIZATION TO TAKE ADVANtage of people's desire for belonging and purpose. As WeWork was blossoming, it seemed as if almost every venture-capital-backed startup in the United States was motivated by "making the world a better place," rhetoric so lofty it made their capitalistic responsibilities to their investors seem like an afterthought. The buzzword was "mission driven," and profit was not the mission—at least in theory.

Facebook wasn't just a social network that made money on ads; it was devoted to making "the world more open and connected." Airbnb wasn't just a booking website for short-term stays in apartments and homes, but a platform that let people "belong anywhere." Financial startups vying to be the next generation of Wall Street giants were determined to democratize investing and expand opportunity to the underserved.

The bombast was in part an outgrowth of Silicon Valley's hippie roots, after the utopian ideals of the 1960s influenced some early leaders like Steve Jobs. But in a highly competitive market, that jargon was also necessary to lure talent. Skilled software engineers and managers had an abundance of tech companies to choose from; some could expect offers of $300,000 a year from the Googles and Apples of the world. To land top recruits, companies needed to offer more than just a salary.

It was a shift from many other corners of the business world. Wall Street traders tend not to preach how they chose Goldman Sachs over UBS because one bank is better at expanding access to credit for the disadvantaged; they often do, however, say one offered better compensation.

But in Silicon Valley, companies managed to marry extraordinary wealth creation with the pursuit of utopianism. It is a mindset that could lead to blind spots. Facebook preached its societal good, so much so it didn't seem to foresee the pernicious effects it could have. Asked about Facebook's effect on terrorism in 2008, Mark Zuckerberg suggested the social network's existence would lead the disaffected youth of the Middle East to come together rather than choose lives of violence. Terrorism doesn't spring from "a deep hatred of anyone; it comes from a lack of connectedness, a lack of communication," he said. (Years later, Twitter and Facebook were forced to combat the rise of terrorist recruiting on their own platforms, particularly by the Islamic State.)

WEWORK'S OFFICIAL MISSION, WHICH REBEKAH NEUMANN HAD crafted, was to create a world "where people work to make a life, not just a living."

This meant more than just offices. Adam Neumann spoke of expanding into hotels, fitness, and even airlines. He was constantly dreaming up a torrent of new plans, even as he ran the company. He often managed on only a few hours' sleep a night. Yet he never seemed tired. He was endlessly energetic, characterized by an unflagging drive. His head was a fountain of ideas constantly overflowing.

Many were not terribly well thought out, nor did they receive much follow-up.

He told staff he was eager to collaborate with Elon Musk, CEO of SpaceX and Tesla, on his plans for Mars, which Musk aspired to travel to and settle. Later, in 2017, Neumann ended up securing a meeting with the entrepreneur. After waiting for more than two hours for an audience at SpaceX's headquarters in Los Angeles, Neumann spent his fifteen minutes pitching Musk on how he wanted to build a community on Mars—when Musk's space transport firm eventually got there. Getting to Mars would be the easy part, Neumann told him. Building community would be hard. Musk, Neumann later recalled to his staff, was unimpressed and lectured Neumann about how getting there was, in fact, the hard part. Musk was an idol, yet he put Neumann in his place, he told his staff. When he recounted the meeting to Rebekah, she told him it was a moment of humility he probably needed.

Plenty of other ideas went the way of WeWork Mars. But by late 2015, the company was moving ahead with one of Neumann's less far-fetched schemes. He had signed deals with two landlords—one in New York and the other just outside Washington, D.C.—to build the first two WeLive locations.

WeLive would essentially be a well-designed college dorm for twentysomethings. Rooms were a bit smaller than a standard apartment, and each floor had giant communal kitchens and game rooms. It was intended to replace the scattershot process of finding roommates on Craigslist, delivering renters an instant community full of the We spirit. WeLive staffers would host happy hours for the renters.

When hyping WeWork to investors, Neumann leaned heavily on the prospect of WeWork taking over the residential sector. The residential sector is a far larger part of the real estate universe than offices, he noted, and expanding into apartments would give WeWork a foothold in a new multitrillion-dollar market. Based on projections from 2014, when WeLive was simply an idea in early stages of becoming real, Neumann showed the mutual funds and other potential investors that WeLive would swell to be one-fifth of WeWork's revenue within a couple years, spitting out $600 million a year by 2018.

Well before the first WeLive was completed in early 2016, Neumann loved to give tours of the twenty-seven-story building at 110 Wall Street. The highlight was a small finished area that was essentially a showroom, giving onlookers a sense of what it would look like upon completion.

To bring the showroom to life, WeWork employees were told to leave their desks during an investor tour and go to 110 Wall. They'd act as models, chatting or playing cards. Neumann specified that when he walked in with an investor in tow, he wanted the Notorious B.I.G. song "Juicy" to be blaring. Given that he was never on time, WeWork employees had to sit with the song on repeat, sometimes for as much as an hour, awaiting their boss and the unknown potential funders.

As an economic venture, WeLive was effectively doomed from the start. One of the reasons WeWork's main business was so appealing was its density. WeWork managed to get two or three times as many people on a floor than in a standard office design. All those extra $800 rent checks from its members meant the company had some money left over after paying its own rent to the landlord and its staff each month.

Apartment buildings, though, can't just absorb three times more people. For one, many cities have regulations meant to avoid the fetid conditions of tenements in the nineteenth and early twentieth centuries. And residents were unlikely to choose a closet-sized room, even if there was a Ping-Pong table down the hall. Existing apartment architecture wouldn't work, so WeWork would have to build from the ground up. Despite all the hype and lofty projections that helped win hundreds of millions of dollars from investors, WeLive never expanded beyond the two locations.

ONE PROBLEM WITH WEWORK'S MISSION-DRIVEN, COMMUNITY-focused rhetoric was that its founder's lifestyle was increasingly at odds with it. In 2015, Neumann moved into the company's new headquarters, a low-profile mid-block building on Eighteenth Street, just west of Sixth Avenue. Inside he had a sprawling office built for himself, where he could switch the glass walls from clear to frosted with a button. He kept a punching bag there that he'd use for his kickboxing lessons; sometimes he'd walk around sweaty and barefoot outside his office after a workout in which he often blared Rihanna. He also had his employees install a "smoke eater," a high-powered ceiling vent that was tied to the HVAC system. Typically a feature in cigar bars, Neumann's smoke eater was meant for marijuana—old tech for a new problem.

In the early years, Neumann would pace around the office, periodically peering at employees' computer screens—occasionally stopping to grill employees on their progress on a certain project. But as the company's head count swelled, he became more removed from the common staffer, known to many only through the all-hands meetings when he addressed them. In his new office, Neumann had a team design an exit for him; with the new door, he could get to the elevators without having to run into his staff in the main lobby.

That's not to say he was completely self-absorbed. Deputies saw him vacillate between thirsting for more wealth and altruism. He often seemed earnestly interested in helping others, particularly small businesses and employees in need. He wanted to make an event called the Creator Awards, for example, at which WeWork would give away money to startups and nonprofits that were making a positive impact on the world. Later, he would launch a company-wide effort to find a matching bone marrow donor for an employee in need.

But as WeWork became more valuable, his charitable side was increasingly overshadowed by his desire to live larger. He began to pile up more homes beyond the town house he and Rebekah bought in 2013. They rented a large apartment near Gramercy Park. And in early 2016, he paid $15 million for a sixty-acre Tudor estate in Pound Ridge, New York.

The added expenditure came as his wife's family finances were under stress. Rebekah's father, Bobby Paltrow, had been sued in the

1980s for successfully soliciting millions in donations to nonexistent charities. While he got off with warnings from the federal judge at the time, by 2014, Paltrow once again drew scrutiny from the same federal judge, this time for not properly reporting his taxes. After pleading guilty to tax evasion on more than $4 million of income, by mid-2015, Paltrow had been sentenced to six months in federal prison in Miami.

It was a stark contrast. Just as Bobby Paltrow's business empire was crumbling, his son-in-law was looking to expand his own investments further. Even though the board had blocked him from personally buying an office building in Chicago in 2013—Neumann was told the conflicts of interest would be a bad look for the company—he became emboldened as the company's valuation rose. By 2015, he was ready to cast aside the board's admonitions and jump back into buying commercial property.

One prospect was the Sarona complex in Tel Aviv, a building WeWork was leasing; he bought a small stake there, a tiny deal, but one in which he again inserted himself on both sides of the transaction.

In Manhattan, another opportunity came up. A fellow Kabbalah Centre attendee, the fashion designer Elie Tahari, was planning to buy a building at 88 University Place in Manhattan and lease it to WeWork—except that his partner dropped out at the last minute. Neumann, eager to get the deal done so that WeWork could get in the building, stepped in himself, putting up the funds for half of the purchase. They paid $70 million, and Neumann guaranteed the loan personally. In the end, it wasn't much of a moneymaker for him—WeWork was given a good deal on the rent—but it still presented the exact conflict of interest that his investors wanted to avoid.

Neumann knew that all this spending—enabled by the huge sums of stock he sold to the mutual funds—was at odds with his company's message. In a meeting with a *Wall Street Journal* reporter, Neumann was asked about a secondhand bit of information a journalist colleague had passed along. The colleague had heard that Neumann had sold more than $100 million of stock, while the reporter had heard separately from a former employee that Neumann had sold more than $35 million. Neumann immediately denied both. Shortly after, when the $15 million home purchase made it into the press, the reporter asked the question again to Neumann's representatives. Neumann again called the reporter to the office and told him, without specifics, that he had only sold less than 1 percent of his shares—an amount equivalent to less than $30 million. In reality, the entity Neumann controlled had sold more than $115 million and borrowed another $23 million, with the lion's share going to Neumann. It was a deception that caused unease among multiple aides aware of the conversation with the newspaper.

Neumann's staff had mostly been kept in the dark about his stock sales. While Neumann had sold his shares to investors for the same price Fidelity was paying—valuing the company at $10 billion—his friends and longtime employees weren't given the same opportunity. Instead, after the funding round, WeWork offered to buy stock from some long-serving employees. Roni Bahar, Rebekah Neumann's brother-in-law Chris Hill, her cousin Mark Lapidus, and Michael Gross all sold some shares, each taking at least $1 million. But the share price was significantly lower than what Neumann was able to sell at—effectively leaving them with 25 percent less than what he received per share.

WeWork said it couldn't pay the same price for tax reasons. But it easily could have structured the sale in a fairer way. Later, WeWork would set up a more egalitarian stock sale in which employees and Neumann were given the same price, a structure that could have been implemented in 2015. When the long-serving employees found out about the disparity in price on the 2015 sale, many were furious.

Neumann saw it differently. It was his company; he was the one who had made it valuable, and he was the one who wrote the rules.

CHAPTER 12

Banking Bros

I N 2015, A DECADE INTO HIS TENURE AS CEO OF JPMORGAN Chase, not only was Jamie Dimon running the country's largest financial institution, but he was often hailed as one of the world's top CEOs, a trusted sounding board for lawmakers on Capitol Hill, and the most recognizable face on Wall Street.

During the financial crisis of 2007–2008, as banks were failing or getting rescued by the U.S. government, Dimon emerged as the most stable figure in the whole wobbly industry. He rescued two dying banks—Bear Stearns and Washington Mutual—and helped stave off a total collapse of the financial system.

But in the years after the recession, Dimon became focused on what he saw as a weak spot in JPMorgan's otherwise formidable reach: Silicon Valley. Technology companies were attracting a torrent of money from Wall Street investors as the economy tilted toward the tech industry. Apple and Google were on their way to supplanting banks and oil companies as the most valuable corporations in the world. By 2016, Facebook's valuation eclipsed that of the 216-year-old bank.

One of the most lucrative and prestigious parts of a global bank like JPMorgan is its investment banking arm. It is the division that aids companies with big financial moves—helping guide a company through a merger or acquisition, or helping a corporation join the public stock markets through an initial public offering. JPMorgan had long been a dominant force in this area—winning coveted advisory positions for acquisitions by corporate giants like General Electric, as well as helping with the IPOs of companies owned by massive private equity firms.

But when the Silicon Valley tech firms wanted advice, Dimon's bank wasn't a company's first call. Instead, its competitors Goldman Sachs and Morgan Stanley had vied for the top advisory role on most high-profile tech IPOs since the financial crisis, including those for Facebook, Twitter, LinkedIn, Zynga, Groupon, and Pandora.

By 2015, the tech sector was primed to explode. A crop of giant, buzzy startups, including Uber and Snap, had stayed private for an unusually long period. Thanks to the rush of private money, Snapchat's maker, Snap, was worth around $16 billion. Airbnb was worth more than $25 billion, more than the hotel giant Marriott. And Uber was worth $51 billion, nearly the size of Ford.

Like moths fluttering around a patio light, the banks rushed to these startups. The companies, after all, were headed for IPOs at some point, and they would all need bankers to advise them. The bankers' task would be to convince stock market investors that these companies' true valuations were even higher than the private investors thought. VCs needed to sell their stock, and new investors wanted to come in. A handful of lucky banks would be chosen to guide the way.

To win this business, bankers laid on the charm—and the checkbook. They'd devote hours of work for free to crunch numbers for founders and their finance chiefs, helping them figure out ways to better portray their businesses. They would help founders borrow money—tying loans to their stock in their companies—and they'd give them below-market-rate mortgages. Banks would even buy goods and services from the startups, such as paying for software that they didn't appear to really need.

JPMorgan played this game just like its rivals, but it still lagged behind them in third place. Unwilling to continue ceding the most valuable and potentially lucrative chunk of the economy to Goldman and Morgan Stanley, Dimon had stepped up his efforts to make his bank central to Silicon Valley.

Dimon had been spending more and more time in California, meeting with entrepreneurs. JPMorgan's rivals marveled at how often they walked into the office of a top—or even midsized—tech company to find that Dimon had just dropped by. Even in Silicon Valley, where there was little regard for staid industries like banking, Dimon had a certain cachet that few other CEOs could replicate. He was known to host dinners on his trips out west that could draw a dozen founders, who were eager to hear what the banker had to say. As Dimon spoke, some attendees scribbled down notes on life and business advice, sharing the top banker's wisdom with colleagues and friends.

Other gestures to the Bay Area economy were bolder and more costly. The Golden State Warriors were planning to move from Oakland to a new $1.4 billion basketball arena in San Francisco. The privately financed venue was to be a flashy symbol of the city's wealth and aspirations. Most expected the naming rights would go to one of the region's giant tech companies, like Salesforce or Google.

It was Dimon, though, who pounced. The bank paid at least $15 million a year for the twenty-year rights: it would be called the Chase Center, a monument to the old order in the heart of the capital of the new economy.

To THE EXTENT THAT JPMORGAN HAD ANY PERSONAL CONNECtion to founders in Silicon Valley, it was largely because of one banker—Noah Wintroub. Lanky, often bearded, and frequently clad in the casual attire and vests of tech entrepreneurs, Wintroub was promoted to the role of vice-chairman in 2015 at the age of thirty-eight. He was well liked and trusted by many tech entrepreneurs, even though few saw him as possessing the kind of clout his rivals at Goldman or Morgan Stanley had.

A Chicago native, Wintroub moved to San Francisco in the late 1990s after attending Colgate University in upstate New York. Shortly after graduating, he went to Silicon Valley, joining a smaller advisory bank, Hambrecht & Quist, in 1999 as the dot-com boom neared its peak. He was an idealist: he often talked about how technology would make the world a better place, and saw his own calling as helping entrepreneurs do that more seamlessly.

Chase bought Hambrecht & Quist soon after, JPMorgan and Chase merged in 2000, and Wintroub joined the giant bank. He spent the waning years of the dot-com boom and its aftermath offering counsel to CEOs and building out his Rolodex. As Silicon Valley faded from Wall Street's priority list, he befriended as many tech entrepreneurs as he could, becoming the bank's contact with founders all over California and around the world.

Wintroub's appeal lay in his blend of techno-optimism and what seemed like a strong moral compass. Many entrepreneurs genuinely liked Wintroub; they believed he cared about them as people. He would call to check in on their families; he would grow teary-eyed when waxing sentimental about his grandfather or his wife and three daughters, or when describing the plight of the homeless in San Francisco. He was unabashedly emotional and admired for the time outside of work that he and his family devoted to social causes.

Wintroub's star rose precipitously at the bank. Dimon and other higher-ups in New York saw him as central to their aspirations for securing key positions in the largest deals. The bank didn't have a deep bench of bankers who had the ears of tech entrepreneurs.

ON A COLD DAY AROUND LATE 2012, NOAH WINTROUB STOOD ON a cobblestoned street in SoHo, listening to Adam Neumann air frustrations about his personal and commercial retail bank—Chase—

while smoking cigarettes in quick succession. Chase is terrible, Neumann told him. He was having trouble with his accounts there.

In New York on a trip, Wintroub had been summoned to meet Neumann at the Crosby Street Hotel, a boutique hotel filled with unique artwork and favored by venture capitalists. Michael Eisenberg, the investor from Benchmark, was visiting from Israel and had gathered a group of entrepreneurs for drinks. He had developed a close friendship with Wintroub over the past few years and wanted to give him an early introduction to an entrepreneur he saw as tremendously promising.

Wintroub joined Neumann outside as the entrepreneur smoked and listened to him as he ranted. Wintroub worked in investment banking—not the retail bank of Chase's sprawling empire, but he'd gladly call customer service himself for the entrepreneur, he told Neumann. On Neumann went. He complained that he was building an enormous company but he couldn't even talk to anyone at JPMorgan about getting a business loan.

Wintroub, chilly in the New York winter, handed Neumann his card and promised to help him.

After their SoHo meeting, Wintroub kept in touch with Neumann. The banker grew more and more excited about the prospects for WeWork to change how businesses use real estate and disrupt the giant industry. He decided that his mentor at the bank, Jimmy Lee, should meet Neumann.

Lee looked more like the Hollywood version of a Wall Street tycoon than Michael Douglas ever did. With slicked-back silver hair, Lee was often clad in pin-striped suits, suspenders, and Hermès ties. His wardrobe and his effusive charm were as legendary as his tight relationships with the CEOs of most major companies and private equity firms. When Rupert Murdoch or Henry Kravis contemplated doing a deal, Lee was often their first call.

Lee, by then around sixty and the bank's top deal maker in New York, was aiding Dimon in his quest to raise the bank's profile in the tech world. He had taken Wintroub under his wing, and Wintroub in turn introduced Lee to his tech CEOs. Despite the region's resistance to men in suits, it was rare that Lee's charm, swagger, and intelligence wouldn't captivate Wintroub's potential clients. The Wintroub and Lee partnership—their inside and outside game—landed JPMorgan key roles, if not yet lead roles, on giant tech deals like LinkedIn and Facebook. They were making progress, and Jamie Dimon was optimistic.

Wintroub asked Lee to meet Neumann. The entrepreneur, Wintroub said, could be the man to transform the entire real estate industry. Lee was skeptical. Real estate's a tough business, he told Wintroub, but he agreed to meet Neumann and tour a WeWork location.

When he arrived at WeWork's lower Manhattan offices, Lee said he had no more than fifteen minutes to look around. He stayed for nearly three hours. Lee declined Neumann's offer of a tequila shot but was impressed by Neumann's ideas for building WeWork locations all around the United States and the world. Before he left Neumann's office, Lee said JPMorgan should consider lending WeWork money so it could expand more quickly.

That meeting led to a crucial deal for WeWork. Each company—one a highly profitable financial institution with origins involving Alexander Hamilton and Aaron Burr and the other a five-year-old, money-losing startup—saw something to like in the other. Hoping to win WeWork's IPO business years down the line, Lee and Wintroub helped arrange a huge credit line for WeWork, one that would eventually grow to give WeWork access to more than $500 million in debt by 2015. The credit line, essentially a loan, would prove critical for WeWork in winning over landlords concerned that the company could become insolvent. Now WeWork would have one of the most storied names in American business, JPMorgan, backing part of its leases.

Neumann saw the power of that money and recognized how much JPMorgan's deep pockets could help him. He also genuinely liked Lee, who carried himself with a confidence that appealed to the name-dropping entrepreneur.

In fact, Lee was quick to remind Neumann that he needed the bank more than JPMorgan needed him. After Lee gave a quote to *Forbes* magazine about Neumann at Wintroub's request, Lee was annoyed that Neumann didn't even call to thank him. "I'm done with Adam Neumann," he told Wintroub, who relayed Lee's annoyance to Neumann. Within four hours, Neumann had sent an engraved gift to Lee's office and said he'd been working on the order for days.

But in June 2015, JPMorgan was rocked when Lee, then sixty-two, died suddenly while exercising on his treadmill in his Connecticut home. His death shocked friends and clients, many of whom were in the middle of deals with him.

Neumann seemed particularly devastated. After attending his memorial service at St. Patrick's Cathedral in midtown Manhattan, Neumann wrote a lengthy tribute on WeWork's website, calling Lee "the last of the old-school bankers who did business with a handshake and made bets that were first based on people and then numbers." He was, according to Neumann, "the best guy you could ever have in your corner."

Neumann continued to speak to Wintroub after Lee's death, but his interest in the bank waned. Neumann liked having the *top* people fawning over him. Lee had fit that bill, but Wintroub didn't. And it seemed to Neumann that Dimon didn't give him enough time.

Other banks were circling, and Neumann made sure that Wintroub knew it. He would mention Goldman Sachs casually in their conversations, which had the desired effect: it drove the bankers insane and made them ever more eager to win his business.

Goldman, too, had been pushing to get close to WeWork as Neumann's star rose. An arm of the bank had invested in WeWork in 2014, and ever since the investment banking team had been happy to offer advice. They flattered Neumann and his team with bullish figures about how WeWork would be valued on the public markets. Doing the work were Kim Posnett, an up-and-coming tech banker in her mid-thirties with a wide network that included celebrity friends, and her colleague David Ludwig, a Goldman lifer who had graduated from the University of Pennsylvania's Wharton business program in 1996.

By late 2015, Neumann was interested in fund-raising once again and surveyed his new investment banking friends for advice on valuation and next steps. Wintroub was skeptical he could raise even more money at a higher valuation—Neumann had just raised $400 million from Fidelity and others—but Neumann persisted.

When he turned to Goldman, he got a different answer. The firm was bullish. The Goldman Sachs team drew up charts that WeWork used for its presentations to its board. The message reinforced what Neumann had been preaching all along: WeWork could be even more valuable than its $10 billion mark when it traded on the stock market. To justify this, Goldman picked companies it said were similar: superfast-growth tech companies, like Netflix and Amazon, among others.

With Jimmy Lee gone, JPMorgan suddenly seemed to sparkle less. Goldman Sachs, on the other hand, was hitting all the right notes.

Moreover, Goldman had deep connections in Asia, a whole region full of funders that WeWork hadn't even tried. Neumann gave the bank the green light to set up a fund-raising trip to Asia.

The banks were looking west. WeWork was looking east.

CHAPTER 13

Taking Over the World

ADAM NEUMANN WAS ADDICTED TO FUND-RAISING. FRIENDS saw he loved the rush of finding new pockets of cash: the thrill of clinching a deal for hundreds of millions of dollars; the euphoria of seeing WeWork's valuation and his net worth rise. He would become jittery and overbearing as his staff tried to reel in funders. Sometimes after a good meeting with a potential investor or landlord, he'd have a big grin on his face, as though he knew he'd won over another convert.

"It was almost like he was a young guy and trying to date these hot chicks," a WeWork staffer, who had watched Neumann woo deep-pocketed investors, said. If one wasn't charmed, there was always another.

Each success emboldened him. Back when WeWork was worth $1.5 billion, few of his lieutenants and advisers thought he'd be able to raise a round at a $5 billion valuation, yet he did. Then he did it again at $10 billion, further defying skeptics. McKelvey told a gathering of real estate professionals in 2015 that Neumann was "probably one of the best at raising money in the world."

Beyond the adrenaline rush, friends saw another aspect of the fundraising that appealed to Neumann. For him, the company's valuation was a measuring stick for how he stacked up against the known names in Silicon Valley. At $10 billion, WeWork was one of the biggest and hottest startups of the moment, along with Uber, Airbnb, and Snapchat. The bigger the valuation, the more thoroughly WeWork and Neumann had earned their seat at the table among the greats in Silicon Valley; the more magazines called with plans to put him on the cover; the more celebrities were excited to join his events; the more heads of governments and industries sought him out. At $10 billion, WeWork was ranked ahead of Spotify, which had an $8.5 billion valuation. It was in a different league from the messaging service Slack and the ride-sharing company Lyft, which were worth $2.8 billion and $2.5 billion, respectively, in late 2015. This world order—reinforced by websites and newspapers that ranked large startups by valuation—played directly to Neumann's insecurities and narcissism. WeWork's valuation, he always thought, needed to be higher.

By the fall of 2015, after talking with Goldman Sachs, he devised a plan. The world's second-largest economy was bursting with investors who wanted to get in on ascendant global companies. Neumann was obsessed with bringing WeWork to the most populous country in the world; he frequently told staff that anyone trying to build a global company needed to be in China. Looking to China also gave WeWork a good excuse to raise more money. It was a novel move previously executed by Travis Kalanick of Uber, who launched ride hailing in the country in 2014 and was in the process of raising more than $1 billion just for his China operation.

Neumann's existing investors weren't happy to hear about his fund-raising plan. Bruce Dunlevie of Benchmark and Michael Eisenberg—who had left Benchmark to run his own firm—had been pushing him to improve existing operations. They urged him not to overreach. Why not stay focused on the main business? Many of the investors simply wanted Neumann to go public. Being a public company tends to bring much-needed scrutiny; it might hold Neumann accountable to his flights of fancy, they reasoned. Further, if WeWork went public, they'd have the ability to sell their shares and harvest the enormous returns that appeared on paper.

Benchmark, which initially put in $15 million followed by a bit more in subsequent rounds, had a stake worth well over $1 billion on paper at WeWork's $10 billion valuation. So long as WeWork was private, it would be hard to sell any of it.

Of course, Neumann didn't have to listen to their advice. The company was firmly in his control, and the board members had shown that they would eventually bend to his will on even the most consequential decisions. "No" votes simply didn't happen; even when directors were irked, they went along in the end.

So Neumann pressed ahead. He told aides he wanted to raise at an increased valuation—between $15 billion and $20 billion. It didn't matter that nothing had changed about the business from May. WeWork was now a hot company—one of the most valuable startups in the world. He would be able to persuade someone to invest at that level.

The task faced numerous obstacles. Beyond the obvious— WeWork had just months before raised at $10 billion and just raised before that at a $5 billion valuation, so why should its valuation go up past $15 billion now?—air was beginning to come out of the Silicon Valley startup bubble.

One pinprick came in October 2015 when *The Wall Street Journal* published an exposé on the $9 billion blood-testing startup Theranos, whose black-turtleneck-wearing founder was often compared to Steve Jobs. The piece by John Carreyrou said that many of Theranos's central claims about its technology were false. It was a piercing indictment of Silicon Valley's hype machine, where innovation and disruption were ascendant and critical questions were often dismissed as obnoxious cynicism.

At the same time, numerous highly hyped startups were beginning to miss the superambitious targets they'd used to lure investors. Suddenly companies like the cloud storage startup Box and the payment processor Square were going public at valuations that were *lower* than when they last raised money from investors—a concept nearly verboten in startup land, where everything was supposed to be "up and to the right." Anything else was a crack in the facade of success.

Some were raising concerns about the amount of money poured into the sector, with the occasional voice even openly calling it a bubble. Among those was Bill Gurley, the Benchmark partner who invested in Uber. Gurley was a highly respected figure in Silicon Valley, a lumbering former analyst with a Texas twang who warned on his well-read blog that "late-stage investors, desperately afraid of missing out on acquiring shareholding positions in possible 'unicorn' companies, have essentially abandoned their traditional risk analysis," he wrote. "We are in a risk bubble."

Neumann was not pleased to hear this line from one of his own investors. He confronted Gurley at an event hosted by a bank in Las Vegas. Neumann admonished Gurley, telling him that the boom atmosphere helped both of them, lifting WeWork's value.

Neumann had reason to be defensive. WeWork's growth until that point was enabled above all by its ability to attract ever-larger sums. If the fund-raising machine ever turned off, so, too, would WeWork's growth, and with it its lofty valuation.

The company needed more and more money at higher valuations because its losses kept getting larger. In 2014, WeWork took in $74 million of revenue yet reported an operating loss of $88 million, its own records show. This came even though WeWork, just a few months before the end of 2014, told investors it expected an operating profit of $4.2 million. Into 2015, it veered further off its path of projected profits. Instead of the $49 million operating profit it had predicted, it ended the year with a $227 million operating *loss.*

For whatever reason, be it a lack of attention or compelling excuses by Neumann, the investors weren't particularly troubled by these missed profit targets. WeWork was hitting its *revenue* targets and opening locations just as fast as it had promised.

Some of WeWork's mutual fund investors did start to have other concerns, but they were more focused on Neumann himself.

T. Rowe Price was frustrated with Neumann's move to consolidate control over the company in 2015. It was the start of what would be a mounting number of worries at the fund manager about WeWork's governance.

Neumann quickly spooked Fidelity, too, after its investment. When the deal was announced in June, Neumann told *The Wall Street Journal* that he didn't hunt for the funding—that investors came to *him*. "We didn't seek this out," he said. "We kept having offers and kept ignoring them."

This was news to the Fidelity portfolio manager Gavin Baker. He had invested in WeWork only after hearing about its fundraising round from a JPMorgan banker who was trying to help WeWork find investors. Baker was incensed. After reading the story, he called Neumann to express his displeasure. Not only did it make Fidelity look bad, he told Neumann, but it was simply inaccurate and embarrassing. (Baker quickly forgave the slight and provided regular counsel to Neumann.)

Now Neumann was eager to put these past misrepresentations aside and start hunting for funds around the globe. As usual, he had a particularly adept nose for where to find money. Despite some air coming out of the balloon in Silicon Valley, there was still a lot of money in China eager to get into U.S. firms. Tech had been on a tear in China, and many investors—as well as homegrown behemoths like Alibaba and Tencent—were trying to spend more globally, particularly in the United States. All Neumann had to do was find the right match.

IN THE FALL OF 2015, NEUMANN FLEW WITH MICHAEL GROSS TO China. In two successive trips over a month, the pair zigzagged around the country on a private plane, bouncing from meetings with landlords to pitches with potential investors, all arranged by Goldman Sachs.

Gross, who had been the CEO of the struggling boutique hotel chain Morgans Hotel Group—and before that spent years working in finance at banks and hedge funds—was now a constant sidekick and close friend to Neumann. Having moved on from serving as WeWork's CFO, his title was vice-chairman, but his value add at the company was largely in helping Neumann shine in fund-raising meetings. With his youthful good looks, the Cornell graduate exuded a polish that Neumann lacked. He had an ability to charm the Wall Street and private equity crowd by seeming like one of their breed. Like Neumann, Gross didn't use a computer in his normal course of business—an ironic feat for the two men integral to convincing investors that WeWork was a tech company.

Neumann would often sour on his deputies, but since he joined WeWork in 2013, Gross had been a near-constant friend and crutch. At first, Gross had helped bring some flourishes of boutique hotels to WeWork, impressing on Neumann the importance of the mood and music of the common spaces. In fund-raising pitches, he translated Neumann's grandiose language into digestible terms for investors, making them see dollar signs after Neumann talked about bringing the world together.

In part, his task was to warm up the room—to get investors interested so that Neumann could reel them in. Later, he repeatedly called himself Neumann's "fluffer" until Jen Berrent, WeWork's legal chief, told him to stop. He livened up company events and even routine investors meetings by choosing 1990s hip-hop songs. (Neumann would describe Gross as "vice chairman—and also head DJ.") Once, he and Neumann were wooing an investor from Tiger Global at Gross's beach house in the Hamptons. After flying in by helicopter, the investor, Scott Shleifer, drank so much with the duo that he threw up on Gross's fluffy dog. Tiger didn't invest.

In China, their pitch meetings followed a similar pattern. They were often held in five-star hotel conference rooms in Shanghai and Hong Kong and bolstered by Neumann's infectious confidence about where WeWork was going. Three years earlier, only a handful of well-known investors had put money into WeWork. At this point, Neumann could point to two of the largest banks in the world—Goldman Sachs *and* JPMorgan—as backers. Potential investors were primed to see WeWork like Uber or Airbnb, not some office space company like Regus.

Neumann was particular about where each guest would sit; he would ask his staff to arrange and then rearrange the seating before they arrived. He showed off promotional videos made by WeWork staff that made the offices seem like vibrant hives of fun-loving millennials enjoying their jobs.

Alcohol was almost always on hand—in greater quantities than is customary in Chinese business meals—and often played a starring role in the fund-raising conversations. The plane trips between meetings were filled with drinking. For early morning meetings, Neumann would often arrive late, looking hungover. In the middle of one meeting with the Chinese co-working company UrWork, waiters burst into the conference room with trays of tequila and beer that the attendees proceeded to consume.

His pitch seemed to strike particular interest with Hony Capital, a private equity firm that was a spin-off of the state-backed investment company Legend Holdings. Hony was led by John Zhao, a balding, friendly former tech executive who studied physics before turning to business, receiving an MBA from Northwestern University. Eager to go global, Hony had recently made two splashy investments that crossed borders: it had bought the British pizza chain PizzaExpress and plowed money into a new U.S. film studio, STX Entertainment.

Zhao, then in his early fifties, and Neumann clicked almost immediately. Just a few minutes into Neumann's pitch, Zhao was sold on the business, he would say later. He loved to talk about the fusion of global businesses and local ones—"glocal"—a concept Neumann quickly warmed to as they repeated the term to each other.

Between pitches Neumann raced around the streets of Shanghai and Beijing, looking at buildings. In between meetings Neumann conducted rapid-fire interviews with candidates for jobs in China, taking them in his car and then dropping them off at his destination.

By the end of the second weeklong trip, Goldman Sachs surveyed the funding landscape and found relatively little interest. Neumann had been aggressive in his pitches, making it clear that he expected a valuation above $15 billion, rather than the standard practice of playing coy on price. Driving a hard bargain had the effect of scaring away most of the potential investors. One private equity firm was potentially interested in a valuation below $12 billion. No other bids came in.

Zhao, though, was intrigued. Without setting a specific price, he indicated he was interested in buying a stake at above a $15 billion valuation. It was a huge premium compared with the only other real interested party.

Neumann was thrilled. Hony was agreeing to give WeWork a burst of hundreds of millions of dollars, which could allow the company to launch a big expansion into Asia. It would be transformative, he believed. WeWork could be the truly global company Neumann imagined.

The two agreed to do a deal. The final valuation, both sides agreed, would be figured out soon, when Zhao came to New York.

Later, the companies would work for months to complete the deal. The WeWork team thought the Hony staff junior to Zhao were skeptical of the investment. As was the case at Fidelity, it seemed that the lower-level number crunchers were unclear why the valuation was so high. In the end, though, Zhao's zeal for Neumann won the day. Zhao would go on to round up money from a series of other big-name Chinese investors, including Alibaba's founder, Jack Ma, to invest alongside Hony. Not long before the deal closed, Zhao was in New York, and he and Neumann celebrated. Neumann invited him to a staff party at a new WeWork location; late into the night, Neumann invited a crowd up to the roof of the building at 110 Wall Street. Shots of tequila were passed around, and Neumann pulled out a fire extinguisher, spraying the foamy discharge on the crowd, dousing Zhao.

But before the months of negotiations and due diligence, while Neumann was finishing his China fund-raising trip, he and Zhao decided to have an initial celebration of their impending partnership. Neumann and Gross were in Hong Kong at the time, so Zhao brought them to the Chariot Club, a stodgy, members-only establishment modeled on the exclusive social and business clubs in London and Manhattan. The group secured a private room and ordered the Peking duck. As they waited for their food to come, and as the alcohol hit their empty stomachs, the decibel level rose, as did the energy. Gross pulled out a Bluetooth speaker, blasting Jay-Z so loudly that guests outside the room could hear. By the time everyone got up to leave, the group was heavily intoxicated. Keeping the speakers on as they walked across the dining room—as sedate, suit-wearing diners stared at them—Neumann and Gross stumbled toward the elevators; a car waiting outside would take them to their private jet. Sill in earshot of the dining room, the two together began to chant.

"We are taking over the world!" they yelled. "We are taking over the world!"

PART III

CHAPTER 14

Friends in High Places

W*HY WON'T HE ANSWER THE DOOR?*

A gaggle of WeWork executives and aides were pacing in the lobby of the ITC Gardenia in Bangalore. It was around 8:00 one morning in January 2016. They had made the nearly twenty-hour trip to attend a conference called Startup India, the brainchild of Prime Minister Narendra Modi, who was eager to make India a more inviting place for entrepreneurs.

Coming shortly after Neumann's adventures in China, the trip was intended to be far more than a junket. Before the official kick-off of the conference, Marc Schimmel, an early investor and adviser to Adam Neumann, had arranged a series of meetings with potential investors and partners in different cities around the country.

Now, as the team of WeWork emissaries waited in the ornate lobby of the five-star hotel, the clock was ticking down to the appointed hour for the first investor meeting. There was a big problem. Nobody could wake—or find—Neumann. While Neumann often ran late for meetings, this radio silence was rare and unnerving.

Several of the executives and Neumann's assistant tried calling their boss, again and again.

The group included the new communications chief, Jen Skyler; the chief revenue officer, Francis Lobo; and Rebekah Neumann's nephew Luke Robinson. Lobo and Robinson exchanged nervous looks. The pair had been up with Neumann later than the rest the night before, happy to have a rare occasion to bond with their boss. They shared stories as Neumann poured tequila shots at the hotel pool, then retreated to Neumann's hotel room, where they continued drinking. There, Neumann began calling friends and employees back in New York over FaceTime, joking and heckling them during the middle of their workday.

The group in the lobby grew more anxious with every passing minute and finally turned to hotel security. The security team went to unlock the door to Neumann's room. Inside they found Neumann: passed out but alive.

Schimmel tried to justify the seeming lapse to the group: "You don't understand all the pressure on this man." He has a giant business with a crazy valuation. He has four kids. This is the way he unwinds, Schimmel said.

By the time Neumann was finally roused, the planned meeting had come and gone. Neumann spent the afternoon recuperating at the spa.

BY EARLY 2016, WEWORK'S BREAKNECK GROWTH HAD SWELLED its location count to sixty-five. Most were still in U.S. cities, but the company had made inroads into Europe and Israel, and its investment from Hony Capital meant it would soon be a player in China. Now Neumann saw an opportunity to make a move in the world's second most populous nation.

When Neumann had fielded an invitation from the prime minister's office to speak at Startup India, he told his team he'd go on the condition that he could secure a one-on-one meeting with Modi. Neumann had always known how to extract maximum value from such meetings. In the room, one-on-one, he could charm and connect on a deeply personal level. Afterward, he knew how to wave around his bond with the well-known figure, however fleeting his interaction, to spur yet more connections. Prime Minister Modi had a name worth dropping.

On Neumann's penultimate day in India, he finally got his chance to sit down with Modi, who ran as a pro-business candidate. Neumann surprised his team when, days before the meeting, he invited his father, Doron, to fly from Israel and insisted he join him for the meeting in New Delhi. It wasn't a terribly in depth-conversation. Modi, in addition to taking in Neumann's pitch for WeWork's expansion into India, asked Neumann for help solving his country's housing crisis, Neumann recounted to others. Neumann pledged that WeWork would find ways to do so. Neumann would later tell his staff that WeWork would solve not only India's housing crisis but the world's.

The next day, Neumann ascended the stage at the Vigyan Bhavan conference center. He wore a flowing white shirt and a high-collared navy-blue vest nicknamed the Modi vest because it was the prime minister's attire of choice. Before an audience of hundreds, he was introduced by a local CEO as "the quintessential entrepreneur" with a rags-to-riches story who had overcome failures before hitting it big. It was just the kind of intro Neumann liked. Rocking in his chair as he spoke, Neumann told the crowd just how much WeWork had grown in six years and how it was getting ready to explode across the globe.

"We're in nineteen cities, we're in seven countries, we're on three continents, and we're just getting started," he said. Citing its abundance of young workers and startups, he declared that India "could be bigger than Europe" for WeWork. Fund-raising, he told the rapt audience, wasn't a big concern. "If your business is the right business, raising money will not be the difficulty."

Sitting in the audience, nodding along, was a self-possessed Japanese businessman who was starting to write some of the largest checks India's entrepreneurs had ever seen.

Masayoshi Son was the founder and CEO of the Tokyo-based tech conglomerate SoftBank Group. Clad in a black blazer and white shirt, the fifty-eight-year-old had a contagious smile and slight build. He was there to make his own mark on the tech scene: Son would take to the same stage later in the day, where he described the future of India in euphoric terms, declaring it "the beginning of the big bang." Son had recently invested $2 billion in India-based companies. Onstage, he pledged to accelerate that number in the coming years.

But Son's ambitions ran far larger. With a portfolio that extended from the telecom giant Sprint to stakes in ride-hailing startups in India and China, SoftBank was already one of the world's best-known tech investors, having survived through several ups and downs. Son, known in tech circles simply as Masa, liked to tell people that he was the world's richest man in 2000 for three days before losing almost everything—more than $70 billion—in the dot-com bust.

Son's most famous investment was a propitious bet on a fledgling Alibaba in 2000, when he led a $20 million round of financing into the Chinese e-commerce company. By 2016, SoftBank's 32 percent stake in the then-giant tech company founded by Jack Ma was worth around $40 billion and growing fast. But Son had yet larger targets in his sights. He yearned to be one of the richest men in the world and for SoftBank to be one of the most valuable companies on the planet.

Son, two decades older and roughly a foot shorter than Neumann, shared many traits with the entrepreneur. Both had extreme ambition and unflinching optimism. Son eschewed many conservative Japanese business traditions, including suits, often wearing Uniqlo vests or casual sweaters. While flashing a wide grin and speaking calmly, he employed a brashness and directness unusual in Japan.

While he earned his vast fortune betting on technology, Son was never a computer geek or even a deep study of the industry. Instead, he focused on forging ties to people with expertise and people in power.

Son had taken up golf with a fanatical fervor in his early twenties on the advice of his doctor when he was recovering from a serious illness. His father had cirrhosis, so Son abstained from alcohol to persuade his father to follow his lead. He barely had a drink until his early forties. Still, he knew how to wine and dine potential business partners, building his fortune by persuading people in high places in business and government to collaborate with him. The Japanese press in the 1990s called him "Rojin-kiraah," or "Old-Man-Killer," because of his ability to woo older titans of business.

Son loved an entrepreneur with a vision, and Neumann idolized hard-charging self-made billionaires. Despite the odd-couple look, those who knew both predicted instant chemistry.

BORN IN 1957, SON HAD GROWN UP IN A FAMILY OF OUTSIDERS. His grandparents immigrated to Japan from Korea, which meant that Son was not entitled to citizenship. Korean immigrants who arrived before 1945 or the end of World War II were often referred to as Zainichi, which roughly translates into "staying in Japan." Because of their ancestry, Son and his family were also banned from holding government jobs.

His father, Mitsunori, made a home for the family in a shack in a poor, small rural village on one of Japan's southwestern islands. Through pluck and thrift, they clawed their way to the upper-middle class. Many of Mitsunori's ventures were considered unseemly, including bootlegging hard liquor and building out a chain of small gambling establishments, known as pachinko parlors. His parents changed their family name from Son to Yasumoto to obscure their Korean roots, a relatively common practice in Japan.

By the time Son was a teenager, the family was living in one of the larger houses in the cosmopolitan city of Fukuoka. A friend remembers it being a rare house in the area large enough to fit a Ping-Pong table. His father also had saved up enough to send Son to a short high school exchange program at the University of California at Berkeley. His brief stint in the United States motivated Son to return to America to complete high school.

Once Son touched down in Northern California, he moved at the kind of frenetic pace that would define his business life. After learning English for several months and then entering high school as a sophomore, he persuaded the principal to let him take a college entrance exam, which he passed. As he later told his biographer, he left high school in 1974 without graduating to avoid wasting precious time.

He soon enrolled at a community college near San Francisco, where he joined his future wife, Masami Ohno—also an exchange student from Japan—whom he'd met after arriving in California. After less than two years there, Son returned to UC Berkeley. College coursework, including engineering classes and economics, held little allure for him. Friends and associates remember Son's fixation on making money. Son said he'd brainstorm one idea for an invention a day.

Aided by cash from his father—who regularly sent him money over the next few years—Son urged Hong Lu, his friend and one of the few other undergraduates at Berkeley from Japan, to become his business partner instead of taking a job he had lined up with an ice cream company. To convince him, Son called Lu multiple times a day—pestering his fiancée and her family, too. In increasingly grandiose terms, he outlined how much money Lu would make in a yet-to-be-determined business endeavor.

One endeavor involved putting arcade games like *Space Invaders* that Son imported from Japan, with help from his father, in restaurants and bars all over Berkeley. Soon they were generating so much cash that Son and Lu bought their own arcade, Silver Ball Gardens, just off campus.

Another moneymaking gambit, an electronic text-to-speech device, proved more complex.

Forrest Mozer, a physics professor at Berkeley, had created a device that would let users select common phrases, and it would speak them in another language, with correct pronunciation. Son was big on the idea and had a plan to sell the devices in airport kiosks in Japan. With the device showing good potential, Son, who had minimal technical expertise himself, hired a team of part-time researchers to build prototypes of other devices he was dreaming up. Even as he continued his undergraduate classes, Son flew regularly to Japan with Lu for meetings with electronics companies about his product pipeline. Son eventually sold the patent for the translator to Sharp for about $1 million, he boasted later.

Mozer only found out that Son had sold the device decades later when he read about it in a newspaper feature on Son. Mozer was never paid for his work or for use of the device. (SoftBank has denied this, saying Son remembered paying Mozer.)

By the time Son graduated in 1980, he felt compelled to go back to Japan. His father was sick, and Lu bought out Son's stake in their joint company for $2 million. In 1981, back in Japan and bolstered by his check from Lu, Son formed SoftBank, the company that would eventually become the vehicle for realizing Son's grandiose visions. Son described the company as a bank where people could buy or sell software, and he quickly lined up deals with national and international software companies, often pushing them to become their sole distributor in Japan.

Son noticed that the software distribution business was similar to the arcade business—only on steroids. Once he struck the deals to license software, he could quickly find buyers all over the country, and the business generated mountains of cash.

But that wouldn't be large enough for Son's broader ambitions. He soon expanded his company's focus into computer-industry trade publications, buying the Japanese editions of *PC Week* and *PC Magazine.* On its face, these were head-scratching investments: Son had no particular interest in print journalism, and the publications weren't even profitable. But they were excellent at increasing SoftBank's brand awareness, as well as Son's personal brand.

Obsessed with Microsoft's Bill Gates, Son decided to put him on the cover of one of his magazines in 1987 and flew to Seattle to conduct the interview himself. After their hour-long meeting, Gates gave Son a tour of Microsoft's headquarters and told Son that he read the computer magazine *PC Week* (the U.S. edition) religiously to understand the industry. Within a decade, Son would buy that publication, too.

Over the next decade, Son expanded his empire inside Japan and grew richer and richer. Still he yearned for more. Son would not be satisfied until he was in the orbit of Bill Gates and other tech magnates. To get there, he decided to literally buy the stage they most coveted.

SON RETURNED TO THE UNITED STATES REGULARLY ONCE HE started SoftBank, keeping close tabs on developments in technology. A visit to Las Vegas for a week in November was a critical part of that. Once a year, more than 100,000 people would fly into Nevada to attend Comdex, a conference founded back in 1979 that had evolved into the world's fair of the personal-computing industry, growing in size and stature along with the tech industry. Tech glitterati like Gates, Oracle's co-founder Larry Ellison, and Intel's CEO, Andy Grove, vied for key speaking spots, while companies unveiled their latest gadgets and futuristic-seeming products like high-density compact discs, Intel's Pentium Pro computer chips, and Plasmatron monitors. It all gave Comdex goers an early glimpse—sometimes as much as a year in advance—into consumer technologies that might soon come to market.

By 1993, Comdex's co-founder Sheldon Adelson was seeking to sell the trade-show business. During the conference that year, Son approached Adelson and several members of his executive team at the famed Sands casino—a property that Adelson had recently purchased—with a proposition. Clad in a neat gray suit, Son walked solemnly into a meeting room, bowing as he greeted Adelson and

his team. Son praised them for creating the world's greatest technology conference. Now, he said, it was time for SoftBank to run it.

Adelson and his partners stared at Son quizzically, knowing little
about his background or his wealth. I can make the business better,
Son said. You charge too much, and there's too much red tape, he
told them. Adelson told Son to raise more money and come back.
They could talk more if he did.

Adelson walked Son to the door, shut it behind him, and rolled
his eyes. "It was hard to take him seriously," said Jason Chudnofsky,
a Comdex executive who had been working with Adelson on the
sale.

Less than a year later, Son had more than enough cash at his
disposal. In July 1994, he took SoftBank public on the Japanese
stock market. His roughly 70 percent stake in the company was
worth more than $2 billion.

He returned to Las Vegas in early 1995, this time with plenty
of money to spend. Adelson had been looking to sell Comdex
for at least $300 million but struggled to find a buyer. While Son
could be a fierce negotiator, he was also developing a tendency to
become so enraptured by an idea or a founder that he ended up
paying a price far beyond what a seller might even think about.
SoftBank agreed to pay roughly $800 million. Son was convinced
it was the next step in his quest for respect. He told Chudnofsky
at the time, "If I own the communications tools, I'll own the
industry."

Financially, Son's investment in Comdex didn't go well. The
trade conference's parent would end up in bankruptcy by the early
years of the twenty-first century. But it did prove to be a conduit
for key relationships, and Son began to stoke friendships with Gates,
Ellison, Grove, and others at the nodes of global power. In Japan,
he had become a celebrity.

Armed with his new, powerful tech social circles, Son raced into
deal-making mode, rapidly gobbling up companies at high prices

that stunned American investors. SoftBank spent nearly $2 billion to acquire the publishing company Ziff Davis, which owned *PC Magazine,* and then another $1.5 billion months after that to buy Kingston Technology, which made computer memory boards.

Son was just warming up. By the late 1990s, he had gone all in on the internet, snapping up stakes in burgeoning dot-coms. He created what was then one of the world's largest startup investment funds, with nearly $2 billion to spend, and ended up investing in a shockingly large number of companies—more than 400. While he had billions in cash from SoftBank's IPO, it wasn't enough. He grew enamored with debt. He piled loans onto SoftBank and sometimes borrowed more himself—using his own stock in Soft-Bank as collateral—in order to fund larger and larger bets.

As the dot-com bubble inflated, Son kept pouring money in. He created a separate venture capital fund in California that used both SoftBank's own money and cash from outside investors. Money rushed into websites of all flavors: the e-commerce site Buy.com, the online stock site E★Trade, and the web-hosting service GeoCities. He made huge bets on instant delivery. He backed Kozmo.com and the online grocery-delivery company Webvan. He told *Forbes* in 1999 that he owned roughly 7 to 8 percent of the publicly listed value of all U.S. internet properties.

SoftBank's shares peaked in February 2000 at a valuation of roughly $190 billion, a crest that coincided with the broader peak in tech stocks.

Then came the bust. Investors fled internet stocks as they realized the magnitude of the bubble they'd created, and companies like Webvan and Kozmo that hemorrhaged money swiftly disappeared. The man who was deemed—or at least aspired to be—Japan's Bill Gates or Warren Buffett watched much of his wealth evaporate. Having relied heavily on debt to fund all his giant bets, Son was in a precarious spot, highly leveraged and vulnerable to a downturn. By the end of the year, as the dot-com bubble popped,

SoftBank's shares had lost more than 90 percent of their value. He lost more wealth than anyone ever before.

SoftBank's portfolio included some of the worst busts in terms of investor dollars lost. One of its largest bets—Webvan—discontinued operations and declared bankruptcy, losing roughly $850 million in investors' money and laying off two thousand workers.

For all of SoftBank's losses in the dot-com era, one winner offset a large portion of them: the search engine Yahoo. After first investing in 1995, Son pushed Yahoo's founders, Jerry Yang and David Filo, to take $100 million—more than what they said they wanted or needed at the time. When Yahoo went public in 1996, SoftBank owned roughly one-third of the company's shares. SoftBank later helped Yahoo's founders set up in Japan, and kept a 60 percent stake as the company grew to be far more valuable than the U.S. arm of Yahoo.

JUST BEFORE THE DOT-COM IMPLOSION, SON MANAGED TO PLANT what would turn out to be the seeds of his comeback that would grow out of the smoldering ashes of his empire. In January 2000, SoftBank led a $20 million investment in a company run by a budding, energetic Chinese entrepreneur named Jack Ma.

Son likes to tell people he bet on Ma, the founder of Alibaba, because he liked the glimmer in his eyes. "We didn't talk about revenues; we didn't even talk about a business model," Ma said at the time. "We just talked about a shared vision. Both of us make quick decisions."

Alibaba at the time was a nascent e-commerce company in China that connected manufacturers and buyers across the country. It would go on to transform the internet and retail in China. Son's investment would become known as one of the best single investments of all time.

Apart from this investment, Son hunkered down in Japan in the early part of the millennium and plowed his efforts into building a high-speed internet network in the country. He found a challenge in the bureaucracy, and at one point he was so frustrated he walked into Japan's telecommunications ministry and threatened to set himself on fire with a lighter unless the ministry helped him. Within four years, this company—Yahoo BB—had increased Japan's internet speed far beyond the U.S. average, and he'd built a lucrative franchise.

In 2006, Son's rehabilitated SoftBank expanded into the mobile industry, spending roughly $15 billion to buy Vodafone's business in Japan—a distant third-place carrier. By negotiating directly with Steve Jobs, he landed exclusive distribution rights for the iPhone, quickly vaulting his mobile phone company into the top tier.

By 2012, the itch had returned. Son yearned to become a force in the United States again. He turned back to his mobile phone playbook and started trying to buy *both* Sprint and T-Mobile—a move to compete against AT&T and Verizon. He announced a $21.6 billion deal in late 2012 for 70 percent of Sprint. Apple's Tim Cook and others assured him that a deal to buy T-Mobile as well would pass muster with U.S. regulators, he told others. As if to announce his return to the Silicon Valley elite, Son bought one of the most expensive houses ever sold in the country, spending $117 million for a nine-acre estate in Woodside, California, a stone's throw from the epicenter of venture capital on Sand Hill Road.

His ambitions ran further still. He frequently talked about a three-hundred-year growth plan for SoftBank that would make it the world's top technology company—at the forefront of every major shift. In one slide presentation to his investors, he charted the path over the next three decades for SoftBank and technology. Humans and robots would grow symbiotic; brains and computer chips would be interdependent. SoftBank, he told investors, would help cure sorrow and increase people's happiness. One slide showed a future human life expectancy of two hundred years.

"The saddest thing in people's life is loneliness," one slide read. "SoftBank works to increase people's joy."

By 2013, Son's goal to create the top mobile carrier in the United States had failed. While he was able to buy Sprint, the U.S. government blocked him from buying T-Mobile. Winning the U.S. mobile market had been a critical piece of Son's master plan for SoftBank to become the most valuable company in the world. Associates said he took that ambition very seriously, and with the failure to combine Sprint and T-Mobile, he became morose.

Still, his wealth continued to grow. Alibaba had become enormous, and SoftBank owned a huge chunk. Son began hunting elsewhere, scanning around the world for places to invest. That is what brought him to India at the start of 2016. Having vowed to invest billions more in Indian companies, he was eager to get to know them.

As ADAM NEUMANN'S TIME IN INDIA WAS NEARING AN END, NOT only had he met Modi, but he'd made inroads with potential partners in the country who could be key to WeWork's expansion. Son invited Neumann to a reception SoftBank was hosting for several hundred guests on Neumann's last night in the country. There, at a restaurant overlooking New Delhi at the Leela Palace, one of the nicest hotels in India, Son gave Neumann a rapt audience.

At a banquette slightly away from the cocktail party, the two entrepreneurs leaned forward, barely taking a breath for half an hour as they discussed their respective business visions. After they wrapped up, Neumann continued to socialize with the attendees, amusing SoftBank's other key executives, Nikesh Arora and Alok Sama, with outrageous stories and off-color jokes. His team could tell Son was taken with Neumann.

Soon, their paths would cross again.

CHAPTER 15

It's Tricky

THE PRIVATE JET WAS HEADING EAST FROM NEW YORK, OVER the Atlantic, with Adam Neumann and a handful of staffers inside.

Their destination was San Sebastián in northern Spain, a small city in the Basque country west of France, where the Atlantic Ocean flows into the Bay of Biscay to create an enviable surfing locale.

The WeWork crew had indeed come for waves—but not in the ocean. They were there to kick the tires on a young startup called Wavegarden, run by a Basque engineer, Josema Odriozola.

The nine-year-old company made surf pools—aquatic venues larger than an Olympic-sized pool that created eight-foot waves on demand, a product that had the potential to open up surfing to anyone in the world, regardless of their distance from a beach.

Surfing had become a new passion for Neumann. He honed his skills on Long Island, out east in the Hamptons, where he and his wife, Rebekah, had bought a house in 2012, and sometimes closer to the city in the Rockaways. Surfing cleared his mind, he told friends; it lifted his spirits. He especially loved surfing in Hawaii, where he'd hire crews of well-known surfers on Kauai's north shore to coach him and show him the best waves in the island's famed Hanalei Bay. Surfing was a passion he shared with Rebekah, who joined him on many trips.

Artie Minson, who had joined WeWork in 2015 as its president and chief operating officer, learned how deeply attached his boss had become to surfing one day while the pair was working late into the early morning. Around 1:30 a.m., Neumann told Minson how it had been a while since he'd surfed. He missed it. Minson offered up his beach house, a short drive out of the city on Long Island, telling Neumann that he could go whenever he wanted. Minson eventually left the office to sleep for a few hours before trudging back in the next morning bleary-eyed for an 8:00 meeting. He was startled to find Neumann in the office already, looking bright and energetic, wearing a bathing suit. Neumann had already been to Minson's house to surf.

For all Neumann's enthusiasm, however, some rituals of the sport did not meet his liking. A key element of the sport is paddling. Typically surfers start at shore and paddle out into the surf on their boards. Then, as they wait for a good wave, they paddle more before popping onto their feet as the wave catches them. Paddling is the platform on which all other skills are built—the pain before the reward.

It wasn't for Neumann.

He took a far less patient approach; for many of his surfing excursions, he would hop on a Jet Ski helmed by one of his surf coaches. The motor would blare as they pushed farther out into the ocean, towing a board off the back. Once he was taken to an ideal location, Neumann would simply wait for a good wave—a technique called "step off."

"The way I surf, I don't have time for paddling," he once said to a colleague.

Most surfers consider Jet Ski drop-offs cheating—like a mountain climber hopping a ride on a helicopter most of the way up. Some surf spots in Kauai even forbid them, though Neumann, with his well-respected local surf coaches, was able to skirt such regulations without much trouble.

The love of surfing was what brought Neumann to the Basque

country in early 2016. Earlier, Neumann had asked his longtime deputy Roni Bahar, who jumped from one new initiative to the other at WeWork, to look into the nascent business of surf pools. Like Neumann, Bahar was prone to dreaming big. He bought into Neumann's vision for an all-encompassing WeWork that involved far more than office space rentals.

Bahar had observed a new fervor among millennials for sports like surfing. Wavegarden, he thought, had a technology that could open up the sport to even more people. You no longer needed to be near an ocean to surf; you could build a surfing destination in the middle of Texas or Illinois. As WeWork rapidly expanded, Bahar thought a Wavegarden facility could be offered as an amenity to anyone with a WeWork membership—a perk as WeWork evolved into more of an all-encompassing lifestyle brand. Neumann, who told friends he saw surfing as a great way to build community, was into the idea. WeWork could even construct surf pools as part of campuses for giant office complexes.

In Spain, the crew tried out Wavegarden's technology. The surf pool was larger than a football field, with a mechanical spine in the center attached to a snowplow-like arm that pushed water into wave after wave.

Neumann liked what he saw. After months of negotiations, by May 2016, the deal was done: WeWork paid $13.8 million in cash and stock for a 42 percent stake in the company. That didn't give WeWork full control, but gave it plenty of influence.

To outsiders, the investment was beyond puzzling. One such person was Jamie Hodari, the CEO of the co-working company Industrious. In a meeting with his smaller rival, Neumann—seemingly trying to impress Hodari—told him WeWork's latest purchase was "making waves." At first, Hodari assumed it was a metaphor—until he watched a video Neumann showed him. Hodari thought it was absurd.

If the deal puzzled outsiders like Hodari, it didn't seem terribly strange at WeWork. Neumann's vision had intoxicated his staff. If the boss's vision was to buy a stake in a surf pool company as a way to create community, he must be onto something. The board approved the deal, too. WeWork was getting into the surfing business.

As WEWORK POURED MONEY INTO QUESTIONABLE VENTURES LIKE Wavegarden, the company was still struggling to make money in its main business of subleasing office space.

Despite the rosy talk of WeWork's revenue growth, the more the company expanded, the more money it lost. WeWork needed to keep raising large amounts of money every year or so. To maintain the kind of rapid growth that gave Neumann license to compare WeWork to a tech company, it needed more funds. If WeWork was a rocket ship, it was one that needed constant midair refueling sessions.

Of course, this wasn't the plan WeWork put forward to investors. Nor was it WeWork's internal plan. At the start of 2015, WeWork projected that its revenue would grow 153 percent, to $202 million, but it only planned for its expenses to grow 37 percent, to $220 million—just like a software company that can throttle back on growing expenses once clients are buying its products en masse.

But WeWork's financial reality at the end of 2015 looked nothing like a software company's: revenue was almost exactly as projected, but expenses were $414 million, rising just as fast as revenue. WeWork was spending $2 for every $1 it took in—not a sustainable pattern. In the first six months of 2016, it was a similar story: it lost $191 million on $178 million of revenue. The company was losing $1 million *a day*. Back in its inaugural year of 2010, the company barely even spent $1 million in the whole *year*.

So far, Neumann had largely succeeded in persuading private investors, time and again, to breeze past these inconvenient losses, chalking them up to the inevitable cost of rapid growth. Instead, he guided their eyes to the future he painted for them—one of a dis-

ruptive tech company that would spout out giant profits as it became the workplace of choice around the globe. After all, other
darling startups like Uber, Lyft, and Snapchat were losing gobs of
money, too. These companies were all just trying to break into big
industries, he contended, and doing what it took to get there. And
unlike many of these startups, WeWork had no clear sizable competitor on a similar trajectory.

This was a substantial change from the traditional way of funding startups. Startups historically would raise two or three rounds of
funding from venture capitalists, at which point they were profitable or (hopefully) close to it and would head to the public stock
markets. There, they would conduct the IPO—revealing all their
financials and risks to the public markets—and then start trading
publicly on stock exchanges, where it is easier to raise money. Amazon took just three years to go public after it was founded. Apple
went public after four years.

Now, however, startups were finding that they could afford to
stay private for years longer, thanks to the giant roster of investors
trying to get into hot startups. By 2016, Uber was already seven
years old, with no defined plans on when to go public. WeWork
was six. Airbnb was eight. Staying private meant an easier life for a
founder—without the scrutiny one faced from the press and investors over quarterly earnings reports.

The lack of scrutiny let problems fester inside these companies.
Companies like Uber and Lyft got used to losing money without
much concern from their investors. The entire culture of many of
these startups was based on revenue growth, not on curtailing ex-
cessive spending. It was a formula that worked so long as the CEOs
could persuade big investors in one-on-one meetings to keep giving them more money at higher valuations. It also meant that
founders could spend more time on pet projects that might seem
wasteful to outside investors—Airbnb's Brian Chesky would later
push the company into the film production business; Uber started

a flying car division. It was a prolonged adolescence, living under the roofs of abiding VC parents.

By mid-2016, however, it seemed that Neumann's freedom in the private markets was coming to an end. He had largely run through the entire global Rolodex of giant private investors willing to douse startups with cash. And at its current spending and expansion trajectory, WeWork was going to need an enormous amount of money in the future to keep operating.

To Neumann and his staff, an IPO seemed the logical next step. The stock markets would be enthusiastic about a fast-growing company like WeWork, they figured. The other benefit to offering shares to the public, of course, would be that WeWork's investors and employees would be able to sell shares and start spending their paper fortunes. Employees who were around when Benchmark came in, particularly those in senior roles, had seen enormous gains on their stock options. Many had millions of dollars in paper wealth.

Staff began to prepare, and they quickly concluded the company needed to improve its loose spending habits. While WeWork's board wasn't laying down the law on the company's missed targets, the public markets might not be as forgiving as private market investors.

Neumann had executives, including Dave Fano and Jen Berrent, scrutinize the company's finances for ways to improve its operations. Fano worked on finding cheaper and faster construction techniques to help slash the cost of new desks, a huge source of expenses.

Meanwhile, Neumann increasingly began to trust Berrent, WeWork's chief legal officer, who came from the corporate law firm WilmerHale. She was clearly sharp on issues beyond just law and helped guide him in his successful effort to secure more voting control with investors. As her stock rose, Neumann added to her portfolio, giving her WeWork's culture department, and had her take steps to reorganize staff, saving costs on head count.

WeWork's staff also had exploded in size; it had more than 1,000 employees, up from roughly 250 a year and a half earlier. Senior staff realized WeWork needed to trim a lot of fat, and Neumann agreed. Less than a month after paying $13.8 million for the stake in Wavegarden. WeWork fired 7 percent of its staff, or about 70 people in the organization, and put new hirings on hold. Employees who received low marks on evaluations from their bosses were particularly vulnerable, with many shown the door. Bloomberg broke the news in a June 3, 2016, story and followed soon after with another piece on the company's missed targets.

Such drastic cost-cutting maneuvers jolted a workforce whose culture had been predicated on optimism and cheerleading. A couple of weeks after the firings became publicly known, Neumann addressed the elephant in the room at an all-hands gathering. Standing in a big open space in the headquarters, he struck a more somber tone than usual, telling staff the cuts were tough but were necessary if the company was to fulfill its mission. Some were poor performers, and WeWork aspired to have a culture of excellence. The company would be better off in the future, he declared.

Then, on a dime, the mood changed. Neumann called out for a surprise guest to join him onstage. From the back of the room, Darryl McDaniels from the pioneering hip-hop group Run-DMC came to the front of the room and embraced Neumann. He then launched into a set, including hits like "It's Tricky." As Neumann clapped in the front, staff burst into the crowd with big metal trays filled with plastic shot glasses, pre-poured with tequila, circulating through as the set went on.

Stumbles in the rearview mirror, the party raged on.

CHAPTER 16

One Billion Dollars per Minute

MASAYOSHI SON WAS GETTING ANXIOUS.

He'd been building SoftBank for three decades, and by the summer of 2016 his personal fortune was estimated at around $17 billion. He'd trade the number one spot on the *Forbes* Billionaires' List in Japan with Tadashi Yanai, the founder of Uniqlo, over the course of the year.

But it wasn't enough. He was fifty-eight years old and rarely mentioned in the same breath—or even conversation—as the biggest names in tech like Jeff Bezos, Mark Zuckerberg, and Bill Gates. He still longed to fulfill his vision of building the world's largest company within his lifetime. However, the main vehicle he was relying on to vault SoftBank into the upper echelons of U.S. business circles—mobile carriers—wasn't going well.

SoftBank had purchased Sprint for nearly $22 billion in 2013 with a plan to consolidate it with T-Mobile and make it a clear force in U.S. wireless—following a playbook he'd executed successfully in the Japanese telecom market. But Son was blindsided by the Obama administration's hostility to the deal. By 2016, Sprint was a weak player, hemorrhaging money and saddled with debt.

Buying companies and operating them wasn't getting Son where he wanted. The way forward, it seemed, was to turn to others—to focus on investing. SoftBank had long been among the most active players in tech investing. Now Son envisioned investing on a far grander scale than he had in the past. He would raise a venture capital fund larger than any that had ever been raised before. It would have so much money, he thought, that it would be able to anoint winners and losers in a given industry solely by throwing money at one startup and withholding it from competitors. Pre-emptive strikes in a winner-take-all world. The winners, he thought, would go on to be extraordinarily valuable—ideally giving SoftBank a big stake in a company that would turn into the next Facebook or Google.

To create a fund of this unprecedented magnitude, Son would need to use other people's money, not just his own. He'd need more money than anyone else had ever raised for a private investment fund. He'd need *tens* of billions of dollars.

Son had rehabilitated his reputation following the dot-com bust—mostly thanks to his investment in Alibaba. But now he wanted to raise more than the biggest names on Wall Street in private equity were raising. Blackstone Group and Apollo were the heaviest hitters in private equity, and even they had never raised more than $25 billion for a fund. The biggest venture capital fund ever raised had been only around $3 billion.

What's more, it would be nearly impossible to round up that money in the traditional way venture capital firms raise funds. The pensions and endowments that invested in those funds typically did so in chunks of a couple hundred million dollars at most. Only one kind of investor was in a position to offer the type of money Son sought: extremely wealthy nations.

To tap that wealth, he would need a leader to take a risk on him. Such giant sums would take more than just a technocrat at a democratic nation's pension fund. It would take a head of state, or close to it—a leader with immense power willing to put enormous trust in Son and his vision to help grow the nation's wealth.

That narrowed the list further. There were only a few such candidates in the entire world.

. . .

Rich on fossil fuels and light on democracy, the middle East's cluster of monarch-led petrostates—the United Arab Emirates, Qatar, and Saudi Arabia—each had giant sovereign wealth funds that could theoretically devote tens of billions to an investment they truly believed in.

Son initially set his sights on Qatar, a tiny landmass in the Persian Gulf physically smaller than the state of Massachusetts but filled with wealth from natural gas. On the private jet ride to pitch the Qataris, Son was paging through his presentation. He wanted the Qataris to commit to a big chunk of the total fund size, which he set at $30 billion.

But when he came to that figure in his presentation, he hesitated and started to edit. Son deleted the 3. Then he replaced it with a 1, and then added a zero at the end.

One hundred billion dollars.

He told his deputy Rajeev Misra, "Life's too short to think small."

The Qataris were noncommittal, so Son began to set his sights elsewhere. Saudi Arabia, the most populous country in the region, had traditionally been a less enthusiastic investor than its neighbors. While Qatar and Abu Dhabi invested heavily in industries around the world, the Kingdom of Saudi Arabia invested its wealth fund mostly in domestic companies. But Son and his aides watched as changes started brewing in the kingdom's old order. There was a new king and an ascendant prince, Mohammed bin Salman, a thirty-one-year-old who wielded great power within the country and seemed destined to one day lead the nation. Like Son, Prince Mohammed was thirsty to make a dent in the world.

Son needed to land a meeting

Deputy crown prince mohammed's rise to prominence in Saudi Arabia had been swift and unexpected.

Prince Mohammed's father, Salman bin Abdulaziz Al Saud, became king in January 2015, assuming control of a generations-old
monarchy known for moving slowly and conservatively. Big decisions tended to be made by consensus among descendants of the
state's founder, Abdulaziz bin Saud, with key government roles split
among different factions of the extended family.

But King Salman, then seventy-nine, began to break from the
slow, steady, and predictable Saudi way. In 2015, he handed his
twenty-nine-year-old son, Mohammed—known to be his
favorite—control of Saudi Arabia's economy and the military. Both
positions were extremely powerful posts, traditionally split between
different family lines.

Tall and burly with a megawatt smile, Prince Mohammed was
charismatic and engaging. Known as MBS, he toted around an
iPad, showing off his command of technology, and made known his
penchant for working at all hours of the day and night, drawing a
contrast with his older relatives in power. Prince Mohammed
lacked the pedigree and worldliness of his relatives. While most
Saudi male royals attended elite universities in the United States or
England, Prince Mohammed was solely educated in the kingdom,
but he had proven himself a shrewd businessman, doing deals with
Saudi companies where lines between the royal family and corporations were blurry. As he stepped into the key government positions following his father's ascendance to the throne, Prince
Mohammed was eager to assert the Saudi state as the dominant
power in the Middle East.

He quickly began to shake up foreign policy, risking upsetting
the volatile region's precarious balance of power. He accelerated a
long-standing proxy war with Iran—the Shiite Muslim power to
the north—bombing neighboring Yemen to oust rebels with Ira-
nian links. He stoked tensions with the Obama administration,
which was trying to reestablish relations with Iran.

Similarly, he decreed that the Saudi economy was due for a
major shake-up. Ever since oil was discovered beneath Saudi Ara-

bia's sandy surface in the 1930s, the kingdom had been the archetypal petrostate. Citizens got ultracheap gas and decent state services as a result. While neighboring states tried to lean heavily into other industries—tourism, aviation, trade—they were never prioritized in the Saudi capital of Riyadh.

But Prince Mohammed was coming to power just as another bubble a few states away from Silicon Valley was popping. A years-long boom in hydrofracturing had filled the landscapes of western Texas and North Dakota with so many new oil wells that the world faced an oversupply, causing prices to plunge by nearly two-thirds. It was a huge hit to the kingdom's lifeblood.

Prince Mohammed decided the country needed to diversify its wealth away from oil, putting eggs in other baskets. He began to speak of a future in which Saudi Arabia would be central to the new world economy. He bundled his ideas in a plan called Vision 2030, announced in 2016. To fund the vision, he decided that Saudi Arabia would sell a huge stake in its state oil business, Aramco, to investors through an initial public offering. To give it worldwide prominence, he was said to favor the New York Stock Exchange as the trading venue, putting the kingdom on the global economic stage. By selling shares through an IPO, he said, the kingdom should be able to raise roughly one hundred billion dollars to plow into the country's sovereign wealth fund, which would invest in other businesses around the globe. "Undoubtedly, it will be the largest fund on Earth," he told Bloomberg that April.

Suddenly, based on what many saw as an impulsive announcement by a young, power-hungry royal, Saudi Arabia was the most significant potential client in the world for Wall Street banks and giant fund managers, who quickly sought ways to get to know the prince.

In a series of power moves fit for a king, Prince Mohammed would demand that bank CEOs and senior executives fly to Riyadh on little notice to walk through their projections for Aramco's IPO. One night in late 2016, he kept the CEOs of Morgan Stanley, Evercore, HSBC, and Moelis—along with one of Jamie Dimon's top deputies—seated in a small antechamber from midday until around 8:00 p.m. before kicking off a series of individual meetings, finally summoning certain CEOs in the middle of the night.

As for where to put that expected IPO windfall, Prince Mohammed was particularly taken by the dazzle of Silicon Valley. He loved the concept of emerging technology and later planned a futuristic $500 billion city called Neom that he envisioned as a showcase of the world's most cutting-edge technologies, complete with flying cars and robotic dinosaurs.

He wanted only the best. In June 2016, as the kingdom was still early in plotting the Aramco IPO, he directed the Saudi sovereign wealth fund, the Public Investment Fund, to write a $3.5 billion check to Uber. It was the largest international investment the country's wealth fund had ever made, and one of the largest single investments ever in a U.S. startup, giving the PIF a seat on the company's board. If he was trying to get Silicon Valley's attention, it worked.

The deal was to be the start of a new era. The PIF, headed by an affable private banker named Yasir al-Rumayyan, began adding staff, gearing up for a wave of investment in companies well outside the fund's norm of Saudi energy-related corporations. Still, some concerns remained about the fund's abilities: members of Uber's board, bankers, and fund managers were often baffled meeting with al-Rumayyan, because they felt he didn't seem to have a sophisticated understanding of finance yet was in charge of one of the largest funds in the world.

In September 2016, Prince Mohammed undertook a whirlwind foreign policy tour of Asia while on his way to the G20 in China. Before the conference, he swung by Japan to meet with the prime minister but would have time for some other meetings.

Son's aides saw their time to pounce. Running point was Misra, a former Deutsche Bank executive often trailed by a cloud of vape smoke from his nicotine pen. The New Delhi–raised operator had climbed his way up in the SoftBank hierarchy and was set to oversee the forthcoming fund. He turned to his former Deutsche Bank colleagues who had even deeper ties to Saudi Arabia and who had launched a fund that would later become known as Centricus. They tapped their connections and managed to get a win: the Saudi prince would have time to meet Son while he was touring Japan.

Centricus would ultimately get a $100 million payday, just for connecting the dots.

PRINCE MOHAMMED ARRIVED IN JAPAN IN SEPTEMBER 2016 WITH an entourage of roughly five hundred people that required thirteen separate planes—the middle stop of an Asian tour sandwiched between Pakistan and China.

He met Son at the Akasaka Palace in central Tokyo, an ornate, nearly 120-year-old compound built for a Japanese crown prince.

Son, tieless and wearing a casual beige blazer, sat down next to Prince Mohammed. Holding his twenty-page pitch deck, he quickly explained how SoftBank's proposed fund could help wean Saudi Arabia off its reliance on oil—by getting in early on the world's next great technology companies.

Son told the bearded, six-foot-tall Prince Mohammed he could give him and the kingdom a $1 *trillion* gift and put Saudi Arabia at the center of the technology revolution that was rapidly transforming every imaginable industry. To accomplish this unprecedented feat of investing, Son said, all Prince Mohammed had to do was give him $100 billion.

He pointed to his Alibaba investment as well as other SoftBank success stories. He painted a picture of how a new supersized fund would get them into the hottest firms early and allow them to shape entire industries. He outlined for Prince Mohammed his plans for moving entire nations away from electricity and into solar power and for positioning SoftBank to win in a world where technology and artificial intelligence dominated. (Son often spoke of the Singularity, the idea that the intelligence and capabilities of computers would at some point in the future greatly exceed those of humans.)

With this power and Son's nose for promising startups, he could return tenfold what Saudi Arabia invested.

The pitch worked.

Prince Mohammed agreed to give him $45 billion. It wasn't the full $100 billion, but it was an astronomical sum—the largest ever commitment to any venture capital fund, or even any private equity fund—and an extraordinary win for Son. He would instantly be the most influential funder for startups in Silicon Valley and globally.

Soon, Son would need to fill out the full $100 billion fund—he ultimately got another $15 billion from an Abu Dhabi fund and put up more than $30 billion from SoftBank itself—but in Tokyo it was time to marvel at the accomplishment. While Prince Mohammed had been made aware of some details of Son's proposal before the meeting, it was a jaw-droppingly fast decision, given the size of the check. SoftBank's internal team and a consulting firm they employed were shocked when Son left his first meeting with Prince Mohammed and was promised such a large sum.

Son would later boast in an interview that he had received "$45 billion in forty-five minutes." He added, dryly, "One billion dollars per minute."

EVEN BEFORE THE CHECK FROM SAUDI ARABIA HAD CLEARED, THE $45 billion the prince promised was burning a hole in Son's pocket.

After another meeting with the prince in Riyadh weeks later in October 2016, Son flew with a deputy, Alok Sama, to India, where he was to meet the CEOs of several companies SoftBank had invested in. The CEOs of these companies, including OYO, Snapdeal, and InMobi, were nervous. Son's former expected successor, Nikesh Arora, had directed investments into India and had been their main contact at SoftBank. But Arora had abruptly been pushed out of SoftBank months before, so these CEOs were in the dark about SoftBank's future plans to back them.

Son was soon sitting inside a boardroom at the Leela Palace, the five-star hotel in Delhi where he first met Adam Neumann, with the CEOs who had been waiting for more than an hour for him to arrive. Breathlessly, Son apologized for arriving late and then told them, speaking much more rapidly than they were used to, "I had the most amazing meeting with the prince of Saudi Arabia." The prince, he said, would give him $45 billion, and he'd have $100 billion to invest and build the future. It would be the biggest fund ever, he said giddily.

Any one of them could get access to that money, but they had to prove themselves winners. If they could show how they could become the number one player in their industry, they'd get "unlimited money." Otherwise, they'd get nothing.

Son also had big ideas of his own to foist on them. Minutes before arriving at the hotel, he'd called Bhavish Aggarwal, the CEO of the car-hailing company Ola Cabs. If I gave you another $100 million, Son asked, would you create one million electric vehicles for India? At that point, Ola connected drivers and riders in a manner similar to Uber but didn't own vehicles. We can build out those vehicles, and it will change transportation in India, he said breathlessly.

It was all a bit much to take in. The founders seated around him asked him a few questions about the fund and what exactly he wanted to see from them. Son's answers were vague, but his pronouncements were bold. He now had the money to build the biggest companies in the world—firms that could alter virtually every industry.

The message to those in attendance was clear: Son was going to be the one who could fund the race and anoint the winners. He was going to be a kingmaker.

CHAPTER 17

Neumann & Son

O N DECEMBER 6, 2016, MASAYOSHI SON WAS ON HIS WAY TO Trump Tower, having flown to New York to meet the president-elect. Much of the world was still in shock over Donald Trump's surprise victory over Hillary Clinton. Son, however, was eager to gain favor with the incoming administration, particularly after the Obama administration had dashed his hopes for a Sprint/ T-Mobile deal.

Son would join a long line of dignitaries, ranging from business titans like Jack Ma to celebrities like Kanye West, as well as those angling for jobs in the administration, all of whom would make the very public pilgrimage to the president-elect's gilded penthouse.

While his wealth might have granted him an audience with Trump anyway, Son had an intermediary set up the meeting—an old business counterpart, Sheldon Adelson. The casino magnate had been instrumental in funding Trump's campaign. Decades earlier, Adelson had sold Son the Vegas-based Comdex technology conference business.

Before taking his turn at the Trump spectacle, Son would make a stop at Eighteenth Street and Sixth Avenue. There was a promising potential investment he wanted to see. It wouldn't take long.

· · ·

At wework's eighteenth street headquarters, a group of top staffers had been preparing for Son's visit. Prospective funders were constantly being whisked through WeWork's offices, but for Son, the deepest-pocketed startup investor on the planet, Adam Neumann and his staff pulled out all the stops.

Since his meeting with Son in India, Neumann and his team had kept tabs on SoftBank, hoping for a shot with him. Neumann and Gross tapped one of their key advisers, Mark Schwartz, the chairman of Goldman Sachs's Asia Pacific operation, who had just helped them raise their China round. Schwartz, who was a member of SoftBank's board and a longtime confidant of Son's, worked behind the scenes to help Neumann land this New York meeting.

On the appointed day, everything was scripted. The energy had to feel right—no empty desks—as did little things like the music. Even the smell mattered. Executives tasked one employee with making waffles in the main kitchen so the bakery odor would waft through the space.

But there was a problem. Son arrived late. Very late.

"I'm so sorry, but I only have 12 minutes," he told Neumann when he finally pulled up, an hour and a half after the appointed time.

Neumann gave him a whirlwind tour, whisking Son around the office. One point of focus was WeWork's R&D kiosk, an area that WeWork used to demo new products—as if to show off its tech bona fides. There was a desk that rose and fell to a member's preferred height. A phone booth had temperature and lighting that automatically adjusted to a preferred setting. A screen depicting the globe allowed users to zoom in on WeWork's projects in a given city.

In reality, the gadgets were marginal aspects of WeWork's business—the desk would later be scrapped—but for Neumann they served an important purpose: Son was a tech investor, and Neumann was determined to show him that tech was in WeWork's DNA.

As the minutes ticked by, Son wanted to keep talking. He suggested Neumann join him in his car; Son was due at Trump Tower, thirty-eight blocks north.

Toting a printout of his slide deck, Neumann slid into the SUV alongside the Japanese investor, ready to make a final pitch. But, to the WeWork founder's surprise, Son had already seen enough. His best bets had come as a result of pure gut, and he was convinced that Neumann was something special.

Son made an offer. He wanted to invest over $4 billion in We-Work, he told Neumann as their car maneuvered north through the crowded Manhattan streets.

It was almost incomprehensible. WeWork had raised $1.7 billion in total to date, and that was an incredible feat. Each time Neumann found someone new—a new investor willing to put in tens of millions, and then a few hundred million—it was like pulling a rabbit out of a hat. His fund-raising coups had shocked his advisers time and time again. And now, after a twelve-minute tour and during a brief car ride, Son wanted to put in more than $4 *billion*?

It was a huge offer of money—one of the biggest ever in a startup. As the car inched uptown, Neumann and Son took a scrap of paper and sketched out a deal—Son in red ink, Neumann in blue.

SOON AFTER, SON WAS IN THE LOBBY OF TRUMP TOWER, SMILING with the president-elect as they strode out from the gilded elevators to address a phalanx of cameras and reporters. Trump, who wore a bright red tie and a suit, lightly placed his hand on the back of Son, who was wearing a red tie and a red sweater underneath his suit.

"This is Masa, of SoftBank, from Japan," Trump said. "He's just agreed to invest $50 billion in the United States, and fifty thousand jobs. And he's one of the great men of industry."

Details were light. Son appeared to be just repackaging existing plans as though they were a consequence of the press-obsessed president-elect's victory.

As Son stood there, outlining his plans for U.S. spending, few in SoftBank knew that their boss had just committed more than $4 billion to Neumann's company. Had they known, they would have been shocked. After all, SoftBank had looked at WeWork before—and passed. It was over a year earlier—and the idea didn't play well with SoftBank brass at the time. Son's longtime deputy Nikesh Arora was well known to have strong resistance to WeWork. He had berated one of SoftBank's fund managers when he first pitched WeWork as an investment, telling the fund manager he was an idiot for trying to say a real estate company with no profits could ever scale like a technology company. But Arora left SoftBank in mid-2016 amid a power struggle.

The same fund manager had tried to sell Son on the deal in Son's Tokyo office, but he apparently didn't have Neumann's magic embedded in his pitch. Son looked visibly bored as the fund manager spoke, and they quickly moved on to other potential ideas.

As SON POSED WITH THE FUTURE PRESIDENT IN TRUMP TOWER, Neumann raced back to headquarters, jubilant. During the car ride back, he called Steven Langman, a friend, board member, and one of his earliest investors. Neumann told Langman he was at first shocked by the amount of money and then was tempted to push Son higher. "I could just hear you in my ear saying just take it. Just say yes."

When he arrived at WeWork, Neumann bounded into Artie Minson's office waving the scrap of paper with red and blue writing on it and talking so quickly it was almost nonsensical. Minson couldn't quite figure out what was going on; he didn't realize the piece of paper represented over $4 billion in new financing. Neumann pulled Jen Berrent from her office to his.

Neumann took pictures of the piece of paper. The scribbles were actually relatively complex. Neumann and Son agreed that the globe would be divvied up into a number of separate entities—

each with its own funding for the region—allowing for local inves-tors in places like China and Japan. Berrent and Minson handed the actual paper to WeWork's general counsel, Jared DeMatteis, to make it an official document.

As the enormity of the funding deal was setting in, Neumann was running behind for a *Business Insider* conference where he and his co-founder McKelvey would speak.

Clad in a black blazer and a shirt that said, "Live Better To-gether," Neumann jumped into a van where McKelvey, members of WeWork's PR team, and his chief of staff were waiting. As they drove toward Lincoln Center, Neumann showed the evidence of the impromptu contract from his phone to his co-founder. He and McKelvey gave each other hugs and high fives.

The giant infusion of cash was the answer to how WeWork would swiftly become an unstoppable global real estate behemoth. The executive team and most of the board joined in Neumann's giddiness. Mark Schwartz, who would soon join the board as a SoftBank representative, offered up a note of caution to Neumann and a few executives.

Masa runs very hot and cold, Schwartz warned them. He's very hot on this right now, Schwartz said, but if he turns cold, it could be a problem for WeWork.

CHAPTER 18

Crazy Train

ADAM NEUMANN WAS PANICKED. IN A FEW HOURS, HE WAS set to leave on a predawn flight for Tokyo to complete the first chunk of SoftBank's monster investment, but he hadn't thought to bring a gift. Masayoshi Son was putting $4.4 billion—the number they'd finalized—into his company, and he didn't have so much as a bottle of scotch to say thank you.

Neumann paced around his headquarters, talking through what he could possibly give Son. It needed to be bold—to be amazing. Then he saw it: a giant collage that took up much of one wall in his office.

The company had commissioned the piece in 2015 from the Israeli artist Lovka. It was a mixed-media work, with WeWork spelled out in lowercase white letters in a slight serif font across almost the entire width inside a white frame. Between the letters and the frame, almost every inch was filled with objects referencing the history of technology and art—a keyboard, a paintbrush, circuit boards, batteries, calculators. Lovka had described the piece as representing the effects of innovation and rapid obsolescence of products. To many visitors, it was mesmerizing.

There was a problem, though. The piece, eight feet in width, would never be able to fit on the private jet they were renting for the trip. As they were leaving for the airport, around 5:00 a.m. on Wednesday, Neumann told his team they had to find a way to get the collage to Tokyo by Friday before they returned to New York.

It was beyond a tall order; giant freight shipments don't work like passenger travel, where one can just buy a ticket online at the last minute. They need to be arranged weeks in advance. Staff at WeWork scrambled, pleading with their logistics contractor for help. The contractor, Logistics Plus, managed to find a way to get the piece on a cargo flight to Helsinki, where it would have an eight-hour layover before getting to Tokyo, through customs, and somehow to SoftBank's headquarters by 5:00 p.m. Friday.

It made it—at 4:54 p.m. WeWork paid roughly $50,000 for the effort. (Logistics Plus was so proud of the feat the company's CEO later detailed the odyssey in a blog post that attributed quotes to both Muhammad Ali—"Impossible is nothing"—and Winston Churchill: "Never, never, never, never, never, never give up.")

It was a telling sign of how Neumann and Son—with legions of staffers and piles of money at their disposal—were able to force the impossible into existence.

In the months leading up to neumann's trip to japan, we-Work worked to ensure that Son's casual car ride commitment of billions would actually go through.

Key to the deal was getting through SoftBank's due diligence process, during which the company made sure WeWork's numbers were in order.

It turned out many at SoftBank weren't at all thrilled about the deal their boss had cut. When Son had informed members of his staff in late 2016 of his handshake commitment to put more than $4 billion into WeWork, underlings were aghast. The Vision Fund was supposed to supercharge the world's future tech giants, so what was Son doing putting it into an overvalued real estate company?

The SoftBank Vision Fund executive Vikas Parekh was tapped

to finalize the deal. An alumnus of Boston Consulting, KKR, and Harvard Business School, the prickly San Francisco–based executive, who was in his late thirties, was wary of the assignment. Parekh had heard stories about Neumann's behavior and the company's financials—red flags. His own interactions with WeWork counterparts during early negotiations didn't alleviate his concerns.

The SoftBank due diligence team turned up some worrying problems. They found WeWork's prior projections that forecast huge near-term profits, but it was clear that WeWork was instead experiencing larger and larger losses. The company had wildly missed its goals. All that red ink wasn't a good look.

Neumann scrambled to clean up other potential sources of concern. One particularly noxious problem came from one of the mutual funds, T. Rowe Price. The once gung ho investor was proving meddlesome, frustrating Neumann because it raised objections to his moves to strengthen his control over the company and to sell additional stock to fund his lavish lifestyle. T. Rowe had also recently started publicly reporting the value of its stakes in private startups. After WeWork raised money from Hony at a $16 billion valuation, T. Rowe's own appraisal of its WeWork stake gave the company a valuation of around $12 billion—not $16 billion. It was a figure anyone could see, and Neumann was displeased.

Neumann took his anger straight to T. Rowe. He and Artie Minson got on a call and made their case for why T. Rowe should increase its valuation of WeWork. The executives at the Baltimore-based firm demurred. Other parts of the organization are responsible for valuation, they told Neumann. Still Neumann persisted. When it became clear he was getting nowhere, he dropped off abruptly, leaving Minson to finish up the chilly call.

In the end, it turned out none of the red flags mattered. Within SoftBank, the reasoned objections of underlings might as well have been shouted into a black hole. Once Son made a decision, his team was expected to execute the deal, not question it. Son wanted to move ahead.

. . .

By MARCH 2017, THE MAIN DETAILS HAD BEEN IRONED OUT, AND it was clear the deal was going to happen. Neumann, joined by Jen Berrent, Michael Gross, and a cadre of other executives, flew to Tokyo—trailed by the giant piece of collage art—to meet with Son and finalize a contract for an initial $300 million payment.

The deal that took shape was more or less what had been agreed to in the back of Son's car a few months earlier in Manhattan. The $4.4 billion would go into two main buckets. The largest chunk, $3.1 billion, would be new money to WeWork to fund expansion. Some of that was further divided between various regions around the world—China, Japan, and others in the Pacific. In all, We-Work's valuation would rise to $20 billion as a result, and SoftBank would get two board seats, though Neumann would remain in full control.

SoftBank would spend another $1.3 billion buying stock from existing investors and employees. The so-called secondary offering would be a massive windfall for those who could sell up to roughly 10 percent of their holdings, while also allowing SoftBank to expand its stake. WeWork was still far from turning a profit and far from going public, where the stock markets could weigh in on whether the trendy company really deserved a tech valuation. Yet plenty of the executives and investors involved planned to take profits for themselves in this deal.

Benchmark would sell $128 million worth of stock, giving Dunlevie's fund a huge return on the $15 million it initially put in. Marc Schimmel and Samuel Ben-Avraham, whom Neumann had met at the Kabbalah Centre, together would sell well over $100 million of stock.

The biggest winner was Neumann. The entity he controlled—which also held Miguel McKelvey's stock—would sell $361 million, an enormous return for the entrepreneurs who put their relatively paltry savings into the company in 2010. Taken with the more than $130 million sold in earlier rounds, the cash-out marked one of the most lucrative sales of stock of any U.S. startup CEO before an IPO or sale.

When all the paperwork was done on the first $300 million chunk of the deal, Neumann surprised those present in the Tokyo conference room by announcing that he wouldn't sign until the person who negotiated the most on his behalf was there to enjoy the moment: the chief legal officer, Jen Berrent. Son was suddenly agitated. Where was she? She needs to be here now, he demanded.

Berrent's star at WeWork had risen high since she joined the company as its chief counsel in 2014. A workaholic with straight brown hair who was captivated by the founders she worked with, Berrent devoted herself to carrying out Neumann's directives and vision. Her serious demeanor and drive didn't make her terribly popular internally; she would walk past her direct reports inside WeWork's headquarters and not say hello; and she readily admitted she had a lack of empathy. She did have fans, including the lawyers who worked under her and who often hailed from top firms, and even her detractors respected her intellect.

Moreover, she was a zealot for Neumann and the company, so much so that she married her wife in a WeWork. She would tell others how she'd stay up late, after she put her son to sleep, to keep the WeWork machine moving forward. Employees were often surprised if she didn't respond to an email within five minutes—at any time of the day or night. Beyond helping Neumann secure more voting power, Berrent was a critical player in the fund-raising process. With Minson, she structured the SoftBank deal in a way that made it hard for the Japanese conglomerate to pull out.

So when she arrived for the signing in Tokyo and saw that Neumann had held it up, she told him he didn't need to wait for her.

"We did," he replied. "You did the deal." It was a touching moment for Berrent, giving her a sense of belonging, she later told the whole staff.

With Berrent in the room, Son and Neumann signed the paperwork, securing the $300 million and setting the stage for the remainder to fall into WeWork's bank account.

Soon after, the group retreated to Son's main dining room, the size of a typical midtown Manhattan restaurant, except there were only a handful of tables. The views of Tokyo through the nearly floor-to-ceiling windows combined with the minimalist space gave attendees the sensation they were floating over the city.

Rather than have a private celebratory lunch, Son wanted Neumann to meet someone: he brought along Cheng Wei, the CEO of Didi Chuxing. Didi was China's main ride-hailing company—one that engaged in a bloody territory battle with Uber for China, eventually emerging victorious, causing Uber to sell its operations in the country to Didi. Wei was one of the biggest beneficiaries of Son's investing largesse. He had already received numerous rounds of funding and was in the middle of conversations with Son about putting $6 billion more into the company. Son said he was excited for the pair of entrepreneurs to meet. Wei, who wasn't fluent in English, was accompanied by a translator.

For Son, it seemed there was a lesson he wanted Neumann to learn. After effusively praising Wei to Neumann, Son looked straight at Neumann and told him that Wei beat Travis Kalanick, Uber's CEO, in China not because he was smarter than Kalanick. Wei was crazier, Son said.

"In a fight, who wins?" Son asked Neumann. "The smart guy or the crazy guy?" Being crazy is how you win, he continued. "You're not crazy enough."

To Neumann's aides in the room, the words seemed foreboding. Neumann was already the craziest person most of them knew. Neumann even knew he was crazy. Now a man who agreed to invest $4.4 billion in Neumann's company after a twelve-minute tour told Neumann he needed to be even more bold and rash.

It was a fateful moment for the seven-year-old company. The words were immediately imprinted in Neumann's mind. He was eager to broadcast to others the marching orders given to him by this oracle of tech investing. He called friends from Tokyo, marveling at Son's advice to him. When he returned to the United States, he repeated the story constantly.

And as time would go on, he would live up to the request. Almost impossibly, he and WeWork would indeed become crazier.

THE TRIP WASN'T ALL CELEBRATORY.

Amid the smiles and big plans, SoftBank made one request of Neumann—a request that came close to scuttling the whole partnership.

On the second day of the trip, Son said it was important that Neumann meet Son's biggest investors in the Vision Fund, representatives of both the Saudi PIF and Mubadala, of Abu Dhabi. Son was still hammering out the final details of their investment in the Vision Fund, but he wanted to make sure they were excited about WeWork. They'd be giving WeWork billions of their dollars.

Neumann walked into one of SoftBank's boardrooms. Inside were dozens of representatives from SoftBank, Mubadala, and the PIF, including Yasir al-Rumayyan, the head of the Saudi fund. Neumann, as he often did, said shalom—a Hebrew greeting—and added, "Salaam alaikum," a similar Arabic greeting meaning "Peace be upon you."

Taking a seat at the giant oval table, Neumann then launched into his pitch about WeWork's ambition to become a dominant global force in real estate, with Son chiming in. The WeWork employees in the room who had heard this pitch many times before were struck by how, with no prior planning, Son and Neumann, despite stark differences in their accents and idioms, spoke as if in a common voice about the future. They seemed fully aligned on where WeWork was going, using similar rhetoric.

Before leaving, Neumann had a far less harmonious interaction.

Neumann told several others at the time that SoftBank asked if he would consider making a pledge not to give any of SoftBank's money to the Israeli military. No Arab state had ever invested so much in a startup run by an Israeli before, and, SoftBank told him, the Middle East investors were concerned that if Neumann redirected their money in such a way, it would be problematic for them. (A SoftBank spokesperson denied that the company made this request.)

Neumann and his team boarded their plane back to New York, and he vented to his staff about the shocking—and somewhat bewildering—ask. While Neumann had no intention of giving money to support the Israeli armed forces, he was offended and enraged by the question. He felt it smacked of anti-Semitism.

Somehow the global significance of the $4.4 billion deal had escaped him until that point, but suddenly Neumann felt the weight of the geopolitical implications of taking Son's money and, by extension, that of Saudi Arabia and the UAE. Neither Arab country had diplomatic relations with Israel at the time, nor were Israelis allowed in either country. What's more, both countries presented plenty of human rights concerns; women were forbidden to drive in Saudi Arabia. None of this jibed well with WeWork's rhetoric of inclusiveness and equality.

Despite having just signed for the first $300 million installment of the larger deal, Neumann threatened to walk away.

"We're taking toxic money," he said.

Berrent and other aides scrambled to calm him down and persuade him not to overreact. It was too big a deal, and they were too far along, to blow it up over this, they thought. Saudi Arabia's money is everywhere, they told Neumann. Berrent was emotional. I'm Jewish and gay, she told Neumann. I'm not accepted in several different ways by the Saudi government—and many other groups of people. Let's take their money and do something good with it.

Neumann would wrestle for months with the implications of taking the money. In long meetings back in New York, gatherings that sometimes bled late into the middle of the night, he would discuss what it might mean if WeWork did so well that the Soft-

Bank Vision Fund made back ten times its original investment. Would he be personally responsible for funding the Saudi government and anything negative they might do with it? How can we ever be sure that won't happen?

He backed down. While he made no pledge on how he'd spend the money, the team would soon start working to finalize the rest of the giant investment.

CHAPTER 19

Revenue, Multiple, Valuation

THREE POINT ONE *BILLION* DOLLARS. THE AMOUNT WAS STAG-
gering just to utter out loud. The new cash at WeWork's
disposal—the amount of SoftBank's new investment, minus the
portion that went to buying out existing shareholders—was the
second-largest private investment ever made in a U.S. startup, bested
only by Saudi Arabia's investment in Uber. It was four times more
than WeWork spent in all of 2016, and twenty times more than it
spent in all of 2014, when it attracted mutual fund money. It was
enough to fund the entire San Francisco public school system for
nearly five years or to buy an airline: Virgin America sold for $2.6
billion the prior year. It was more than the market capitalization of
The New York Times. It was twelve *Washington Post*s, at the $250 mil-
lion price tag Jeff Bezos paid for the paper in 2013.

Adam Neumann was eager to start spending. The moment
marked the beginning of a new chapter for Neumann and We-
Work, one in which the company's costs began to spin out of control, with money plowed into spurious and tangential initiatives
with no clear connection to WeWork's core business.

Fueling the coming spending spree was Neumann's desire to
deliver on his promise to SoftBank, other investors, and his employees that WeWork was far more than just a real estate company.
The problem, though, was that as Neumann began spending heav-

ily to build out a broader vision for WeWork, he never seemed to have a clear picture of what the company *was,* only what it *wasn't.*

Depending on whom Neumann was pitching over the years, WeWork was a community company—one that was ushering in a new way for people to work and live where you bond and do business with your neighbors at the office. Or it was disrupting the world's real estate market, even though it was not a real estate company. Neumann frequently called it a tech company—one that just used offices the way Uber used cars—but not always. Above all, he was obsessed with having it appear *like* a tech startup in its rapid growth and big ambitions.

Even as late as mid-2017, in an onstage interview at a *TechCrunch* event, Neumann struggled to answer the simple question of what type of company WeWork was. "We used to view ourselves as a community company, but we are starting to figure out now that we ourselves are still discovering what is the best type of company that we want to be," he said, adding it was neither real estate nor tech.

Whatever it was, Neumann was insistent that WeWork would have a high valuation compared with its revenue—referred to as a company's "multiple."

Neumann offered various explanations to account for the high valuation. "You're going to see a very exciting multiple for companies that really treat other people the way they want to be treated," he told the audience at *TechCrunch* in 2017. Later that year, he explained to an interviewer that WeWork's valuation and size were "much more based on our energy and spirituality than it is on a multiple of revenue."

For a company that was seven years old to still not be able to explain its core business with clarity was unusual. Further complicating this murky image was that WeWork's financials still looked very much like a real estate company's. Almost all its revenue came from office rentals, termed "membership fees," while other revenue sources were marginal at best.

WeWork's high valuation, and the marketing that got it there, were important for reasons beyond vanity. The valuation was central to WeWork's existence, as well as its quandary. WeWork was spending so much money to open buildings and expand its global footprint that it had to continue raising larger and larger sums to keep up its rapid pace of growth. But investors were only investing in the company *because* of its rapid growth. If they looked at it as a more mundane real estate company, they would never have valued it at $20 billion, and certainly no one would have given it $3.1 billion.

Others were starting to notice this paradox.

"If you had positioned this as a real-estate company, it wouldn't be worth this," the renowned real estate investor Barry Sternlicht, of Starwood Capital, told *The Wall Street Journal* in 2017. Neumann "dressed it up and made it into a community, and that turned it into a tech play."

By the time SoftBank's money was coming in, WeWork's identity crisis stood to be a potentially big problem. If Neumann couldn't shake the lingering suspicions that it was just a real estate company, future investors might question its current valuation, much less any higher valuation Neumann would seek in the future. For years, Neumann had been pitching a compelling *story* about his company—one that would create a whole new global behemoth based on a changing millennial workforce that would look to WeWork for not just office space but all aspects of their lives. It was the story—not WeWork's particular financials at the time—that endeared it to so many investors.

Neumann even said as much out loud. In one meeting with executives from the real estate brokerage startup Compass (which would itself later raise hundreds of millions of dollars from SoftBank), he asked the CEO and his staff why they thought WeWork was valued at so much more than Compass compared with their respective revenues. After everyone in the room went around with an answer, he told each of them they were wrong.

The real reason for the difference? "My story," Neumann told them. It was far better than theirs, he said.

NEUMANN BEGAN USING SOFTBANK'S MONEY TO TRY TO SPEND the story into reality.

Internally, for as much time as its leaders spent denying WeWork's identity as a real estate company, the problem was that its revenues and expenses continued to make it look like one. To put the company in good shape for an eventual IPO, Neumann and his staff wanted to show how they could get money from things other than just office space—how they could make more money from their *community.*

So Neumann looked outside WeWork to bolster its story, turning to tech companies—firms that might be able to help WeWork show future investors how it was, in fact, a tech company. It wasn't terribly strong ground for Neumann, who had a novice-level understanding about technology; those around him were amazed he was able to talk about concepts like artificial intelligence so clearly to investors while having so little fluency himself.

But Neumann had a knack for latching onto big concepts, and he liked what he saw when he came across Meetup.com, an event planning website. By startup standards, Meetup was old and rusty, nearly set out to pasture. It was founded in 2002, a year that was a comparable drought in between floods when it came to Silicon Valley hype and investment. The site let people plan events and invite their friends and strangers; it was used by supporters of the presidential campaign of Howard Dean in 2004 and took off among people organizing games and events around hobbies. At the conceptual level, it shared an ethos with WeWork: it sought to enable in-person social interaction amid an increasingly disconnected era.

Neumann saw other potential benefits, too. Meetup had a huge email database. WeWork sites could host Meetup events and then turn all of those visitors into members, Neumann reasoned. Meet-up's finances weren't great; despite fifteen years in business, it wasn't producing a ton of revenue.

Neumann went for it. He directed WeWork to pay $156 million for the company, a sizable slug of the $3.1 billion that hadn't yet arrived in WeWork's bank account.

Another early acquisition was Flatiron School, a "coding boot-camp" that offered crash courses on how to program apps and other software—often used by those looking for a career switch to tech. The school, a favored prospect of WeWork's COO, Artie Minson, wasn't a standout tech company either. It was due to have just $11 million in revenue in 2017 and lose $2 million. But Minson pushed it as a way to help fill desks, among other reasons, because its class-rooms needed space. WeWork paid $28 million for the company in a mix of cash and WeWork stock, with plans for a big expansion.

The two acquisitions were puzzling and seemingly arbitrary. If WeWork wanted to be a tech company, why were its first two big acquisitions a struggling decade-and-a-half-old online event web-site and a for-profit vocational school? Neither offered much to existing members. Neumann began sending arrows in numerous other directions. WeWork opened a gym, called Rise by We, in the former headquarters of Goldman Sachs. Neumann and Fano pitched Barry Diller, the legendary entertainment and media titan and chairman of the travel website Expedia, on designing and building a new headquarters in Seattle for the company. Neumann tried to sell Diller on putting a Wavegarden surf pool next to the office space on its campus. Diller declined, but the company let them try redesigning a small Expedia outpost in Chicago.

Perhaps the boldest idea was starting a new elementary school. In this case, the project's mastermind was Rebekah Neumann, who told Bloomberg in 2017 that the concept was to raise "con-scious global citizens" who "understand what their superpowers are." The company commissioned Bjarke Ingels, the energetic

Danish "starchitect" who was designing a new headquarters for Google, to conceive its inaugural space.

WeWork's board was skeptical but let the deals go through. While the board was pliant in WeWork's early years, SoftBank had changed the whole dynamic. With two new board seats, SoftBank's presence diluted the influence of old directors like Bruce Dunlevie of Benchmark. SoftBank, with the $20 billion valuation it assigned, had big dreams for WeWork, and Son encouraged Neumann to deliver far more than just offices. As Neumann reminded the board frequently, he was the visionary.

It was a good audience for that message. For many Silicon Valley investors, such scattershot spending could be a sign of a visionary CEO. Adherents of this founder exceptionalism would invariably point to Jeff Bezos, who spread Amazon into e-book readers, cloud storage, and film production. (Of course, Amazon had begun to turn a profit by the time Bezos spent heavily on these new far-flung ventures.) Meanwhile, Mark Zuckerberg negotiated Facebook's acquisition of Instagram himself, informing his board the company would be shelling out $1 billion only after the basics of the deal were ironed out.

For every success story, there were far more lemons at large money-losing startups, which often cited a founder's vision when they barged into large new areas outside their expertise. Airbnb's CEO talked of reinventing air travel and made a push into film production. The scooter company Lime launched a retail store and a car rental business. Still, Neumann's behavior stood out for the amount of money he put into such initiatives, particularly given how much the company was losing on its core business.

IN ADDITION TO QUESTIONABLE NEW BUSINESS VENTURES, SPENDing on WeWork's own offices for its staff and executives had ticked up. In the fall of 2017, WeWork agreed to *buy* the Lord & Taylor flagship department store on Fifth Avenue and Thirty-Ninth Street. Neumann envisioned converting the iconic building into a new headquarters that would symbolize the arrival of new power brokers in the city's real estate. As the era of grand department stores was on its last embers, WeWork would climb into Lord & Taylor's shell. Bjarke Ingels was also tapped to redesign this building.

In San Francisco, Salesforce Tower became Neumann's obsession. A rounded obelisk that resembles a thousand-foot-tall missile, the tower being built by the developer Boston Properties was set to be by far the city's tallest, a skyline-defining beacon of San Francisco's economic ascendance. Salesforce had leased half of it, and the landlord was asking some of the highest rents in the city.

Neumann *needed* to be in the tower, he told his staff. WeWork would set up its own office there as a West Coast headquarters. WeWork ultimately signed three floors for seventy-six thousand square feet at a price north of $80 per square foot—a pricey rent by WeWork standards. As the company renovated the space, the budget grew and grew, with Neumann envisioning an atrium that had a big airy, open staircase connecting the floors. Such changes required huge structural reinforcements, pushing the costs of the renovation beyond $500 per square foot—roughly triple the price of a standard WeWork location.

WeWork's expansion tear wasn't limited to these grand spaces. Seemingly every few blocks in midtown Manhattan, black flags bearing WeWork's logo were unfurled outside new offices; locations were also under way in cities from São Paulo to Frankfurt to Mumbai. By mid-2017, WeWork counted more than 120,000 members spread across six million square feet of space. That's the equivalent of two Empire State Buildings, or about 188 times the size of its initial SoHo space at 154 Grand. The company itself had more than 2,500 employees, ten times the 250 or so it had just three years earlier.

Keeping up the pace of this growth was starting to get harder.

Neumann wanted to keep doubling every year—a task that required an enormous amount of leasing and money.

With the economy booming again, commercial landlords were no longer desperate for tenants, and many of the best deals—beautiful warehouse-like spaces—were gone, so WeWork had to lease in traditional boring office towers. The changing office market meant WeWork's most basic cost, rent, had in many cases doubled from the early years, while its membership fees had not.

Neumann, frustrated that the real estate team wasn't meeting its ambitious goals, called an 8:00 meeting one night in June, rolling in around an hour late as bleary-eyed colleagues in Europe stayed on waiting for him. Clearly drunk, he amped up his standard performance.

He first sought to energize the room, passing around plastic shot glasses and tequila stowed nearby, instructing employees to down shots. Then, in a happy-drunk mood, he went around the room and checked in with every manager seated there. For each region, he yelled and coaxed them to push harder—to sign more leases. He shouted out new, even harder goals, clearly made up on the spot.

One attendee scribbled down the numbers as Neumann said them. At the start of the meeting the goal had been to sign leases for enough real estate for 225,000 desks by the end of the year; now it was 275,000, the employee realized. Neumann had just increased the annual goal by more than 20 percent, seemingly on a whim, while evidently intoxicated. Although reaching high had helped motivate employees in the early years, the night of impromptu goal raising was hardly an idle exercise: the targets were entered into WeWork's internal systems, making a benchmark for the employees that could affect compensation.

Of course, more desks meant WeWork would need far more bodies to fill them.

For its first locations, WeWork was able to find members through Craigslist and word of mouth. Then it added a constant stream of tech mixers and other events where WeWork drew in potential tenants and showed off its space. Then it leaned on referral bonuses, online ads, and calls to people based in a Regus office. It eventually started paying brokers commissions to bring in tenants.

Neumann initially loved to boast about how he spent nothing on marketing, showing how WeWork was spreading virally, like Facebook in its early days. But by 2017, it was spending heavily. To get real estate brokers interested, it offered big promotions like 20 percent of the value of a lease—*double* the market rate paid by competitors like Regus. (A shorter-lived promotion offered some brokers 100 percent of the value of a lease.)

Adding pressure were the competitors that popped up and were sprinkling the country with WeWork-like offices. Neumann was eager to crush these companies, and steal their tenants, before any presented a real threat.

One fast-growing competitor was Industrious, led by Jamie Hodari, an engaging Brooklynite who had degrees in law and public policy and had previously run an education nonprofit in Africa. Neumann invited Hodari to join him for a trip to Atlanta to look at some buildings, part of a courting process in which he was trying to strike a deal with Industrious. In late summer 2017, he told Hodari to join him on his private jet the next morning, in the Hamptons. Hodari took an Uber around 4:00 a.m. and met Neumann, who arrived late, at the plane.

Over Bloody Marys and fruit as the plane zipped toward Atlanta, Neumann laid out a preview of what was going to happen to Industrious. He had hundreds of employees ready to launch an assault, he said.

"When I push the button, they're going to start reaching out to all your customers, letting them know they can come to WeWork for free," he said. They will offer a full year's rent for free, he said. "You'll lose one-third of your customers," he told Hodari as they sat next to each other. For the rest, he'd then up the ante, offering them two years free.

Hodari was intimidated but figured it couldn't be real. They barely even competed: Industrious was much smaller, and there were plenty of tenants to go around. No business could act so economically irrational simply to mess with a competitor, he thought.

But Neumann wasn't bluffing. Soon after, Hodari's staff started receiving offers passed along by their tenants, showing that WeWork was indeed offering huge discounts to anyone who defected. Similar assaults were launched on numerous other competitors, even small single-location co-working companies.

ALL OF THE SPENDING ADDED UP. WEWORK IN 2017 RECORDED $1.8 *billion* in expenses. Those expenses were growing even *faster* than revenue, which in 2017 totaled $866 million. Seven-year-old startups are generally supposed to show that losses are shrinking, if they even still have losses at all.

The growing losses and continued missed projections should have been alarming to investors and staff around Neumann, let alone Neumann himself. But the ever-inflating valuation was blinding for all involved; it was easy to believe that everything was working fine because everyone was getting richer on paper.

Instead of dwelling on the losses, the top priority for Neumann was growing revenue. The reason was obvious to those around him: investors were easily beguiled by Neumann's talk of WeWork's propulsive growth rate. The company had been valued in the SoftBank deal at twenty times its revenue—a generous revenue multiple even for a software company, let alone a real estate company. (Regus was still less than two times.)

"He would oftentimes do his napkin sketch on revenue, multiple, valuation," one senior executive recalls. "He would say, we have to get to $10 billion in revenue, because we'll get $200 billion in valuation."

The bigger the revenue, the bigger the valuation. Little else mattered.

. . .

SOME OF NEUMANN'S SCATTERSHOT EFFORTS TO GROW PAID OFF.

In 2016, WeWork had begun an experiment: subleasing space to large companies. Initially led by Roni Bahar, WeWork's enterprise division began contracting with corporations to take entire floors, or even entire buildings. It was a whole different setup, because they wouldn't even interact with other random companies working together in a WeWork.

The experiment turned into a big business—one initially re- sisted by the board but insisted upon by Neumann. Amazon quickly became the company's biggest subtenant, taking thousands of desks in cities from San Francisco to Bangalore. Microsoft, Salesforce, and Facebook all hungered for desks. WeWork could give these companies whole floors within months compared with a typical drawn-out leasing process with a ten- to fifteen-year commitment— an appealing proposition for fast-growth companies.

While the pitch landed Neumann big-name clients and a new ticket to fast growth, the focus on corporate clients ended up un- dercutting one of the very tenets of WeWork that Neumann was already struggling to augment: community. These companies were typically physically separate from WeWork members, on their own floors with their own conference rooms—drinking their own fruit water. The enterprise clients were using WeWork as an outsourcing company—one that would just lease, build, and manage space for them. The physical social network wasn't benefiting.

Even in WeWork's more traditional spaces, with smaller compa- nies, problems were brewing. At Neumann's direction, the com- pany's own research department conducted a study in late 2017 that looked at the strength of some of the community aspects of the company in its spaces. The study, which surveyed 554 members around the company about their interactions with other members, was titled "Are Our Members Friends?"

The answer was no.

"There is less of a community at WeWork than we imagined," the study said. Other than co-workers, 69 percent of WeWork members in the study didn't have any friends at WeWork, even based on a generous definition of the word "friend." The study—an academic-style report that was posted to WeWork's internal network—echoed a prior study by a member that found a similar problem. Even in spaces with open offices geared specifically toward encouraging collaboration, few people even knew many others' names. "The average WeWork member isn't socially connected with others in their building," the report found.

It was a shocking result, even for the research team leading the study, the authors said in the report. They went back to all the respondents and asked follow-up questions, believing they must have phrased the questions wrong. When the follow-up questions came back with the same result, they began to accept the unpleasant reality. All the hype about community in the company's marketing was just that—hype, a sober contrast to the early days of tight-knit offices in Manhattan.

"This result was incredibly surprising since it contradicts a lot of our rhetoric about the strength of our community," stated the study's authors.

Still, the results didn't turn many heads. Within the company, it was hard to dislodge a widely held belief. WeWork spaces *were* communities, staff believed. Neumann preached it; managers repeated it. It felt real.

CHAPTER 20

Community-Adjusted Profit

DESPITE BEING AT THE COMPANY JUST THREE YEARS, ARTIE Minson by 2018 had already survived several near-death experiences on the stomach-churning and turbulent ride of WeWork senior leadership.

Minson was hired in 2015 to be an adult in the room at We-Work, a move pushed on Neumann by investors, including Benchmark and Michael Eisenberg. Neumann made him the president and chief operating officer—akin to Facebook's Sheryl Sandberg, the deputy to Mark Zuckerberg. By year two, Minson had fallen from grace. Neumann cited frustrations over delays in new building openings as he pushed Minson to the sidelines. His new role was a more narrow one as chief financial officer—a humiliating reassignment.

Until then, Minson had enjoyed a nearly friction-free upward career trajectory. Raised in Queens blocks from the beach in a middle-class enclave of Irish immigrants, Minson excelled academically, which helped him land a coveted spot at Regis High School, the tuition-free, all-boys Catholic school in Manhattan that was widely regarded as one of the city's best. Students learned Latin; many glided into Ivy League colleges and universities. Minson, a cross-country runner, did well academically and won acceptance to Georgetown.

After college, Minson climbed the ladder of corporate finance, spending time at the accounting firm Ernst & Young and AOL before he became CFO of Time Warner Cable. When Neumann recruited him—promising him a front-row seat at one of the country's most disruptive startups—Minson's boss at Time Warner Cable, Robert Marcus, called him "the finest CFO in America" in a press release announcing his departure to join WeWork.

When he got to WeWork, Minson was a clear contrast to Neumann. He had a serious demeanor and rarely, if ever, downed the tequila shots regularly passed around headquarters. Typically showing up at work in a blazer and button-down shirt tucked into jeans, he stuck out in the casual WeWork HQ. Some employees started calling Minson "Dad."

After being relegated to the sidelines, Minson made efforts to re-endear himself to Neumann, including by helping him with a favorite personal pursuit: getting more money. When Neumann wanted to borrow nearly $100 million from JPMorgan, in 2016, Minson helped him figure out the details of the loan, which was tied to his WeWork stock. It was an unusual tangle of personal and professional—so much so that when one of JPMorgan's bankers negotiated with Minson, the banker was confused as to who Minson was. Why would the company's CFO help negotiate a personal loan for the CEO? the banker wondered. When the loan was completed, Neumann got a call from Mary Callahan Erdoes, a top JPMorgan executive, congratulating him.

During the company's annual Summer Camp in 2017, McKelvey interviewed Minson onstage. With a smirk, McKelvey complained about the chore of submitting his personal expenses and having to worry about costs. McKelvey asked him, why can't finance be more fun? Later that night, Minson watched from the sidelines as more than a dozen members of his finance team played rounds of flip cup on about six Ping-Pong tables and complained about McKelvey's dis. Many rounds into the game, his deputy Mark FitzPatrick jumped up onto a Ping-Pong table and started chanting, "Finance is fun."

Eventually, Neumann warmed to Minson again, and the CEO hosted a party for the finance department in the penthouse of 110 Wall Street, the WeLive location in lower Manhattan. By the end of the night when they were near the hot tub on one of the upper floors that looked out over Lower Manhattan, Neumann and a few others grabbed Minson's shoulders and legs and threw him into the hot tub fully clothed, with his wallet still in his pocket. A WeWork rebaptism of sorts.

Minson was generally happy to serve as Neumann and We-Work's hype man. In early 2018, at the all-company Global Summit at the theater at Madison Square Garden, Minson took the stage wearing a New York Knicks uniform. He told the staff, which by then numbered in the thousands, that they were working for the fastest-growing company ever. He showed slides of WeWork's growth and compared them with some of the fastest-growing companies in the S&P 500 throughout history. WeWork, he said, blew every other company away.

BECAUSE OF THAT RAPID GROWTH, THOUGH, WEWORK HAD A constant need: more money.

By 2018, as the company was guzzling through SoftBank's billions, Minson saw an opportunity to raise money in a different form from a standard investment round. He wanted to do it through Wall Street's bond markets—a form of debt that is traded almost like stock between investors.

It would be a big lift, almost like a junior varsity IPO, requiring a full disclosure of WeWork's financials to a wide range of potential investors. The goal was to give WeWork legitimacy with Wall Street and the big investors that buy public stocks—to pave the way for a future public listing. The move would allow WeWork to borrow hundreds of millions of dollars without selling a slice of the company. Minson would chart the course.

The sooner the better, he thought, because WeWork would

need to go public eventually; almost every big company does. Minson had kept in close touch with bankers like JPMorgan's Noah Wintroub and Goldman Sachs's David Ludwig, who continued to tell him WeWork was on track to perform well on the stock market, based on its growth. A public offering was the obvious endgame: employees and investors could sell their shares, harvesting their WeWork riches, and WeWork would be able to raise more money from stock investors. SoftBank's money wouldn't last that long, after all, especially as their losses kept growing.

A potential roadblock could be Neumann himself. Neumann always seemed to have some discomfort with the idea of going public—it was hard to imagine him holding dry finance-laden conference calls with analysts every three months—and Minson was thinking of ways to acclimate him to the dynamic. A bond offering, he thought, could help grease the wheels as a kind of stepping-stone to an IPO, forcing WeWork to report numbers quarterly to investors and to be more disciplined about its spending.

Normally a money-losing company like WeWork couldn't take on large loads of debt. Bond investors wanted to see a company generating cash to repay its debts, or at the very least have some assets that they could seize if a company wasn't able to make its interest payments. But these weren't normal times. Low interest rates had emboldened investors to take on risky bets for the promise of higher returns. By 2016, another money-losing startup, Uber, had raised $1.15 billion by tapping the debt markets.

Still, Uber's numbers looked better than WeWork's. Even though Uber was hemorrhaging money—it was effectively losing money on every ride, subsidizing consumers with venture capital money—its finances were at least headed in the right direction. Losses were shrinking as a percentage of revenue. WeWork, meanwhile, was spending *twice* as much as the revenue it took in, a problematic formula that didn't get better even as WeWork grew. Minson was relatively sanguine about WeWork's finances, but he realized having such a large loss—100 percent of revenue—could be problematic. He and Neumann sought to convince people that the losses weren't what they seemed.

One way was to not talk about losses at all, or even to talk about something WeWork didn't have: profits. Neumann frequently mentioned WeWork's "profits" in public and private. In 2015, he told *The Wall Street Journal* that WeWork was "profitable." In 2016, he told his whole staff, "We don't need to raise any more money. We're in an amazing place. We have a profitable business that's going to only get better." In 2017, he told a *TechCrunch* conference that the company liked to "hover around" breakeven on one measure of profitability. WeWork would lose more than $190 million that year based on that measure.

Minson chose his words much more carefully. When investors asked questions about losses, Minson often told them they didn't get WeWork. The company lost money only because of its growth rate, he would say. If they simply stopped expansion or slowed it down, the company could become instantly profitable. Once each of WeWork's locations was filled, it took in far more in rent from members than it paid in building and staff expenses. Aides believed this was what Neumann meant when he would say WeWork was profitable—even though he didn't always give the disclaimer.

To bond investors, WeWork was going to need something more direct. A problem was that WeWork needed to disclose profits and losses as dictated by accounting rules. So to show some measure of profitability in addition to those standard figures, Minson turned to a formula that they'd been showing to investors and in internal projections and infused it with WeWork branding: "community-adjusted EBITDA."

As traditionally understood by investors, EBITDA was short-hand for "earnings before interest, taxes, depreciation, and amortization." While the term isn't the cleanest acronym—it's pronounced "ee-bit-dah"—it is a widely used metric that gives investors a sense of how profitable a business is while stripping out accounting charges that fluctuate, and other items, like taxes. In essence, it often shows how much cash a business is making or losing on a quarterly basis, before accounting adjustments.

Unlike EBITDA, the term "community-adjusted EBITDA" was not a measure sanctioned by the main government regulator of the investment world—the Securities and Exchange Commission—and it had some misleading qualities. First, it erased a huge array of other expenses, like the cost of WeWork's design department and its tech team as well as all its general and administrative costs. To Minson, this omission was meant to give investors a crisp number to show them how the individual locations were spitting out far more money than they cost to run and WeWork was showing a big "net loss" only because of other costs related to its rapid growth. In reality, the metric also stripped out costs that made these buildings successful, like sales and marketing.

Its biggest trick, though, was a complex maneuver related to the way WeWork paid rent. When WeWork signed a ten- or fifteen-year lease, landlords typically gave the company the first year free, not unlike an apartment owner offering the first month free. Given how fast WeWork was growing, that meant a huge number of its locations—upwards of 40 or 50 percent—wouldn't be paying rent at any given time. Yet at the same time, WeWork was taking in monthly rent from its members. On paper, that allowed some We-Work locations to look super profitable, because the company's enormous cost of rent wasn't yet being paid.

Given that these rent holidays can mislead investors, regulators require that when companies report their income, they spread the benefit of that year of free rent across the entire ten-year lease, a move called "straightlining." That means instead of reporting zero rent in year one and 100 percent of rent in the rest of the years, a company has to report paying 90 percent of the rent in every year, even though it actually didn't write a check to that landlord for the first year.

Community-adjusted EBITDA gave WeWork an avenue to circumvent those accounting rules—fully legally, with full disclosure to investors—thus allowing it to show a healthy "profit." In effect, it was simply a formula to show Wall Street what Neumann had been saying for years. He frequently touted WeWork's amazing margins, saying how its buildings were generating 30 or 40 percent more money than it cost to run them.

Few understood the gravity of this move. The average bond investor likely isn't steeped in the intricacies of real estate leases. But the effect was extraordinary. By normal measures, WeWork's revenue doubled to $866 million in 2017, and its losses more than doubled to $933 million that year. But using Minson's new definition, WeWork had actually generated $233 million in profits.

Minson and FitzPatrick thought this metric highlighted how WeWork's buildings could become geysers of cash. Minson would often tell his team and outside investors that WeWork's business model was a lot like the cable business. It cost a lot to string miles of cable on telephone poles and into people's homes. But once customers signed up, the cable boxes in people's homes eventually spewed money month after month. With community-adjusted EBITDA, Minson had found a way to distill the ethereal nature of WeWork's profitability down to a formula that could be served up to Wall Street.

As they met with potential investors for the forthcoming bond sale, the metric appeared well received. Neumann was pleased with the progress. Then the 254-page document used to sell the bonds spelling out all of WeWork's financials got in the hands of the media, with *The Wall Street Journal,* the *Financial Times,* and others alerting the world to WeWork's unusually aggressive, and amusingly named, metric. "Community-adjusted EBITDA" was mocked relentlessly online. On Twitter, users questioned whether WeWork was the next Pets.com, a 1990s dot-com flameout. The blog *Dealbreaker* called the metric a "rage-inducing Silicon Alley pile of thought horseshit."

Neumann was caught flat-footed, unprepared for any public blowback—on WeWork's finances or community-adjusted EBITDA.

Until this point, he had enjoyed years of largely fawning press. Just months earlier, *The New York Times* ran a splashy weekend feature on WeWork titled "The WeWork Manifesto: First, Office Space. Next, the World," that delighted PR staff.

This time, though, Neumann's personal touch couldn't fix the coverage. It was the first time that WeWork's numbers—even with their embellishments and adjustments—sat in front of the media, as well as a wide number of investors who hadn't also been dazzled directly by Neumann's sales pitch.

Still, plenty of investors remained keen. In late April as they were getting ready to finalize pricing, JPMorgan's bankers told Minson there was enough demand for WeWork to raise about $200 million more than the $500 million amount they initially expected. In a world of low interest rates, investors were willing to take a gamble on the company for slightly higher returns. Did WeWork want to sell even more debt? their bankers asked.

Minson called Neumann. It was Neumann's thirty-ninth birthday, and he was in a hot tub surrounded by friends at his sixty-acre "farm" in Pound Ridge; Minson explained the demand and asked if he was willing to take on $700 million in debt. Neumann thought, then called out to his friends loudly: What is 39 times 18?

The number 18 is effectively a lucky number in Judaism. Neumann ended up doing the quick math, delivering the answer to Minson. WeWork should increase the amount of debt to $702 million, he said.

The champagne was uncorked prematurely. Within a day of raising the debt, the price of WeWork's bonds began to fall. They dropped to 97 cents on the dollar by the third day of trading and then to 94 over the next two weeks. A 100 mark essentially means investors expect to be repaid in full. Dropping below that mark so quickly is highly unusual, and a sign that the market didn't like WeWork as much as expected. Minson became obsessed with the bond price. During meetings, he'd check the price every five to ten minutes.

Neumann saw it as a public relations disaster, however, not a financial one. Angry and embarrassed, he called his finance team and his communications team into several meetings in the days that followed. How could they solve this? he demanded.

Neumann asked if they could buy back some of the bonds themselves. It was a strange request; companies almost never bought back their own debt so soon after raising money. But the finance team said it was technically possible and would likely boost the price, just like a company buying back its own stock. Neumann green-lighted the idea.

It took a number of months, but after going through the trouble of selling $702 million of bonds to investors, WeWork eventually spent $32 million to buy back a chunk of the very same financial instruments it sold.

CHAPTER 21

Adam's ARK

I WANT TO BE A BILLIONAIRE SO FUCKING BAD." IN WEWORK'S early years, Michael Gross would occasionally blast the rap ballad "Billionaire" by Travie McCoy for Neumann as a way to pump him up. On one cross-country plane trip on a private jet, Gross blared the song as he bellowed its lyrics.

"I wanna be on the cover of *Forbes* magazine," he yelled as Neumann reveled in the moment.

By early 2018, with SoftBank's money in hand, not only was Neumann a billionaire—he was now worth around $5 billion, on paper—but he had indeed been on the cover of *Forbes*.

With once-wild dreams seeming to manifest themselves before his eyes, Neumann's ambitions became more hyperbolic. WeWork, he told others, was going to be the world's first *trillion*-dollar company. (It was actually Apple that would become the first company to achieve this milestone, which it did in August 2018.)

If WeWork was going to become the most valuable company on the planet, however, it needed to do more than just rent property. Neumann believed it needed to own it. Ever since WeWork's founding, he'd had landlord envy. He looked at buildings and saw that landlords were the ones that reaped the rewards when values rose, a dynamic that irked him. *He* was the one adding value to the building, he carped to landlords, while they were the ones getting richer.

He had dabbled before, buying slices of a few buildings We-Work leased, though he didn't do it much because of the pushback from his board. Still, he yearned for WeWork to get in the owner-ship business. He would tell others that if Starbucks or Whole Foods had bought the real estate around their stores as they became global giants, they would have made billions upon billions, given that their mere presence helped raise values in a neighborhood. Why couldn't WeWork do the same? he wondered.

In 2016, Neumann struck a deal with Steven Langman, his longtime board member and friend, to start a private equity fund devoted to buying buildings where WeWork was leasing. The two created a company called WeWork Property Investors—owned and run jointly by WeWork and Rhône Group, the private equity firm Langman founded—that would raise money from other investors and then buy buildings leased to WeWork.

The concept had some merit. Buildings with lots of vacancy tend to be less expensive. Once a tenant signs a long-term lease, the value of a building can shoot up substantially. In theory, the fund could take cheap empty buildings and make them valuable almost instantly by getting WeWork to sign a lease.

Neumann, Gross, and others saw the approach as a way to build a giant business that would benefit WeWork in numerous ways: it would have a friendly landlord—itself—and it would also make money running the fund. They envisioned it would be a giant arm of WeWork, one that would raise tens of billions of dollars from other investors in the next few years. The numbers they were throwing around were so lofty they would have made WPI one of the biggest real estate private equity funds on earth.

As usual, the reality was far more complex. The business was a tangled knot of conflicts of interest, in which WeWork was on both sides of every deal. Theoretically, Rhône would want WeWork to pay high rents for its buildings, while WeWork would want to pay low rents. It was as though two money-obsessed friends jointly owned a house but only one of them lived there—a recipe for a fight over the cost of rent.

WeWork the tenant would be striking a deal with WeWork the fund manager and Rhône the fund manager simultaneously. Meanwhile, Rhône was an investor in WeWork and Langman was on its board, while Neumann both oversaw the WeWork staff negotiating the lease and had 50 percent control of the entity they were negotiating with for leases. The intertwined involvement of Rhône and Langman was unusual, and multiple WeWork executives found the whole ordeal messy and frustrating, expressing concern to each other over all the conflicts. Of course, the conflicts were disclosed to investors, and some of those conflicts were even part of the appeal of the fund. The investors were essentially buying buildings that had a guaranteed tenant in WeWork, a valuable proposition. Still, Rhône faced its own internal problems: two real estate executives were upset with the strategy and voiced concerns to others in the real estate industry about the conflicted structure. Both were reassigned, withdrawing from work on the fund, and later left Rhône.

As the fund invested, WeWork executives indeed ran into conflicts. After the fund agreed to buy a building in London called 51 Eastcheap, WeWork real estate executives balked at the rent WPI was asking them to pay. WPI, however, had paid the price of $61 million for the building under the assumption WeWork would pay the rent needed to support such a price, which WPI felt was justified for the building and the neighborhood. Ultimately, Neumann stepped in. Seemingly wanting the nascent fund to do well on its early investments, he told WeWork he thought the price was right. They paid up.

DESPITE THE DEAL MAKING AT WPI, NEUMANN WAS STILL REST-less and nervous that he wasn't moving fast enough to satisfy Son. By early 2018, the billions of dollars he hoped WPI would raise from pension funds and other investors hadn't materialized. Naturally, Neumann shifted to even more grandiose planning. He imagined yet another company within a company: he began confiding to others his idea to create the largest real estate investment firm on the planet—from scratch. If funded well, it could buy a huge amount of the real estate WeWork needed to lease to keep up its exponential growth; it could also get into constructing buildings from the ground up.

The new fund would have a biblical name to meet its biblical-sized ambitions. Neumann dubbed it ARK, a reference to Noah's ark. By pushing into the property ownership business, WeWork could expand faster and more efficiently—floating the company to financial riches, the thinking went. To some, Neumann also disclosed another inspiration for the name: the three letters stood for Adam, Rebekah, and Kids. Even top staff weren't sure if he was kidding.*

Unlike the Rhône fund, which started with a few hundred million dollars, Neumann had enormous ambitions for the real estate venture. He wanted to raise $100 billion by the end of 2018. To put that into perspective, Blackstone, the world's largest real estate fund manager, had only recently surpassed $100 billion in real estate assets—more than three decades after the firm was founded and following years of stellar performance. Neumann wanted to get there overnight.

His deputies nonetheless cooked up a plan to raise funds from giant investors around the globe. The biggest ask would be to Saudi Arabia, from which they wanted to request $100 billion for the fund. It was a comically large number. Saudi Arabia had indeed

---

* Neumann's use of a fund with the initials for his family has an eerie parallel to Enron. One of the key facets of the fraud that sank the high-flying energy company was a small entity named LJM that bought assets from Enron at inflated valuations. It was created by Andy Fastow, Enron's CFO, and stood for the first initials of the names of his wife and two children. (John R. Emshwiller, "In Enron Trial, LJM Is a Double-Edged Sword," *Wall Street Journal,* Feb. 22, 2006.)

committed $45 billion to Masayoshi Son for the Vision Fund, but it's not as if the country had unlimited stores of scores of billions lying around. The entire size of the country's sovereign wealth fund—the bulk of the money the country had to invest—was $230 billion as of 2017. Aides traveled to Saudi Arabia to show off the plans for a $100 billion fund, though no deal ever materialized.

Other candidates were an array of top mutual funds, sovereign wealth funds, and banks. The fund-raising plan was to go along with another round of investment WeWork was planning for the business, but an internal presentation urged those involved to tell investors WeWork didn't *need* the money; it was just trying to get more investors into the fold before a future IPO. "We don't need more capital," the presentation said on a slide titled "Control the Story."

Neumann had an endless number of related grand plans. He wanted WeWork to co-develop 2 World Trade Center, the final tower to be built on the World Trade Center site, and struck a tentative deal with the owner, Silverstein Properties. It later fizzled.

While Neumann loved the idea of owning real estate, others at WeWork saw potential in ARK for other reasons. Berrent and Minson saw the fund as an opportunity for financial engineering. The two executives—both still quite bullish on WeWork—recognized that its losses couldn't keep growing forever. One way for WeWork to turn toward profitability would be to find someone else to pay for the costs of renovating and constructing their offices—one of WeWork's biggest expenses.

ARK, they figured, could be that savior. The idea was that ARK—using funds raised from real estate investors around the globe—would treat WeWork more like a hotel operator, like Marriott, which generally doesn't own or lease any of its hotels. Instead, hotel landlords spend the money building out hotels and then pay a hotel company like Marriott to manage the building. It was their plan to become "asset light."

Neumann had financial engineering plans of his own. In addition to the benefits he saw in the business, ARK offered a way for him to get an even more lucrative remuneration package. He had staff devise a plan that would give him a personal ownership stake in the fund—one that came on top of the billions in paper gains he planned to see indirectly, as WeWork's largest shareholder.

It was an audacious money grab. His stake wasn't going to be that of a mere investor in the fund. He wanted a piece of the "promote"—the tool private equity managers use to get an out-sized chunk of any profits a fund returns. Typically, the company behind the fund would get that promote—meaning WeWork would gain if the fund did well. But here, Neumann was prioritizing his own wealth over WeWork; he wanted it *personally.*

The move would mark a far brazen conflict of interest than his other property purchases, giving Neumann a potentially large interest in every property the WeWork fund bought. To critics, the concerns would be legion. If WeWork ever hit financial trouble and needed to back out of some leases, it would be in a position of effectively choosing to stop paying rent to its CEO—a near-impossible scenario to imagine.

Eventually, staff convinced Neumann that the conflicts would be too extreme. Instead, ARK would be headed by people appointed by Neumann, and he would have no special ownership stake in the fund. Executives set out in the spring of 2018 to start to raise money for the fund and scout out new buildings in a bid to make property ownership a whole new pillar of WeWork.

Yet soon, Neumann's ambitions would reach further still. One new pillar wouldn't be enough.

CHAPTER 22

The $3 Trillion Triangle

O NE BY ONE, CEOS OF THE HOTTEST STARTUPS IN SILICON
Valley made the pilgrimage. Some flew to Tokyo, where
they waited in a hotel room for hours until they were summoned.
For others, the journey was just a short Uber ride to Woodside,
California, not far from Sand Hill Road. If they were lucky, the
meeting would include a meal.

As SoftBank started spending its $100 billion Vision Fund, the
startup world took note. Never before had such a massive new
spigot of funding opened on the tech sector. It was an amount
more than the annual budget of Ireland, more than the value of the
vast majority of tech companies, save the largest giants. The fund's
billions had the potential to reshape fledgling industries, to determine winners and losers with a check. And it was all controlled by
a single person. Masayoshi Son wanted to have a personal hand in
selecting every recipient.

As he saw it, his instincts and his gut—the vibe he got from
a founder—were often far more crucial deciders than data and
analysis.

"Feeling is more important than just looking at the numbers,"
he said of his investment strategy in startups. "You have to feel the
force, like Star Wars."

So Son began to spend. Wildly.

His main target was unicorns, the category of $1 billion–plus startups. Already, many saw the sector as overvalued, full of companies long on promises and short on profits. But he wanted to dive in.

As Son put it to investors, "We are unicorn hunters."

SoftBank staff were tasked with surveying the unicorn landscape and finding prospects. Before investing, staff would labor to create long books of due diligence on these companies—highlighting their risks and their virtues. But given that the decision most important was Son's, deal after deal had a similar type, one that Son was particularly likely to yearn for: a brash, even arrogant man with an extraordinarily bold vision.

The meetings with Son tended to follow a similar pattern. Son would meet the entrepreneur in an office or one of his mansions in Tokyo or California—sometimes giving a tour, showing off a prized painting of Napoleon he owns—and ask about the business and what the supplicant was seeking. Then the founder might say, "We want $150 million."

Son, in response, would say something like "You aren't thinking big enough. You need to double your growth," despite seeming to know little about the company or industry. He'd tell founders they needed to invest more in sales and that they needed to dominate their sector before a rival did—even if it wasn't the type of business where that logic seemed to apply.

Eventually, in the span of the brief meetings, sometimes just twenty or thirty minutes long, Son would persuade the founder to take a larger check. The $150 million request might turn into an offer for $500 million. If the founder seemed reluctant, the offer could turn to a threat: Son would point to how he could fund rivals if the founder refused his money. Losses were rarely discussed; he figured they would be wiped away when a company beat out its peers, like how LinkedIn and Facebook were able to become profitable after their networks became huge.

Money went to startups like Plenty, an indoor farming company that had a thirty-minute meeting with Son and walked out with a

$200 million commitment, double what it requested. Money flew to the delivery app DoorDash, to the online home-buying company Opendoor, to the real estate brokerage Compass. Son bet billions on driverless cars, even as concerns grew that self-driving technology was not anywhere close to prime time. He pumped $375 million into Zume Pizza, a company that pledged to have robots make pizzas and delivery trucks cook them en route; its pizza operations shut down a bit more than a year later.

Son dreamed of a synergistic relationship among the startups in his herd of unicorns. SoftBank's companies would do business with one another and collaborate. The common denominator, he said, was AI—artificial intelligence. Yet in reality, AI was a marginal tool at a large chunk of the companies he showered with money. But Son either believed founders who exaggerated its utility or simply saw something more than the facts supported. For instance, he boasted to investors how WeWork was an AI company—how the combination of sensors placed throughout its buildings and AI would meaningfully help its business. "WeWork will be analyzing how people can communicate," he said, and "recommend what to buy."

Vision Fund staff became adept at coaching founders ahead of meetings with Son to increase their future revenue and profit targets—dramatically.

Silicon Valley investors grumbled that the company's approach was reckless and would end badly, though most would only do so privately. Son's cash blitz was lifting valuations overall, and it would often allow existing investors to cash out some—meaning that VCs who invested early could make some immediate profits, no matter what happened to the company in the end.

By 2018, the pause in startup mania that had occurred in late 2015—when WeWork had to turn to China to raise money—was history. Valuations were rising again across the board as money grew far faster than good ideas. With SoftBank dominating the late-stage startup market, earlier-stage investors were leaping before they looked—fighting to push money into young startups with a singular big idea, no matter how little the track record. Vision had become everything.

EVEN AMONG THE BRASH CEOS IN SON'S PORTFOLIO, ADAM NEUmann stood out.

Neumann had a particularly innate sense of ambition and fearlessness—one that bordered on recklessness. They were traits shared by Son himself, and Son seemed smitten with Neumann.

Neumann's relationship with Son quickly became a source of personal angst for the WeWork CEO. Son was Neumann's genie and his master. SoftBank's money gave Neumann the potential to build the world of "We." Son told him he'd be the next Jack Ma, the founder of Alibaba, whom Son backed early.

Neumann, Son told him, would have *unlimited* access to SoftBank's money. It was a pledge that surely made Neumann's head spin—imagining all the possibilities. SoftBank's investment gave him the green light to focus only on the issues Son seemed to care about—revenue growth—and not worry about profits. It was a license to spend. The potential downside, though, was huge. If Neumann stumbled and lost Son's trust, it would be difficult to find any partners deep-pocketed enough to bail him out. Neumann's only choice was to keep dreaming big and impress Son.

NEUMANN AND SON MET FREQUENTLY THROUGHOUT 2018. IN March 2018, Neumann, Jen Berrent, Artie Minson, and a trail of other executives found themselves sitting cross-legged on the twenty-sixth floor of Son's private dining area gazing over Tokyo.

Not long into the dinner, Son clicked on a video. The WeWork crew watched as a flat-screen monitor flashed a promotional presentation from SoftBank-backed OYO Hotels, run by the wiry twenty-four-year-old CEO Ritesh Agarwal. OYO had been expanding rapidly all over the world, and its revenue growth rate—the key indicator for Son—was even faster than Neumann's.

"Your little brother is going to beat you," Son told Neumann. "He is being bolder than you."

Neumann's reaction was muted, but to the others sitting there on the WeWork team, it was clear what Son was doing. Neumann was not only highly competitive but deeply insecure. Now a father-figure type was goading him—telling him he wasn't good enough and his "little brother" was doing even better. It was almost like bullying, they thought.

And it worked. WeWork executives dreaded Neumann's meetings with Son for the edicts that would inevitably follow.

By mid-2018, WeWork had 300,000 members—more than the population of Buffalo, New York. It had around six thousand employees, one and a half times the workforce of Twitter. It was on pace to take in $1.8 billion in revenue. A total of one million members—once seen as a fantastical goal—was in reach.

Still, it wasn't enough.

IN THE LATE SPRING OF 2018, NEUMANN CALLED A FEW SENIOR executives into a meeting. He took out a sheet of paper and a pen. He scrawled out three lines—forming a simple triangle. This, he told them, was WeWork's future.

One corner of the triangle signified WeWork's main office business. Another was ARK, the real estate arm he'd recently started, which Neumann expected to become the world's largest owner of property. And then on the third corner were services—the sprawling set of businesses like brokerages and cleaners that help the real estate sector hum along.

Next to each corner, he wrote "$1 trillion." Each arm of WeWork, he averred, would be a $1 trillion business on its own.

Neumann had recently had an epiphany, he told those assembled. He was dominating the office sector but still paying landlords rent. Meanwhile, he had pondered buying the real estate brokerage Cushman & Wakefield and realized the full extent of just how much money there was in the real estate services business. Brokers were getting huge commissions leasing WeWork space. Management companies were getting rich cleaning the lobbies and running security at building entrances. What if someone owned the *whole* system? What if WeWork vertically integrated it all? WeWork would own buildings, it would build buildings, lease buildings. It would rent apartments, expanding WeLive. WeWork would advise companies on their office space—becoming the sole solution. If companies wanted to stay in their own buildings, WeWork would design them; then it would lease them desks, run their coffee machines, sell them software. A WeWork ID could open WeWork-run security gates. If tenants wanted to lease with someone else, WeWork would find them space and get a brokers' fee. It could be huge.

Unlike his earlier scattershot acquisition strategy—surf pools, Meetup.com—executives around him saw in this vision real potential to disrupt the entire real estate sector. The triangle strategy would require truckloads of money, but it could reshape everything if it worked. Neumann was ecstatic with the promise. Meeting after meeting internally was convened to discuss the plan. What started as one triangle then became two, with different business lines subbing in and out for the various sides. There was WeLive, WeGrow. Perhaps they'd do retail.

Sometimes Neumann scrawled a triangle with light emanating behind it—giving the diagram a secretive, Illuminati-like feel. For a while, Neumann wanted to put one of the equilateral triangles upside down, lying atop the other. It was a Star of David.

The staffers around Neumann were wary of the overly religious overtones. Berrent persuaded him to drop it.

NEUMANN AGAIN FLEW TO MEET SON IN MID-2018. THIS TIME HE wanted to continue discussions with Son about a modest new investment to keep WeWork's expansion machine running. Bankers from JPMorgan, including Noah Wintroub, had continued to hover around WeWork in hopes it would eventually IPO, so Neumann brought Son estimates from JPMorgan about WeWork's valuation. Pointing to the bank's projections, Neumann told Son that WeWork would be worth far more than the $20 billion valuation where Son last invested.

But quickly, Neumann sensed Son was in a good mood. It was time to drop the bigger idea. Rather than talk about an investment of just another few billion, Neumann laid out his triangle plan. Together, he told Son, they could take on the *entire* real estate market—to rapidly seize it. They would become the go-to provider for space for companies around the world, making money as a landlord, as a tenant, and as everything in between. They'd take on the apartment market, the brokerage market, the construction industry; all of it would be their playground. They could build something worth *trillions,* by far the largest company on earth.

It was the exact type of big-thinking vision Son was looking for. He was intrigued. He wanted to learn more—to think about how to do a deal.

The Tokyo pitch kicked off a series of meetings throughout the summer involving senior staff from both companies who raced into high gear putting together a giant plan code-named Project Fortitude. In Tokyo, in New York, and in San Francisco, Neumann, Son, and their respective staff repeatedly met up to hash out just what the plan would look like and just how much money WeWork would need.

It was a lot. To accomplish what he wanted and envisioned, Neumann told Son in a meeting in New York at the start of July, he wanted $70 billion. It was a gargantuan number. The entire Vision Fund was $100 billion. Uber—which raised more than any startup ever—had raised about $12 billion total in its existence.

Neumann and his team showered Son with projections of voracious growth that WeWork was planning, should a deal come together. Neumann gave Son a presentation that showed how WeWork was already growing faster than it planned in 2018, and thus it now expected faster growth for years to come. He sketched out how WeWork was set to have 14 million members in 2023—more than the population of Belgium—up from 420,000 in 2018. It would mean around one billion square feet of real estate, more than twice the size of the entire Manhattan office market. WeWork's enterprise business was thriving, he showed Son. If its largest subtenant, Amazon, kept its growth rate up, it would have 200,000 desks with WeWork by 2023—a rather heady projection for any company.

All of this would be lucrative, Neumann explained in his presentation. WeWork's main business alone would hit $101 billion in revenue by 2023, up from the $2.3 billion they planned in 2018. Together with ARK and the services arms of WeWork, the projections called for a jaw-dropping $358 billion in revenue in 2023. (Apple, by comparison, had $266 billion in revenue in 2018.)

The giant numbers—the asks for unprecedented sums—didn't scare off Son. He saw WeWork as his chance to guide a company to ubiquity around the world, and he could be even more involved than with Alibaba.

He wanted to dream even bigger.

Impressed by the efficient growth of WeWork's enterprise businesses, he told Neumann that WeWork needed to have ten thousand salespeople, up from the hundreds it employed at the time. It should also aim for ten thousand buildings and ten thousand real estate employees—fantastical numbers.

To illustrate why WeWork needed to build so many buildings, he made an analogy for the WeWork team relating to the chicken and the egg. WeWork had to build first—show the world a finished product—and then demand would follow. The chicken—the finished product—came first.

It was a strained metaphor, but he wanted to memorialize the moment. He took out his iPad and pulled up a picture of Yoda from *Star Wars,* bracing a green light saber. "Chicken first!!" he scrawled on the image in yellow, adding, "10k! 10k! 10k!" He signed at the bottom, "Masa," and sent it to Neumann.

The duo fed off each other's excitement, dreaming bigger and bigger. Son seemed eager, fully sold on Neumann and his chance to turn WeWork into a massive home run. In a room in WeWork's headquarters, working alongside Neumann, Son pulled up on his iPad WeWork's chart that showed a hockey-stick-like growth curve for WeWork's main business. Turning on the draw function, in purple, he extended the growth curve for another five years—the hockey stick of revenue growing even higher upward—and then scribbled down some math. By 2028, he wrote, WeWork's main business would have 100 million members and hit $500 billion in revenue. Then he assigned it a valuation, adding together what he projected for ARK and services.

He scribbled in yellow ink, "$10 T," and underlined it twice. With SoftBank's support, WeWork would be worth $10 trillion by 2028.

THE TWO WERE A COMBUSTIBLE COMBINATION. TOGETHER, THEY assumed the world's financial sector would bend and stretch to meet their aims. The plan they were discussing was on a scale beyond the audacious, yet they seemed to view it with a sense of certainty. In 2018, the entire value of the U.S. stock market was $30 trillion, yet Son scribbled out some calculations and presumed WeWork would be worth $10 trillion in a decade.

To the two of them, the world's financial system was a chessboard where pieces would move as they wanted. With ARK, for instance, billions were penciled in from sovereign wealth funds. One slide in one of WeWork's presentations called for $10 billion from Saudi Arabia, $5 billion from Norway, $4 billion from two Canadian funds. Another slide from WeWork showed how ARK's growth plans depended on $593 billion from investors and lenders—an amount that would represent a sizable chunk of the United States's entire commercial real estate finance system. Another showed how the two companies could invest $40 billion themselves into ARK, but take more than $500 billion in profit after the buildings increased in value. The bulk of the investment that went in would be others' money. Just whose wasn't clear: wealth funds, banks around the world, or perhaps private equity, they thought. Both Neumann and Son had shown the ability to part the financial seas before; surely this time would be no different.

Sufficiently bullish on WeWork's future, Son agreed to do a deal. It wouldn't be as big as the $70 billion Neumann wanted, but it would be something giant. Eventually, they settled on a plan: Son would buy out all of Neumann's existing investors for about $10 billion and put *another* $10 billion into WeWork, giving SoftBank ownership of most of the company while leaving Neumann as the only other large owner remaining. Son was proposing the largest ever buyout and investment of a U.S. startup. To get the deal in motion, WeWork had SoftBank commit to giving it another $3 billion—a nonrefundable deposit, of sorts. The valuation would equate to roughly $47 billion.

WeWork wouldn't need to go public. It would just live off Soft-Bank's money as it grew bigger and bigger.

Neumann instructed a legion of staff and lawyers to get to work on the deal. Together, he and Son would own WeWork. Together, they would rapidly build a behemoth, one that would gobble up the world's real estate market.

CHAPTER 23

Summer Camp

O NE DAY IN THE MIDDLE OF AUGUST 2018, ABOUT SIX THOU-sand members of WeWork's staff, the majority of the global workforce, were sitting in a giant field in the English countryside outside London, watching with bewilderment as the spiritual guru Deepak Chopra delivered a didactic, New Age jargon–infused lecture on a stage in front of them.

WeWork's employees had gathered—thirty-four hundred miles from its headquarters—for the company's seventh annual Summer Camp. New Yorkers and staff from outposts around the globe had arrived hours earlier at Heathrow, filing into a caravan of charter buses, before heading south and east to the chosen venue, Eridge Park. It was a stunning and sprawling preserve of rolling hills and woods set on thirty-six hundred acres, the former estate of an eighteenth-century British earl once used for nobles' deer hunts. Bleary-eyed from their journey, the jet-lagged employees watched as Chopra gave an invocation to open the weekend that centered on mindfulness, spirituality, being true to yourself—anodyne themes for the millennial startup crowd.

But his speech—and a video—grew weighty and weird. Chopra, whom Rebekah Neumann had been courting to partner with WeWork's new school, started talking about life, death, rebirth, and creation. As he spoke, the giant screen above the stage displayed an image of a fetus and eventually a baby. It was *creepy,* employees thought. And difficult to discern. Some wondered if Chopra was condemning abortion. (He had written publicly that he leaned more toward the pro-choice side.)

They were confused and rattled. And starving. Many of the employees had endured sleepless overnight flights and a bus ride to the fields where they'd be staying in six-person tents for several nights, sharing communal bathrooms in trailers. Dozens of food cart vendors had been hired, but they were told not to serve dinner until Neumann had wrapped up his introductory remarks, which followed Chopra's and would go on for more than an hour. This came after a monsoon-like rain that fell as they arrived and flooded many of the thousand-plus tents.

It was an ominous start to an event that had been an integral part of the company's fabric since 2012, when Adam Neumann first trekked the tiny staff to an upstate New York lake for a weekend. Like WeWork at the time, it was scrappy—canoes were stuffed with ice and cans of Coors Light—and somewhat intimate. Work was sprinkled amid play; Neumann once led an introspective discussion with thirty people about what was working and what wasn't inside WeWork. At night he'd party with everyone.

In the years since, it had ballooned into a massive production—part music festival, part Burning Man, part corporate development retreat—all caked in exuberant partying and cultlike self-adulation. It was meant for staff for the first half, then opened up to WeWork members, too, to party alongside the employees.

Startups and money-losing tech companies had become notorious for injecting their workplaces and off-site events with perks that seemed more out of a frat house than a workplace. For many, it meant events like margarita Mondays and for more lavish spenders a retreat featuring a music act.

But as it did with so many other trends and tropes in Silicon Valley, WeWork took standard tech startup revelry and added an exponent. The landscape of tents at Eridge Park looked like a me-

dieval army camp on a battlefield. Giant colored flags evoking the
Middle Ages—or perhaps *Game of Thrones*—lined the tent-covered
fields.

The long weekend was packed with every event imaginable—
kayaking, canoeing, and paddle boarding. On land, there was yoga,
martial arts, and flower crown making. One could pet mini horses,
learn to make pottery, or tie dye T-shirts. There was soccer, zip-
lining, and jumping at each other in giant inflatable-ball outfits.
Available to all, constantly, was alcohol. Bartending stations lined
the ground, offering beer and wine. Staff had to wear bracelets that
bartenders scanned. These wristbands imposed some theoretical
limit on alcohol, though few could figure out what it was. Regardless, rather than wait in a long line every time you needed a refill,
the drink of choice became a full bottle of rosé; everyone seemed
to have one in tow.

At night, everything got crazier. One big-name act after another
took to the main stage in front of screaming and dancing WeWork
staff. The singer Lorde, the indie pop band Bastille, the Swedish DJ
Alesso. After the main acts ended, two *additional* stages kicked into
gear. WeWork staff could head to an EDM-themed tent or a tent
where a DJ played pop hits. Marijuana smoke filled the air. Harder
drugs—while not sanctioned—were easy to come by.

As budgets grew since WeWork's early years, company organizers had gradually booked bigger and bigger names, often acts poised
to break into the mainstream: St. Lucia, Chromeo, the Chainsmokers, and the Weeknd. For 2017, when camp had moved to a larger
site in England, the company had tapped even more well-known
and expensive acts. The Roots performed songs from *Hamilton*
with its creator, Lin-Manuel Miranda, who was paid nearly
$500,000 for his time, which included both a performance and an
onstage interview with Rebekah Neumann.

By 2018, the point of the festival seems to have boiled down to
celebrating the extraordinary awesomeness of WeWork. Thomas
Hobbs, a reporter for the U.K. real estate publication *Property Week,*

bought a ticket to the camp for the portion that included outsiders and wrote a piece called "The Cult of WeWork," quoting some anonymous staff members who defended the deity-like figure of Neumann. "Adam wants to build a better world. Everything he does is to galvanise human beings," one employee told the publication. Rebekah Neumann told the staff: "A big part of being a woman is to help men manifest their calling in life."

The co-founder of Flatiron School, which had been acquired by the company in 2017, showed off his new tattoo. It was the WeWork company logo—a serif-font "We" surrounded by a black circle—inked on his left pec. Neumann encouraged staff who were couples to have "We babies," suggesting they could get free education at WeWork's schools. One community manager proposed to his girlfriend, who'd come for the trip, in front of a cheering crowd of his colleagues.

For all the talk of "we" and egalitarianism, the Neumanns made their place clear. While nearly all WeWork's employees shared tents and used bathrooms where showers and toilets regularly overflowed, they could look up to the top of a hill and see a mini compound of luxury trailers for the Neumanns, including their five children, and McKelvey, among others. For the Neumanns' compound alone, the grocery list given to aides was eye-popping: four hundred plastic shot glasses, twelve cases of Don Julio 1942, and two bottles of Highland Park scotch that sold for more than $1,000. They also requested two bartenders, a "signature Range Rover," and a Mercedes V-Class, according to the list obtained by the journalist Reeves Wiedeman. When Neumann ventured down the hill, he was trailed by security guards.

The weekend of fun wasn't optional. It was mandatory for staff to attend, and one manager the prior year had even been fired after she left a day early. (Adam Neumann, having just had his fifth child, also left early that year.) While the millennial crowd that dominated WeWork's staff generally seemed to love the event, it wasn't for everyone. Many older employees resented it. One recounted waking up to hearing someone pee on the side of her tent. "I am not here to get peed on," she told *New York* magazine.

And then there was the food. Specifically meat—there wasn't any.

Shortly before the 2018 event, Adam Neumann surprised the entire company with an edict: WeWork was banning meat. The policy seemed to be motivated by his and Rebekah's interest in environmental sustainability; he also said WeWork would be going paperless. With little detail or direction from Neumann about what the ban would mean, a bewildered group of senior executives quickly huddled to figure out a policy: Meat could be eaten within WeWork but wouldn't be served at company events, nor would employees be able to expense it for business meals. Fish was okay. Chicken was not. (Soon after, Neumann sparked internal dissent when he was spotted eating a lamb chop inside WeWork's headquarters—one of numerous episodes of carnivorous consumption employees noticed after the ban. The paperless policy, which never was well adopted, also didn't apply to Neumann, who didn't use a computer.)

In subsequent weeks, staff met with Neumann to hammer out more details of the ban. McKelvey was happy with the changes and decided to become vegan. Discussing Summer Camp, Neumann directed staff to come up with ways to illustrate the impact We-Work was having by going vegetarian. He suggested commissioning an art piece to memorialize all of the animals that were being saved. Perhaps a pile of chickens, he said.

The chicken sculpture did not materialize, but the Neumanns were fully embracing new roles they'd created for themselves. Long known for his partying ways, Adam Neumann had begun cultivating a more serious persona as a CEO, global statesman, and guru—at least in public. Rebekah, whose role in co-founding WeWork was trumpeted by her husband during most of their speeches, was cast as the enterprising humanitarian who was reimagining education.

The litany of speeches peppered with world-saving rhetoric and onstage interviews with celebrities and gurus seemed to mirror the Neumanns' evolving sense of identity. Adam Neumann referred to WeWork almost in the past tense—as a company nearing peak operational performance that could basically run on its own so that he, his wife, and the employees gathered before him could tackle bigger societal issues that really mattered.

In the middle of the second day of Summer Camp, the Neumanns, sitting alongside McKelvey on the main stage, spoke in a way that casually flicked at some of those world-salvation plans. Rebekah, wearing large black sunglasses, a silky black button-down shirt, and black pants, told the crowd in a low, weary monotone, "Just so you guys know one of my biggest dreams for We is that we'll be able to build communities around the world where children who are not in the right situation could come and live forever basically and feel like they are part of a family."

Adam, speaking more rapidly, seemed to be trying to make up for Rebekah's low-energy delivery: "With our members around the world we could wake up one day and say we want to solve the problem of children without parents in this world. We can win and do it within two years."

He was just getting going. "And from that we can go to world hunger," he said. "There's so many topics we can take one by one."

The couple's presentation gave employees a glimpse into their mindset: they were thinking about far more than running an office space subleasing company.

Fueling their ever-rising and perhaps ever-more-erratic ambitions was the forthcoming deal with Masayoshi Son. The deep-pocketed investor's recent commitment was going to mean a whole new volume in the story of WeWork, a full partnership with the world's most active tech investor, who had seemingly endless billions of dollars to spend on dreams. Neumann couldn't see a scenario where this deal, Project Fortitude, wouldn't go through.

It was a curious name. According to the traditional rules of making money, WeWork was shaky, not strong. The foundation of the business had never been stable, and WeWork had lost more than $600 million in the first six months of 2018 alone. At each juncture when Neumann and his team might have been forced to figure out a viable business model that could be profitable, more money came in, and Neumann would persuade everyone to build higher. The wobbly foundation didn't matter so long as the cash reserves kept getting replenished in bigger and bigger quantities.

As 2018's camp came to an end, negotiations with Son were humming along. Neumann's main task as he saw it—and Son reinforced—was to just keep dreaming bigger.

CHAPTER 24

Shoes Off, Souls Inside

I N HINDSIGHT, JOSHUA SHANKLIN SHOULD HAVE KNOWN SOME-thing was off from the start.

In the summer of 2018, he and a group of colleagues at We-Work's headquarters filed into a spacious bathroom attached to Adam Neumann's former office. Inside, the scent of burning incense filled the air. A makeshift altar decorated with fruits and flowers sat next to Neumann's sauna and shower.

As each employee entered, a twentysomething spiritual guru—who gave off a Jesus vibe to some—whispered a word or mantra in their ears. They then walked back to Neumann's former adjacent office to ponder what they'd just heard.

It was mid-summer 2018, a few weeks before WeWork was set to open the doors to its new private elementary school, WeGrow. Shanklin and the others lining up for the brush of enlightenment were its teachers and administrators. As they readied for WeGrow's inaugural set of students, they were told to sit for numerous daily sessions with the guru, Hunter Cressman, during which they were implored to get in better touch with their souls. Cressman, whose previous experience consisted largely of private meditation classes with wealthy Manhattan clients, had been tasked by Rebekah Neumann with creating a mindfulness curriculum inside the school.

Shanklin, the grandson of a Pentecostal preacher, was now set to be the school's lead teacher, but he found the whole experience off-putting. The sessions with the guru were the culmination of a lengthy period of training for the staff. The WeWork offshoot had been conceived by Rebekah Neumann, who was distressed over the lack of suitable education options for her own children. She and Adam had decided to create their own school—naturally, under the auspices of WeWork.

In a city where parents plotted their children's private school options in utero, Rebekah could find no single New York school that checked off the critical items on her wish list for her children. She wanted a progressive school where her children could learn Hebrew and ideally study Judaism in a beautiful setting with healthy food. None of the schools in Manhattan or in the surrounding area were right or even close to it.

WeWork took off after the company found a void in the office space market. Rebekah was certain she'd found a similar hole in education. If she couldn't find what she needed for her children, certainly others were having the same problem. What's more, WeWork's ideals of sharing and empowering people to do what they love would surely translate to education. The Neumanns were trying to find more and more ways to export their ideas and infuse them into new areas.

Since WeWork's founding in 2010, Rebekah had jumped between roles in marketing, branding, and design, while taking lengthy maternity leaves around the births of her five children, including twins. It wasn't enough for her. She made it clear to employees that she wanted more recognition for her role at the company, particularly given the long shadow of her husband. After Adam appeared on the cover of a magazine, she told WeWork's public relations staff that she hoped there wouldn't be more profiles like that one: she was the one who had to live with his growing ego, she complained.

By 2017, she had finally landed on her own mission inside the company. WeWork would build a bespoke school, one that would serve not only their children but others'. They would fix education in the United States and around the world.

The school, which would initially accept students ages three to nine, would cost up to $42,000 per year, though because of Rebekah's desire for socioeconomic diversity, many students would attend with financial assistance. It would operate out of the third floor of WeWork's headquarters on Eighteenth Street. The school's guiding philosophy was a mix of the Montessori method—in which instead of being taught standardized subjects, children largely direct their own educational path—with elements drawn from the couple's own lives. Even the youngest children would learn the principles of entrepreneurship; they'd go to the Neumanns' house upstate to learn farming, and they could take Hebrew classes. The Neumanns' children didn't eat meat and rarely ate animal products. The school's food options would be vegan. Parents were forbidden to pack meat for their own children's lunch. Instead, the school offered child-friendly recipe suggestions such as the "cheezy sprinkle," which was a mix of hemp, pumpkin, sunflower seeds, raw cashews, smoked paprika, sea salt, and nutritional yeast.

There was a heavy dose of mysticism and spirituality. Just as Rebekah, a student of Buddhist tradition and Kabbalah, had spent decades practicing meditation and yoga, now so would the school's students.

SHANKLIN, A BOYISH-LOOKING FORTY-TWO-YEAR-OLD MIDWESTerner, had come to WeGrow as a seasoned veteran of the Montessori tradition. A faculty teacher at Xavier University's Cincinnati-based teaching school, he'd also been working as a consultant to schools around the country that were looking to build their own Montessori programs.

In early 2018, Shanklin came to New York to observe the experimental class Rebekah Neumann had been operating out of a school in Tribeca since 2017. He offered her a slew of recommen-

Adam Neumann and his sister, Adi, on the Israeli talk show *Good Evening with Guy Pines* in 2001. His hair cropped short from his time in the Israeli navy, Neumann boasted about moving to New York, where he wanted to go to school and follow Adi into modeling.

After Neumann moved to New York, he started Krawlers, a baby clothes company that sold pants with padded knees to protect babies while they crawl. The startup struggled financially, and Neumann yearned for a bigger idea.
Roy Ramon

In 2008, Neumann partnered with Miguel McKelvey, an Oregon-raised architect, to create Green Desk, a small Brooklyn co-working space that was a precursor to WeWork.
Andrew Toth via Getty Images

Neumann married Rebekah Paltrow in 2008. She later said that the second she met him, she knew he "was going to be the man who would hopefully help save the world."
Astrid Stawiarz via Getty Images

WeWork opened its first location in 2010 at 154 Grand St, with McKelvey overseeing design. The spartan space filled quickly with small businesses and the self-employed, including a lawyer and a photographer.
Lisa Skye

As WeWork expanded, the locations began to take on a uniform aesthetic. Light streamed in through the glass walls, giving the interiors a light and airy atmosphere.
Jamel Toppin / The Forbes Collection via Getty Images

Continuing to grow, WeWork sought to add experienced executives. Michael Gross (left), the CEO of Morgans Hotel Group, started as WeWork's CFO in 2013 and played an integral part in WeWork's rapid-fire fund-raising.
David M. Benett via Getty Images

Neumann recruited Artie Minson, the former CFO of Time Warner Cable, as president and chief operating office in 2015 but later limited his oversight to WeWork's finances.
Bloomberg via Getty Images

Jen Berrent, a former partner at the law firm WilmerHale, was hired as WeWork's chief legal officer in 2014. Known for working around the clock, she eventually became the company's chief operating officer.
Bennett Raglin via Getty Images

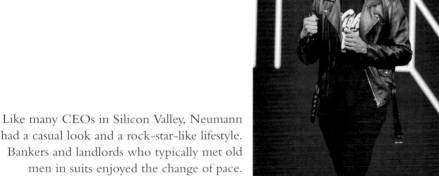

Like many CEOs in Silicon Valley, Neumann had a casual look and a rock-star-like lifestyle. Bankers and landlords who typically met old men in suits enjoyed the change of pace.
Jamie McCarthy via Getty Images

As he promoted his vision of WeWork to investors, the charismatic CEO often concluded his pitches with wild partying. After one funding round over shots of tequila on the roof of a building, Neumann sprayed his new investor with this fire extinguisher.
Ilana Blumberg

At another party, Neumann threw a tequila bottle through his office window. After the first pane shattered, a colleague threw another.

SoftBank's Masayoshi Son (left), who long pined to be considered in the same league as technology titans like Bill Gates and Steve Jobs, raised $45 billion from Saudi Arabia, striking a deal with then deputy crown prince Mohammed Bin Salman, money he used to invest in companies including WeWork.
Bloomberg via Getty Images

Son implored Neumann to dream big, once telling him to hire ten thousand salespeople, and underscoring the message with a crudely composed iPad image of Yoda wielding a lightsaber. Son wanted WeWork to expand rapidly, saying demand would follow.

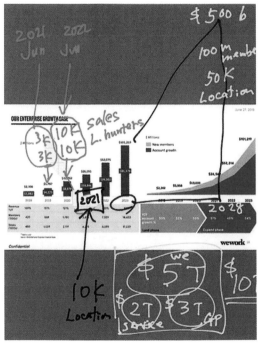

As he pondered a bigger investment in WeWork, Son pushed WeWork's already ambitious financial projections into territory unprecedented in business history. During a meeting with Neumann, he scribbled out a vision for a company worth $10 trillion.

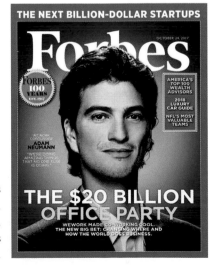

For years Neumann enjoyed glowing press coverage. To reporters, as it did to investors, WeWork portrayed itself as a disruptive, technology-driven startup reshaping the world's real estate sector.

As the company grew, so did its parties. In 2018, WeWork flew thousands of employees to England for its "Summer Camp." At the corporate retreat in the guise of a music festival, staff played games, listened to inspirational speakers, and partied in the evenings.
WeWork

As WeWork's valuation grew, Neumann sold a large amount of shares and took loans, worrying investors. He used that money to finance an increasingly lavish lifestyle. He bought a $21 million home, with a room shaped like a guitar, just north of San Francisco.
Photography by Jacob Elliott

Neumann hated flying commercial. In mid-2018, WeWork paid $63 million for a Gulfstream G650ER private jet.
Paul Denton

To keep funding its heavy losses, and with diminished options left for private funding, WeWork decided in 2019 to raise money through an initial public offering. JPMorgan's CEO, Jamie Dimon, was eager for the bank win the lead underwriter role, a position the bank had struggled to land on tech deals.
Bloomberg via Getty Images

JPMorgan's main liaison to Silicon Valley–style startups was a banker named Noah Wintroub, who took the lead in courting Neumann and WeWork and eventually won the prized assignment.
Bloomberg via Getty Images

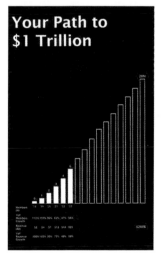

Goldman Sachs also vied to run the IPO for WeWork. During one presentation, Goldman bankers showed a deck including this slide that played to both Neumann's hunger for a giant valuation and his affinity for simple visuals.

WeWork's IPO prospectus was filled with inspirational quotes and photos that Rebekah Neumann and a group of staff members spent months putting together. The company was panned for the document's new-age language and the steep losses it revealed. In the summer of 2019, *The Wall Street Journal* published a series of articles that raised questions about WeWork's a corporate governance and revealed unsavory details about Adam Neumann's personal financial dealings, as well as his penchant for partying.

As the IPO faltered, Neumann watched as his empire began to crumble around him. Days before being ousted as CEO, he was on the streets of Manhattan, barefoot and on the phone, just across from his home, a condo building the Neumanns effectively controlled thanks to having bought so many units in it.

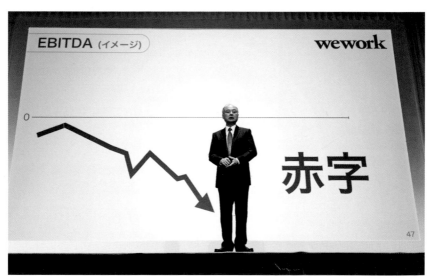

After WeWork's implosion and Neumann's ouster, Son's SoftBank bailed out the company, giving it a valuation of $8 billion—$39 billion less than its peak. Son apologized to his shareholders, saying he erred in his judgment. SoftBank said it would buy nearly $1 billion of Neumann's WeWork stock, a promise SoftBank tried to back out of and ultimately curtailed to less than $500 million.
Tomohiro Ohsumi via Getty Images

dations for how she could improve the school. "It was pretty much a mess," he recalled.

Rebekah, sitting in her office, outlined her plans for WeGrow. The expansive vision involved building schools all over the world that would "re-create the traditional classroom environment," giving children a greater say in their education and more direct experiential learning. She told Shanklin she was impressed by his feedback—so impressed that she wanted to offer him a job. "No one is honest with me," she told him.

Shanklin was taken aback. He and his wife had just adopted a toddler and had two daughters in high school in Cincinnati. Moreover, as part of his current job at Xavier, his children were entitled to a tuition remission there.

In a separate phone call, Adam Neumann gave Shanklin a sales pitch. Shanklin would have the chance to shape not just WeWork's school but the entire future of American education. "If this is your destiny, there will be no challenges," Adam told the speechless midwesterner.

Adam dangled the offer of WeWork stock, telling Shanklin the company's valuation was growing so quickly that it would soon be worth far more. Adam warned him that if he waited too long to decide, he would never have an opportunity like this again.

IN JUNE 2018, SHANKLIN AND HIS FAMILY SETTLED INTO A HOUSE in Millburn, New Jersey, a suburban community about an hour from WeWork's headquarters. Forty-five students, ages three to nine, were set to arrive at WeGrow in less than three months. They still needed to find more teachers, to turn an entire floor that once housed WeWork employees into a school, and to finalize the curriculum.

It was a formidable timetable, but Shanklin was emboldened by the challenge. He'd never seen teachers and staff with such impressive pedigrees—from some of the best public and private elementary schools and universities. The resources at their disposal were astonishing. Shanklin would get to work with Bjarke Ingels's team to build out the school's space.

Throughout the summer, the ten thousand square feet of office space was starting to transform into what Rebekah Neumann would later tell *Architectural Digest* was "more of a universe or village than a traditional classroom." The space resembled a meadow with green mushroom-shaped sofas in the middle and an open floor plan. Curvaceous wooden shelves delineated classroom spaces, and small cocooned wooden hives hung from the ceiling and sprang off the floor functioning as reading nooks. There was also a vertical garden where plants grew along the wall, tables that were essentially big jigsaw puzzles, and special lighting that changed in intensity throughout the day. The perimeter of the space was designed as a track where children could run at the times of their choosing. A sign stood at the entrance: "Shoes off, but souls inside."

Rebekah had tapped Adam Braun as the school's chief operating officer. Braun was dazzling. He was just thirty-four, but he'd already founded a nonprofit, Pencils of Promise, that built hundreds of schools in India, Nicaragua, Ghana, and elsewhere, and he'd written a best-selling book. He was from a family of high achievers; his brother Scooter was Justin Bieber's manager. Braun had started another company, MissionU, which was seeking to upend college and university education by offering a free one-year degree in exchange for a portion of a graduate's income over the next few years. WeWork had just acquired it to bring him on board.

With the promised resources of WeWork and the Neumanns and the star power of Braun, Shanklin felt inspired. The things Rebekah Neumann would say "would all sound so beautiful," he recalled. "There was so much optimism. We felt like what we were doing would change education forever."

.   .   .

It didn't take long before problems began popping up.

As WeGrow's staff ushered students and parents into classrooms on the second day of school, Rebekah Neumann couldn't get an elevator to take her and a few families up to the third floor. A special key card was required to access the WeGrow floor, and neither Neumann nor the parents had one on them. They were stranded briefly in the lobby before they were all escorted in.

A short time later, as students were beginning the school day, senior staff, including Shanklin and Braun, were told to meet in Rebekah's office on the sixth floor. When they arrived, she was crying. That was humiliating, she screamed at them. This makes it look as though the school doesn't work, she said.

The staff was stunned. Confrontations like these might be normal in the high-stress startup world, but not in the more measured world of private childhood education. Shanklin had immediate flashbacks to his time working as a student manager of Indiana University's basketball team under Bobby Knight, the coach famous for his success and his temper.

He apologized calmly. It won't happen again, Shanklin told Rebekah. She took a few minutes and caught her breath. She thanked Shanklin. "I'm not a hysterical person," she said, as if shocked by her own outburst.

It wasn't the end of it.

After the school day wrapped up, Rebekah called another meeting—this time for the entire WeGrow staff. How could the elevator incident have happened? she asked, locking eyes one by one with the employees.

From that moment on, teachers and administrators became particularly sensitive to any incident that might similarly set Rebekah off.

It was a somber close to what had been two positive days with the children. For some of the senior staff, simply getting children into the classroom felt like a miracle. They'd been struggling with

Rebekah's constantly changing ideas about the design and the curriculum.

The Montessori teaching method espouses giving students "freedom within limits." Rugs are particularly important because they outline spaces for students to sit together in morning circles and to do their own work.

With this in mind, Rebekah wanted to find the perfect rugs—all in white. Over the summer, they received multiple shipments of white rugs and mats. Soon after the rolled-up rugs were unfurled at WeGrow, she'd send them back. The shade of white would be wrong. Or the texture. Or both.

Shortly before the first day of school, the teachers were terrified looking at the empty floors, and they discussed going to Ikea to find alternative mats. To Rebekah, even the word "Ikea" was blasphemous. For the first several months, while she continued to seek out the right white rugs, the teachers used masking tape to outline places for students to sit.

But the toughest part was finding teachers who fit Rebekah's criteria. She wanted teachers who had Montessori training and could teach Hebrew. It wasn't an easy hiring process. Staff watched as Rebekah dismissed many potential hires, citing her concerns that the otherwise seemingly qualified candidates had the "wrong energy."

Before the school year started, one teacher asked whether they would have non-gendered bathrooms. Rebekah Neumann didn't think it was appropriate for children of different genders to share the same bathroom and demanded that the teacher be fired. Rebekah would later say that she was worried that the teacher was too focused on her own agenda rather than the mission of the school.

DESPITE THE BEHIND-THE-SCENES HICCUPS, STUDENTS AND PARents at WeGrow were largely excited by their educational experiment and awed by the sheer beauty of the space. In the mornings, students meditated. Music and dance were incorporated into classes throughout the day. Children could run around the track if they felt antsy, and even the youngest ones had a lot of autonomy over how they spent their time and directed their studies.

Many weeks, students would ride for nearly two hours—in traffic—on a limo bus with reclining leather seats to the Neumanns' house in Bedford, New York, where they learned about farming and grew fruits, vegetables, and flowers. The music teachers accompanied them on these trips, singing songs along the way, and teachers could have one-on-one time with students. After their days on the farm, the students sold leafy greens and produce inside WeWork, a sort of child-run farm stand that delighted the mostly millennial staff.

There were plenty of bright spots for staff, who bought into Rebekah's rhetoric about building an educational movement. Children were developing and a community was coalescing in the school. Still, there were constant reminders that WeGrow was, at heart, the Neumanns' school.

Teachers arrived on several different Monday mornings to see waste strewn around the floor. Chairs were in the wrong classrooms; nothing looked the way staff had left it the previous Friday.

The cause of the disorder: Adam and Rebekah had hosted a dinner over the weekend for their family and their friends' families inside the school. Not only would teachers have to frantically clean up the school before the students arrived, but they'd often spend the first few days of the week reprimanding the Neumanns' children and several children of their friends to observe rules regarding climbing on the hives or swinging from them. The children would protest: We were allowed to do that this weekend. Why can't we now?

When staff brought this up with Rebekah, she apologized and swore it would never happen again. The staff was relieved until a few Mondays later when they found the school once again a mess.

Clashes also occurred over HR issues. Despite Rebekah Neumann's struggles to find teachers and staff whom she deemed a good fit for WeGrow, she became agitated by her staff's requests for raises. When she saw the head of HR's plan to offer modest raises of a few thousand dollars per staffer, she called a meeting with senior staff. Why were teachers getting paid so much, and why did they want more? It's an honor to be a part of this, she said. We don't want staff who are just doing this for the money. The teachers shouldn't be trying to take advantage of us, she told them.

In a subsequent meeting about the raises, Adam Neumann started discussing the cost of living in New York City—rent and groceries and transportation and even nights out. Staff members were surprised by Rebekah's seeming ignorance of how much anything cost in New York. Eventually, she relented: the teachers could get their raises.

Pay wasn't the only area where Rebekah sought to intervene. As the school year progressed, Rebekah's ideas about the curriculum changed daily. She took to questioning the teachers on day-to-day decisions, often based on feedback from her children.

Shanklin was getting uneasy. He and the staff were put in an impossible situation, he felt. They were serving the whims of the Neumann family rather than doing what was right for the other children at the school. Moreover, his family was miserable.

He approached Rebekah and told her he would leave in the coming months. She was sympathetic to his concerns, telling him she respected him for putting family first.

Still, she had a request to keep him on: Would he ever consider moving to Hawaii to set up a school there? The Neumanns loved Kauai and wanted to spend more time there. It could be a nice lifestyle, she told him. Although he pondered the prospect, Shanklin turned the offer down.

Soon after Shanklin told Rebekah of his final decision, Adam Neumann came into her office and questioned him on his move. You need to teach your children to be resilient, Neumann told him. Then he started to tell a story about the history of Israel—

about how Israelis had to be fighters. What are you teaching your children, he asked Shanklin, by taking them out of New York and giving up?

It was yet another off-putting interaction that cemented his dissonance with the Neumanns, who clearly thought extremely highly of their own advice. In a prior conversation with the couple, after Adam walked out, Rebekah turned to Shanklin and said, "Isn't he amazing? Some people think he's the Messiah."

Ultimately, it was a cordial end, though Rebekah did ask Shanklin to leave quietly. She didn't want his departure to spook the parents and children in the school. Before his last day, the Neumann children themselves were leaving for a vacation. He'd grown attached to them and wished he could say goodbye. Just before they left, one of the daughters looked at Shanklin quizzically, sensing that something was amiss. She asked him if she should know something.

He demurred and simply wished her a good vacation.

It was the last time he'd see any of the Neumanns.

CHAPTER 25

Flying High

IT WAS THE SUMMER OF 2018, AND THE GULFSTREAM G650ER was sprinting toward Israel, packed with Adam Neumann's friends. While it was a personal trip—not for work—a typical We-Work in-flight scene was under way. Booze was flowing, and marijuana was passed around as the jet cruised over the Atlantic Ocean.

Soon after touching down in Israel, Neumann and his entourage set off away from the airport. After they were gone, the crew of the plane—which was owned and operated by Gulfstream—opened a closet on the aircraft to find a cereal box. Stuffed inside was a stash of marijuana left for the return flight.

It wasn't welcome cargo. Smoking on board was one thing, but transporting marijuana—an illegal drug in New York and Israel—across borders into a foreign country might expose Gulfstream to serious risks. The crew reported what they found to superiors, and Gulfstream decided to pull the jet. It swiftly left Israel without Neumann, and the company complained to WeWork over the incident. Neumann and his friends were left stranded, ultimately renting another private jet for the trip back to New York.

NORMALLY, GULFSTREAM—AN AIRCRAFT MANUFACTURER—wouldn't be running a flight for Neumann. But he was buying a jet for WeWork from the company, and the jaunt to Israel was something of an extended test-drive he negotiated as he waited for his plane to be delivered.

Until that point Neumann had been flying on a rented Bombardier Global Express. The $56 million jet could travel from San Francisco to London without refueling, and its operator, VistaJet, boasted that its on-board meals came from Michelin-star restaurants like Nobu. For Neumann, though, there was a problem with this arrangement. Other corporations *owned* their own aircraft for executive travel. He wanted his own status symbol—a shiny beacon of extreme corporate wealth.

It was a symbol of his rising ambitions—and growing ego.

For most corporations, such transportation is hardly a rational choice. The cost difference between flying private and commercial is simply extraordinary, making it extremely hard to justify economically. (VistaJet's list rates on the Bombardier Global Express started at $16,000 an hour, so a trip from New York to Tokyo would cost more than $200,000.) An NYU economist even found that the stock performances of public companies with jets underperformed those without. One theory is that the decision to buy a jet is indicative of broader bad financial decision making, suggesting that a CEO is a poor steward of investors' money.

Neumann insisted to colleagues that buying a jet made more sense than renting, though few were convinced. There was no obvious reason he needed the top-of-the line version. Other private jets cost tens of millions of dollars less.

Buying or renting, there were some practical benefits of private travel for Neumann. At six feet five inches, he felt cramped on commercial flights, even in business class. A private plane accommodated his chronic lateness and let him bring his fluid way of working into the air. On impromptu trips, he sometimes encouraged staff mid-meeting at headquarters to simply follow him to the airport and continue a conversation or have a longer meeting at forty thousand feet. These passengers would end up as far away as

San Francisco and be forced to find their own way back home. Still, some relished the opportunity to get his undivided attention for multiple hours. Shiva Rajaraman, who oversaw WeWork's tech, once flew to China with Neumann, mostly just to get time with him to talk. Others hated riding with him to Europe because sometimes he would want to work through the night, forcing his companions to stay awake, too.

Then there was the partying. Particularly when a few of Neumann's friends or close colleagues were on the plane, booze flowed heavily. Shots came out quickly, as did pot. One friend brought along for a few rides found it redolent of a rock band tour bus. "It was like being a groupie," he recalled thinking.

On one round-trip flight Neumann took to Mexico City in 2015, the charter company was instructed to keep two bottles of Don Julio 1942 on board for the morning flight down ("even though it's early," the charter company was told). After the trip, the charter operator, Gama Aviation, complained to WeWork that one of the passengers became sick "throughout the cabin and lavatory" and the plane needed extra cleaning. Further, the charter company said in an email to WeWork, "Passengers were spitting tequila on each other" and the "crew was not tipped."

Such antics continued as WeWork grew. On one flight Neumann took, there was so much marijuana smoke in the cabin that the crew was forced to pull out the jet's oxygen masks and put them on. VistaJet was frequently left to deal with the effects of Neumann's onboard partying. The company told WeWork employees it repeatedly had to take jets out of service to clean or fix the interiors, following alcohol spills and vomit. On multiple occasions, Neumann or one of his companions tore down a curtain divider between two parts of the jet.

In early 2018, Neumann informed WeWork's board that the company was planning to buy a Gulfstream G650ER, the latest top-of-the-line aircraft. The plane—whose white shell was accentuated with thin blue and gray stripes—could seat up to thirteen passengers and fly eighty-six hundred miles without refueling. It would cost $63 million.

It's virtually unheard of for a venture-capital-backed startup to own a private jet before going public. Many investors would be aghast that their money was going toward such a lavish expense, particularly at a company that lost nearly $900 million the prior year.

Yet WeWork's board approved the purchase—unanimously. Board members seemed to be growing weary of pushing back on Neumann, and in the scheme of a company worth $20 billion, a jet didn't seem worth a fight. Regardless, Neumann had a powerful supporter of the purchase. Masayoshi Son said he was fine with the idea, Neumann told board members.

Some WeWork staff, though, fretted that if the public ever found out, it would be a horrible look. Beyond the hypocrisy for a company that cited environmental sustainability when it banned meat, Neumann often enacted cost savings by demanding cuts to travel budgets other than his own, forcing some executives to fly coach on international trips.

Staff managed to bury the agreement to buy the jet in the bond documents, simply calling it unnamed "assets" that cost $63.4 million. Public relations staff held a series of meetings to come up with talking points to justify Neumann's need for it, if its existence ever became public. When *The Wall Street Journal* wrote about the jet in 2019, an executive explained that WeWork had numerous executives constantly flying around the world, when in fact only Neumann had the privilege. Neumann even referred to the jet to some staff as "*my* jet," leaving one executive under the erroneous impression that he paid for it himself.

One exception was for the maiden flight, when the Neumanns wanted some other executives—including Sebastian Gunningham, a new top executive lured from Amazon—to ride it first. Staff was under the impression that Neumann wanted the plane to get some miles on it before his family would ride inside.

One of the first trips of the plane was to Summer Camp. When a few top executives were planning to leave early and return to New York, they ran into a problem: It was a Saturday. Neumann was becoming more religiously observant, and he was observing rules around not working on the Sabbath. The same rules, he decreed, would apply to the jet, even if he wasn't on board.

The Neumanns' work accommodations on land were getting upgrades as well. The company was renovating the entire sixth floor of the headquarters at 115 West Eighteenth Street, moving Neumann and other executives up from the fifth floor. Neumann's new office was outfitted with a giant personal bathroom, featuring walls of pale green tile, a sauna, and an ice plunge. The latter addition was a new obsession of Neumann's. The ice plunge consisted of a metal tub filled with cold water and ice that one stands in, freezing, to refresh one's legs. Neumann extolled the virtues of the ice plunge to anyone who would listen, once even showing the entire staff a picture of him and a cadre of male deputies in one.

Rebekah Neumann took the office next door. To furnish it, she chose an L-shaped pink-and-yellow couch and a white sheepskin rug. She saw six different iterations of the decor and the layout, weighing in on each one. Still, when she walked into her finished office space, during an early morning tour, she questioned why it felt cramped and complained that it was smaller than Adam's.

"My soul can't breathe," she told the designers.

ICE PLUNGES, JETS, AND PINK COUCHES WERE JUST A REFLECTION of the times. Mission creep in 2018 was everywhere, particularly with the promise of the giant deal with SoftBank that would bring billions more into the company. It sometimes seemed as though the story Neumann had long been telling investors and staff about We-Work spreading into myriad other aspects of life was already true. He began frequently referencing Jeff Bezos's transformation of Amazon from a website that sold books into the dominant internet retailer.

Offices to us are like what books were to Bezos, he would say.

But what was the other half of that analogy for WeWork? What was WeWork's equivalent of developing the dominant global e-commerce platform?

The vision was still eminently hazy, despite eight years of growth and billions of dollars of investment. Neumann was unable to stay focused on the expansive yet specific triangle strategy he presented to Son, in which WeWork would seek to control all sides of the commercial real estate market. Not only would WeWork help companies with their real estate, but he wanted it to sell them software, to sell them food, to provide their workers with housing, to educate their children. In the near future, he wanted to go even bigger. He wanted to get involved in city planning, perhaps even take over chunks of cities with large urban campuses, and he would soon hire a senior executive from Google to oversee the division. It was a vision that left countless open questions. Even so, Neumann's charismatic delivery of it, for all its uncertainty, created a ripple effect of excitement.

"We are here in order to change the world—nothing less than that interests me," he told the Israeli newspaper *Haaretz* the year before.

This ambiguous credo led to increasingly puzzling acquisitions and new lines of business. A common link was simply that Neumann got along with the founder and then extolled to his staff the synergies of the company.

Conductor was one such purchase. Neumann and its founder, Seth Besmertnik, had both gone to Baruch College. While they weren't particularly close in school, they ran into each other years later, and Neumann took an interest in Besmertnik's company. The New York–based search optimization startup, founded in 2007, helped businesses market their products online. It had basically zero

connection to WeWork's core business. But Neumann told his staff
to buy it, saying large businesses using WeWork could benefit from
Conductor's services—a logic that implied basically any company
that offered services for other businesses qualified as a potential acquisition.

The WeWork executive overseeing technology, Shiva Rajaraman, was impressed by some elements of Conductor's tech but figured it would just be a small purchase—along the lines of $10
million. Neumann had a much higher sum in mind: $113 million,
mostly in WeWork stock. During late-night negotiations that often
took place in his office over drinks, Neumann emphasized to Besmertnik that once WeWork hit $25 billion in sales in four years, his
stake would be worth even more. (Besmertnik put a framed copy
of the sheet with the deal terms in his house alongside a picture of
him and Neumann.)

Ideas for other acquisitions abounded. Brainstorming sessions were frequent—with executives suggesting a wide array of
well-known companies and startups, sometimes seemingly at random. Some were buzzy. Executives once pondered trying to buy
MoviePass, the notorious money-losing company that charged
users just $10 a month for unlimited movie tickets.

Neumann was taken by Sweetgreen, the healthy salad chain out
of Los Angeles. He offered to buy it for around $1 billion, but the
deal never went far. Other moves were even bolder: Neumann
considered buying Regus, the serviced office giant and WeWork
predecessor, which had changed its name to IWG. As of mid-2018,
IWG had 145,000 more desks than WeWork, but WeWork was
worth around five times more than IWG. Neumann met with
Mark Dixon, the CEO who had been frustrated by Neumann's
rise, but no deal resulted.

WeWork held talks to buy the real estate brokerage Cushman &
Wakefield, and also considered buying the giant real estate management arm of CBRE. It came closer to buying a giant property

maintenance services company, BGIS, for $1.3 billion, but it was the runner-up bid.

Through Neumann's lens of valuation, such deals made sense. The market—which at this point was largely SoftBank—was clearly valuing WeWork based on its revenue, not its losses. If WeWork could dramatically increase its revenue by buying a company like IWG, the thinking went, WeWork's valuation would theoretically go up even more.

Further afield was the potential investment in the ride-hailing company Lyft. Neumann told his deputies he hoped to buy Lyft, and he met repeatedly with John Zimmer, its president and co-founder, about a possible investment by WeWork. It would have been a rather strange marriage: two aging startups, both bleeding money, with one investing the venture capital dollars it raised from SoftBank into the other. (When Masayoshi Son later found out about the talks, he was furious with Neumann and forced him to shut the discussions down. SoftBank was a backer of Lyft's rival Uber. Neumann told aides he preferred Lyft, in part because it was still run by its founders. He had less respect for Uber, run by a professional CEO, after Uber's co-founder Travis Kalanick was forced out by the company's board.)

Beyond buying and investing in esoteric companies, WeWork started some of its own projects in far-flung areas. It launched its own autonomous driving robot division—a scrappy team of a few staffers who set out to make a small robot that could greet guests and deliver packages to offices. Working out of a former flower shop in Palo Alto, the team felt constrained without more staff. But with the help of a robotics company to which they outsourced some work, the team cobbled together WeWork's own small robot prototype, complete with lidar, cameras, and other sensors.

The ambitions of WeWork's main business continued to grow as well. By the fall of 2018, WeWork had surpassed JPMorgan to become the largest private tenant in all of New York City—a feat it also accomplished in London. While WeLive was seemingly on a perennial hold—a rare sign of financial prudence, given that the two initial locations were performing poorly—staff contemplated other lines of revenue. For months, staffers hunted for sites where WeWork could establish a large conference center. The idea was to build a corporate "off-site" retreat for companies with millennial employees where they could surf amid team-building exercises. The company began negotiating with Suffolk County on Long Island to get subsidies to put a center there, where a Wavegarden surf pool was planned next to the conference center.

The board did little to hinder Neumann's moves, however erratic. The investors were seemingly focused on the SoftBank deal; some stood to make billions selling their holdings.

WEWORK'S SPRAWLING AMBITIONS REFLECTED ITS FOUNDER'S growing ego. For Neumann, it wouldn't be sufficient to just be running the world's largest business. He saw himself playing a bigger role in society. As he explained to a founder of a smaller startup, it wasn't enough for WeWork to just have a big valuation. It needed to have the *biggest* valuation. That way, he said, when countries started shooting at one another, he'd be the one they'd have to call to solve their problems.

He seemed detached from reality, musing about the impossible. His mind often appeared to be living in the future he envisioned— where WeWork was ubiquitous across the globe, pervading all aspects of society and the economy. Based on the deal he and Son had sketched out, WeWork was on track to be worth many trillions of dollars in a few short years, and he'd own nearly half. He'd be a trillionaire—the world's first—if all went according to plan.

Earlier in WeWork's rise, Neumann would ruminate about one day running for prime minister of Israel. But by 2018, he looked at it differently. When multiple people asked him if he'd ever run for office, he replied that if he was going to run for anything, it would be "president of the world."

The world was reinforcing his megalomania. Elected officials were eager to meet Neumann as his star rose, particularly mayors who liked the sparkle of innovation WeWork would bring. He had a prime speaking spot at the U.S. Conference of Mayors' January 2018 meeting, where he dazzled city leaders by telling them the world was moving more toward "we" and away from "me." Following an introduction by future Democratic presidential candidate Pete Buttigieg, he told them WeWork would bring them everything they needed, creating a thousand jobs per location. "We won't just bring you jobs," he declared in a nearly half-hour interview onstage, "we'll bring you a place to live, we'll bring you education."

On a trip to Washington, D.C., he went to the U.S. Senate and met Chuck Schumer, the Democratic minority leader from New York. (Schumer's brother Bob was Neumann's personal lawyer on the deal with SoftBank, helping him negotiate his compensation and terms over his control.) Neumann reveled in the visit with the powerful senator and the marble hallways of the Capitol. He tried to walk into the Senate chambers and onto the Senate floor, only to be stopped by security.

As he was leaving the Capitol, he turned to his aides and said he was done with meeting with heads of cities. "No more mayors," he said, "only senators from now on." Mayors, of course, were crucial, given that WeWork was physically based in cities, so the ultimatum was short-lived.

Still, he seemed to lack the concept of deference even with a head of state. He had one meeting with the Canadian prime minister, Justin Trudeau, and the prime minister's office wanted him to come to Ottawa for another. WeWork was set to announce a planned expansion in Canada. They scheduled a date, but less than a week before the event Neumann decided he needed to reschedule. The request was effectively a snub in the hierarchical world of politics; the prime minister of Canada shouldn't have to rework his schedule around an indecisive CEO of an ambitious but decidedly midsized company. He never got another meeting.

The Canadian faux pas came after a near humiliation of the U.K. prime minister, Theresa May. In September 2017, her staff cobbled together a last-minute event with business leaders at a We-Work amid her visit to the city for the United Nations General Assembly meeting. The event, though, coincided with a promise Neumann had made to Rebekah to speak about entrepreneurship to children at the experimental precursor school to WeGrow. Rebekah, livid that he was planning to back out of his commitment, screamed at Neumann so loudly that others heard—telling him to skip the meeting with May. WeWork's staff intervened, begging Neumann to meet the prime minister. They prevailed. He showed up in a suit, fidgeting in his seat as he spoke with her.

In Neumann's mind, he was on the same plane as prime ministers and other leaders. It was a grandiose lens on life, as well as on his company. He envisioned WeWork staying in his family for hundreds of years—passing to his children and their children. He would talk about WeWork as a company that would last for three hundred years. Or a millennium.

At the same time, he aspired to live forever. Humans will be able to solve the problem of death, he told staff; it was just a matter of time. To help fulfill this aspiration, Neumann became a major investor in Life Biosciences, a Boston-based startup working on technology that would extend lives. The company even called him the co-founder. (The company's website dropped any reference to Neumann as a co-founder in late 2019.)

This aggrandized sense of self was common to both Neumanns. When Rebekah was asked on a podcast in the fall of 2018 to imagine she'd live as long as she wanted, she cut in. "That might be forever," she said. Rebekah helped sow the seeds of his outlook. On the same podcast—hosted by the former athlete and lifestyle guru

Lewis Howes—she recounted that when they met, she realized there was "no ceiling on his potential or our potential together."

That interview offered a rare, candid glimpse into the couple's ambitions. In her eyes her motivations were completely pure. The two of them were committed to making the world better—creating a more just society, a more sustainable one.

"Our vision and dream and goal," she said, "would be [to] be around the entire planet."

"We want to create a whole We world, where everybody is unified and happy and together. That's the intention, but we need the help of the whole world to make that happen."

As ADAM AND REBEKAH NEUMANN'S EGOS ESCAPED GRAVITY, THE people around them generally didn't sound alarms.

To some, Neumann's messianic ambitions were just an amped-up version of Silicon Valley founder megalomania. Well before Neumann and WeWork, there had long been a cult of the CEO that existed more broadly in American business, where the charismatic chief executive was held up as a figure to be revered. Charismatic leaders like Jack Welch and Jamie Dimon were idolized and idealized in the media for creating highly profitable empires at GE and JPMorgan. The cult extended to stories with rough endings, too. Jeff Skilling was cast as the archetypal smart, charismatic, profit-generating CEO for his leadership of Enron—until the company unraveled.

Silicon Valley added on the notion of a visionary—of someone who could create a new product that delighted and disrupted. Through this lens, Steve Jobs was the ultimate deity—one whose vision defied the paper-pusher CEO image and allowed him to boldly dream of the iPhone.

The Neumanns once had dinner with Walter Isaacson, Jobs's authorized biographer. Afterward, Isaacson emailed Neumann about a WeWork deal he'd read about, comparing the deal to something Jobs might have done. Neumann proudly read the email aloud to a group of senior executives. One day, Neumann told staff, he wanted Isaacson to write a biography about him.

It was like a frog boiling in water: he always had an ego, and those around him didn't realize how absurd some of his thoughts were becoming. That, and it wasn't quite clear how seriously to take these things. Did he *really* think he'd live forever? Or maybe he just thought he'd find a way to live a bit longer. After all, it's not as though he could really run for "president of the world."

That was just Adam being Adam, one executive thought at the time.

It was easy to overlook his crazier side for the good things We-Work brought them. Relatively unseasoned executives were given huge responsibilities—far larger than if they worked for an established company like Google or Facebook. And they were all slated to get very rich if things continued apace. It wasn't an environment where anyone wanted to throw cold water on the leader.

Among founders, Neumann was far from alone in his highfalutin rhetoric. Brian Chesky of Airbnb penned an open letter to staff saying the company "will have an infinite time horizon" and its goal was to have "a world where you can go to any community and someone says, 'Welcome home.' Where home isn't just a house, but anywhere you belong." The founder of the online fitness class company Peloton wrote to investors that his company's mission was "to better ourselves, inspire each other, and unite the world through fitness." Making the world a better place was a common CEO aspiration.

LITTLE EMBODIED NEUMANN'S GROWING SENSE OF HIMSELF BETter than his perceived place in the Middle East. A year earlier, the CEO had huge misgivings about working with the Arab state investment funds behind SoftBank—nearly calling off the deal. But at the time, advisers around him, including Jen Berrent, urged him to take the dissonance over the pairing of an Israeli founder and the Saudi wealth fund and use it as an advantage. By 2018, he had started to see WeWork as a force so big and good that it could transcend the region's troubles—putting him in a unique position to work with all sides on issues of global significance.

That spring, Mohammed bin Salman, who oversaw the Saudis' investment into SoftBank's Vision Fund, was on something of a post-coronation tour of the United States, having just consolidated power at home and been named crown prince. Mobs of security and aides in black Mercedes limos darted from small gatherings with dignitaries and CEOs from one major city to the next. On its California leg, the delegation took over two separate Four Seasons hotels—one in Los Angeles and one in Palo Alto. Aiming to modernize his country and diversify Saudi Arabia away from oil, Prince Mohammed was plunging money into the U.S. startup scene, not only via the Vision Fund but also through investments in companies like Lucid Motors, an electric car company. The techno-optimist was happily received by top venture capitalists and tech giant CEOs. Tim Cook of Apple, Sergey Brin and Sundar Pichai of Google, and Mark Zuckerberg of Facebook were all photographed with him.

Neumann managed to secure his own meeting. On a stop in Los Angeles, Prince Mohammed was holding court at a mansion, sitting down with people like Oprah Winfrey. Neumann and Roni Bahar traveled there and met with the crown prince as well as the head of the PIF, Yasir al-Rumayyan, for around an hour. The two principals were a clear match: both huge dreamers and visionaries bounding with energy. They talked about the region and WeWork's ambitions for expansion there. Neumann told him his plan to open Flatiron School coding academies in Saudi Arabia, but starting just for women. He wanted to partner with the Saudi state on it—an idea Prince Mohammed seemed to embrace. Neumann felt a bond and had a common friend in Jared Kushner, an early WeWork landlord and now the son-in-law of the president of the United States.

He made a bold statement to the crown prince, he later recounted to WeWork staff.

He told him, you, me, and Jared Kushner are going to remake the region.

Neumann would frequently psych up executives before a meeting—telling them about WeWork's broader ambitions, how it would have a "seat at the table" in big world decisions in the future, an amorphous, far-reaching declaration. He brought up his desires for brokering Middle East peace in his meeting with Isaacson, and he once told a group of executives that a Middle East peace treaty would one day be signed in a WeWork. Neumann's staff even played a small role in the Trump White House's attempts at facilitating a new Middle East peace plan. Kushner was running the process and was lining up help from the private sector for an economic development-focused summit in Bahrain. Neumann dispatched Roni Bahar to help. Bahar suggested a video—and put the White House team in touch with a production company. The result was a short video that opened the summit, a computer animation that showcased the potential for a Middle East transformed by the economic boom that could follow peace in the region.

Some of Neumann's aides were concerned about doing business with Saudi Arabia. Staff worried about the kingdom's patchy history with human rights and treatment of women. It could be a bad look for a company that espoused progressive values, they told Neumann.

In October 2018, six months after Prince Mohammed's goodwill tour to the United States, the *Washington Post* columnist and Saudi government critic Jamal Khashoggi was dismembered in the Saudi consulate in Turkey. The Turks revealed evidence that pointed to Prince Mohammed and his top aides as the masterminds behind the attack, a claim later supported by the CIA.

The grisly incident made for an incredibly awkward situation in Silicon Valley. Prince Mohammed, via SoftBank, had become the largest funder of startups in the world. Suddenly he was an international pariah. While a handful of CEOs who took SoftBank Vision Fund money publicly condemned the incident, the vast majority stayed quiet, despite pressure from their staff to speak out.

Neumann didn't grasp the political gravity of the situation. The Saudi government had planned a giant conference in Riyadh—hosted by Prince Mohammed and dubbed Davos in the Desert—which had attracted top CEOs, bankers, and money managers the previous year. Following the news of Khashoggi's death, attendees were swiftly dropping out of the conference, yet Neumann wanted to go. Numerous aides pleaded with him to stay home, and We-Work's public affairs team even had him talk to Stephen Hadley, national security adviser under George W. Bush who became a consultant to corporations. He cautioned Neumann about the perils of going to the conference. Eventually, Neumann relented and called off the trip.

It was a tough decision for Neumann, who relished the proximity to the powerful crown prince and his vision of the modernized Middle East. Prince Mohammed just needed better guidance, better advice, Neumann told Hadley.

Who could offer such counsel? the veteran foreign affairs official wondered.

Without hesitation, Neumann replied, "Me."

CHAPTER 26

Both Mark and Sheryl

IN SILICON VALLEY, IT HAD BECOME CONVENTIONAL WISDOM that a visionary founder should hire a business-focused right-hand operator to bring the business into shape. Under Mark Zuckerberg at Facebook, there was Sheryl Sandberg. At Google, the co-founders, Larry Page and Sergey Brin, tapped Eric Schmidt, and later Sundar Pichai, to be their CEO while the founders took more ceremonial roles or pursued pet projects.

Adam Neumann, though, trusted few. Why would he cede control? As far as he was concerned, he was the one with the skills needed to run WeWork—from vision to detailed operations.

He repeatedly told lieutenants, "I am both Mark and Sheryl."

He wasn't. For much of WeWork's existence, the business had functioned shockingly well despite a management structure characterized by chaos. Executives switched roles constantly, and responsibilities were shifted around from one manager to another. Lower-level employees would often find they had a new boss only when they looked in the company's official HR system. Neumann, struggling to delegate, wanted to be involved in a litany of decisions.

Early on, his personal involvement and indefatigable work ethic were actually quite effective. By setting extremely high goals—and yelling when he was upset—he had a way of forcing subordinates to deliver on demands or deadlines that seemed impossible. His attention to detail and obsession with hitting certain metrics left staff exhausted, though his style undoubtedly helped WeWork grow in its early years. But as WeWork was gearing up for the SoftBank deal in late 2018, this management structure was becoming a hive of dysfunction. With more than eight thousand employees, WeWork was simply too big for Neumann's chaotic approach.

Neumann continued to resist the push by advisers to delegate power to a deputy. The list of former heirs apparent was long. While Neumann and Miguel McKelvey were partners in the earliest days, McKelvey, who had little interest or aptitude for managing the expanding employee base, had been largely relegated to working on smaller roles related to WeWork's brand, culture, and environmentalism. After McKelvey, there was Michael Gross, followed by Artie Minson, who quickly lost the approval of Neumann and was moved to the CFO role. There was also Rich Gomel, a real estate executive who was later put in charge of ARK; and Dave Fano. The résumés grew increasingly impressive. In 2018, Neumann recruited Sebastian Gunningham, a senior executive at Amazon whose turf included operations and technology at the e-commerce giant, to an amorphous role with the title of vice-chairman. Soon after arriving, Gunningham told a colleague he'd never seen a company that focused so much more on its valuation than its product.

Neumann had told many of these deputies they would eventually take over as CEO, as he would one day migrate to a more distant chairman position. Yet none would sustain his approval even as a viable number two.

Without a deputy, Neumann was key to most every big decision.

For most WeWork executives, the charismatic leader was like a drug. Having his ear made them feel alive and successful. They would jostle with each other to impress him and boast about how great their teams were doing. And when he liked someone, the sun would beam on the person. Suddenly the in-favor executive was appearing in key meetings. They were asked to surf with him; to use the ice bath with him; to join him on the plane. In earlier years, he'd invite them to sessions with his Kabbalah teacher. He would rave to others about how a new executive was brilliant and how everyone should listen to what this person had to say.

Then, inevitably, Neumann would turn on them. His optimism would fade. Numerous managers at WeWork over the years described this feeling of a cold front swiftly setting in. Perhaps the manager had missed a quarterly goal, or an internal competitor had whispered concerns about the person (almost always a man) into Neumann's ear. Suddenly others were being invited surfing. Through WeWork's glass walls, the out-of-favor manager could watch as others were being called into important meetings instead. It was deflating—even depressing. Some would sit outside his office for hours for a scheduled meeting, only to watch as his assistant called in others.

At an executive retreat in 2017, Neumann gathered a few dozen of his top staffers for a lunch at the Surf Club in Montauk to talk about WeWork's operations and management. Waiters started to bring out the food, but Neumann sent them back: he had more to say. He went on about the value of working with people you know. He turned to Michael Gross, sitting next to him.

"What's that word you like?" he asked Gross.

"Nepotism?" Gross responded.

Neumann raised a glass. "To nepotism!" The staff dutifully raised glasses of Don Julio 1942.

Ever since WeWork's early days, nepotism was a common theme. By 2018, despite WeWork's transformation into a massive global corporation, it was still everywhere. Important roles throughout the organization were filled by friends and family. These extended well beyond Rebekah Neumann.

Chris Hill, Rebekah's brother-in-law, held senior roles, including chief operating officer and chief culture officer, between 2011 and 2016, before becoming CEO of WeWork Japan in 2017. The company's head of real estate for years was her cousin Mark Lapidus. Her nephew Luke Robinson was a top enterprise executive. Adam Neumann's sister, Adi, was the paid star of the show at numerous Creator Awards events, acting as emcee. Adi's husband, a former professional soccer player in Israel, ran the company's fitness arm. His childhood friend oversaw security. Arik Benzino—Adi's modeling agent when she was a teenager—oversaw the entire North American and Israeli operations of WeWork offices. Two of Miguel McKelvey's "siblings" from his commune worked at the company. The board of directors was full of ties of its own. At various points, the children of three directors—Bruce Dunlevie, Steven Langman, and John Zhao—worked at WeWork. Mark Schwartz, the director who pushed SoftBank to invest, intervened to help a WeWork employee move locations. He persuaded senior executives to give her a cushy job in New York.

Executives had their own nepotistic ties. For years, WeWork relied heavily on a construction firm owned by the brothers of its head of construction.

Some were qualified for their jobs or, like employees at many startups, moved into jobs not clearly correlated with their résumés and excelled. Many did not. But even among the high-achieving ones, the extraordinary amount of nepotism created a cultural problem within the organization. Low-level staff, and even executives, say they were afraid to push back against those who had a familial tie or friendship with the Neumanns.

Beyond nepotism, other aspects of Neumann's approach to management would make a business school professor gasp.

To executives in HR, he railed against perceived "B-players" who had proliferated throughout the organization. As WeWork's head count swelled in 2018, he arbitrarily decreed that WeWork should be firing 20 percent of its employees a year. HR executives were bewildered by the demand, as such mass firings tend to be reserved for companies in dire financial straits. Further, they realized it would be extremely challenging to find that many people to fire without causing major problems for the business: they successfully pleaded to modify the 20 percent mandate so they could include those who left voluntarily, too. As pink slips flew out in bundles, the HR team even had to create a whole online system to keep track of the firings and see if they were on target. They missed the goal, coming up just shy of 20 percent.

Executives were scared to speak up. The previous fall, in 2017, Neumann caused a scene at an executive retreat when he learned the company had paid many thousands of dollars for a self-serve espresso maker. Apparently unaware the machine was intended to reduce costs by replacing human baristas, he shouted at his executive team, demanding to know who was responsible. The staff sat there silently, looking around uncomfortably: no one raised their hands.

The next day, WeWork's placid, affable head of HR, John Reid-Dodick, brought up the subject of Neumann's outburst with a collection of other top staffers, and while some defended Neumann, many others shared stories of how it was impossible to have rational conversations with their CEO. Soon after the impromptu complaint session, Reid-Dodick was unceremoniously stripped of most of his key responsibilities and moved to a different job—a move that had been discussed before but accelerated after the event. Friends believe he would have been fired if not for McKelvey's intervention on his behalf.

It was just one of many consequences of a C-suite culture in which saying no or voicing criticism was implicitly discouraged. Neumann encouraged junior and senior members of his staff to give him a heads-up on what executives said about him in his absence, creating a climate of paranoia. Executives said they were scared to push back against Neumann when he asked for the impossible; if you said no, he'd push you out of the way and give your duties to someone else, they worried. Neumann encouraged bravado; lower-level employees said executives seemed to be constantly "peacocking" around Neumann rather than warning him of hazards or impressing upon him the dangers of WeWork's growing red ink.

Still, Neumann preached a certain gospel of acceptance, and his team was schooled in the rhetoric of inclusivity. With the onset of the #MeToo era, as tales of sexual harassment dominated discussion in American corporations, Neumann became particularly expressive with staff. He said that he had been abused growing up. He offered no specifics about who or how, but it was a vulnerable side of him that he rarely offered, even to close friends.

Women, he frequently said, were integral to WeWork's success. "We usually do better with women executives," he said at a public event in 2017. "It has something to do with ego." By the end of the year, he added, he wanted a majority of WeWork's workforce to be women, "just because we think it's better for the company—not for any branding reasons."

But in day-to-day life at WeWork, the reality was quite different. While women filled the ranks of lower-level staff positions, female executives found it hard to get ahead.

One friend of Neumann's within the company became a particular source of concern for some women. Adam Kimmel, a well-known fashion designer whom Neumann had lured to the company, became WeWork's chief creative officer in 2018.

Kimmel took over design and introduced a big revamp of WeWork's look—pushing whiter, brighter plant-filled spaces instead of the existing darker motif. He had a nose for good design, and Neumann was insistent that he oversee the design team, which then numbered in the hundreds.

Kimmel's wife, the actress Leelee Sobieski, a friend of Rebekah Neumann's, would sometimes come into WeWork's offices and sit in on meetings with his design team, offering feedback on their plans. Women at the company noticed that Kimmel would avoid taking meetings one-on-one with them, and even booked separate cabs and hotel accommodations when the design team traveled. Kimmel later told WeWork executives that he took these measures out of respect for his wife.

Multiple women complained to HR, saying they found his apparent policy highly disruptive, making their jobs difficult. After HR looked into it, some in the department thought Kimmel should be fired. Neumann got involved. He shielded Kimmel from getting fired, though he agreed such a policy wasn't acceptable. One of the women who complained was pushed out. WeWork later paid her a sizable settlement.

For many who watched, it was yet another example of the challenging environment women faced in a company dominated by male executives. At that moment, companies throughout Silicon Valley and corporate America were grappling with questions over how women were treated and whether sexual harassment and discrimination had been handled appropriately. The broader cultural awakening to long-standing issues within companies was suddenly leading to the swift ouster of many senior corporate executives. Something, many thought, needed to be done at WeWork.

RUBY ANAYA HAD BEEN AT WEWORK FOR FOUR YEARS BY LATE 2018. The California-raised Anaya had started in WeWork's software team, working on its app, before moving to the company's culture department, where she reported to Miguel McKelvey. The department's job was to infuse the "We" spirit into outposts throughout the world.

McKelvey wasn't enamored of Anaya as an employee. She scored low in performance reviews, and in the midst of Neumann's push for stepping up firings in the summer of 2018, McKelvey made the call: Anaya had to go.

After she was fired, she consulted a lawyer, and in October 2018 she filed a lawsuit alleging, among other complaints, that she had been groped at company events by WeWork employees. According to Anaya's lawsuit, a drunk co-worker at the company's Global Summit grabbed her and forcibly kissed her, before she slapped him. HR investigated, though didn't find enough witnesses or evidence to proceed, she alleged. Her lawsuit painted a picture of WeWork culture in which alcohol flowed so freely at events it was setting the stage for inappropriate and unwelcome behavior. (In subsequent legal filings, Anaya denied that complaints were raised about her performance and said she hadn't been given the opportunity to address concerns with a performance improvement plan.)

Typically, at this point, companies offer up somewhat safe responses, issuing statements expressing a strong commitment to a workplace free from sexual harassment and broadly denying wrongdoing. WeWork's PR department had even drafted such a response in advance of the filing.

But when Neumann found out about the lawsuit, he was livid. He gathered McKelvey and others, including Jen Skyler, the head of communications. Neumann told Skyler the company would issue a statement attacking Anaya. Further, he said, Skyler should leak images to the media that portrayed Anaya in a bad light. WeWork had collected a number of photos from social media and elsewhere that showed her partying.

Skyler was aghast. As with many senior staff, others rarely saw her push back against Neumann. But this time she was insistent. She would not leak to the press photos of her former colleague for suing over sexual harassment, and WeWork should not attack Anaya publicly, she told Neumann.

Shouting ensued, and while Skyler won part of the battle—she didn't leak photos—Neumann directed McKelvey to send a letter to staff attacking Anaya. McKelvey would email the whole company that "Ruby frequently neglected assignments, skipped meetings and didn't show up for her team or for the company."

Email alerts flashed on the phones of WeWorkers everywhere, and employees were horrified as they read the note. Many employees saw McKelvey as friendly, optimistic, and approachable, qualities that gave them hope in WeWork's mission. Now, after one of his employees was alleging sexual harassment, he was publicly denigrating her?

Later, numerous staff would look back on the incident as the moment when they grew skeptical of WeWork's making-the-world-a-better-place rhetoric. Slack channels lit up with criticism, while employees whispered to one another how similar incidents were commonplace. *Finally,* people were talking about some of the hypocrisy they were seeing, many women at the company said at the time.

In the aftermath of the Anaya suit, some members of senior management sought to make changes to allay the staff's concerns. They revamped HR and started receiving and investigating far more claims with allegations of incidents similar to those experienced by Anaya. The company sought to examine compensation and improve any gender pay gaps.

Still, few saw wholesale change. A lawsuit brought in the spring of 2019 would reveal that fifty-eight executives were given new compensation packages worth more than $1 million. Just three were women.

It wasn't just compensation. The board was all male. Nearly every top executive at the company was a man, and executive activities that involved being around Neumann tended to appeal to men, too. Surfing. Sitting in a sauna or an ice bath with him.

It went back years. Early on, he asked multiple potential female hires if they were planning to become pregnant—something barred by employment law. Many former employees say he called maternity leave "vacation."

"I hope you're going to have fun on your vacation while we're here working," he told Medina Bardhi, Neumann's longtime chief of staff, according to an employment complaint she filed. She alleged she was given a lesser job upon returning after maternity leave, unable to keep her old position.

． ． ．

NEUMANN DIDN'T APPEAR TO BE ALL THAT CONCERNED WITH the internal strife and HR challenges at WeWork. They were side issues. Above all, by late 2018, what mattered and what gave him satisfaction was that his We world was falling into place.

His company's logo adorned buildings in most every major city center in the world. It was the biggest private tenant in New York and London, and his clients included most any major company of significance—Facebook, Amazon, GE, Bank of America. Rebekah Neumann's vision for education had become WeWork's, and together the couple planned to reshape schooling for children everywhere. As staff raced to complete the forthcoming deal with Masayoshi Son, WeWork was on track to change the world, just as Neumann had been promising for years.

In the fall of 2018, he spoke to the board of the Presidio, a former army base in San Francisco where he was trying to win the rights to build a WeWork campus. "My personal mission—and Miguel's and my wife that's sitting there—is to make this world a better place."

"You guys have such big companies here in the Valley," he told the board. "What are they actually doing to change the world? I know what they are doing to increase valuation. But what are they actually doing?"

WeWork, he told them, was truly mission-driven.

CHAPTER 27

Broken Fortitude

TOP HEDGE FUND MANAGERS, INVESTMENT BANKERS, AND CEOs filed into the ballroom at the midtown Manhattan Hilton on December 10, 2018, gathering for the annual Wall Street dinner to benefit the United Jewish Appeal.

Lloyd Blankfein, the recently departed CEO of Goldman Sachs, was at the lectern before the dark-suit-clad audience to introduce the keynote speaker, whom he called "my good friend." He moved the microphone higher, saying the adjustment was "to save you the trouble."

Adam Neumann stood up. Wearing a black suit with a white shirt and no tie, he strode past the current Goldman CEO, David Solomon, to take the microphone.

Before the more than two thousand attendees, Neumann discussed humility, saying that becoming more religious—disconnecting from society for Shabbat on Saturdays—made him keep his ego under control. He marveled at the splendor of a country where "an Israeli kid" could come and "build a business and have a life that couldn't be imagined anywhere else on this planet."

Then he gave advice to the crowd.

"Treat other people the way they want to be treated," he said.

"Together," he said, "we actually can change the world."

Neumann was radiant. He had clawed his way to the upper echelons of global society. Here, *he* was being asked to give the night's featured address. A decade earlier he was selling baby clothes, but now he was the orator dispensing life and spiritual advice to the chieftains of American capitalism. Not only was his company continuing to grow at a torrid clip, but he was living a life even more lavish than many of those in the audience—a lifestyle that would have shocked even some of the billionaires sprinkled throughout the ballroom, with his multitude of homes and a top-of-the-line private plane.

Neumann was in the final stretch of negotiations with Son and SoftBank—a couple of weeks away from completing a deal that would buy out all of Neumann's other investors. It was set to be the largest ever investment in or buyout of a U.S. startup. SoftBank was slated to spend $10 billion to buy stock from employees and existing investors, delivering shareholders like Bruce Dunlevie of Benchmark astounding profits. It would give Neumann a partner in Son, who seemed to have unlimited billions to fund Neumann's dreams—someone who believed he could make a company worth trillions. His stake in WeWork was going to be worth roughly $10 billion on paper after the deal.

By the end of the month, he was confident, it would all be done.

UNLIKE HIS EMPLOYEES, NEUMANN WASN'T PLANNING ON GETting any cash in the deal by selling stock. But he did negotiate a gargantuan compensation package.

As Neumann and Son were sketching out Project Fortitude, they agreed on one clear goal: the company should grow as large as possible as quickly as possible. And true to form, the two growth-addicted CEOs focused only on revenue, ignoring profitability. If

WeWork hit $50 billion in annual revenue—a giant number larger than Facebook's revenue in 2018—Neumann would get an enormous stock bonus equivalent to about 9 percent of the company.

At the $1 trillion valuation Neumann yearned for, that meant an extra *$90 billion* of wealth. It would be up to Neumann to divide that $90 billion between himself and the rest of the company's management, but his aides expected he'd take the lion's share.

The level of growth needed to hit $50 billion in revenue was almost inconceivable. It meant doubling revenue every year for the next five years. Such exponential growth might be manageable in the early years, but in a company of WeWork's size it was becoming an extraordinarily onerous lift. Doubling in 2018 meant adding the equivalent of four Empire State Buildings of office space. But if it kept up this growth, by 2023, doubling within a year would mean adding the equivalent of all of the space in every single office building in Manhattan.

Neumann was giddy about the deal with Son. He and Rebekah decided to rename the whole company, as in their minds, it was already far more than an office space business and the shift would only accelerate with the added investment. They chose the We Company, a rhetorical umbrella under which they hoped to build out WeLive and WeGrow, as its new name. Rebekah put forth a new mission statement for the parent company: "to elevate the world's consciousness."*

Neumann also loved the SoftBank deal because it would allow WeWork to stay private, letting him avoid the headache of being a public company CEO. Even though SoftBank would buy more than half the company, Neumann would stay in full control. And

---

* Like some other terms in the WeWork lexicon, the motto's genesis appears to be from the Kabbalah Centre. The Neumanns had broken with the center amid a broader scandal there relating to sexual assault allegations against its former co-director, Yehuda Berg. Yet the language was almost identical to what Berg wrote in his book on Kabbalah, which said the center's goal was "to elevate the consciousness of the entire world."

he would be tied to a visionary who had felt like a father figure to him—one who promised him unlimited capital to fund his ambitions.

"We'll be private forever," Neumann had told senior executives. "We'll pull off what no one has been able to do."

He had always been uneasy about going public. He had clearly mastered the private fund-raising game, saying just what he needed to attain a higher valuation and more money. He *hated* the minimally transparent step of the bond offering and didn't do the quarterly calls with bondholders, leaving them to Artie Minson and Michael Gross. (In addition to talking finance with investors on the calls, Gross was no fan of the hold music for investors before it started: he had a staffer change the unremarkable soundtrack to 1990s hip-hop like the Notorious B.I.G. The prior music wasn't "We" enough, he complained.) Neumann was racked with anxiety and anger over WeWork's sagging bond prices. Aides winced to imagine what a constantly updating stock price would do to the quietly insecure Neumann.

He also made clear he chafed at having a board he had to answer to—even his extremely permissive board. Son, he thought, would stay mostly out of the way.

Throughout 2018, he had become further removed from the board. Neumann, the board chairman, often wouldn't show up at meetings, dispatching Artie Minson or Jen Berrent to serve in his stead for impromptu board sessions and board committee meetings that came up. Regularly scheduled board meetings were quite infrequent between June and December 2018, because negotiations with SoftBank dominated the day.

The board members were eager for the payout. Benchmark first invested at the equivalent of $0.46 per share and now was going to get $55 for every share. It would mean a payout of nearly $2 billion. Bruce Dunlevie and Lew Frankfort—the onetime CEO of Coach who had been a longtime board member and adviser to Neumann—

met with Son to discuss timing and terms. The pair was in charge of negotiations for the board, because the rest of the members were conflicted. Son gave Dunlevie and Frankfort his word that the deal would close, the directors told the WeWork team.

Still, Mark Schwartz, one of the board members who had known Son the longest, gave some candid advice to top WeWork executives. Speaking of Son, he made clear his word was not his bond in a deal and he might walk away at any point.

"He's dangerous," Schwartz warned. "He doesn't have the same moral compass as you or I."

FOR TOP STAFF IN WEWORK'S HEADQUARTERS, GETTING THE DEAL done was the absolute priority for months. Artie Minson's team sorted through the finance aspects, while HR prepared to cut checks to the company's staff for their stock, which SoftBank would be purchasing. Jen Berrent scheduled daily 9:00 p.m. conference calls for senior executives to sort through issues around the deal.

Among Berrent's tasks was negotiating WeWork's future under SoftBank ownership. After four years at the company, she had earned Neumann's trust, in part by carrying out some of his ruthless decrees—like large-scale firings. She had long been in awe of Neumann—naively so, many other executives believed, as even many of his friends could see his glaring shortcomings as a leader. Berrent, though, was a dogmatic believer in Neumann as a gifted visionary. Normally reserved, she would light up when he came into the room. What was good for him was good for WeWork—even if she personally disagreed with him. In a moment of levity and candor, she once described to a group of WeWork lawyers what would occasionally happen when she or Minson would push back on Neumann on something they thought was a bad idea.

"Adam will say, 'I don't fucking care. Do it,'" she said. The few dozen members of the legal team laughed uncomfortably.

Berrent was a big proponent of the deal, excited by what We-

Work might accomplish in a SoftBank-funded future. Still, as the Fortitude negotiations progressed, even Berrent began to notice worrying developments.

By mid-November, Berrent's work on the deal was largely done, yet the talks dragged on: Neumann was endlessly renegotiating his own deal with Son, pressing for more. Aware of potential conflicts, Neumann had hired his own attorneys separate from the WeWork team, using corporate law firm Paul, Weiss, Rifkind, Wharton & Garrison to negotiate his compensation plan and his contract with SoftBank. The delay had little to do with WeWork's success, Berrent observed. The deal should be done, yet Neumann was drawing out the negotiations for his personal benefit.

Beyond his monster compensation package, Neumann wanted assurances that he would stay in control—an unfettered grip, even though Son was putting up all the money. SoftBank, however, wanted clauses so it could remove him under certain circumstances— a reasonable ask. Neumann negotiated to the point where SoftBank wouldn't be able to remove him—without paying a large penalty— if he went to jail on just any felony, for example. His lawyers pushed for a provision where he would have to commit a *violent* felony before SoftBank could remove without penalty.

THE FIRST BIG JOLT OF TURBULENCE FOR THE DEAL CAME NOT IN Tokyo or New York, but in Riyadh, the Saudi Arabian capital.

When Son agreed to a roughly $20 billion deal with Neumann in the summer, he expected he would use the $100 billion Vision Fund to pick up much of the tab. But despite running the fund, Son did not have full control over it. As the principal funders—the Saudi Public Investment Fund put in $45 billion—the Saudis had to approve large investments. At first this arrangement did not seem problematic. After all, Son had dazzled Crown Prince Mohammed bin Salman to secure the investment.

But a few rungs below Prince Mohammed, staff had grown

wary of SoftBank and WeWork. To many of the former Wall Street bankers and fund managers at PIF, the math didn't make sense. Son and Rajeev Misra—head of the Vision Fund—wouldn't show much in the way of specific figures, and PIF's head, Yasir al-Rumayyan, would rarely ask follow-up questions. Because most of SoftBank's investments were private, it was hard for PIF's team to do its own work. The new employees quickly inferred that al-Rumayyan wasn't interested in pointed questions from them about the Vision Fund.

Further raising eyebrows at the fund was a move by SoftBank to pour much of the Vision Fund into ride-hailing companies around the world. PIF had already put $3.5 billion into Uber and didn't want the Vision Fund to dive further into the same industry. Yet Son plowed ahead and bought stakes in Uber clones around the globe.

Soon after, SoftBank informed the Saudi fund and the Abu Dhabi fund Mubadala about the WeWork deal. When both expressed uneasiness, Misra, who had been wary of the WeWork investment from the beginning, didn't push them.

Neumann, who had become friendly with al-Rumayyan, had separately tried to woo him. They had dinner with Michael Gross in London. Gross spooked al-Rumayyan's security team when he snapped pictures with drinks in the frame. (The consumption of alcohol is illegal in Saudi Arabia.) Al-Rumayyan's security team insisted Gross delete his pictures. The charm session didn't yield any checks.

With the Saudis cool on the WeWork investment, the Vision Fund had to stay out. SoftBank had few options to fund the deal, save for one: its own money. The Japanese conglomerate was in the process of preparing an IPO in Japan of its telecom business. That IPO would be one of the largest ever in Japan, and by listing it publicly, SoftBank could sell off its stake there to public market investors and raise enough money to cover a $20 billion buyout of WeWork.

Son was hyper-focused on the WeWork deal and bringing Neumann's triangle to life. He decided to move forward: SoftBank would put up its own money to get it done.

By the week before the christmas break, berrent, minson, and even Neumann were breathing sighs of relief. Neumann's own negotiations over his deal were done—nonviolent felonies and all. Just as WeWork's staff was ready to leave for the holidays, Minson, Berrent, and others spoke to Son's longtime consigliere, Ron Fisher, who was also a member of WeWork's board, to iron out a few minor final terms that they quickly resolved. After months of exhausting work, the deal was done.

Congratulations, Fisher told Minson and Berrent. He'd be sending over some last paperwork to sign, he told the WeWork team. This is going to be amazing, he said.

The executive team retreated for the holidays. They were on the cusp of something huge. Many longtime staff—Minson and Berrent included—were set to get checks for millions. All the investors other than SoftBank were going to get paid out. WeWork's startup journey was about to come to an end. It was ready for a new SoftBank-owned chapter—a future of expansion for years to come.

In tokyo, the mood was less ebullient.

Aside from Son, collective dread had been building inside Soft-Bank for months over the WeWork deal. Misra cautioned against the purchase, as did other top deputies. It was too much money, particularly given that the Vision Fund wouldn't be picking up the tab, they warned Son.

Son spent months brushing them off. He was dead set on getting it done.

"WeWork is the next Alibaba," he told his investors.

By early December, Son saw all the pieces coming together. SoftBank's Japan telecom unit—the piggybank Son would use to pay for the WeWork deal—was set to list on the stock exchange, where SoftBank would sell a huge chunk of its stake for more than $20 billion.

But as the days of the month ticked by, the winds in the stock markets began to turn. After a long rally, investors worried the tech sector overall was overheated, not just in Japan, but around the globe. SoftBank's shares began to fall, and fall. Adding to its troubles were a major outage of SoftBank's own mobile network in Japan and concerns from the Arab investors about the forthcoming WeWork deal, which had been reported in *The Wall Street Journal*. In one day SoftBank's stock fell 4.9 percent. The next day it was down 2 percent. Then 3.5 percent.

Tens of billions in value were vaporizing.

Still, Son pressed on. On December 19, the telecom IPO proceeded. SoftBank raised $24 billion, a decent price and more than enough cash to proceed. But the next morning when the stock market opened, the newly spun-off telecom company's shares plummeted 15 percent, a terrible performance in Tokyo's relatively stable stock market. It was one of the worst IPOs ever in Japan.

Spooked investors pushed SoftBank's stock down further still. It dropped 4.7 percent on December 20 as investors absorbed the news. The next day it dropped another 2.3 percent.

The fall was getting out of control. It seemed as if it could have no floor. Normally, Son wouldn't give the share price so much attention. But he had built SoftBank up by relying heavily on debt—something that always caused his investors concern. Now, if SoftBank's stock continued to fall, the company's lenders could demand SoftBank repay some of the loans, immediately, quickly forcing a cash crunch at the giant conglomerate.

While Son had resisted months of pressure from within his organization, SoftBank's CFO, Yoshimitsu Goto, warned Son that shareholders would revolt further if the WeWork deal went ahead. It could send SoftBank's stock into a downward spiral.

The WeWork buyout was simply untenable, he told him. The deal had to be called off.

Neumann spent the final days of 2018 with his family in Hawaii, relaxing on the island of Kauai. He was spending time with his new friend, the surfing legend Laird Hamilton, in one of the world's most storied surf spots. As he rode the waves, he was exhilarated about what would come next at WeWork. The surfing that week was treacherous at times. Neumann broke his finger while surfing with Hamilton on what he later described as an eighteen-foot wave.

Then, on Christmas Eve, Neumann's iPhone rang. It was Son.

There was a problem, Son said. He explained that SoftBank's stock had gotten hit so hard by the sell-off in tech stocks that they didn't have the money to pay for WeWork anymore. The deal was dead.

Neumann couldn't quite process what Son was saying. The deal was *done*?

Neumann called Berrent and frantically relayed what Son had said. He texted Minson and asked him to call him the following day when he was done celebrating Christmas with his family.

It was a shock to all of them. They huddled by phone. Neumann wanted to try to resurrect the deal. Surely Son could be convinced, he thought. He had been so excited about the promise of buying WeWork. If only Neumann could meet him in person, perhaps he could sway Son once again, Neumann thought.

Son happened to be in Hawaii at the same time, and Neumann quickly flew over to Maui to meet him.

Neumann reverted to a simple pitch that he hoped would play to Son's insecurities: the fear of missing out. Now was a unique moment in time to get such a monster deal done, he told Son. Everything was lined up, and WeWork's business was still booming in

December despite the tech turmoil in the stock market. If Son didn't get in now, he'd miss out on the deal of a lifetime, Neumann told him.

Son was receptive, but told Neumann he simply couldn't do it, blaming the market and his CFO. They talked several times over a few days and discussed what SoftBank could still do. Son eventually agreed to invest an additional $2 billion in WeWork—$1 billion of new cash, $1 billion to buy out existing investors.

It was a small consolation prize, but would at least open up a way for Neumann to put on a good face before the whole staff.

As he explained what had happened to his team, though, everyone realized the unspoken reality. One billion dollars wouldn't go far. Without SoftBank's continued largesse, WeWork was going to need a new way to find billions. SoftBank was the biggest fish in the private markets; there simply weren't others with billions to shower on them.

WeWork, they all realized, was going to have to go public.

PART IV

CHAPTER 28

Diseconomies of Scale

A S A CREW FROM CNBC SET UP CAMERAS IN A CONFERENCE room at the Microsoft Theater in downtown Los Angeles, Adam Neumann and Ashton Kutcher strode through the doors.

It was January 9, 2019, and WeWork's giant Global Summit was in full swing. Thousands of employees had flown to the city, where they would spend three days shuttling among their downtown L.A. hotels, parties, and company seminars. In addition to a big announcement—Neumann had renamed WeWork the We Company—WeWork executives were expecting Neumann to boast about the new investment from SoftBank and turn the narrative away from the collapsed larger deal.

Neumann arrived at the CNBC set looking awful. He was clad in a baggy white T-shirt with "MADE BY WE" written six times in all caps in different bright colors. He had huge bags under his eyes. His hair was frizzy. He was midway through a New Year's detox diet, he told aides—one that apparently sapped his energy. He asked for an espresso with clarified butter to perk up.

He had been a fount of charisma the day before, when he announced to the staff the latest SoftBank funding. But during the CNBC appearance, the only palpable source of energy came from his longtime friend Kutcher. The actor was hosting WeWork's Creator Awards startup contest that week, but in the interview he played the role of Neumann's hype man.

The host, Deirdre Bosa, questioned Neumann about the Soft-Bank buyout collapsing, insisting it must have been a blow to see a $20 billion deal mostly evaporate.

Neumann tried to frame the downsized deal—in which he got $1 billion of new money from SoftBank—as a huge win.

"Our balance sheet has north of $6 billion on it," he told Bosa, looking directly at her. "It's above and beyond what we need to fund the company for the next"—he briefly paused, shifting his eyes down to the lower-right corners as though to do some math—"four to five years."

It was a timeline that suggested WeWork had plenty of room to keep racing forward without worrying about money. But it wasn't true. It wasn't anywhere close.

BY THE BEGINNING OF 2019, WEWORK HAD ACHIEVED ENORMOUS scale. It was gearing up to add more than twenty million square feet of office space that year—nearly the equivalent of the entire office market of downtown Kansas City. By midyear it would have more than 500,000 members, larger than the population of Minneapolis. In midtown Manhattan, it had become like Starbucks during its expansion blitz of the 2000s, with its black flags with "WeWork" written in white popping up outside brick buildings on seemingly every other block. Its swag was also omnipresent. WeWork T-shirts dotted the subways. When it rained, WeWork-issued "Do What You Love" umbrellas sprang up on sidewalks.

This scale should have meant enormous savings. A company adding a Kansas City's worth of office space should be able to ne-gotiate great prices; it should need far fewer people working in administration at headquarters for every office.

WeWork's CFO, Artie Minson, had long touted the financial benefits of this expansion. "This is a business where scale matters,"

Minson told Bloomberg in 2018. "We're building global supply chain capabilities."

He was referring to economies of scale, a crucial elixir for any company aiming to improve its margins and undercut smaller competitors. The reality for WeWork, though, was diseconomies of scale. The bigger the company got, the more it managed to spend. Neumann's desire to prioritize rapid growth above all else meant there was no time to slow down and take stock of what was going wrong.

Spending had topped $3.5 billion in 2018, but revenue that year was just $1.8 billion. WeWork was bleeding cash. Back in its 2014 pitch to investors, WeWork predicted it would have $941 million of operating income—*profit*—in 2018. Instead, the metric was a loss of $1.7 billion. WeWork lost more than $3,000 every minute in 2018.

This was a particularly striking amount of money to lose, given that in 2000 Mark Dixon's serviced office company, Regus, which essentially had the same business model and a similarly torrid growth rate, nearly broke even, reporting a tiny loss of less than $6 million. Even Uber and Lyft—known for their extremely heavy losses—were at least curtailing their losses as they grew. WeWork's losses simply grew with the company, quarter after quarter.

Waste was everywhere. You could reach out and touch it.

Take the bright pieces of modern lounge furniture that adorned WeWork's lobbies, key to the company's image. Some couches were electric blue, with giant cushions. Others were a light orange, the color of an almost-ripe mango. There were simplistic mid-century modern designs paired with minimalist chairs; there were obtrusive, billowy pieces that dominated a corner of a room. They were splayed on the company's Instagram account, its website, its advertisements.

Given the scale of WeWork's operation, it would seem easy, then, to order lots of these couches on the cheap. A whole team of WeWork employees was even devoted to this effort. By 2019, the furniture and fixtures team, in concert with the logistics and warehouse teams, was in charge of sourcing economical couch and chair designs and negotiating deals with suppliers. The idea was to have thousands of pieces of furniture on hand months in advance of when they were needed. Factories in China would make the couches, which would get put into containers, sail across the Pacific Ocean on a giant ship, and then sit in warehouses in places like New Jersey. It was all quite impressive.

But other parts of the sprawling company had different plans. WeWork's chief creative officer and Neumann's friend, Adam Kimmel, the scion of a real estate empire who spent much of his career creating a high-end menswear line of clothing, would decide he didn't like a certain design of furniture that had been ordered from China en masse months earlier. Locations about to open should get different furniture, he would assert. Once, he told his designers to not use any more of a huge order of custom couches due to the color. *Orange isn't working,* he said.

Designers had to scramble. They'd order replacements quickly, sometimes paying retail or near-retail prices for couches. Many would cost multiple thousands of dollars. Sometimes employees would simply go to West Elm and buy sofas, putting them on the company Amex. If couches were running late, they sometimes were airfreighted to make it in time, an outrageously expensive endeavor that could cost thousands of extra dollars per shipment.

Meanwhile, hundreds of pieces of lower-cost furniture sitting in a New Jersey warehouse, prudently ordered well ahead of time, went to waste. Rows of couches would pile up unused—set for disposal. WeWork would sometimes have warehouse sales, inviting staff to rush to New Jersey on a Saturday for the chance to buy $1,000-plus couches from brands like Vitra for $100 or less. One designer put photos on Instagram of her newly furnished apartment, which looked like a pop-up domestic WeWork. Unclaimed brand-new couches that weren't likewise adopted were simply sent to landfills.

Similar tales of cost overruns or rose-colored math adorned the empire.

The real estate team felt unceasing pressure to grow, but it was becoming more difficult to get giant leases at good prices. Employees on the team took to making aggressive projections when they leased some buildings, making assumptions that future members would pay noscbleed prices to rent desks. Construction employees would factor in huge declines in material costs from one year to the next based on little more than optimism.

Duplication was omnipresent. There were once three separate teams working on an "on demand" product for which WeWork members would pay by the hour or day rather than just by the month. Multiple teams were testing separate future ID card access systems. Regional teams sold desks to large corporations, while teams in headquarters did the same. Staffers in regional offices were devoted to digital marketing teams that hunted for new members. Many of their efforts were duplicated by someone else on the marketing team in New York.

Dave Fano's product team was working on a high-end version of WeWork—a more expensive look, feel, and price—not dissimilar to one being developed separately by the U.S. WeWork team under Arik Benzino, or one developed in Asia under Christian Lee. Fights began breaking out among fiefdoms; regional leaders wanted their own teams and sparred with those like Fano who were trying to centralize decision making. Sometimes a third bureaucracy, special products, fought over turf, too. The constant tussling became so much that Fano, who was once running much of the company, was pushed out in the spring. Multiple executives started to call it Game of Thrones.

Budgets swelled and swelled. Over the years, Neumann would frequently look at growing costs and demand cutbacks. But cutting wasn't easy. Affected executives would protest, pointing out that scrapping one initiative or laying off staff would make it harder to grow revenue. If the enterprise division had fewer salespeople, for instance, it couldn't fill as many desks. Presented with such arguments, Neumann often sided with the aggrieved staffer; budgets stayed big.

WeWork's tech staff was a parable for the entire company. As part of Neumann's desire to position WeWork more as a tech company, as he had long contended it was, the number of people it had working in tech swelled to more than fifteen hundred. It was an enormous number. By comparison, the Snapchat maker, Snap Inc., an actual tech company, had fewer than three thousand employees, including many in non-tech jobs. Hundreds of millions of dollars gushed into the tech apparatus at WeWork, where salaries ran high in order to be competitive in San Francisco. Given the steep investment, one might have expected the department to produce revolutionary tech that would supercharge WeWork's office business. But instead, the team was rudderless, with staff scattered between a problem-plagued billing system, an eclectic array of acquisitions like Meetup and Conductor, and other random projects.

What WeWork called cutting-edge new developments had comically simplistic results. For instance, the company boasted about how its artificial intelligence systems and sensors could yield amazing insights about how people used space. The takeaways seemed unremarkable—or even obvious to the naked eye. One set of sensors revealed that members like working near windows in common areas, while another showed long lines at a coffee station. WeWork should add another barista, the AI team concluded.

Other parts of the organization behaved as though WeWork were already a Fortune 500 company. In the spring of 2019, members of the company's video team were dispatched to work on a video to accompany the company's "global impact" report intended to demonstrate how WeWork's members were spurring economic growth. The team flew to numerous cities around the United States as well as the Bahamas, where WeWork didn't have an office, and they spent two days with underwater cameras shooting an organization that worked with coral reefs. An employee estimated the endeavor cost more than $200,000 and amounted to a one-minute video that appeared briefly on the company's home page.

· · ·

Beyond wework's operational inefficiencies, neumann's inclinations for new business ventures—often enmeshed with his personal interests—continued unrestrained.

Neumann gave Michael Gross the green light to hire a top former Disney executive to start We Entertainment, a hazy new business line that sought to rent recording studios and hold movie screenings. Meanwhile, Neumann, Ashton Kutcher, and Guy Oseary, a talent manager famous for representing Madonna, tried to bring WeWork into Hollywood, pitching studios a new *Shark Tank*–like show modeled on the Creator Awards.

Neumann issued bizarre real estate edicts, including directing WeWork to pay nearly $450 million for a 50 percent stake in San Francisco's Parkmerced, a sprawling apartment complex home to nearly ten thousand people. Aides were confused by the idea, given that the apartments, built in the 1940s, were miles away from downtown San Francisco, not to mention that aging rental apartments had nothing to do with WeWork's core business. Hoping to build new apartments on vacant land in the complex, Neumann put down a $20 million deposit, which WeWork lost when it later backed out of the deal.

Sometimes the pursuits were even more peripheral. Gross and Neumann briefly became obsessed with buying a coveted Wu Tang Clan rap album of which only a single copy was made. The disgraced pharmaceutical executive Martin Shkreli had paid $2 million for it, but it was seized by the federal government after he went to prison. Gross and Neumann sent internal emails to other members of the staff to see how they could buy it, but the effort never went anywhere.

More troubling were Neumann's deals with his friends.

On at least two occasions, he used SoftBank's money to invest in companies with little clear connection to WeWork other than that they were run by his friends: Ashton Kutcher and Laird Hamilton, a star of the 1990s pro-surfing scene.

Both ventures were financed from a $200 million pot of money from SoftBank, meant to be a mini venture capital fund. Dubbed the Creator Fund, the concept was pretty simple. WeWork would hunt for startups in the general area of "transformative companies driving the future of work" and give them SoftBank's money, and then WeWork and SoftBank would split the profits. WeWork hired a whole staff for the fund who scoured for entrepreneurs building startups that fit this description, doling out small checks to the best of them, usually for less than $5 million. Many of these investments went to winners of WeWork's Creator Awards in cities around the United States and the world.

Kutcher's and Hamilton's ventures, however, received more than $25 million each, making them by far the largest two investments in the fund. Neither had any clear connection with the "future of work."

The first investment went to Laird Superfood, a tiny startup founded by Hamilton in 2015 that made nondairy coffee creamer, juice, and other "plant-based superfood products" meant to give an energy boost. In the fall of 2018, Neumann struck the deal to lead a $32 million investment. It was an enormous sum for a company's Series A investment; WeWork's Series A was just $17 million, and even that was considered large. The deal was completed not long before Neumann's late-December trip to Hawaii, where—he later told *Fast Company*—he went surfing with Hamilton.

Soon after, WeWork started offering Hamilton's coffee creamer and energy-infused juice throughout the empire. There was a set of Laird Superfood dispensers at 85 Broad Street in Manhattan, which failed to generate much interest.*

Kutcher's involvement came around the same time. Neumann had been hanging out with the star of *That '70s Show* since he first met Rebekah. Kutcher, who was frequently seen in WeWork's of-

---

* Amazingly, Hamilton's wasn't the only energy-boosting coffee creamer in the Creator Fund portfolio: in December 2018 the fund invested more than $4 million in Kitu Life coffee, a small company run by WeWork members. Nearly one-fifth of the Creator Fund had thus been earmarked for the energy-boosting nondairy coffee creamer sector. (Internal WeWork documents detailing Creator Fund investments, WeWork, 2020.)

fices over the years visiting Neumann, had become a successful venture capital investor in his own right. He was an early investor in Uber, Airbnb, and Spotify—a particularly impressive roster for a part-time VC—making him a good face for the Creator Awards. Neumann had enlisted Kutcher to emcee the awards at the company's Global Summit and to help work with WeWork on future Creator Awards.

Now WeWork, at the behest of Neumann, was poised to go far deeper into business with the actor turned investor. Around the time of Global Summit, word came down: WeWork was getting ready to commit $38 million to Kutcher's venture capital fund, Sound Ventures, using $30 million from the Creator Fund and another $8 million from WeWork itself. Staff were confused: Why would they invest money from their own startup investment fund into someone else's venture capital fund?

It wasn't the only benefit WeWork offered Kutcher. Around the same time, WeWork leased a building on Wilshire Boulevard in Los Angeles. The company was in discussions for a deal in which Kutcher's Sound Ventures would get *two years* of rent-free space, an enormously generous concession even by WeWork standards. (The deal never ended up getting completed.)

While at Global Summit, Kutcher loudly sang WeWork's praises. In the same CNBC interview during which Neumann said WeWork had four to five years of money left, Kutcher offered an evangelical take on WeWork. He used to think WeWork was just a company renting space, but recently he'd looked under the hood.

"I realized it was a technology company," he said.

And, without a hint of irony, Kutcher explained how WeWork's unique capabilities would allow it to take a leading role in fixing societal ills.

"Through the technology that this company has," Kutcher continued, "it has a greater capacity than any other company in the entire world to bring people together and close that divide between the haves and the have-nots."

· · ·

IN THE WEEKS AFTER GLOBAL SUMMIT FINISHED UP—AFTER NEU-
mann hyped WeWork's future to the audience at the Microsoft
Theater—a prudent company would have recognized the need for
wholesale change.

WeWork's inability to turn a profit was suddenly dangerous.
Without the money Masayoshi Son had pledged for the larger Fortitude deal, the company was going to need billions to keep mate-
rializing from somewhere. WeWork was still spending as though it
had Son's unlimited bank account.

In less than two years, WeWork had burned through nearly
$3 billion of Son's money, yet it was no closer to becoming a profit-
able, sustainable business. If anything, it was further. Yet no one
seemed to be sounding alarms.

Any concerns insiders did have were typically muted. Jen Berrent, Artie Minson, and multiple board members told Neumann that
WeWork should consider slowing its growth. But none were forceful
enough, and efforts to change course tended to be halfhearted—
or too little, too late.

After Global Summit, for instance, Neumann had the company
scale back on some ventures imagined under Fortitude. His vision
for a Powered by We division that renovated offices for companies in
their own office buildings was largely halted. WeGrow's expansion
was put on hold, and the We Company renaming ended up being
more rhetorical packaging than indicative of any strategic shift.

Still, WeWork's main business continued its frenetic pace of
growth, complete with heavy spending. Everyone involved was
banking on Neumann's ability to keep doing what he'd been doing:
persuading new investors to buy into the WeWork dream at an
ever-higher valuation. All they had to do was convince the public
markets of the promise in an IPO, a move that could provide a wave
of cash to wash away the company's sins.

CHAPTER 29

Guitar House

AFTER THE COLLAPSE OF THE BIG SOFTBANK BUYOUT, GLOBAL Summit, and a stop in Miami—where Neumann spoke at JPMorgan's private conference for the bank's so-called ultrahigh-net-worth clients—Adam and Rebekah Neumann decamped in January 2019 to the serene confines of Marin County in the Bay Area. It was a long-planned trip. They intended to spend months there, hoping to meld into Silicon Valley culture and the tech companies Neumann saw as WeWork's peers.

The family moved into a house they'd bought the prior summer for $21 million in Corte Madera, a ritzy, bland-but-beautiful suburb ten miles north of San Francisco, in the shadow of the area's largest peak, Mount Tamalpais. In the spring, the surrounding hills turn a vibrant green. Nestled amid a grove of eucalyptus trees, the thirteen-thousand-square-foot mansion had views of the San Francisco skyline, topped by Salesforce Tower, where WeWork had its West Coast headquarters. It had a racquetball court and a pool with a giant waterslide. In the house's center there was a room shaped like a guitar—a sinuous-walled recording studio that connected to a skinny guitar neck of a hallway. A prior house on the property—since demolished—had belonged to the rock promoter Bill Graham, and so the press gave the home the moniker Guitar House.

The Bay Area offered Adam Neumann a place to unwind after

the troubles in December. He commuted to the office in the Salesforce Tower, which he conceived as a monument to WeWork's Silicon Valley ambitions. He often strolled barefoot around the halls.

THE CHANGE OF SCENERY CAME AT A TIME IN WHICH NEUMANN
seemed rudderless. In the wake of the SoftBank comedown, he
hunted for some way to define WeWork beyond just offices.

To aides, the failed SoftBank deal seemed to haunt Neumann
for months. The once-energetic leader seemed withdrawn, with
less spark and zeal. He had gotten so close—so close to being tied
at the hip to the deep-pocketed Son; so close to having unlimited
funds and staying out of the public markets. His mindset seemed
confused—not fully accepting the reality that WeWork wasn't on
track to be the $10 trillion company he'd dreamed about with Son.

He tried to make inroads at the big Silicon Valley companies, a
crowd he'd never meshed with. He'd met Ruth Porat, Google's
CFO, and both he and Bruce Dunlevie tried to persuade her to
join WeWork's board, to no avail. He hotly pursued a meeting with
Tim Cook, CEO of Apple. Neumann and his lieutenants pitched
Apple on the idea that a supercharged version of the WeWork key
card could be tied into the iPhone. Eventually, Cook agreed to a
meeting, and Neumann was so excited he asked aides if he should
get his hair done, noting that Cook was gay.

Still, nothing concrete resulted from these meetings—not from
Google, not from Apple, and not even from another startup closer
to WeWork in age and valuation: Airbnb.

In multiple meetings with the San Francisco home rental startup,
Neumann pitched Airbnb's CEO, Brian Chesky, on a plan to re-
invigorate WeLive and spread it around the world. Chesky, despite
a smaller valuation of $35 billion, had much of the credibility in
Silicon Valley Neumann seemed to crave. Airbnb lost less money
and had a more efficient business model; Chesky was respected by
many top venture capitalists.

Neumann angled to cultivate a partnership. He told Chesky that WeWork and Airbnb would build ten thousand apartment units they would rent on Airbnb. Chesky's initial reaction was that ten thousand was a bit small for Airbnb to get involved. Airbnb lists millions of homes on its website, so a big effort for thousands just wouldn't be worth the time. At a subsequent meeting Neumann came back with a new plan: they would build ten *million* apartments. Chesky was bewildered. Where did Neumann think they would get the money to build ten million apartments? he wondered. If each one cost $100,000 to build—a figure they'd discussed—that would mean $1 *trillion*.

They never struck a deal.

As he was engaging in erratic efforts to drum up new business, Neumann showed flashes of anger. He was upset about the SoftBank deal falling apart, and even as he made efforts to revive the deal with Son, he repeatedly told aides he wanted to "fuck Masa up." He was also frustrated when Son didn't let Neumann participate in the $1 billion share purchase he completed for other employees and investors. Son figured Neumann had already taken enough cash out.

The aftermath had other effects. Neumann wasn't humbled by the deal's collapse. Instead, having been abandoned at the altar by his mentor, his insecurity grew. And so did his ego.

Senior executives would be asked to fly to San Francisco with little notice for an in-person meeting with Neumann, only to wait for hours. Sometimes he didn't meet them at all; on several occasions, he had left the country by the time the staffer arrived, or he was there and simply wouldn't have time for the person. Other meetings were endless. Midway through some long executive sessions, Neumann's assistant would walk in and set out silverware and a napkin in front of him, then bring him a meal prepared by his personal chef. As his colleagues continued to talk about the topic at hand without any meals of their own, Neumann would devour his lunch. More than once, co-workers observed him pull his plate up to his mouth and lick it clean.

Neumann continued to flaunt his wealth, a constant reminder to employees that he had been able to sell more of his shares than they had. When staff went to his house, they often found three nannies attending to the five children—sometimes wearing matching white polo shirts with *N* stitched into them.

He became more focused on using his money to buy into other startups, including a medical marijuana company and Selina, a company with a similar business model to WeWork but focused on upscale hostels.

Cars piled up. Neumann was typically whisked around in a Maybach, a superluxury car built by a division of Mercedes-Benz, that cost in excess of $200,000. He also acquired a Tesla, an Escalade, and others. He often drove in a convoy—with a driver in an otherwise empty car or SUV trailing the Maybach. It served a useful purpose for the frequent meetings and job interviews he'd hold in his car. When the meeting was finished, both cars pulled over, his riding companion was ushered out, and the driver took the person back to the office. One executive was shown the door in the middle of gridlocked traffic on the Long Island Expressway—instructed to find the chase car somewhere behind them in the traffic.

Money flooded into the Neumanns' real estate portfolio. Beyond the California house, they expanded their personal real estate empire in New York. They embarked on a renovation of the $15 million Tudor-style home they'd bought in Pound Ridge north of the city, adding two thousand square feet to the existing thirteen thousand. Despite enlarging the residence, they actually reduced the nine bedrooms to just five supersized bedrooms. They also bought another $3.2 million six-thousand-square-foot house nearby—to use during the renovation.

In Manhattan, the West Eleventh Street townhome they purchased in 2013 was constantly under renovation, to the frustration of neighbors. Ultimately, the Neumanns deemed it too much of a security risk. It was too easy to get in off the street, without a doorman. So instead they rented a giant apartment by Gramercy Park as they hunted for a new house to buy. They found it in the fall of 2017, when they paid $34 million for a spread of apartments at 78 Irving Place, a sandy-brick building built in 1920, just off Gramercy Park and only five blocks from WeWork's headquarters.

Even though the building had just been completely renovated by a developer, the Neumanns combined the fifth-floor unit with the sixth and seventh floors, demolishing walls on one of the floors to create a mammoth master bedroom. On the ground floor they combined the two units, creating a space that was frequently an extension of the office, with WeWork employees dropping by for meetings.

The purchase of so many units gave the couple full control of the building's condo board. It was not unlike Adam Neumann's position at his own company: the Neumanns could make changes with seeming impunity, despite the frustrations of neighbors. Neumann asked three key employees to sit on his condo board: Medina Bardhi, who served multiple tours as Adam Neumann's chief of staff; his longtime aide Stella Templo; and another former chief of staff, Joel Steinhaus.

With the Neumanns largely living in California, senior staff back in New York were left to juggle a hot issue with their Manhattan home—one no one was eager to touch. It was a priority for Rebekah Neumann—first assigned to Artie Minson, then passed off to others.

The task at hand had to do with a cell phone antenna next to the Neumanns' new home. It couldn't stay there, the couple declared, and WeWork executives needed to get it removed.

The reason cited was Rebekah's concern about electromagnetism. The advent of 5G cellular technology in particular seemed to scare her. When she was just eleven, her older brother, then twenty-three, died of cancer, devastating Rebekah and her family. Later, she lost several other close relatives to cancer: her father's brother

(Gwyneth Paltrow's father) and his sister. She often spoke of having a number of phobias around wellness and health. Adam told colleagues that they vaccinated their children on a delayed schedule because of Rebekah's wariness over potential health effects. (The Centers for Disease Control and Prevention warns parents against delaying vaccinations.)

As a result of those phobias, she became obsessed with the potential horrors posed by a 5G antenna. (There's little in the way of scientific research to back up such concerns.) As the couple renovated the Irving Place apartment, her children's rooms were given extra electromagnetic shielding in their walls. Rebekah then decided it still wasn't safe enough. The antenna had to go.

Getting an antenna moved is not a simple task in New York. There is no friendly town clerk or manager to simply ring up and start complaining.

Instead, Minson, who was a veteran of Time Warner Cable, was asked to work his connections to get Verizon or Sprint to find a new home for the antenna. The CFO was in the middle of trying to prepare the company for an IPO, though he did tell the couple he made some calls on the matter.

He didn't make much progress, so others within the organization were called upon. Eventually, the request landed in the lap of Maria Comella, a well-regarded political operative who was a top public affairs and policy executive at WeWork. She had been the chief of staff to Governor Andrew Cuomo of New York and a top aide to Republicans, including Governor Chris Christie of New Jersey. Through the spring, she spent a great deal of time turning to the phone companies and others in an effort to get them to move the antenna—all while on the clock for WeWork.

While WeWork staff worked on their home in New York, the Neumanns brought some comforts of WeWork New York with them to the Bay Area. They tasked WeGrow's staff members with teaching their kids and a few others in the area. The location: the Guitar House.

A teacher from New York was moved out to the Bay Area, and local teachers were hired. Filling out the tiny school were the children of a few others connected to the Neumanns through We-Work. The couple asked the family of Conductor CEO Seth Besmertnik to spend a week or two in California with them. They also hired Neumann's surf coach from Hawaii, Dom Del Rosario, as a full-time instructor. Del Rosario had four children, three of whom were school age, who would join the school in California, too.

The Neumanns' absence at WeGrow in New York was a relief to many, offering the staff a brief respite from the constant whirlwind of changes ordered up by Rebekah Neumann. Teachers started calling the time without her "Festina Lente," the Latin term for "make haste slowly." They could focus on the students and learn how best to teach them.

The couple seemed oblivious to the contradictions inherent to their lifestyle. Even as their stock-sale-funded lives grew more luxurious, even as they used the company for unmistakably—and often extreme—personal gain, the couple frequently talked about how they were all part of the same family as their employees and investors. Earlier, after the purchase of their $15 million home in Pound Ridge, Rebekah Neumann boasted to an interviewer that "we believe in this new Asset Light lifestyle," defined by fewer material goods. She added, "We want to live off of the land."

LIKE MUCH OF THE WE UNIVERSE, THE NEUMANNS' BLEND OF personal and professional crept outward. It wasn't simply a matter of saving money. The Neumanns said they would happily reimburse the company for any staff hours spent on their personal projects. But the pledge didn't always get carried out. Sometimes staff were unaware of the procedures; other times, the lines between business and personal were just too blurry.

In San Jose, in the relatively sparsely developed downtown of

America's tenth most populous city, Neumann was quietly accumulating an enormous swath of property with his own money. Using a local developer named Gary Dillabough, he paid more than $33 million for the Bank of Italy building, an elegant fourteen-story brick tower built in 1925. Nearby, he bought a parking lot for $25 million, struck a deal for a site next to a tech museum, and paid $40 million for an office building that he then leased to WeWork. In all he bought well over $100 million of property in San Jose, mostly throughout 2018 and into early 2019.

Behind it all was a hush-hush plan to make a WeWork city within a city—an urban campus filled with WeWork office buildings, WeLive apartments, WeGrow schools, and anything else in the WeWork family.

Bjarke Ingels drew up the master plan, while Roni Bahar was the main driving force for the concept. The vision was a multibillion-dollar collection of offices and apartments that would serve as a test ground of as-yet-unspecified technology, a kind of "smart city," in which WeWork was angling to be a major player. They imagined a $7 billion development effort that would lead to space for more than thirty thousand new WeWork desks and five thousand WeLive apartments.

Neumann was funding the purchases himself because, at this point, he sensed that justifying spending so much money on property for future development would be a hard sell to his investors. But the intermingling still opened up WeWork and its CEO to the same potential conflicts of interest that had plagued him on earlier personal real estate forays. When *The Wall Street Journal* revealed the San Jose efforts and details on Neumann's purchase of other buildings in January 2019, the story was picked up widely in the media, and the reception was sharply negative.

Neumann committed to transferring the properties to WeWork's real estate fund at cost, though he still seemed not to grasp the intensity of the concerns from outside investors and onlookers who were shocked at the brazen, bad look of it all. He told Bloomberg he didn't understand the concerns because he intended to use the properties to benefit the company and that he'd be making a personal sacrifice in doing so. And to *Business Insider,* he said he was fully aligned with WeWork, telling them he was its largest shareholder.

"WeWork is me," he said. "I am WeWork."

AMONG THOSE WATCHING THESE HEADLINES WERE BRUCE DUN-levie and Steven Langman, Neumann's first two outside board members. Both were crestfallen when SoftBank's deal to buy most of WeWork fell apart. They had come to the precipice of extraordinary success—of cashing out their enormously profitable investments.

Now they wanted another way to sell their stake; they wanted WeWork to go public. And quickly.

They had grown tired of Neumann's antics, and he'd long ago stopped looking to them for close guidance and mentorship. It wasn't a particularly fun position for them—sitting on a board where they approved item after item they personally disagreed with, like the surf pool company and the jet. But Neumann effectively had full control of the company, so they approached their seats on the board largely as advisory. Rocking the boat with a "no" vote was a sure way to fall out of favor with Neumann and lose any chance to influence him, multiple directors figured. Of course, if all the directors had banded together, they could have outvoted Neumann, and he would have been forced to take more drastic measures—like adding seats to the board—if he was intent on pushing a measure through. But banding together to vote down the jet—or anything else—didn't come up.

Langman and Dunlevie thought the public markets could provide Neumann scrutiny in a way they couldn't. Neumann, they figured, would be likely to listen to a stock price more than their nudging or complaining. What's more, once the company was public, their job would largely be done. Sometimes early investors stay on for years, but usually VCs sell quickly, and new board members take their seats.

And, crucially, they also knew WeWork needed more money—more fuel to propel its exponential growth. It was clear that absent a change of heart from SoftBank, the necessary funding lay only in the public markets. It was time, they realized, for WeWork's journey in the private markets to come to an end.

So the two investors, well aware of Neumann's increasing proclivity for self-enrichment, devised a plan to turn it to their own advantage, using a mechanism of power they had in their control: pay. The duo oversaw the board's compensation committee.

They offered Neumann a huge compensation package—one that could make him insanely rich if WeWork continued to do well. They would give him nearly ten *million* shares of stock options if he took WeWork public. The IPO-dependent pay package would give him more than $700 million at WeWork's current valuation. Sweetening the pot, the eventual deal would give him *billions* of additional dollars in stock, although only if WeWork's valuation kept growing on the public markets.

Neumann agreed to the deal but still wanted more. His attorneys at Paul, Weiss had shown him a way of reconfiguring WeWork that would allow him to save substantially on his taxes, if he could pay the long-term capital gains rate rather than standard income taxes. Seeing the potential benefit, he ordered a complete legal reorganization of the company—a heavy effort on the part of company lawyers to reclassify WeWork as something called an "Up-C" structure. He designed it so that he and a handful of favored executives received stock packages with the low-tax structure.

The rest of the company's employees weren't so fortunate. Their stock was unchanged—set to be taxed at the standard rate.

CHAPTER 30

The Plunge Before the Plunge

FROM AROUND THE WORLD, A PARADE OF ADAM NEUMANN'S friends and acquaintances converged on the Republic of the Maldives, a tiny nation made up of twelve hundred small islands in the middle of the Indian Ocean. There were Neumann's childhood pals. His top aides from work. His family. A few of his kids' teachers from WeGrow. His hairdresser. His bodyguard. His surf coach. His surf coach's friends. Numerous nannies.

Neumann was turning forty, and he wanted to celebrate.

It was the final stop on a three-week, multi-leg trip to bring his thirties to a close—a tour that also included time in the Dominican Republic and the Mediterranean.

But the Maldives had a particular allure for him: they were a surfer's paradise.

His typical surf excursions included instructors, Jet Ski drivers, and at least one drone photographer to document the action, but the Maldives trip was different. His main surf instructor, Dom Del Rosario, who had joined Neumann's full-time personal staff in early 2019, brought along a whole squad of his colleagues, including some well-known names from the Hawaii surf scene and an instructor from the Dominican Republic. The surfers and a parade of support staff stayed at their own resort, a fairly luxurious spot called Lohis; Neumann and his friends stayed at the five-star resort One&Only Reethi Rah, where picturesque villas sit out on wooden piers in the ocean.

Topping it all off: Neumann rented an enormous yacht that parked off the atoll in deeper waters. During the week, the CEO held court on the 239-foot *Titania,* a five-story boat that featured a crew of twenty-one, an onboard pool, its own spa, and a grand piano. Its list price was more than $500,000 per week.

The yacht made excursions around the islands, and on one jaunt it got stuck on a sand reef. Neumann, who loved discussing his time in the navy, insisted on giving the crew some directions on how to unmoor the ship. (A similar episode happened on another surfing trip to Costa Rica.)

It was an odd time to be partying on the other side of the world. Neumann's company had just kicked off planning for the most consequential financial move in its history: an initial public offering.

WeWork was finally preparing to go public.

A MONTH BEFORE THE MALDIVES TRIP, ARTIE MINSON WAS GROW-ing anxious.

On March 29, Lyft went public and received a warm welcome from Wall Street investors. The company was the first of a wave of large, aging, and money-losing startups to start trading publicly. It had lost more than $900 million the prior year and showed no clear signs of how it would turn a profit. Yet investors valued the company at $24 billion—more than double its valuation just a few months earlier in a private investment round.

To Minson, it was a great sign. Fast-growing companies without profits were embraced by the markets: the window to go public was wide open. What's more, he thought WeWork had a better business. The finance chief had long been an advocate of an IPO and wished it had moved forward with one earlier. With SoftBank tapped out, it was clear to him that an IPO was the company's only real option for the billions it needed in funding.

WeWork, he told Neumann, needed to go public now.

Just before Neumann left on his birthday globe-trotting, he gave the green light to start preparing. Minson, Berrent, and their respective teams started working furiously to put WeWork's finances and the regulatory systems in place for the offering. It would be a giant push.

Neumann, meanwhile, managed to do some work while away. He summoned a WeWork staffer to fly to the Maldives—an eighteen-hour trek, at minimum—to give him a briefing on the team's progress.

On April 29, 2019, from the Maldives, Neumann had staff compose an email to WeWork's employees, letting them know the company was moving ahead with an IPO. "I do not have an exact date or timeline to share with you," he wrote to employees, "but I wanted you to know first that this process has started."

It was welcome news for the staff. WeWork often paid less than other startups. Instead they had sold would-be employees on the mission and the potential riches set to come from stock they handed out. Some who joined in the early years were sitting on millions in paper wealth. Soon, everyone could get rich.

An IPO isn't just a graduation ceremony for a company transitioning from the world of private investment to the public stock market. It is more akin to an election campaign. Companies truly must *sell* themselves to the public, giving public market investors pages upon pages of financial statements, as well as a coherent message about how their companies make money and why they will thrive in the future. A key component is the valuation; a company wants to make sure the number is a high one. The larger the valuation, the more the company makes from each share it sells—and the richer its existing investors become.

Crucial to this laborious process is an investment bank—or several—to serve as middlemen, guides for the company on its months-long, grueling trek to the public markets. The bankers know the investors: they know what they like to hear, what spurs demand, and what scares them. Most of all, they are experts at figuring out what valuation stock market investors will assign to a company.

The role of a sherpa in an IPO is a coveted one on Wall Street—particularly for the highest-profile and most highly valued companies like WeWork. First, there's the likely windfall. On a single IPO the size of WeWork, investment banks generally share a pool of fees that can exceed $100 million.

Beyond the prospect of a big payout, banks covet the prestige and bragging rights associated with leading an IPO. The most important role is the "lead left"—a term that derives from the order of how banks are listed on regulatory documents filed with the SEC. The lead bank is listed to the left of others.

Bankers had been ingratiating themselves for years with Neumann and his team with this in mind. WeWork was considered the most valuable startup in the country after Uber, and bankers at JPMorgan Chase, Goldman Sachs, and Morgan Stanley all hoped their institution would be christened lead left.

By May, WeWork was ready to choose. Back from the Indian Ocean, Neumann and his deputies organized a "bake-off," the term for a long-standing Wall Street ritual in which bankers pitch for a role on an IPO.

In theory, a company would want bankers to come in with a sober, honest assessment of a company's strengths, its weaknesses, and a realistic range of how public market investors might value the company. Instead, the bake-off itself often becomes part of the marketing process. Banks frequently pitch a lofty range of expected valuations to get in the good graces of the executive team, only then to spend subsequent months walking the high expectations back. Uber, for instance, was told its valuation could be as high as

$120 billion in an IPO, though it later went public for roughly $40 billion less.

JPMorgan had been tempting WeWork with extremely bullish projections for years, and Neumann had used them to urge Masayoshi Son to push up the valuation when he invested. Neumann and Artie Minson would talk about the banks' prior projections for WeWork's valuation almost as fact, using them to justify why companies should accept WeWork's stock instead of cash, or why an executive's stock bonus was worth far more than it appeared on paper.

UNDER NEUMANN'S WATCHFUL EYE, A SMALL WEWORK TEAM gathered to weigh the performance of the three banks vying to lead the IPO: Artie Minson, Michael Gross, and Ilan Stern, who had been a hedge fund and venture investor and had recently taken over managing Neumann's personal wealth.

First up for the WeWork ring-kissing was Morgan Stanley, led by its star tech banker Michael Grimes. Grimes had played a central role in the IPOs of most top Silicon Valley companies, including Google, Facebook, LinkedIn, Snapchat, and Uber. He was known for theatrical moves to win over the entrepreneurs. For Uber, he worked shifts as an Uber driver and made a presentation outlining what he'd learned behind the wheel when he pitched their team. Yet, unlike bankers from Goldman Sachs and JPMorgan, Grimes and his team had a more limited history with Neumann.

Still, WeWork's team was impressed by Grimes's knowledge of the business and his insights into how Morgan Stanley would sell the company to investors. The bank had put together a sample video of what WeWork might show potential investors and had already written a draft of an IPO prospectus—the key document companies use to sell themselves to investors and share with the Securities and Exchange Commission. But he offered words of warning: Lyft's stock had started to fall, and Grimes came to We-Work's headquarters in between meetings for Uber's IPO, which would take place later that week. Grimes was frank. Investors were wary about Uber's losses. And they would be even more nervous about WeWork, particularly without the right guidance. WeWork still hadn't proven that it could become a profitable business. He'd find skeptics among investors, he said.

You need us, Grimes told Neumann.

Morgan Stanley's range: Bankers would market WeWork to potential investors at a valuation of between $25 billion and $65 billion.

Neumann thought there would be fewer skeptics than Grimes suggested. "You're not scaling up your enthusiasm as high as it can be," he told Grimes.

NEXT CAME GOLDMAN SACHS, THE BANK THAT PRIDED ITSELF ON having more sophistication and smarts than its rivals on Wall Street.

Goldman had developed deep ties with Neumann over the previous years. The bank helped him raise money in China. Neumann became friends with Lloyd Blankfein before he left as CEO at the end of 2018, meeting him for dinners and calling him for advice. Shortly after Blankfein's successor, David Solomon, took over as CEO, Solomon dined with Neumann and played him some of his music (the CEO was known for his hobby of playing occasional gigs as a dance club DJ). Neumann showed him WeWork's offices at 85 Broad Street, Goldman's former headquarters.

Among those leading Goldman's charge was Kim Posnett, a top tech banker who was based in New York and a particular favorite of Neumann's. After graduating from Yale in 1999, Posnett worked as a math tutor in Los Angeles, where she tried out for a few acting roles. She never gained traction in Hollywood and instead went to Wharton to get her MBA.

The Goldman team handed Neumann a picture-filled book,

tailor-made to appeal to his predilections and his sense of self. They knew Neumann struggled to read because of his dyslexia, so they didn't include much in the way of text—mostly using evocative images. The cover page used WeWork's tagline, "Do What You Love," scrawled in cursive font. Its second page featured inspirational quotations from Mother Teresa, Lin-Manuel Miranda, Steve Jobs, and Bob Marley ("Love the life you live. Live the life you love").

When they did use numbers, they knew the right ones to include. One page was headlined "Your Path to $1 Trillion," drawing out how the company could hit that target over the next decade and a half. The Goldman team compared WeWork to Salesforce, Facebook, and the videoconferencing company Zoom. WeWork, Goldman noted, was growing faster than almost all of them. Of course, each of those companies was profitable, but Goldman didn't dwell on that disparity.

At the end of the book, Goldman laid out its range, which was calculated a slightly different way than Morgan Stanley's. WeWork, it projected, could expect to be valued between $61 billion and $96 billion.

Neumann was elated. He loved the pitch and was thrilled with the valuation projections. Goldman clearly got WeWork, he thought. At $96 billion, WeWork would be worth more than General Electric, more than CVS. It would be worth more than *Goldman Sachs*. Sweetening the pot: Goldman was bullish about WeWork's ability to borrow. It was readying a plan to get WeWork $10 billion of loans.

FINALLY CAME JPMORGAN. THE TEAM WALKED IN THINKING IT had built enough trust with Neumann to win the listing without much trouble. Artie Minson even told the bankers before the pitch that they were the favorites. Jamie Dimon, the firm's CEO, to whom Neumann had often referred as "his personal banker," didn't join the meeting. He sent a letter that told Neumann and his team,

"You have the full resources of the firm as you embark on this phase of your journey."

Pressure was high on Noah Wintroub. The JPMorgan banker, who'd met Neumann six-plus years earlier and helped him with his Chase account, had stayed in close contact with this exact end goal in mind. JPMorgan was still lagging behind its main rivals in the constant battle to win the top tech IPOs. Its team had just lost the lead position on Peloton's IPO to Goldman Sachs even after Wintroub and others had spent years helping the exercise-bike startup raise money. And while JPMorgan did lead Lyft's IPO—only after pledging not to work with Uber for the next eighteen months—the initial euphoria had turned to disappointment when Lyft's stock plunged below its IPO price in its second day of trading.

Wintroub's presentation lacked the pomp of Goldman's. Rather than emphasize the prospect of reaching $1 trillion, Wintroub talked about WeWork's strategic strengths—how the company was on the path to reshaping the way in which large corporations would rent real estate. A follow-up slide deck sent to WeWork called out WeWork's "superpowers" of "scale" and "technology." One slide in that deck noted that WeWork's future cash flow—a form of profit—was "TBD," adding that it will be an "important metric." In his in-person pitch, Wintroub landed on a price that was still high for a real estate company, but sober compared with the expectations of WeWork.

JPMorgan's range: $46 billion to $63 billion.

It landed with a whimper. Neumann was upset with the bank he'd known so well. It was a terrible pitch, he thought. He berated Wintroub, telling him that despite all his years following WeWork, he just didn't understand what the company was about, repeating a common refrain from their earlier meetings. Wintroub didn't believe in WeWork, Neumann told him. Twisting the knife, he told him that Goldman did. They think the market believes in us, Neumann said.

"They're gonna take over," he told Wintroub.

Wintroub couldn't wrap his head around the possibility that he had spent countless hours over the last five years catering to Neumann's every whim, only to end up the loser. Surely Jamie Dimon would be upset. JPMorgan had been investing in WeWork and Neumann for years, not just with hours of wining and dining, but with actual money. The bank's asset management arm had invested in WeWork when it was valued at $1.5 billion and JPMorgan had become a huge lender to the company, as well as Neumann personally. When he wanted a loan tied to his stock, JPMorgan was there. For his most expensive houses, JPMorgan was his lender; it gave him more than $97 million in mortgages and other loans.

At this point, most startups would have made a final decision. Neumann, ever the negotiator, picked another tack. He wouldn't officially appoint any bank the left lead "underwriter" until as late as possible. It was a decision that would pit the banks against one another for months to come—precisely the hypercompetitive environment Neumann liked. In one sense, it was savvy: banks would continue to do backflips to win him over. The unintended consequence, though, was that bankers would hold off on informing Neumann bluntly about reality. Neumann, they knew, didn't like bad news, and tended to look elsewhere for a more optimistic opinion.

PART OF THE REASON NEUMANN WAS HOLDING OUT WAS THAT HE wanted the best possible debt package from his lead bank—billions more to keep WeWork's machine running.

Soon after the pitch, Goldman's bankers, elated they were now the favorites, got to work on a deal to provide up to $10 billion in debt. It was a complex arrangement that relied on the profits coming out of individual office locations—before accounting for costs at headquarters. WeWork's borrowing capabilities would expand over time up to $10 billion. While the overall business was a fire hose of losses, much of that was in the expenses at WeWork HQ—

the legions of tech engineers, the administration, the jet, and the extraneous businesses. Goldman figured if they confined their loans to WeWork's locations, they could take over those offices and limit their losses if WeWork ever failed to pay back its debts.

The plan was pure genius in Neumann's eyes. Goldman had seen the magical elixir of WeWork's business that had eluded others. And more important, $10 billion—even over several years— was so much money they could even consider staying private longer. Clearly Goldman preferred that WeWork do an IPO, but Neumann at least wanted the ability to avoid it or push it off.

Goldman's CEO, David Solomon, indicated to Neumann personally that the deal would get done. Neumann would later tell other bankers that Solomon "looked into his soul and knew what I wanted to do," referring to the debt deal. Goldman was slated to do well itself: the bank told WeWork it would charge $200 million in up-front fees just to make the loans.

But by late June, about eight weeks after the bake-off meetings, Goldman began to waver. Rather than stand behind the full $10 billion itself, Goldman told WeWork it would likely be able to guarantee only $3.65 billion of the debt, and it would work with other banks like JPMorgan to raise the rest.

To Neumann, this failure to commit was a betrayal. Still shaken from SoftBank's last-minute end to their planned deal around Christmas 2018, he couldn't believe that as July 4 approached, he would spend another holiday weekend scrambling to find an alternative for funding. Neumann called Solomon, absolutely livid. "You abandoned me," Neumann told him.

Noah Wintroub had been waiting for this moment. JPMorgan was always skeptical that Goldman could actually put together a full $10 billion debt package, and he still held out hope that WeWork would turn to them instead. Now it was happening.

JPMorgan was asked to move at lightning speed. Minson told them they had thirty days to get the deal done. Wintroub enlisted nearly a hundred people within the bank to work on it, and the bank readied a plan to help WeWork borrow $6 billion.

Unlike Goldman's debt package, JPMorgan's offer required that WeWork complete an IPO. WeWork would need to raise at least $3 billion from the stock market in order to get JPMorgan's $6 billion in debt.

It worked—or so JPMorgan thought. Neumann told the bank they were the favorites—so long as they could raise the debt. Wintroub was back in the driver's seat, and Goldman was in the doghouse. JPMorgan, and other banks that joined it, would be in line for at least $100 million in fees, just from the debt. Taken with the fees for raising money from stock investors in the IPO, all the banks involved stood to get more than $200 million in fees.

Goldman, though, wasn't done. Bankers there had also been exhausting themselves for years in pursuit of WeWork. Winning the debt deal had become an obsession of certain members of the Goldman team. That included Srujan Linga, a wiry, newly minted managing director who impressed WeWork's team as a financial whiz. Goldman's offer, he thought, was a far better deal for WeWork, and Neumann could be pulled back over to their side once he saw that. Neumann asked Linga and another executive, Ram Sundaram, to come to his house in the Hamptons.

When the bankers arrived, Neumann and Michael Gross, who had been working on the debt deal, invited them to his sauna. It was a favored venue, Neumann explained, for thinking and conversation. As the four men sat inside sweating, Neumann told the Goldman bankers why he was going with JPMorgan. It was a sure, safe bet. Dimon had personally promised that JPMorgan could get them $6 billion, Neumann said.

Nevertheless, Linga and Sundaram persisted. Their plan—the modified Goldman deal that Neumann had rejected and considered a betrayal—was the best way for WeWork to get money to keep growing. As Linga and Sundaram thought their message was sink-ing in, Neumann walked them from the sauna toward his ice bath. No one, Neumann declared, could possibly stay in there longer than five minutes.

Linga, who had become friendly with Neumann over several months, protested. He took very cold showers every day after meditating. He'd do it. Linga slid in, while Neumann and Gross kept an eye on the clock and snapped photos. As the ice-cold water enveloped his legs, he joked that he wouldn't get out until Neumann took Goldman's debt deal, not JPMorgan's. As the clock passed five minutes, Neumann watched in amazement.

Finally, Linga emerged shaking. Neumann said he'd spend the weekend thinking through his next steps.

In the end, Linga's playful plea was for naught. Days later, Neumann informed the Goldman team that he was officially taking JPMorgan's deal. Jamie Dimon's efforts had paid off.

WeWork was about to take its own plunge into the public markets.

CHAPTER 31

To the Energy of We

WHEN A COMPANY GOES PUBLIC IN AN IPO, IT'S REQUIRED to give public market investors a handbook. Starting in the spring of 2019, a host of WeWork lawyers, accountants, and executives began to write the document, clearing out a conference room on the headquarters' sixth floor as an IPO "war room."

This document, called an S-1 or IPO prospectus, is a guidebook that mixes a narrative extolling the company's vision and success with pretty graphs with detailed numbers that shed light on its revenue and expenses, and show healthy growth.

For WeWork in 2019, this was a problem: nine years into its existence, the company still didn't have its story down.

The company had long struggled to clarify just what type of business WeWork was, beyond being a giant, fast-growing company that would do good things for the world. The earliest investors didn't need much clarity, given that they were betting more on Neumann than on the company's financials. Later investors were so eager to get into a company they perceived as being the next big thing that they didn't dwell on it either.

It quickly became clear to those assembled in the IPO war room that there was no consensus on how to describe WeWork, only that it wasn't just a real estate company. The problem was that public market investors would want to know: If WeWork wasn't a real estate company, then what was it?

Often Neumann had leaned into his description of WeWork as a tech company. But its efforts in that area were struggling. Its eclectic collection of Meetup.com, Conductor, and other acquisitions had no clear binding glue, and while Neumann had once imagined that WeWork would sell analytics software to clients tracking employee use of space, the effort never got off the ground.

The way Neumann had pitched WeWork to Masayoshi Son in 2018—with the triangle that called for WeWork to take over every part of the property world, from ownership to services—hadn't advanced much either, given that Son hadn't put in the billions of dollars necessary to get it up and running.

So Neumann employed a new strategy. He urged his team to draw upon one of the most overused terms in Silicon Valley—to show how WeWork was a "platform"—a descriptor that implied an online locus of connectivity with few assets, like Craigslist or Reddit. "We are a global physical platform," read one draft.

Artie Minson was pushing a more numbers-based narrative, focusing on the company's core office business and its rapid growth. WeWork could show how every dollar invested in a new office lease would be repaid many times over by members. Investors wanted certainty, he thought, and the various future aspirations of far-out units like WeGrow and WeLive would just confuse them.

Neumann didn't like Minson's conservative approach and had Jen Berrent try her own version. Then he wanted something in between—something with more "We" to it.

WHILE THE IPO TEAM TOILED IN THE WAR ROOM, THE NEUMANNS moved the family out east to the Hamptons for the summer. They retreated to their compound in Amagansett and had a constant stream of WeWork employees and outside advisers commuting between headquarters and their house. Many just took Ubers for the journey, which could take up to four hours in summer traffic. Other employees, weary of the lengthy hundred-mile trek, went by helicopter or even seaplane. Using the Uber-for-helicopters startup Blade, they simply charged the flights to their corporate credit cards.

Upon arrival in Amagansett, they found *two* Neumann homes. One was inland, next door to Gwyneth Paltrow's house, and had a separate cabin where WeWork staff huddled to do work. The other was a newer acquisition, a glassier, flashier house that overlooked the Atlantic Ocean, marking Neumann's eighth home. There, WeWork employees were more likely to be interrupted by the five Neumann children wandering in and out.

Between the IPO cram sessions that summer, Adam Neumann went surfing, hitting the waves with one of his multiple surfing coaches or with visiting friends. Beyond their two main homes, the Neumanns rented three other houses in the Hamptons for their sprawling staff. The surf coaches—who had to sign nondisclosure agreements—got their own house, while the trail of chefs, nannies, yoga instructors, their hairdresser, and other staff would share rooms in the others. Even so, Neumann kept going on tropical jaunts. He went to Costa Rica in June—the jet made two round-trips from New York in a single week—and again in August. By going through the regimented process of becoming a public company, WeWork executives and advisers had long hoped Neumann might grow more focused on fixing WeWork's shortcomings. Instead, the stress and anticipation of the event seemed to accentuate his flaws. Neumann wasn't checking his crazy.

He couldn't even make simple decisions. If given a straightforward request like choosing a stock exchange, Neumann would instead come up with new ideas about how the listing should be done. Staff would throw up their hands after meetings that ended without the resolution of any IPO questions.

Even more maddening to staff, though, was the involvement of Rebekah Neumann. WeWork employees watched as she discussed the IPO and the paperwork around it more as the Neumanns' personal coming-out party. Aides heard the couple screaming over how she would be listed in the prospectus. It looked ridiculous to have so many titles, Neumann told her. In the end, she was listed as a co-founder, chief brand and impact officer, and founder and CEO of WeGrow. In the section about WeWork's founders, she was listed after Adam Neumann and before Miguel McKelvey. (Earlier, when she was retroactively named a co-founder, her name was usually listed after McKelvey's.)

Another pain point for staffers was the "insert," a montage of photos with captions in the middle of the prospectus that defined WeWork's ethos and mission. While she had little to do with the financial part of the prospectus, Rebekah took the lead on this endeavor.

The section began with a title page in 1960s hippie loopy font: "Step into the World of We." Each photograph became an object of obsession. At one point, she suggested the images should appear in the style of Wes Anderson, the quirky director of films like *The Life Aquatic* and *The Royal Tenenbaums*. Photographers were sent around the world to document WeWork members, with countless photos discarded. In some cases, Rebekah and aides pored over thousands of options before making a single selection. "It doesn't feel soulful enough," she said of certain pictures. "Make it look more '70s." By the time the document was finally finished, designers had gone through thirty-seven rounds of revisions.

The back page of the prospectus, Rebekah determined, would feature nature photography with a personal twist. The Neumanns had donated money that helped conserve of millions of acres of tropical forest. A photograph of some of this land, Rebekah decreed, should be featured on the back page of the IPO documents. The Neumanns decided a photographer should fly via helicopter to take aerial pictures of a chunk of rainforest they preserved in Belize: they said they would pick up the bill.

Hokey-sounding phrases were another point of friction. One

paragraph of Rebekah-tinged language defined the company as "a community company committed to maximum global impact" with a mission "to elevate the world's consciousness." A more prominent phrase, though, would prove especially magnetic for mockery a few weeks later: the dedication.

Over the summer, during a meeting with senior executives, members of the marketing team, and WeWork's bankers, Rebekah revealed an epiphany: WeWork's IPO prospectus needed to have a dedication page, just like a regular book. As many on the team nodded in agreement, she suggested that the dedication read, "To the energy of We—greater than any one of us but inside each of us."

It didn't land well. Some executives became intent on persuading her to drop it. Aides worried the gesture could be seen as weird. Something more straightforward, perhaps, they suggested. Eventually, she relented and agreed to take it out, causing the whole team to breathe a sigh of relief. But soon after, when they reconvened for another meeting, they looked at the latest draft: the dedication had been reinserted. Rebekah explained to them that someone told her it was brilliant.

BEYOND THE VISUAL AND RHETORICAL PRESENTATION, WEWORK was struggling to figure out how to even present its numbers.

Adam Neumann would jump back and forth between being willing to divulge more details of the business and fewer.

Strangely, WeWork opted not to disclose a metric known as mature location economics, which might have offered a strong sense of its core business. Perhaps the most basic question of the business was how much WeWork's offices made in profits once they were open and fully leased. It is a number that has long been crucial to understanding the WeWork predecessor Regus, now known as IWG. And it was a number that Neumann and Minson used to boast about to investors and the press—saying they had profit margins of more than 30 or even 40 percent on fully leased offices, before headquarters and other growth costs were taken into account. Yet the prospectus didn't mention it at all. Instead it highlighted the WeWork-invented metric previously known as community-adjusted EBITDA.

Staff working on the document worried it was going to be a mess. They had hoped that the bankers—from JPMorgan in the lead role and Goldman in second position—would bring some order to the chaos. While the bankers did have some constructive advice, they too were deferential to Neumann, reluctant to give him tough news.

The JPMorgan and Goldman teams flattered Neumann frequently. Wintroub and his partner Michael Millman moved to the East Coast, leaving their families in California for months to be on call for Neumann. The two banks appeared endlessly competitive with each other—afraid one was being trusted by Neumann more than the other.

Neumann added to their insecurity. Aides watched as he got one piece of advice from Wintroub, hung up, and immediately called David Ludwig from Goldman Sachs with the same question. Each bank constantly felt it was being undermined by its rival, rather than part of the same team. Even though JPMorgan had been christened the lead, neither bank seemed to feel secure, given Neumann's propensity for change. Still, their jousting came despite WeWork's promising the two of them the same fees, regardless of which was considered the lead. Ego was at stake.

An IPO of this size actually required more than just two banks. They'd need an army of bankers to find buyers for the billions in stock being sold and teams of analysts to produce research to help potential investors. Given how hungry banks throughout Wall Street were to participate, the Neumanns figured they could try to extract some changes tied to their own stated values, particularly around sustainability.

This effort became a task for Miguel McKelvey. The co-founder's role had become nebulous over the years. His relationship with Rebekah was tense. He'd stayed publicly quiet as the Neumanns rewrote the company's history to make her one of the cofounders or as she took over roles that had once been his. One of McKelvey's executive assistants, however, grumbled to other employees that Rebekah would swoop in and steal her boss's ideas.

His team tried to exact concessions from the banks to overhaul their own environmental practices, because they hoped the banks so lusted to take part in the IPO that they would ban meat or pledge to be carbon neutral. The gambit didn't work: bank executives didn't agree to any major changes.

WeWork did prove successful with another target: the stock exchanges.

In August, the Neumanns summoned the heads of the NYSE and the Nasdaq, Stacey Cunningham and Adena Friedman, out to the east end of Long Island to make their respective pitches.

When Cunningham arrived, Neumann told her he wanted the biggest party ever. He asked Cunningham whether the NYSE could help them close down the streets around their building in lower Manhattan for a giant outdoor block party. Before Cunningham left, Neumann asked her to speak with Rebekah, who ate lunch as she chatted with the stock exchange chief in their kitchen.

While Cunningham was only about a year into her role at the helm of the NYSE, Friedman had courted Neumann for years. They bonded over their athletic interests. During one earlier visit to Neumann's office, he asked Friedman, who has a black belt in tae kwon do, to show him some of her moves. Friedman, while demonstrating a roundhouse kick, ripped her dress.

Friedman was so eager to get the WeWork listing that she proposed creating an entire index of companies named for WeWork. It would be the "We 50," and only companies that stood out on issues of environmental sustainability could gain admission, with WeWork helping set the terms. Investors could then literally buy into not just WeWork but also a broader group of companies that lived up to WeWork's ideals.

Despite Friedman's ingenuity, neither she nor Cunningham got an answer right away. Just as he had been doing with the banks, Neumann pushed the decision to the last possible moment.

AS WEWORK STAFF JOUSTED OVER PHOTOS AND VERBIAGE THAT summer, the winds in the market were changing, and not for the better.

For much of the decade, Silicon Valley had been hypnotized by the "growth at all costs" approach—believing that companies like WeWork, Uber, and Lyft could spend whatever they wanted, so long as revenue kept soaring. Driving it all was an assumption that public market stock investors were so starving for fast-growing companies that they wouldn't care about losses; they would value these companies even higher than SoftBank and other private market investors. It had been the guiding thesis years earlier for the VCs and mutual funds as they plowed their cash into these companies. The public markets, they figured, were playing the same game.

But by summer, that foundational thought—the creaking wooden stage packed with unicorns—began to buckle.

Lyft's stock had plunged after an initial good first day. By July, it was down more than 50 percent from its IPO. Then Uber—once hoped to trade at a valuation as high as $120 billion—was a huge disappointment. It ended up around two-thirds of that figure. Its shares opened below $43, even lower than the $48 price investors paid *four years* earlier—a terrible performance for what had been by far the hottest startup of the decade.

It quickly became clear that stock market investors didn't just want a company that showed fast growth. Losses—to the surprise of many in Silicon Valley—were seen as a bad thing. Uber lost $3.8 billion in the twelve months before its IPO, a record for a U.S. startup. Even the far smaller Lyft was a broken water main of cash, losing more than $1 billion in the year before its IPO, a record before Uber. While companies like Uber loved to compare themselves to Amazon, Amazon lost far less in its first decade combined than Uber lost in the year before its IPO. These losses were without precedent. And suddenly they were a black mark.

The bankers at JPMorgan and Goldman realized WeWork wouldn't be immune to the market chill. In a meeting with Neumann and other executives in the summer, the bankers gave Neumann a primer on the mechanics of the IPO process, and within it they had a slide that implied WeWork would have a $30 billion valuation. That number was a sharp pullback from the far rosier projections they'd given to Neumann months earlier. It was also a sharp drop from the $47 billion mark from SoftBank in January. WeWork staff in attendance assumed they were trying to slowly walk back their big promises.

Neumann lost it. He berated the bankers when he saw the number, demanding answers.

The bankers demurred. They simply said it was an illustrative valuation—nothing to do with the reality of WeWork.

Optimism reigned elsewhere. Artie Minson made multiple presentations to staff and executives over the summer about the company's stellar finances—its large cash pile, the strength of the enterprise business, and its unabated growth. The message was clear: WeWork was in a great position heading into the IPO.

But as WeWork hurtled toward its public debut, there were some other changes Adam Neumann wanted, beyond just the way the company was marketed in its S-1. He wasn't content with his current level of power—of firm control. He wanted the assurance that WeWork would stay in his family for generations to come. As always, he wanted more.

CHAPTER 32

Twenty to One

YOU SHOULDN'T DO IT, JAMIE DIMON TOLD ADAM NEUMANN.
The CEO of the nation's largest bank was firmly advising
WeWork's founder by phone that he should stand down: he was
asking for too much. The issue was Neumann's plan to double the
potency of his already supercharged shares to give them twenty
times the votes of a standard investor. The scheme, which would go
into effect in the IPO, would cement his already solid grip on the
company, giving him the ability to sell billions of dollars' worth of
his own stock while still wielding full control.

Dimon, the long-running JPMorgan Chase chief, thought it
was a terrible idea.

Taken with numerous other measures Neumann was pushing
for, it wasn't fair to his shareholders, Dimon told Neumann. In
business, he told him, there's "what I *should* do" and "what I *could*
do." Grabbing more power from shareholders through the restructuring, Dimon advised him, just wasn't the right thing to do.

Neumann, though, had observed that a handful of CEOs had
similarly favorable setups. Snap Inc.'s CEO, Evan Spiegel, managed
to sell stock to the public that had no voting rights at all, establish-
ing the Wall Street equivalent of an absolute monarchy. In Neumann's view, if someone like the CEO of a social media app could
do it, he *certainly* deserved it, too.

Dimon's pleas left him unmoved. Neumann hadn't learned his own lesson. In late 2018, his unrelenting negotiation of his contract and compensation with SoftBank had ended up delaying the completion of the giant planned buyout so much that the deal fell apart when the market changed. Now he was pushing again.

As Neumann's staff was toiling to clean up the company over the spring and summer of 2019 to make it look appealing to public market investors, the CEO was effectively doing the opposite. He was obsessing over new tools that would give him more money and more power—tools that would ultimately act as repellents to investors.

WeWork had already gained some notoriety for its lax corporate governance. Stories in *The Wall Street Journal* earlier in the year on Neumann's ownership of buildings leased to WeWork and the company's investments in his personal interests—like surfing and an elementary school—had painted a picture of a CEO who was prioritizing himself over the company. Grabbing even more power just wouldn't be a good look.

Many of the noxious features he sought were financial benefits particular to Neumann. Earlier in the year, he had ordered the complete legal reorganization of the company, which would generate huge tax savings for Neumann and a handful of other senior executives on new chunks of stock they were awarded.

Then there was his borrowing. Banks had long been lending Neumann millions—money that he had been spending on his lavish lifestyle, on homes for his family and his extended family, and on his personal investments in commercial real estate in places like San Jose.

Eyeing an eventual IPO, banks desperate for WeWork's business had lined up to offer Neumann personal loans. He secured deals over several years that let him personally borrow up to $500 million from a group of banks including JPMorgan, UBS, and Credit

Suisse. The banks would get WeWork stock if he ever couldn't pay it back. By July 31, he had drawn down $380 million of the full amount. While it was less than he initially wanted—he told others he'd hoped to borrow around $1 billion—it was a staggering amount for the CEO of a pre-IPO startup.

Such borrowing is very uncommon among publicly traded company CEOs, and for a good reason: large loans tied to stock stand to warp CEOs' decisions. If a company's stock falls significantly, the lenders can seize the CEO's own shares, so CEOs with big loans can be motivated above all else to avoid this, sometimes taking actions that aren't in the long-term interest of the company.

Neumann's new loans came on top of the extraordinary amount of money he had garnered by selling his shares. The entity he controlled—We Holdings—had sold a total of nearly $500 million since WeWork started. Most of that had taken place when SoftBank had bought out the shares of some existing investors. But it also included over $130 million in sales that were tailor-made just for him as part of earlier financing rounds. It's not known exactly how much Neumann pocketed versus McKelvey and other small investors in the entity, but the bulk went to Neumann. A 2017 internal WeWork document indicated that Neumann owned 83 percent of We Holdings. While the amount of stock sold represented only a relatively small percentage of the total stock Neumann owned, it was one of the largest amounts ever withdrawn by a U.S. startup CEO before an IPO.

Most every new financial arrangement that benefited Neumann meant another disclosure in the S-1 spelling it out, and the list was starting to get long. Already there were plenty of concerning practices that most hygienic public companies avoid. Most don't have a long list of relatives of the CEO and his wife working at the company. Most respected corporations don't lease property owned by the CEO. Most don't have a board member whose private equity firm is getting fees to help oversee a real estate fund with the company.

However, as WeWork prepared the S-1, those drafting the prospectus didn't mention Neumann's stock sales. Those sales came into the public view only as the result of a *Wall Street Journal* article revealing that Neumann had taken out more than $700 million between sales and loans. Though the number was actually closer to $1 billion, Neumann dispatched his internal PR team to fight the story. When it eventually came out, he went ballistic.

He screamed at aides that the piece—particularly the headline's use of the term "cashed out"—made him look as if he were extracting money from the company because he thought it was overvalued. In his mind, he was bullish on the company and borrowed hundreds of millions—instead of selling—because of that.

By now, even neumann's most loyal allies and staunch defenders were growing tired of his circuitous defenses. That weary group included Jen Berrent. As the IPO neared, her relationship with Neumann became strained. Earlier in the year, she had urged Neumann to cut back on growth and spending, given that Soft-Bank wasn't around anymore, and she'd fought him on some HR issues. Neumann started to grow colder to her, gradually stripping away her duties overseeing operations, leaving her largely to focus on the IPO. As the S-1 drafts continued, staff frequently heard the two screaming at each other in his or her office, voices booming through the glass walls. She winced as Neumann pushed to weaken the already lax corporate governance she'd created for him. Very late in the game, she was waking up to the fact that what was good for Neumann wasn't necessarily good for WeWork.

She tried small-scale moves—to little effect. Berrent scheduled what she called "governance week" for the IPO team, hoping that Bruce Dunlevie and other board members would fly in to coax Neumann to back down from some of his more questionable moves. Dunlevie declined the invite, and others on the board didn't seem terribly concerned. Dunlevie's former colleague and Neu-

mann's longtime mentor, Michael Eisenberg, had grown so wary of
Neumann's behavior during 2019 that he traveled to New York
from Israel multiple times to speak to him directly. But Neumann,
convinced that public investors would be eager to buy shares of his
company, shrugged off Eisenberg's warnings.

So as the summer progressed, Neumann sought to secure even
more power.

Neumann's shares already had the power of ten votes—a level
that gave him a very healthy majority control, given that he held
about 30 percent of the company's stock. He had become obsessed
about the handful of CEOs of lesser companies who had even more
potent shares. The CEO of the fitness bike company Peloton had
twenty votes per share, he carped to lieutenants. *Peloton*. Surely he
deserved twenty, too.

Neumann wanted the ability to sell lots of stock and stay in control, he said. He wanted to give at least $1 billion to charity over the
next decade, a pledge he'd make in the prospectus. He even wanted
to ensure that Rebekah and his children would take over the company if he were to die.

For Berrent and the banks, these were concerning asks. Many
stock market investors would balk at these arrangements, and it
would clearly affect WeWork's valuation, they thought.

Jamie Dimon began to get more involved.

As the CEO of the largest U.S. bank, with more than 250,000
employees and about $2.7 trillion in assets, Dimon usually left ques-
tions about the fine print of an IPO to underlings. This one was
different. WeWork was expected to be one of the largest ever
startup IPOs and, if it went well, could help raise the bank's profile
in the Silicon Valley IPO market, giving it more credibility as a
potential lead adviser. JPMorgan also was finally poised for a windfall for its years of mostly free advisory work for the company and
cheap loans it gave to Neumann personally.

Neumann had been one of the bank's most high-maintenance
and challenging clients. He often grew frustrated with Noah Win-

troub, so Dimon dispatched Mary Callahan Erdoes, the fifty-two-year-old CEO of JPMorgan's wealth-management division and one of a handful of executives mentioned as a possible Dimon successor, to work on the deal.

Erdoes was one of the top women on Wall Street—a good match for Neumann, who demanded to work with those high up in any org chart. She looked far more the part of banker than startup founder: she had shoulder-length blond hair and was frequently outfitted in designer suits and striking pearl earrings. In meetings with WeWork, she often was firm, one of few willing to try to push back on Neumann—to a certain extent. One time, she told Neumann that no company had ever been showered with so much attention by the bank. And she was competitive: at a meeting at Neumann's house, she was seen leaving in a huff after she saw others waiting for Neumann dressed in suits, and she seemed to assume they were rival bankers. It turned out the well-dressed visitors had nothing to do with the IPO.

When Erdoes began to take stock of all of Neumann's power and money grabs that would be disclosed in the prospectus, she realized it was going to be a big problem. On top of changes in the market and WeWork's heavy losses, these corporate governance issues were going to hurt demand for WeWork's stock—they'd hurt the valuation. Investors wouldn't be happy to just give up more control. Neumann simply couldn't have it all.

Sitting him down, she and others at JPMorgan told him that the abnormal, Neumann-friendly governance provisions could mean a hit to WeWork's valuation of as much as 30 percent. Aides had endlessly watched Neumann obsess over valuation as long as they'd known him, so they expected this argument to resonate. Yet Neumann simply shrugged it off. Any hit to valuation would be a temporary dip, he said. After WeWork went public, the markets would see its extraordinary growth continue, and its valuation would soar, he told them.

Neumann was becoming even more detached from reality. His

years of starry-eyed predictions had kept WeWork's valuation rising—and new money flowing—so much so that he didn't absorb the harm his quest for personal wealth and power was doing to the company. He seemed to see his demands as reasonable, lacking the self-awareness to see how much everything in the IPO had become all about himself. The final prospectus even was literally about him: the name Adam was mentioned 169 times.

In hindsight, the bankers, despite their warnings, didn't themselves fully grasp how bad the cocktail of giant losses and bad governance would play. They could have refused to participate, given the extreme nature of some of Neumann's actions. After all, the banks' names were going on the S-1, too. But largely they just raised concerns rather than going to the mat.

As the date to unveil the prospectus began to draw closer, Neumann still pushed for the expansion of his own voting rights, despite the warnings from Berrent, Dimon, and others. Following the Dimon call, WeWork held a board meeting at which Neumann was planning to push through his plan to grant himself greater power through numerous changes, including the twenty-to-one share changes. Just as he resisted warnings from the leader of the biggest bank in the country, he won over the pliant board. Steven Langman cautioned him that WeWork was giving investors lots of reasons not to invest in the company; they shouldn't add on more.

But in the end, the directors all acquiesced to Neumann, save for one small change: Rebekah Neumann would no longer have full control of the company if Adam died; instead, she would be on a committee to choose a successor.

On the whole, as it had for years, the board showed it was unwilling to take a firm stand against Neumann's wishes. Some of the directors had long realized there were problems but hoped that the public markets would solve them, teaching Neumann some caution they had been unable to impose. Now, they thought, they were in the final stretch of WeWork's life as a private company.

Neumann, having spent days endlessly arguing with Berrent

over the twenty to one and other issues, told her after the meeting that his success with the board proved him right: "You almost let your fairness get in the way of what we can get."

AT THE END OF THE ROAD TO AN IPO, A SINGLE BODY HAS UNLIMited discretion over the offering: the U.S. Securities and Exchange Commission. The SEC needs to green-light every item in a company's paperwork before it can sell shares to the public. Like WeWork, most companies now file paperwork confidentially with the SEC to keep their correspondence with the agency, including over financial metrics, private. Most companies submit multiple drafts before the SEC blesses their documents.

By August, nearly nine months after WeWork first submitted documentation, the SEC still wasn't comfortable with numbers the company wanted to show the public. A key sticking point was WeWork's community-adjusted EBITDA, the much-derided figure that WeWork invented and used in its bond sale that purported to show how much money WeWork sites were churning out before other costs were taken into account.

Neumann was obsessed with keeping the metric. While by most every other measure the company was showing big losses, community-adjusted EBITDA was still showing "profits." Of course, this was largely because the figure failed to account for months of free rent from landlords. The effect was to make buildings seem far more profitable than they would have been under generally accepted accounting principles, or GAAP, the gold standard for all public companies.

In one draft after another, the SEC criticized the metric. WeWork tweaked it in an attempt to mollify the regulators, changing its name to "contribution margin," a more standard term. But the SEC was concerned about the underlying accounting issue rather than the name. WeWork countered by renaming the metric again, calling it the rhetorical mouthful "contribution margin excluding non-cash GAAP straight-line lease cost." Further, it agreed to put it alongside another metric that adhered to GAAP. The formerly named community-adjusted EBITDA produced 25 percent profit margins in the first half of the year; the new figure that ran alongside it showed paltry 10 percent margins.

Still, the SEC wasn't satisfied, and Neumann was frustrated. The 10 percent margins were a far cry from the 35 percent–plus margins he had boasted about a few years earlier.

With the SEC and WeWork negotiators at a stalemate over terminology, Neumann—against the advice of some advisers—declared that he wanted to talk to the SEC himself. Jen Berrent was somewhat relieved to have him address the agency directly, thinking he might be able to persuade agency officials to let WeWork use its own measure of profitability. Neumann, after years of winning over venture capital investors, was certain he could get a few government bureaucrats to see things his way. He opted to bring Berrent and a few other key staff members to Washington but left his CFO, Artie Minson, behind in New York.

The WeWork emissaries flew to Dulles on August 1. Running late, they rushed into the agency's downtown Washington, D.C., headquarters. Inside, Neumann walked through a presentation with SEC accountants, making his case that WeWork's own measure of building profitability would help investors understand the business.

The accountants were receptive and polite, but unmoved. The effort failed.

Later that month, the SEC instructed WeWork, "Please remove disclosure of this measure throughout your registration statement."

FOR WEEKS, THE WEWORK IPO TEAM HAD BEEN CONSUMED WITH disclosures that were sure to reflect poorly on Neumann when they came to light in the public version of the S-1. Jimmy Asci, WeWork's head of communications, worked with his team to compile a twenty-plus-page list cataloging all the high-risk items that the press could pick up on that would look bad. Restructuring the company for Neumann's tax benefit, the giant pay package, the properties leased to Neumann, the twenty to one—they were all in there.

Also mentioned in the list was a brief disclosure on page 199 of the document that received scant notice internally: WeWork had purchased the rights to trademarks relating to the word "We" from We Holdings LLC, Neumann's LLC, paying the entity $5.9 million in stock. Years earlier, Neumann and Miguel McKelvey had taken out some trademarks tied to the word, but never transferred them to WeWork. Now was a good time to clean that up, the lawyers decided. Neumann's personal lawyers at Paul, Weiss figured Neumann should be compensated for the value of the trademarks, given that there could be tax implications, so WeWork's lawyers—thinking relatively little of it—agreed. Neumann was informed but didn't even seem to notice it. At a meeting where it was briefly mentioned to the two co-founders, McKelvey expressed surprise, joking he could buy a car with the proceeds.

At most any other company, the CEO personally profiting off a trademark he's selling to his company would easily stand out. Even if it were just a few million dollars, it would be a huge deal—an obvious conflict that would convey a terrible image for the company and the CEO. Bankers and executives would insist it come out. Staff might gossip about it. Add onto that the heavy level of irony—the CEO of a company that casts itself as devoted to sharing was literally personally profiting off the word "We"—and alarms would go off.

WeWork, though, was drowning in terrible images related to Neumann. The bankers, the lawyers—everyone had become calloused to Neumann's grabs for money and power. A $5.9 million deal just didn't stand out to Neumann or anyone else.

The public, though, wouldn't prove so forgiving.

CHAPTER 33

WeWTF: The S-1 Sh*t Show

W HEN WEWORK OPENED UP ITS FINANCIALS TO THE WORLD on August 14, 2019, Adam and Rebekah Neumann, We-Work's communications team, and its senior finance executives breathed a collective sigh of relief.

WeWork's IPO documents were made public on the SEC's website around 7:00 a.m. For the first few hours, the headlines were relatively benign. Commentators and news outlets marveled at the sheer size of WeWork's losses—$1.37 billion in just the first six months of 2019—and how closely the expansion in losses tracked revenue growth. The WeWork team had expected this pushback.

The team was pleased that Neumann's decision to take twenty-to-one voting control—up from ten to one—didn't immediately raise hackles among the media or investors. Neither did the board's decision to give him a bonus to take the company public. As the morning wore on, there was some mockery about the language in the nearly three-hundred-page document, including the title page containing the Rebekah Neumann–authored dedication to "the energy of We" that was "inside each of us." But none of these initial headlines were all that damning.

The first sign the news cycle could turn came when Jim Cra-mer, a popular CNBC host known for screaming about stock picks on his nightly show, *Mad Money,* jumped onto CNBC and started talking about Neumann's greed and what Cramer said was the offensiveness of what Neumann was trying to take from investors.

Neumann couldn't believe what he was seeing on TV. Cramer's my friend, he told WeWork executives on the phone. How can he say this about me? Cramer would later say on another segment, "As much as I like Neumann it doesn't matter."

The dressing-down on CNBC was like the breaking of a dam. The world had begun to digest more of the filing, and news outlets, potential investors, and curious readers started pointing out one egregious term or disclosure after another.

The hypocrisy was irresistible.

Twitter exploded. Online pundits began to home in on just how much wealth Neumann had amassed already; the $500 million *personal* line of credit from three of his underwriting banks; and all his questionable entanglements. The company that was literally named We seemed to be all about *him.* Not only was he named 169 times, not only did the prospectus specifically call him a "unique leader who has proven he can simultaneously wear the hats of visionary, operator and innovator," but he *personally* was profiting off the word "We."

Journalists, investors, and countless casual observers piled on, raising unflattering parallels to Enron, the HBO satire *Silicon Valley,* and Elizabeth Holmes's disgraced blood-testing company, Theranos.

"This company is not even interested in concealing its role as a medium to funnel money from investors towards Neumann's pockets," wrote one Twitter user.

Neumann's own phone and emails—relayed through assistants— were blowing up with questions about the payment for the trademark.

Neumann called Minson and Berrent and screamed at them, asking why that payment was in the prospectus. *Why didn't you tell me?* Berrent told him that she had gone over everything in the prospectus with him multiple times. Neumann insisted he had never seen it.

The Neumanns were rattled. Rebekah had expected to generate headlines for her philanthropy: the prospectus outlined the Neumanns' pledge to give away $1 billion over ten years. But even that gesture became a joke on Twitter, given the tepid penalty for breaking the vow: if they failed to follow through, Neumann's shares would have only ten times as many votes as the standard shareholder, not twenty.

Savvy financial spectators kept finding shocking nuggets as they combed through the document during the day and after.

Matt Levine, a Bloomberg columnist who writes a detailed and witty daily email dissected by Wall Street bankers, had been on vacation when the prospectus went live. The following Monday morning, he wrote in his email that the "We" trademark news was "the news item that caused me to absolutely lose my mind—the item that, if I were a slightly more dedicated financial columnist, would have had me on the next helicopter back to the office."

Then there was Scott Galloway, an NYU marketing professor, entrepreneur, and best-selling author and a well-known, acerbic voice in Silicon Valley circles. On August 16, he penned a piece on WeWork titled "WeWTF." It was brutal. Galloway ticked off the litany of governance concerns debated by the bankers weeks earlier, giving emphasis to Neumann's profiting off the word "We." "YOU. CAN'T. MAKE. THIS. SH★T. UP," he wrote. "Any Wall Street analyst who believes it's worth over $10 billion is lying, stupid, or both."

As WeWork's PR staff scanned the responses to the IPO prospectus, they were dejected because it was a sea of only negative news. Typically, even for much-maligned companies, there are some defenders—someone to point out the good. The only thing that came close in this case was a post by the respected tech analyst Ben Thompson on his blog *Stratechery* that laid out what a bull case might be for WeWork, yet ultimately concluded that investors should stay away. Still, his mere mention of some positive attributes of the company brought him so much blowback from readers that he subsequently issued multiple mea culpas to his subscribers. He later called the post his "nadir" of 2019.

The response caught employees off guard. They'd sat through one company presentation after another that extolled WeWork's finances and its unprecedented growth. The expectation of a giant payday at the time of an IPO made it easier for many of them to justify the round-the-clock hours their jobs demanded. Suddenly, many were trying to understand why the business model was mystifying the broader public.

The blowback also took a toll on Rebekah Neumann, who hadn't realized how much vitriol was brewing for the rhetoric-heavy, loss-heavy company. She turned to PR aides and told them to stop sending daily summaries of all the press mentions to her. It's too much, she said. In another meeting, she asked aides why the press hated her and Adam so much. We're just trying to help the world, she said.

In the past, media skepticism had been something Adam Neumann could glide over. Sometimes he'd cozy up to a reporter, or he'd rebut a narrative by landing a story in a favorable publication. And he could always point to his storied roster of top investors who had already bought his vision. As Neumann told a reporter at *Wired*'s U.K. edition in 2018, "When the best investors all agree on the same company, trust me that they've done their math, they know our returns, they know exactly what Wall Street pays when a company goes public, and they are sure that they are going to get a return."

Now, though, not only was a decent chunk of the financial sector making fun of him, but he had no way to fight back. Because of SEC rules, Neumann and WeWork were barred from responding publicly to the negative stories and criticisms following the S-1 release. The prospectus, the SEC believes, has to speak for itself.

And given how the public reacted, that wasn't a good thing for WeWork.

To wework's bankers and executives, it was clear the hostile reception to the S-1 was going to hurt the company's valuation. The negative press coverage reflected how investors would look at the company and quoted many questioning its merits. The bankers, once skittish about walking back their projections of up to $96 billion, quickly began to give WeWork executives a dose of reality. The number, they now told WeWork, would be far lower than even the $47 billion mark from the SoftBank investment nine months earlier. Now it was going to be less than $30 billion, perhaps considerably less, they told him.

Beyond the embarrassment of a giant valuation drop, suddenly the task of the IPO got much harder. JPMorgan structured its debt deal so that WeWork would only get access to $6 billion in debt from a consortium of Wall Street banks if WeWork raised at least $3 billion in the IPO—an enormous number. The more WeWork's valuation fell, the harder it would become to raise that much money.

And the company would certainly need money one way or another: WeWork was continuing to burn through its cash. Completing the IPO was more than just a badge of honor: it was critical for the company's future. WeWork's losses were still extremely high, and Neumann had ordered the company to accelerate its growth for the final three months of the year, hoping to show good numbers to Wall Street. But faster growth costs money—and WeWork needed more of it.

It was foreign terrain for Neumann. He was going to need to charm investors anew, but this time from a position of weakness. The team prepared for a busy few weeks, setting up meetings with deep-pocketed investors who might sign on. WeWork was on track for a mid- to late-September IPO. Neumann would need to change the narrative and find some believers in the next week or so, before the company kicked off its two-week official "road show" with presentations to potential investors. What he'd need most were a few committed believers willing to write huge checks.

Just then, a familiar face reached out to Neumann. Masayoshi Son wanted a meeting.

CHAPTER 34

A Setting Son

MASAYOSHI SON WAS GETTING WORRIED. READING REACtions to the IPO prospectus from his office in Tokyo, he was beginning to see that WeWork's IPO was going to be ugly. Public market investors, he realized, didn't view WeWork the way he did. They weren't going to value it anywhere near the $47 billion mark where Son had made his most recent cash infusion into the company—not even close.

The timing couldn't have been worse for the man who aspired to be known as the Warren Buffett of tech. For the first half of 2019, Son had been trying to make good on his plan to launch a successor to the original Vision Fund. He saw the first fund almost as the pilot episode of a series. The second Vision Fund would firmly establish SoftBank as *the* dominant tech investor on the planet. From there more funds would follow, allowing SoftBank to spread its reach further and further into every aspect of the digital economy.

Earlier in the summer, he announced a huge milestone: he had already rounded up investors who made commitments totaling $108 billion, making it even larger than the first fund. The commitments came with a big caveat: the investors hadn't yet signed anything obligating them to pay up.

Actually converting those pledges into real money was proving harder than expected. The first Vision Fund had no obvious break-out successes so far, despite investing almost $80 billion. Mean-while, numerous other high-profile companies in the fund like Uber and the semiconductor company Arm Holdings were signifi-cantly lagging behind expectations.

Still, Son decided to forge ahead with the second fund. To drum up interest from others, he began crisscrossing the globe trying to persuade his existing investors in the first Vision Fund to kick in even more for Vision Fund 2. He once again turned to Crown Prince Mohammed bin Salman and the Abu Dhabi fund Mubadala, which together had given him $60 billion for the first fund, asking if they would put in money again.

Saudi Arabia's PIF was noncommittal. It was unclear how much money the kingdom would raise from the IPO of Aramco, and it didn't have another $45 billion just lying around. The Saudis' wari-ness around a new financial commitment was a particular blow to Son, who had publicly stood behind Prince Mohammed after the killing of Jamal Khashoggi. Son had expected that his loyalty would be rewarded when it came time to raise funds again.

Officials from Mubadala were more positive. They told Son they were willing to put $25 billion into the new fund, up from $15 billion in the first Vision Fund. It was a start. Working with a series of high-paid bankers and consultants to advise him, Son then went looking for more pools of capital to tap—Kazakhstan's wealth fund, a Singapore wealth fund called GIC, and Canadian pension funds.

One advantage Son had was opacity. Most Vision Fund–backed companies hadn't gone public yet, so it was hard for outsiders to value them. In early August, SoftBank said on a conference call that the Vision Fund's profits were up 66 percent in the second quarter of the year—a figure that would be hard for anyone on the outside to corroborate. Son said he'd start investing the second Vision Fund in the next several months.

But once WeWork's IPO prospectus landed, everything changed. Potential investors and even executives at Mubadala and Kazakhstan's funds started to ask SoftBank pointed questions about Adam Neumann and WeWork's corporate governance. "Every conversation would immediately digress into WeWork," said one attendee of the fund-raising meetings.

When employees of Kazakhstan's fund started grilling advisers to the Vision Fund about WeWork's corporate governance, they were disheartened. In these advisers' view, the former Soviet republic's own fund didn't have much in the way of governance. Yet these employees of the Kazakhstan fund were so moved by WeWork that they felt a need to call out such flaws in a flashy American startup.

In the last week of August, Son reached out to Neumann. He asked him to come to Tokyo to see him. As soon as possible.

Neumann was still racked with disappointment from Son's abandonment of him eight months earlier when he backed out of the Fortitude deal. Things had grown chilly between the once tight pair, but Neumann figured Son could help turn around the narrative about WeWork ahead of its IPO, which was looking more challenging with every day of negative attention.

Neumann summoned Noah Wintroub, who had spent most of the summer shuttling between WeWork's Manhattan headquarters and Neumann's Hamptons homes. Wintroub was planning to go back to San Francisco to spend part of the week before Labor Day with his family. Now Neumann insisted that Wintroub come to Tokyo with him. Along with a handful of other staff, including Ilan Stern, who oversaw Neumann's personal finances, they trekked across the Hudson River to Teterboro Airport and hopped onto the G650ER.

As the WeWork Gulfstream sprinted north over Lake Ontario and toward the Arctic Circle, Neumann thought Son might ask him to call off the IPO, but he expected that along with that request, Son would also offer to make a large investment, giving him the funds WeWork needed to keep growing. During the flight, Wintroub sought to reassure Neumann, who had seemed even more on edge than usual since the S-1 flipped. Wintroub told Neumann he loved him, something the effusive banker told those around him often, and that they'd figure it out. They'd get through this rocky patch together.

It would be a quick meeting, they resolved—only a few hours and they would hop back on the plane that night.

When the group arrived in Tokyo, they drove right to Soft-Bank's soaring headquarters. The entourage entered the tall glass tower and went up to Son's massive executive floor.

They were surprised to find one of Goldman Sachs's bankers already there—Dan Dees, the global co-head of investment banking, who had been a key adviser to Neumann. In Son's executive chamber, where a samurai sword hung from the wall, Dees and Son were seated at a long table, drinking red wine. Seeing Dees in Soft-Bank's office with no warning spooked Neumann. He became immediately suspicious that there was some sort of backroom dealing between Goldman and SoftBank. Dees had been there for a prearranged meeting with the team at SoftBank.

After exchanging pleasantries, Son got to the point. WeWork wasn't ready to go public, he told Neumann. It was clear from the reaction to the S-1 that if WeWork went ahead, it wasn't going to go well. Neumann needed to delay, work on his messaging, and try again later.

Those weren't the words Neumann wanted to hear.

Neumann and his bankers had a follow-up question: Where was WeWork going to get the money to keep funding its operations if it delayed? The company was nearly out of cash and was expecting billions from the IPO.

Son then introduced a surprise guest, a forty-two-year-old banker with a boyish face and a toothy grin. He was Lex Greensill, an Australian whom Son introduced as someone who would be able to fix WeWork's need for billions. He breezed over a plan whereby the banker's company—Greensill Capital—would provide WeWork with a loan.

The offer was immediately greeted with skepticism by the WeWork team. Were they really going to rely on someone they'd never heard of to give them billions of dollars? There were also eyebrow-raising tangles of potential conflicts: SoftBank had just invested in Greensill's business. Neumann directed Greensill to talk to his personal banker, Stern, in another room. (Stern left that meeting wary of WeWork borrowing money from Greensill. Neumann and Wintroub would later refer to him as "Lex Luthor.")

With Stern and Greensill off on their own, Son sat at the head of the table with Neumann seated next to him. Neumann turned to Son and made clear he was planning to go ahead with an IPO. Without any real, viable alternative, WeWork would proceed.

Son, whose intensity was usually masked with a smile and a few jokes, grew stern. You need to call off the IPO, he told Neumann repeatedly. You're not ready. You'll embarrass yourself and the company. Take the money from Greensill, Son told him. Get the company in better shape, and start over in a few months.

No, Neumann said, clearly agitated.

Son wouldn't let up. It was clear he viewed Neumann as his pupil—a pupil who was now completely out of line, spurning his mentor. The normally calm and collected billionaire started growing red in the face. His breathing changed, huffing; he was visibly infuriated.

"I will not let you do this," Son barked at Neumann. He threatened to use his influence to block the IPO if Neumann pushed ahead—to hurt WeWork if he didn't fall in line.

The others in the room shifted uncomfortably in their seats. Son rarely raised his voice, much less got this flustered. Neumann, by contrast, was agitated at times during most negotiations, but the tenor of the conversation now grew even louder.

Finally, Son took Neumann aside and into another room to continue the conversation.

Neumann would later tell senior WeWork executives that Son said he was going to "fuck up" the IPO. It was clear SoftBank had already lost billions of dollars on WeWork, given the new, low valuation the bankers were expecting in the public listing. Son, Neumann told others, threatened him, saying that a bad WeWork IPO was going to destroy the second Vision Fund.

Neumann left the office irate. He and his entourage raced to the airport, set to return to the United States after their meeting, which had gone on longer than expected. Once they all boarded the plane, the door closed, and the pilot readied for takeoff, awaiting clearance from the airport to leave. After a few minutes, the pilot was told to turn around. It was 11:00 p.m., past the deadline to take off for the night. They'd have to return the next morning.

Neumann wondered aloud whether Son had pulled the ultimate power move and instructed Japanese authorities to ground their plane for the night.

Exhausted, they flew back the next morning, having solved nothing. They still needed to round up an enormous herd of buyers for the stock. WeWork's existing investors were counting on it. The company's employees—now numbering more than fifteen thousand, or around three times the size of Twitter—were counting on it.

CHAPTER 35

Paranoia

A FEW DAYS AFTER RETURNING FROM JAPAN, ADAM NEUMANN walked into Fidelity's Boston headquarters. Four years had passed since the sunny reception Neumann had received back when he first wooed the mutual fund in 2015 and it helped lead a $400 million round of financing. Gavin Baker—Neumann's key backer, who had been bullish on WeWork from the moment he met Neumann four years before—was gone, having left the firm in 2017. A *Wall Street Journal* story published after his departure said that women accused him of sexual harassment.

Those who remained at the firm were no longer so happy to see Neumann. Over the years, they'd grown disenchanted with him, concerned about his growing list of conflicts and his self-enrichment, and more and more skeptical of the business. Years earlier, portfolio managers at Fidelity had asked WeWork for some specific data points about WeWork's business. While they initially took it in stride when Neumann glossed over the details, with each meeting they grew frustrated as promised figures never materialized.

Now Neumann wanted Fidelity to invest again—this time in the IPO. Fidelity was a crucial buyer in the IPO process for any company—one of a handful of giant funds that pumped in substantial chunks of money and then held on to their stock for years. Another WeWork investor—T. Rowe Price—had become so embittered with WeWork and its unpalatable corporate governance that they told the company's bankers they wouldn't meet with Neumann and certainly wouldn't buy stock in the IPO. Fidelity, Neumann realized, was going to be crucial.

This time, Neumann's pitch wasn't working. The Fidelity team peppered him with questions, which he mostly didn't answer to their satisfaction. The mutual-fund employees left the meeting exasperated.

In the first half of September, Neumann pitched numerous potential IPO investors in similar encounters. In conference rooms of deep-pocketed hedge funds and mutual funds, he tried to stoke interest in the company before the official two-week investor road show kicked off. And in meeting after meeting, Neumann was on his back foot—uncharacteristically off. He was defensive, preemptively addressing concerns about his corporate governance issues or the company's losses. He seemed to be trying *too* hard. He filled much of the hour-long meetings with his own meandering monologue, leaving little time for questions from the investors—who had many. Rather than seeing the nodding heads and smiles across the table he was used to, he sensed an apprehension in the air; the investors' faces screamed of skepticism. By the end of meeting after meeting, interest in WeWork was scant.

His aides and bankers watched and winced. He's floundering, one person in the IPO team thought. He was all over the place, trying to show a firm command of the business and proving he was the visionary—*both Mark and Sheryl*. And no one was buying it.

For nine years, Neumann had succeeded in one-on-one meetings, convincing a growing roster of the world's top investors and bankers, through the sheer force of his charisma, that WeWork had all the characteristics of a thriving tech company. In these in-person meetings, he dripped with confidence. He made those across the table see the future he saw. They nodded along and smiled, focusing on the vision Neumann painted.

It was, at its heart, a magic trick. Benchmark, Harvard's endowment, T. Rowe Price, Fidelity, Goldman Sachs, JPMorgan Chase, and so many others—he'd managed to get them to look away from the cold reality that WeWork was in the office space subleasing business and to view it as something else. Something tremendously valuable.

Now Neumann's magic had worn off.

The cacophony of WeWork skepticism and mocking—the blatant hypocrisy of his pushes for personal wealth and power at a company that was supposedly about community and sharing—was too much for Neumann to overcome. Some investors indicated they would buy at a lower price, while others seemed to feel it was too toxic to invest at all.

Neumann sought out Michael Gross to join him at several IPO pitch meetings, surprising investors who expected the CFO. Gross, the vice-chairman, had moved to California and had been playing a more peripheral role in the business. He wasn't involved much in the preparation of the S-1, and when Neumann struggled to answer investors' questions, Gross didn't have those answers at the ready either. Jamie Dimon personally counseled Neumann to drop Gross from the pre-IPO pitches. Beyond his good looks, how exactly does Gross help you in your meetings? Dimon asked.

Neumann, meanwhile, was behaving erratically. There is a litany of rules regarding what a CEO can and can't say in these pitch meetings. Generally, the pitch has to be tied to the specifics already in the S-1 and any other presentations made to all potential investors. Neumann was told to stick to a very specific script and let the bankers handle the follow-up.

Instead, Neumann started calling some investors after the meetings. He'd ask them what they thought of the company—what would it take for them to get comfortable? A move redolent of a car salesman pushing an uninterested buyer, the needy calls seemed to shatter any remains of his once confident facade. Further, they even threatened to throw a legal wrench in the IPO, if what he said was outside the strict bounds of what was allowed. WeWork's bankers were furious with him and told him to cut it out. When he didn't listen, Dimon had to instruct Neumann personally to stop.

Neumann began to get desperate. He flew to San Francisco to see if Marc Benioff, CEO of Salesforce, would invest. The marketing software giant had recently invested in the IPOs of Dropbox and SurveyMonkey, and Neumann considered Benioff a friend and mentor. A Salesforce commitment would have been a great name to have to attract others. But Benioff demurred.

Neumann jetted to London, where he turned again to Saudi Arabia. JPMorgan, which was also advising Saudi Arabia on the IPO of its oil company, brokered the meeting. Yasir al-Rumayyan, whom Neumann also considered a friend, said PIF could indeed be interested in a big anchor investment, but he would want a lot from it—highly preferential terms. It wasn't the answer Neumann needed.

Neumann also tried to reshuffle aspects of the prospectus in an effort to deflect the onslaught of criticism about WeWork's corporate governance, among other issues. WeWork had only male board members—another source of criticism for a company that purported to be devoted to equality and fairness.

In early September, Neumann announced that Frances Frei, a professor of technology and operations at Harvard Business School, would become the board's first female member.

WeWork's board had rarely been rattled enough to say something to Neumann or reprimand him; this decision was an exception. The board members learned that Frei would be part of their group only from the press release. Neumann then didn't even bother to show up at the next board meeting. Along with numerous missed board meetings in the prior year and a half, the directors had finally had enough. Steven Langman barged into Neumann's office after the board meeting ended. His disengagement was unacceptable, he told Neumann.

Neumann showed up at the next meeting days later, apologized, and pledged to attend all future meetings.

. . .

By mid-september, the planned ipo was around two weeks away, and few investors were signaling an intent to buy shares. Something needed to change: WeWork needed to go public and the less interest there was from investors, the harder it was going to be to pull it off.

At WeWork's headquarters, on Thursday, September 12, 2019, around 7:00 p.m., Neumann finally walked into a planned 4:00 p.m. meeting in his office with bankers from JPMorgan and Goldman; WeWork's main lawyer from Skadden, Arps, Slate, Meagher & Flom; Jen Berrent; and WeWork's communications chief, Jimmy Asci. JPMorgan's Noah Wintroub and Michael Millman told Neumann that the company needed sweeping changes to its corporate governance for investors to buy the stock, noting that Jamie Dimon was insistent on such changes. Crucially, Neumann had to loosen his grip on the company; Rebekah couldn't have a role in choosing his successor. He also needed an outside director, they told him.

WeWork executives had prepared a list of potential changes that were beamed onto a large screen inside his office. As the group discussed the wording of each change to the S-1, Neumann grew agitated and combative. "I don't understand why I have to do this," he said. "I don't want to do this." He stormed out of the room.

For months, WeWork's team had watched bankers capitulate when Neumann didn't like their suggestions. After Neumann returned, the night wore on and Wintroub surprised the weary group by taking a firm stand, exploding at Neumann.

"Do you want to go public? This is what it is going to take," he barked.

Neumann stayed petulant, rushing out of the room in protest multiple additional times. WeWork was his company; he didn't want to loosen his grip simply because the public didn't *get* WeWork yet.

His advisers had finally reached the point of exasperation with the obdurate CEO. They were telling him that his company might not be able to go public unless he gave up some of his own personal benefits, and yet he was unwilling to do something that could so clearly benefit the company overall.

Eventually, as the clock approached midnight, Neumann finally relented and settled on a list of changes. WeWork would promise to appoint a lead independent director to the board; Neumann's voting rights would be chopped back down to ten votes per share, from twenty; Rebekah Neumann would no longer play a role in choosing her husband's successor; and Neumann would also undo the $5.9 million trademark transaction.

It wasn't a satisfying victory for the advisers. It had been a rough few weeks. Few investors were showing interest, and the company was a target of derision from the broader public. Most everyone inside Neumann's office except Neumann looked queasy. By the time the CEO signed off on the changes after fighting each one, there wasn't much to say. Left unspoken was that the changes were unlikely to counteract all the damage the S-1 had already done. Had the bankers stood firm earlier, WeWork's weak position might have been avoided. But prior to the prospectus becoming public, bankers and other advisers had continued to shower Neumann with praise—giving him criticism too infrequently and too meekly. These advisers either ignored or danced around the company's obvious warts and red flags.

Now, at the eleventh hour, they finally spoke up. But the IPO was already on life support.

QUICKLY, IT BECAME CLEAR THAT THE GOVERNANCE CHANGES were indeed too little, too late. As bankers continued to gauge interest, the expected public valuation for WeWork continued to fall, and fall.

After the S-1 was made public, bankers believed WeWork was likely to be worth more than $20 billion, maybe even $25 billion. But as the days ticked by, and with little good news to change the downward spiral, their expectations for the price tag sank further. It began to look more like $15 billion. *Fifteen billion dollars.* This was the news coming from the same bankers who'd collectively told Neumann that WeWork was worth upwards of $96 billion just five months prior. The Goldman Sachs "path to $1 trillion" no longer seemed so attainable.

For a man who saw valuation as a scorecard for success, it was tough to swallow—particularly as the clock was ticking. WeWork needed to launch the two-week investor road show the next week; if the company was to complete the IPO before the Jewish New Year, as Neumann wanted, it needed to start officially marketing to investors within days.

Stress began to take its toll. Neumann was acting more unhinged than usual—anxious, angry, and increasingly paranoid. Upset with negative press and livid that details about what was discussed in private meetings were quickly filtering into news articles, he was convinced he had leaks everywhere. One day when senior staff was gathered at his "carriage house" on the first floor of his apartment building, one executive, Arik Benzino, was talking to Rebekah Neumann on the sidewalk. Suddenly Adam burst outside and urgently whisked them in. He raced to shut the windows and peered outside.

People were probably spying on him right now, he said. There was a man walking with a cell phone on the block—he might have been listening, trying to get information, he told the group.

Neumann was cracking, some in the room worried.

Neumann was insistent on pressing ahead with the IPO, concerned that it was his one shot at a stable future with $9 billion of funding. If WeWork could raise $3 billion at the IPO—regardless of its valuation—it got access to the $6 billion in debt put together by JPMorgan. That was enough money to right the ship—to keep WeWork running for a long time to come.

By contrast, if WeWork waited, the banks were unlikely to lend like that again now that WeWork's flaws were so apparent. WeWork needed billions to keep running, let alone to keep expanding.

For once, valuation wasn't his obsession; getting the IPO done was. It was essential for the company. He told staff to get ready to press on early the next week: the road show would go ahead.

As staff readied for the marketing blitz in coming days, on Friday, September 13, *The Wall Street Journal* sent WeWork a long list of questions and points for fact-checking for a forthcoming profile of Neumann and his leadership of WeWork. The points in the story, the staff realized, could be extremely damaging at a precarious moment.

The *Journal's* piece—the company could deduce from the fact-checking questions—would clearly spark questions about Neumann's fitness to lead WeWork. The profile, based on reporting that had been pieced together over the prior nine months, would paint a picture of Neumann as an erratic, impulsive leader. Anecdotes in the story would include how Neumann wanted 20 percent of the staff fired at one point; how he had WeWork's own maintenance people work on his home; how he told none of the senior executives of the meat ban before he impulsively announced it. The *Journal* piece would offer glimpses of Neumann's delusions of grandeur—how he discussed being president of the world and his aspirations to cure world hunger.

Perhaps most damning, it included the anecdote about the private jet trip with Neumann and his friends in which marijuana was left in a cereal box upon arrival in Israel, causing the owner to recall the aircraft.

WeWork's communications team, Jen Berrent, and Artie Minson were rattled. Bankers at JPMorgan and Goldman Sachs pulled their own internal communications team members into meetings to discuss the story and whether they could work to dial it back.

.   .   .

As the IPO team fretted over the forthcoming story, they were still scrambling to get ready for the road show, set to start by Monday, September 16, or at the latest, Tuesday. One big task was outstanding: Neumann still hadn't shot his promotional video.

A video is central to IPO storytelling—giving executives a chance to showcase certain parts of the business and the company's history in their own words. It's usually played at the opening of investor meetings and posted online for investors.

Typically, such videos are shot *months* in advance, or certainly weeks even for the procrastinatory crowd. The rest of Neumann's executive team had filmed their own contributions over the prior weeks.

Neumann, though, couldn't be pinned down to record his part. On at least four different occasions, WeWork's team set up shoots that were canceled. During two separate times in previous weeks, WeWork had hired a full professional film crew and set up a stage with light and sound equipment. To get Neumann in the right frame of mind, they summoned dozens of WeWork staffers to sit in bleacher seats in an expansive room. Neumann, they were told, performs better when there's more energy in the room.

So the staffers waited. And waited. For at least three hours each session. Neumann never showed. There was always an excuse. Several of the failed shoots cost around $200,000. WeWork's internal video team made sure senior executives saw the tab for each canceled shoot—a subtle missive about the waste.

On Sunday, September 15, 2019, the clock had run out. Neumann had to shoot the video. The audience was scrapped, and he cleared out a part of WeWork's headquarters. Rebekah stood off to the side with Michael Gross, who brought his signature portable speaker and played Drake's "Started from the Bottom" to pump Neumann up. Then, for several hours that afternoon and into the evening, Neumann walked through a roughly thirty-minute presentation that included WeWork's history, the company's mission, and its financials. It wasn't dissimilar to the presentation he'd given to investors many times before.

But the master showman couldn't land his lines. The team tried cue cards and a teleprompter. He tried simply winging it. Once he seemed to be landing part of it, they had to start over because the lighting changed. It dragged on. And on.

Senior executives and bankers grew bored and went home, leaving Neumann in front of the cameras, with Gross, who was meandering around while drinking vodka, and mostly a crowd of junior WeWork staff and bankers.

Meanwhile, Neumann seemed on edge—anxious.

By around 11:00 p.m., the daylong ordeal for a thirty-minute clip was finally over.

Neumann thanked everyone. They were ready for the road show, he said, to a mostly somber room of employees. The remaining team members diligently lined up and took shot glasses, downing the obligatory drinks.

CHAPTER 36

The Fall of Adam

THE NEXT MORNING, MONDAY, SEPTEMBER 16, JEN BERRENT and Artie Minson met in the lobby of JPMorgan's headquarters at 383 Madison. The two longtime Neumann deputies were due to meet with Mary Callahan Erdoes and Noah Wintroub soon, but they needed to get on the same page.

They sunk into chairs in the black-and-white-tiled lobby of the octagonal building—one built for Bear Stearns before its rapid collapse—which was adorned with screens flashing JPMorgan marketing materials. It had been a rough couple of weeks for the two senior WeWork executives. Berrent, normally unflappable, felt a constant cloud of anxiety as things began to look increasingly bleak for the IPO.

Soon after they began talking, they both realized it was time to acknowledge reality. Things weren't going well. Their ship was taking on water faster than they could bail it out, the two agreed. Both longtime Neumann defenders had lost faith in him.

WeWork had become a laughingstock. The corporate governance problems, the investor meetings where Neumann's pitches fell flat, Neumann's inability to stay on script—it was all too much. Adding to the pressure was the forthcoming *Wall Street Journal* story that looked as though it would highlight Neumann's erratic leadership. If WeWork went ahead with its road show and then the *Journal*'s article on Neumann came out, it could be a disaster. WeWork might have to pull out of its IPO plans at the last minute. That could be a hugely damaging event, preventing the company from ever coming back to try again, Minson worried. Berrent had other concerns. Neumann's inability to stay on message when talking with investors presented a huge legal liability; they could be sued if it happened during the road show, she feared.

A glitzy video wasn't going to save this. It was time to pull the plug before they reached the point of no return, the two concluded. WeWork wasn't going to be able to pull off its IPO.

It wasn't their decision to make, but they needed to tell others.

The two zipped up the JPMorgan elevator to meet with Erdoes and Wintroub. In Erdoes's conference room atop the office tower, they outlined their discomfort with Neumann's recent erratic behavior and their fears about the IPO.

Before they got far, though, Erdoes and Wintroub offered a new wrinkle. A junior banker from Goldman Sachs who was present the prior evening at the road show taping told the IPO team that Neumann had smoked pot during the taping—a wildly irresponsible move on the cusp of an IPO, if true. Taken with the *Journal*'s marijuana anecdote, it could even invite legal questions for the bank and its ability to take WeWork public.

Minson and Berrent were exasperated but not surprised. They all agreed that Neumann needed to be persuaded to call off the IPO. Berrent and Minson decided to call Neumann. He should come to the bank, Berrent told him.

When he arrived, Neumann was already furious—upset they were meeting without him.

Minson quickly took Neumann aside to question him about the previous night. Were you smoking pot while you were filming the video? he asked. Neumann vehemently denied doing so.

"No," he told Minson—absolutely not. Minson was skeptical.

Wintroub asked the same question inside the conference room. Neumann looked at Wintroub directly and told him he had not smoked pot while he was filming.

"I swear on my life and my children I would never do that," Neumann told him. (Subsequently, multiple others present at the filming backed up Neumann's version: they didn't think he smoked marijuana that night.)

They moved on. Neumann wanted to highlight some progress. He insisted everyone watch the video he had filmed through the marathon session the day before. The result was "amazing," just watch, he told the group.

But as they watched the video together with Neumann in JPMorgan's office, Neumann's words rang hollow. The man atop WeWork, who was once able to hypnotically paint a picture of an empathetic global business that would transform how people worked and lived, was coming off as manic, unhinged, and slightly incoherent. For Minson, Berrent, and Wintroub, it was as if Neumann had broken the fourth wall—the invisible barrier that separates actors from their audience. They could at once clearly see the weakness of his theatrics alongside his delusions that it was a riveting performance. While his dysfunctional behavior and antics had caused resentment in each of them at different times over the past few months, the video was especially painful.

The team told him what they'd discussed. Their recommendation was to stop the IPO—for now. They could get temporary financing and wait a month or two—or more, they said. With more time, they could figure out how to better cast the company—to somehow win over investors who viewed the company as toxic.

Then Erdoes—who had devoted much of her summer to Neumann and WeWork—said out loud a thought that had popped into the minds of most every senior person involved with the IPO. Maybe it would be best for WeWork if you aren't the CEO, she said. Many potential investors don't think you should be in that role, she told him. The focus of all the problems, the investor concerns, the negative press deluge, Neumann was the tie that bound them all.

Neumann seemed struck by a train. It was hard to process. Seconds later, Minson walked in the room—he had stepped out for a minute while Erdoes was speaking—and Neumann started yelling.

"Mary, tell him what you said," Neumann said, looking back and forth between Erdoes and Minson. Erdoes recounted her suggestion, while Neumann looked on, wild-eyed in disbelief. "Do you think I should resign?" he asked Minson, incredulous.

Minson demurred, telling him it would be best if he calmed down. Neumann ran into Jamie Dimon's office a few doors down in a panic. There, he found the chief of the nation's biggest bank similarly aligned against him. Dimon agreed with Erdoes, the veteran bank CEO told him. Neumann didn't know what to do. He had built WeWork. It was *his* company.

Eventually, Neumann calmed down. The group agreed to defer the decision for the time being. Goldman's team, including Kim Posnett and David Ludwig, had told Neumann earlier in the day that they saw a way for the IPO to move forward. There was still a price—maybe not a great one for Neumann or WeWork—at which investors would buy in.

Neumann considered his options. Eventually, he relented and agreed to a pause. WeWork would delay the IPO for a month or two and reconvene. Neumann would remain the CEO. Neumann even became contrite. I'll get this right and fix it all with you, Neumann told his closest advisers, showing a rare vulnerable side. It seemed like a sincere appraisal of the situation—an apology for his own mistakes.

LATER THAT AFTERNOON, WORD GOT OUT. THE *JOURNAL* FIRST reported that WeWork's troubled IPO was off, and the news ricocheted.

The roster of other banks working on the IPO in lesser roles—

like Bank of America, Citigroup, UBS, and Credit Suisse—had been eagerly awaiting updates. (Morgan Stanley, whose top tech banker Michael Grimes had warned Neumann months earlier that investors could be wary of WeWork's business model, was one of the only major banks to opt out of working on the company's IPO.) Yet for much of the day Sunday, the eve of the expected road show kickoff, WeWork wasn't telling them anything about the status. Bankers weren't getting calls returned; WeWork had gone dark. Then Monday afternoon, the bankers saw the headlines and shook their heads. Some had already flown in from California.

At WeWork's headquarters, rank-and-file employees were gobsmacked. Their company had been in the spotlight for weeks, and none of the news was good. But canceling the IPO was an unexpected blow. Staff traded rumors Monday evening, waiting for updates from the company. Those with stock options began to wonder if they'd ever be able to cash in any of their WeWork shares. The only official communiqué the staff got was a late-night email inviting them to watch an all-company webcast the next morning at 11:00.

IN LONDON, MASAYOSHI SON'S DEPUTIES RAJEEV MISRA AND Munish Varma attended a small dinner with a group of investors, including Ibrahim Ajami, the head of Mubadala's venture arm, and executives at Saudi Arabia's sovereign wealth fund, in the pink-walled, flower-lined private dining room inside Annabel's, a tony members-only club. Throughout the dinner, where they all shared bottles of wine and ate Parmesan-crusted salmon, the conversation turned to WeWork and where the IPO might price. One attendee—Court Coursey, a managing partner at TomorrowVentures, Eric Schmidt's venture firm—said that investors were more likely to buy in if WeWork was valued around $7 billion to $8 billion. Misra—who excused himself several times during the dinner to take urgent phone calls—and the other SoftBank executives glared at him.

Eventually, the conversation became more subdued and awkward. They'd all seen the headlines flash. WeWork would be postponing its IPO.

No one stayed for dessert.

ADAM NEUMANN STOOD STIFFLY IN HIS OFFICE TUESDAY MORNING, feet planted behind a clear lectern with "We" imprinted on its front.

It was a different Adam Neumann from the one the company was used to.

He wasn't speaking to a crowd—just staring straight into a camera that was piped into the livestream on phones and computers throughout the We empire. The shot was backlit; light poured in from windows behind him. And Neumann was clad in a gray suit and bleach-white shirt with the top button undone, his neck-length hair flowing back behind him. He looked like a kid from junior high forced to wear a suit to a cousin's wedding. "We've been humbled by this experience," he said.

WeWork would still go public, he told his employees. It would just be a bit later—perhaps October or November. He listed off stats to extol how great WeWork was doing, and he pledged to step up communications with everyone. He'd hold weekly all-company meetings for the rest of the year. WeWork would improve; the trick was simply figuring out how to understand public market investors.

As Neumann spoke, it was clear to some that he hadn't absorbed exactly what went so wrong—why the public markets didn't accept him the way the long roster of private market investors had in years past. All he knew was that things were different.

WeWork, he said, "played the private market game to perfection."

As for the public markets, he added, WeWork was still learning the rules of the game.

. . .

THE NEXT DAY, WEDNESDAY, ON THE OTHER SIDE OF THE COUNtry, Masayoshi Son was hosting a three-day summit for the Vision Fund's portfolio companies and its investors at the posh Langham Huntington in Pasadena, a five-star hotel originally constructed in 1907 that sits beneath the San Gabriel Mountains.

The event was a celebration of all things Vision Fund, and Son was putting on a show. John Legend would perform, and the fund's investors, CEOs, and advisers—from PIF's Yasir al-Rumayyan to OYO's Ritesh Agarwal to Arianna Huffington—would attend. The gathering was part of Son's effort to convey excitement about the Vision Fund, just as he was trying to drum up interest in another $100 billion–plus for a sequel fund.

But that morning, with guests already chatting about the woes of WeWork, the *Journal* published the story Neumann and his bankers had been bracing for. "Adam Neumann was flying high," the article began. As WeWork had feared, it painted a portrait of a hard-partying, erratic leader of a troubled company—one who pushed for his own interests over others' and had something of a messiah complex. The story was quickly passed around the Langham, and the crowd buzzed anew about their troubled SoftBank-funded sibling.

Now Son was being humiliated by events during his own conference. A company he was loudly evangelizing just months earlier was undergoing a spectacularly high-profile implosion. He'd directed $10 billion into WeWork. He had two seats on the company's board of directors. WeWork was one of the largest investments of the Vision Fund, and just as he feared earlier that month when he met Neumann, a failed WeWork IPO would ruin his attempt to raise money for Vision Fund 2.

Not only was it clearly a disastrous investment, but it undermined his thesis about the genius of founders—about giving them money with few strings attached, simply trusting their vision. If that wasn't enough, the article's lead anecdote of the jet trip to Israel was a particularly bad look for Son. Marijuana use—and its cross-border transportation—isn't viewed as permissively among Japanese investors as it is in the United States.

One attendee walking through the conference overheard Mark Schwartz—one of two Son allies on WeWork's board—in a corner speaking Neumann's name loudly with expletives mixed in. Schwartz, investors, and CEOs gave Son advice on the sidelines of the conference.

Neumann, they told him, had to go.

FOR ALMOST A DECADE, NEUMANN'S BACKERS THOUGHT HE could do no wrong. He had shifted people's perception of reality, persuading one after another of the world's top investors to come along for the ride, boosting WeWork's valuation and pumping the company with more money every time.

Little else mattered so long as WeWork's shares were going up in value. It didn't matter that Neumann publicly said WeWork was profitable when it wasn't or that he took out hundreds of millions of dollars to spend on homes and staff that trailed him around; it didn't matter that WeWork was spending $2 for every $1 it took in; it didn't matter that WeWork was a real estate company. None of it mattered because Neumann was able to convince the market that WeWork had extraordinary value—that its future as a ubiquitous world-changing corporation was inevitable. Millions became billions on paper—so long as everyone was buying what Neumann was selling.

Now, though, his magic was gone. He was no longer a visionary able to move mountains. He was a meme—a caricature of an irresponsible CEO, driven by avarice and narcissism. Now that the public market investors had made clear they didn't think WeWork was even a $15 billion or $20 billion company, it was obvious the billions on paper had vanished. Neumann's power—his invincibility—plunged with it.

So the knives came out.

Board members, long in Neumann's thrall, began talking to one another as the week progressed—without Neumann on the calls. It was clear something needed to be done. Any action would be tricky and likely require Neumann's eventual assent. While the board of directors had the power to fire Neumann, Neumann also had the power to fire the board of directors—to wipe it clean and appoint new ones himself. That's what founder control meant.

Still, Neumann's invincibility wasn't absolute. His iron grip was undermined by the giant losses he'd allowed WeWork to accumulate under his watch. The reality was that WeWork would need more money. Lots of it. If Neumann became enmeshed in a lengthy legal battle to fire his board, it would be unlikely that anyone would fund WeWork as its cash ran out.

SoftBank's Schwartz, who had recently praised his leadership in board meetings, was among the most eager to push Neumann out. On the question of removal, he and Ron Fisher were clear yeses.

The other power center of the board was the early investors, Benchmark's Bruce Dunlevie, Steven Langman, and Lew Frank-fort, the former CEO of Coach who hadn't been closely involved with the company for a few years.

Dunlevie had the most at stake, and the others were likely to follow the lead of the respected Silicon Valley investor. Not only did Benchmark own around 9 percent of the company, but this was the highest-profile investment Dunlevie had ever shepherded at the tremendously successful firm he'd co-founded more than two decades earlier. He'd long believed that Neumann's vision and salesmanship outweighed his flaws. He figured the public markets could make him into a better CEO; all he had to do was get there.

As Neumann's antics and WeWork's finances became increasingly indefensible, partners at Benchmark grew frustrated. Bill Gurley and others at the firm believed that Neumann was out of control, but Dunlevie continued to take a soft touch, voting to approve purchases like the jet and power grabs like the twenty-to-one share structure, even as he voiced criticism. It was a particularly bad look, given that Benchmark was an early investor in two other high-profile startups that had been criticized for governance or culture problems, Snap and Uber, where Benchmark eventually pushed to remove CEO Travis Kalanick.

Dunlevie had his limits. With the company clearly unable to IPO, he felt he couldn't trust Neumann anymore—not to lead the company, or even to tell him the reality of what was happening inside it. Neumann needed to step aside.

He wanted to tell him in person and asked Neumann to meet him for dinner in New York on Sunday. Langman would join, too, as would Michael Eisenberg, Dunlevie's onetime colleague. Eisenberg, while not on the board, had been working the phones in recent days, staying in touch with much of the board and senior staff. He, too, came to the conclusion Neumann had to go. They all booked flights to New York.

NEUMANN COULD FEEL THE COUP COMING. HIS BOARD PLAYED their cards close, but ever since Mary Callahan Erdoes had posited the notion of his stepping down, the idea hung in the air.

Frazzled, he holed up mostly at his home in Gramercy, with a brief weekend trip to Amagansett. He called many trusted aides to hunker down with him in his home office as he tried to figure out what to do. He didn't want to lose WeWork. His initial instinct was to fight.

The head of Neumann's personal investments—Ilan Stern—raced to understand Neumann's legal rights and what a fight with the board might look like. He had spent several days in a WeWork conference room with two deputies shuttling between bankers and WeWork executives, immersing himself in the details of Neumann's stock holdings and how his wealth was intertwined with the company. Meanwhile, Bob Schumer, Neumann's personal lawyer at Paul, Weiss, dived into the issue. Neumann even began to keep a

PR person—Laurie Hays from Edelman—close by his side, separate from WeWork's PR team. His interests were diverging from
the company's.

He paced around the streets near his building, calling allies,
friends, and investors. On one such jaunt, he was wearing black
jeans and walking barefoot on the gum-tarred Manhattan sidewalk,
barking into a phone, his hair frizzy. An onlooker snapped a photo.
When it was uploaded to Reddit days later, it spread swiftly around
the internet. It captured the mood perfectly: a onetime tech guru
looking frazzled and unhinged.

THE OPENING SHOT WAS HEARD THROUGH WEWORK'S PR DEPART-
ment. On Friday, the *Journal* was working on a new story—that
SoftBank wanted Neumann out as CEO—and it called the company for comment. The harried Neumann raced to shore up the
board members he thought were his allies. He called Dunlevie,
who was vague and noncommittal.

It was a bad sign. When friends and allies paid him a visit at his
carriage house Saturday evening, it seemed like a wake. He was
quiet, lacking exuberance. It was clear he had little support at the
company.

Neumann began to openly ponder stepping down. He asked
Berrent and Minson to come over Saturday night. He sounded
them out on who might step into his role. Would Berrent leave if
Minson got the job? he asked.

On Sunday, the *Journal* published its story. It was just focused on
SoftBank and its desire to push out Neumann, but he could feel the
walls closing in. His allies on the board were clearly not offering
him vocal support.

A battle with the board wouldn't be pretty. Stern, having re-
searched the matter all week, told Neumann it would end badly for
everyone. If the rest of the board wanted Neumann to go, Neumann would need to fire the board to keep control of the company,

and a legal fight would likely ensue. Then WeWork would soon need a heavy injection of money. If Neumann were in the midst of a brawl with his board, no reputable investor would be willing to give WeWork a few billion dollars. Instead, WeWork would likely just keep bleeding cash until it ran out. Neumann understood that if he fought, WeWork would go insolvent, rendering the vast majority of his potential fortune worthless.

The scenario could get darker still. Banks including JPMorgan had lent him $500 million tied to his stock—potentially giving them additional levers of power over Neumann. Perhaps they could require him to repay the loan. His eight homes and his string of surf instructors and other staff—everything could be in jeopardy.

On Sunday afternoon, Neumann trekked to midtown to see Jamie Dimon in JPMorgan's Madison Avenue office. He was still considering what to do—whether to fight or go. Everything had crashed so quickly.

When Neumann arrived, Jen Berrent was already there. So were Stern and a handful of other members of WeWork's legal and finance teams. Dimon had been waiting for him. WeWork's IPO was supposed to put JPMorgan on the map among tech companies, but over the past several weeks Neumann had humiliated Dimon and his bankers.

Dimon was direct with him. "You're your own worst enemy," Dimon told him. JPMorgan couldn't take the company public with him as CEO. The reasons were obvious. Investors wouldn't buy the stock, and Neumann had become toxic as a leader. Dimon didn't demand that Neumann leave his post, but explained why it was critical for the future of WeWork for him to do so.

The big question for Neumann and Dimon was whether Neumann was going to fight to keep control.

Dimon counseled Neumann to go quietly. The more gracefully he walked away, the better it would be for WeWork, he told him. And what was good for WeWork was good for Neumann—even if he wasn't CEO. "Save your child. Save your baby," Dimon said.

Neumann, defensively, protested to Dimon. He'd listened to everything the bank suggested, he said, and yet it still all fell apart.

That wasn't true, Dimon told Neumann. "You listened to nothing."

THAT NIGHT, NEUMANN WALKED INTO A RESTAURANT NEAR MIDtown to meet his three closest investors and advisers since he first took venture capital: Dunlevie, Eisenberg, and Langman.

As he sat down with Dunlevie and Eisenberg—Langman was running behind on a flight from London—the two investors made clear what had become obvious at that point: Neumann had lost their support. He had lost the whole board's support. Dunlevie, normally unflappable and genial, was angry—upset with Neumann for letting WeWork go so far off the rails. He told him he needed to go. WeWork would go insolvent if he resisted; Neumann would be hounded by personal lenders and could lose everything, he told him.

By the time Langman arrived, Neumann seemed to have caved. He had little other choice. In the end, staying in power wasn't rational. He didn't want to lose everything. If he stepped aside, he could still be a billionaire. He seemed surprisingly sober about the decision, mostly focused on how he could restructure his own personal loans. Neumann asked the others for advice on that and what relationship he could have to the company going forward—exactly what he could still negotiate.

Dunlevie and Eisenberg headed to their hotels, while Langman headed home with Neumann to keep talking. They sent out an email to the other directors: a call with board members was set for the next morning.

THROUGHOUT THE NEXT DAY, MONDAY, AND INTO TUESDAY morning, Neumann's friends and allies—including his co-founder

McKelvey—filed into the carriage house in Gramercy Park. Adam Neumann had made his decision. And he was holding a living wake.

Rebekah Neumann came in and out. Despite the lingering bitterness toward her and her role, especially over the past several months, many in the room simply felt bad for her in the moment. She looked as if she hadn't slept in weeks. She seemed as though she'd come down to earth—vulnerable. She was still asking why everyone was out to get them.

For those inside the carriage house, the mood was tense. It was a contrast with the climate at the company's headquarters, where work had simply ground to a halt. The office was dominated by employees speculating on Slack or text messages as to what the future might hold. All anyone could do was read about WeWork in the news.

WEWORK, MEANWHILE, NEEDED SOME ATTENTION. DECISIONS had to be made. And fast. On Monday in a meeting at Steven Langman's Rhône offices in midtown, the board met without Neumann and decided that Artie Minson and Sebastian Gunningham would take over as co-CEOs. Neumann was in favor of the decision and had prepared both for the move. Minson had the institutional knowledge and investor relationships, while Gunningham had experience with running operations at Amazon. Later that day, Neumann got to work on details—negotiating his deal with the board, the mechanics of giving up his role and his potent voting shares. He wanted to keep some control—to keep a strong hand over the board if he was going to step aside. The directors agreed he would stay on as chairman, and he would have three votes per share. The company began working on an announcement to the press.

On Tuesday morning, Neumann walked into one of the offices in his house by himself and called into the WeWork board meeting.

On the phone call, he stuck to his pledge to go gracefully, though he wanted to settle some scores. He'd begun to turn angry at Berrent, perhaps resenting her pushback against him in the IPO process. She should be stripped of her largely ceremonial title as president, he told the board, just left to be chief legal officer.

Eventually, there was a vote on his position as CEO. One by one each board member voted in favor of Neumann's stepping down.

When it was Neumann's time to vote, he simply voted alongside everyone else for his own ouster. He pledged to help the company in any way possible. After weeks of mounting tension, he went out not with a bang but a whimper.

Everything was buttoned up by Tuesday midday.

Word leaked out, and *The Wall Street Journal* and *The New York Times* posted stories on Neumann's ouster, with news rapidly reverberating around the internet.

At 1:45 p.m., the official press release went out, titled "WeWork's Board of Directors Announces Leadership Changes."

"While our business has never been stronger, in recent weeks, the scrutiny directed toward me has become a significant distraction," Neumann's quotation in the release said. "I have decided that it is in the best interest of the company to step down as chief executive."

INSIDE WEWORK'S HEADQUARTERS, ARTIE MINSON AND SEBASTIAN Gunningham prepared to address the staff. They sent out a note to all employees, announcing that "Adam has decided to take on a new role as non-executive chairman." They were the new CEOs, they said, warning of "difficult decisions ahead."

At a meeting on WeWork's fourth floor minutes later, the two looked out at rows of glum staffers gathered there to listen. It was a somber coronation—a dramatic departure from the high-energy all-hands meetings of old. Flanked by Michael Eisenberg and Mark Schwartz, Minson began talking.

"Today has been an interesting day," he said. He apologized. For the IPO. For the drama. For the negative press attention that they'd probably been forced to explain to their family and friends for weeks. All of it.

Then he planted seeds of hope. "I believe in a comeback," he told them. He'd been through near-death experiences at other companies, and they'd turned around to become successful companies. WeWork, too, was going to be a comeback story.

CHAPTER 37

DeNeumannization

ADAM NEUMANN WAS BARELY GONE A DAY WHEN MAINTE-nance workers got to the sixth floor at WeWork's Eighteenth Street headquarters and approached the glass walls outside his office. The glass was frosted—so no one could see inside—with white waves imprinted on top of the coating. The workers began to scrape. Gradually, the office became transparent to those who walked by. Other workers were packing up Neumann's things: a photo of him riding a surfboard, other art—all was due to be removed. Down the hall, the pink couches in Rebekah Neumann's office were pulled out; it was being made into a conference room.

It was a new era. The DeNeumannization of WeWork had begun.

Moving swiftly, Artie Minson and Sebastian Gunningham set to work from their new, higher perches, trying to wrest control of the foundering giant. Urgent tasks were piling up. They would need new financing, given that the billions they had been counting on from the IPO weren't coming. They also needed to get WeWork's costs under control—a task no one had been able to do under Neumann, but one the public markets clearly demanded. Finally, Minson and Gunningham needed a strategy—a story that they could tell to investors about how they were going to fix the company.

First came further symbolic moves. Neumann's office was turned into a common lounge (the bathroom and spa were closed off, though curious employers peeked inside.) The jet would be put up for sale. More than fifteen people who were considered Neumann's wingmen—many with ill-defined jobs—were swiftly pushed out. WeWork's vice-chairman, Michael Gross, Neumann's constant sidekick at investor meetings and frequent drinking companion, was unceremoniously shown the door. So was Chris Hill, Rebekah's brother-in-law and the chief product officer. Neumann's drivers and numerous executive assistants were out, too. Staff in Neumann's outer office all packed up their things in boxes, clearing out a vast area in the headquarters.

Gunningham asked workers to sweep Neumann's office and its surroundings for bugs—wondering if the press was getting leaks via electronic listening devices inside the office. (None were found.)

The two new CEOs quickly settled on a strategy. WeWork would shear off all the new limbs it had grown in the past few years—surf pools, elementary schools, Meetup.com, WeLive—and slim down to its core trunk of office space subleasing. They would sell off the acquisitions—likely at big discounts.

They would halt growth immediately, though it would still take six to nine months to open up the new spaces they'd already leased.

Storm clouds and a cash crunch still loomed. Gunningham and Minson determined WeWork still needed job cuts—thousands of them. Managers were told to pull back job offers they'd recently extended; human resources even made a script for how staff should rescind offers.

Employees were glued to Slack, trying to make sense of the disorder that had fallen upon them. One of them was Andrew Walters, a twenty-four-year-old who had joined WeWork in August 2018 to work on marketing data.

The Seattle-raised corporate neophyte knew little of the company when he joined, but it seemed super successful—ubiquitous in New York. A colleague at his last job was joining, and he wanted a seat on the rocket ship, too. Still, it didn't take long before the sheen wore off. Walters found that the lofty rhetoric disguised a far less impressive engine under the hood. None of the tech in the company's demo area for investors and visitors seemed integral to WeWork's business. Management was in constant chaos; colleagues' titles changed six or seven times a year.

More than anything, he couldn't figure out what the magic was; it actually just seemed like a real estate company.

"There's no there there," he recalled thinking to himself. "It felt like we were just throwing money at fancy buildings and booze." As the IPO began to falter, he watched as more and more of his co-workers absorbed the reality of the business, reading one negative story after another. Once Neumann was ousted, onetime evangelizers pulled a 180. They were sad—upset with the reality of the company, now that they saw WeWork for what it was. Neumann became the butt of jokes.

"People were making fun of him," Walters said. It was a complete "emperor has no clothes" moment, he said.

Employees like Walters speculated about the forthcoming layoffs; rumors flew that it would be 20 percent, 30 percent of the staff. Some were still believers, certain the valuation drop would be temporary and their stock options ultimately would bring them riches. But for most, the reality was slowly setting in: WeWork wasn't a life-changing tech company at all; the market had called its bluff.

Not only did it mean their stock options were worthless, it also meant the mission they'd bought into—the soaring rhetoric about changing the world—had just been lip service. If WeWork wasn't a $47 billion tech company, what was it?

Neumann had frequently boasted about how if WeWork wanted to be profitable, all it had to do was slow its growth by half. "So all that talk about simply stopping expansion to be instantly profitable was smoke and mirrors?" one staffer asked on Slack. Someone else cropped the photo of Neumann walking barefoot near his house to make his bare feet an emoji on Slack; staffers could react to posts by posting the bare feet—the way they would a thumbs-down emoji.

NEUMANN'S FALL HAD AN IMPACT FAR OUTSIDE OF WEWORK'S OFfices.

For Silicon Valley, the implosion of the company quickly went from a schadenfreude-infused spectacle to a bomb that rained fallout upon the entire world of money-losing startups. The dominant thesis of the era—that giant losses didn't matter so long as companies had big vision and revenue growth—suddenly looked naïve. The public markets, it turned out, wanted real businesses, not dreams.

It was also true for Uber, the most hyped startup of the past decade, which had once seemed unstoppable and had been hailed as the future of transportation—something that would replace mass transit, personal cars, and even some walking. It hemorrhaged billions recruiting drivers and subsidizing rides in the name of continued growth, and nine months earlier its backers and bankers thought its valuation could soar past $100 billion. But by the time of Neumann's resignation, investors had a more sober view. Uber was worth around $50 billion; investors who pumped in money in a private round in 2015 were down more than 35 percent. If they'd just put their money in the Nasdaq, they'd have been up more than 60 percent.

A similar story went for Juul, the nicotine vaping company built out of Silicon Valley that had reached a $38 billion valuation from a monster investment by the tobacco giant Altria in late 2018. The day after Neumann was ousted, Juul's CEO resigned to make way for an Altria veteran. Slowing growth and regulatory pressures indicated that the vaping startup wasn't the golden ticket investors once thought. Soon after, Altria would reveal a $14 billion drop in Juul's valuation.

With tens of billions having vanished in value from just a few onetime heralded unicorns, bankers made clear to the rest of the unicorn herd—particularly those with similar loss-heavy business models—that the winds had shifted. Public market investors weren't buying what Silicon Valley was selling. The laws of gravity were back in effect.

The investment chill was felt widely, instilling fear in the backers of food delivery companies, scooter companies, and mattress start-ups. Co-working companies and other real estate startups with similar business models scaled back their plans and ambitions. Suddenly CEOs started talking about the need for a "path to profitability" rather than growth. Venture capitalists penned blog posts and Twitter threads recognizing a new era—pontificating that high-margin firms like business software companies were, in fact, the best bets for venture capital. The flaw of WeWork, they said, was its low margins that didn't improve with its scale.

In reality, Silicon Valley was recognizing something more elementary: that software investors should look for software-like profits from software, not from industries like real estate. The fact that venture capitalists suddenly pushed companies to show a "path to profitability" at all was telling: in normal times, a business model that doesn't call for profitability—let alone a "path" to it—isn't a business at all.

FOR SOFTBANK, IT WAS A BITTER PILL TO SWALLOW. IT HAD INfused a fleet of companies with billions. Masayoshi Son's stated strategy at the Vision Fund was that companies should accelerate their growth and not dwell on losses.

Son began to pivot. As WeWork was flailing, SoftBank executives instructed many of the companies they funded to do the opposite of everything they had preached. They should be focused on getting to profitability and even consider layoffs if necessary. SoftBank officials were no longer implying that fast-growing companies, particularly those with big losses, should expect more funding. While this missive was mostly likely insulting and frustrating to the CEOs who accepted SoftBank's money, it didn't make much sense. If getting to profits was the focus, what was the point of all the money SoftBank gave them? Spending money, by definition, tends to mean larger up-front losses.

Not all could pivot on a dime, and many in SoftBank's herd of unicorns began to grow frail. One after another—the dog-walking app Wag, the car rental company Fair, the hotel company OYO— quickly fell under the microscope of a press that had grown far more skeptical of vision-heavy startups than a few years earlier. The original $100 billion Vision Fund had so far found few standout stars, but had a roster of duds. The biggest investments went into ride hailing—where valuations were far lower than a year earlier— and autonomous driving, where a frenzy had cooled. The onetime dream of turning the fund into a $1 trillion home run now seemed a distant memory.

WeWork and the Vision Fund's promise were unraveling at the very time that Son was trying to raise a second, even larger Vision Fund. This was to be Son's future—a whole fleet of Vision Funds that would put him in charge of the largest sums ever raised—to be the kingmaker for all of tech. While he and Rajeev Misra had already said they'd rounded up $108 billion in tentative commitments for the sequel to the Vision Fund, these commitments weren't yet finalized.

Now one of the fund's biggest investments—the one Son used to extol on SoftBank earnings calls as his marquee bet—was shown to be a house of cards. It was disastrous timing. The various sovereign wealth funds, hedge funds, and pension plans Son was trying to round up immediately began to question his judgment, particularly given how obvious WeWork's warning signs looked in hindsight. If he thought WeWork was a $47 billion tech company, why would investors trust him with even more billions?

Mubadala, the Abu Dhabi fund that just months earlier had said it would put $25 billion into the second Vision Fund, now demurred. Son and Rajeev Misra tried another push with Prince Mohammed bin Salman, snorkeling with him in the Red Sea off two super yachts. Yet he didn't bite: Saudi Arabia remained on the sidelines, and other funds that had expressed interest stalled or said they could no longer commit.

The Vision Fund dream was all crumbling around Son.

First, though, Son had a more urgent problem. WeWork needed even more cash, and if it didn't get it soon, it could bring his investment to zero.

CHAPTER 38

Bread of Shame

D AYS AFTER TAKING CONTROL OF WEWORK, ARTIE MINSON and Sebastian Gunningham summoned the board of directors to a meeting about the company's future. The orderly setup represented a break from the past. An agenda had actually been sent out the night before so that directors knew what was going to be discussed. The co-CEOs were looking to get the directors' blessing for their plan to shed extraneous businesses, stop growth, and focus on existing offices.

As Minson kicked off the meeting, Steven Langman scanned through the agenda and materials before him and realized the WeWork nightmare wasn't over yet. Seemingly surprised, the private equity investor and longtime friend of Neumann's piped up to his fellow board members with a sound of alarm in his voice.

"We're going to run out of money."

AS RECENTLY AS THE SPRING OF 2019, WEWORK EXECUTIVES, IN-cluding Minson, had boasted about their impressive cash pile, saying they had billions to spare. But after Neumann was ousted and the IPO was called off, company leaders came to a different realization: WeWork was broke. It was burning cash at an astounding rate and was on track to run out of money in less than two months, more than five months faster than even cynical analysts had pro-jected.

The cash crunch was so severe that they *couldn't even afford layoffs*. They realized they didn't have enough money to pay the severance costs associated with the thousands of job cuts they planned.

Internally, finger-pointing began. Minson should have seen this coming for months and demanded a pullback in spending. Neumann—beyond the simple fact of presiding over a company that doubled its losses each year—had urged a particularly reckless strategy in 2019, pushing the company to fill new desks even faster, in a move to impress the markets during the fourth quarter. This came at a cost—rushing construction jobs is expensive—that fur-ther dwindled the company's savings. And the bankers and lawyers likely should have included a warning about the perilous cash posi-tion in the S-1.

Culpability aside, WeWork needed to move swiftly to save itself. It was staring down the prospect of bankruptcy if it couldn't raise the needed billions within weeks. The board took the lead, with two directors—Bruce Dunlevie of Benchmark and Lew Frankfort, the former Coach CEO—forming a special committee to raise the new money. In turn, they needed a banker to assist. Peter Wein-berg, a former partner at Goldman Sachs and CEO of the boutique investment bank Perella Weinberg, got a call from Mark Schwartz, the former Goldman executive on the board. WeWork desperately needed help. Could Weinberg do it? Weinberg had helped compa-nies like Wachovia and Chrysler navigate their own near-death ex-periences during the financial crisis. Now another troubled former giant needed his help.

When the board met a few days later to discuss more of its fi-nancial options, Schwartz wanted to address the group. The long-time Neumann booster could be awkward in one-on-one interactions, but he was also a gifted orator prone to giving didactic speeches.

"I've stayed silent too long," he declared. "We have to be cold-hearted about where we are going," he said. "No more fantasies."

IT QUICKLY BECAME CLEAR TO THE BOARD THAT WEWORK'S options were limited. SoftBank had already said it would put more money into WeWork to save the company, but that didn't mean it was the best course of action. Many of WeWork's remaining top executives had little but scorn for the conglomerate, blaming Masayoshi Son for accelerating WeWork's insanity under Neumann in the prior two years. They worried SoftBank would use We-Work's troubled position as a way to take over the company at a fire-sale price—balancing some of the billions it put in when the price was far higher.

The obvious alternative was JPMorgan. Despite the black eye it incurred with the failed IPO, it was still willing to help and put a group of debt bankers on the deal. Still, its offer was far less aggressive than a few months earlier. Its prior pledge to lead a $6 billion debt package at relatively low rates—contingent on the IPO—was history. WeWork was now a toxic asset, and JPMorgan didn't want to put its own money at risk. It only wanted to help arrange a deal in which it would find other debt investors, and those debt investors weren't likely to be willing to offer cheap interest rates.

Both suitors burrowed themselves into WeWork, dissecting the company's numbers and peppering the company with questions. A host of SoftBank employees camped out in WeWork's headquarters, which irked WeWork executives, especially Minson. The company gave us $10 billion, and *now* they're asking basic questions about the company's finances? Shouldn't they have done that earlier? he grumbled to others.

Minson, though, was hardly a bystander when it came to We-Work's current precarious position. The finances he oversaw as CFO weren't pretty; they portrayed a company that had reached the limits of its rapid growth. Overall rents were falling around the empire; teams were struggling to fill desks, even as they layered on incentives and discounts to get people in seats. Many buildings in China and elsewhere were performing terribly—not even covering the costs of their own expenses even before counting headquarters and administrative costs.

And things were set to get worse. WeWork had become an aircraft carrier, not a speedboat, and changing course would take time. Because the company had to sign leases months in advance of opening locations, it had already committed to a massive expansion, another 580,000 desks yet to be opened—a commitment that would require WeWork roughly doubling in size.

Now the potential debt investors got to see a key figure that was never included in WeWork's IPO prospectus: the profit margins of *mature* locations that had been open two years. Unlike community-adjusted EBITDA, mature location margins are a standard indicator in the industry that show how much average buildings generate in profit, excluding costs at headquarters. Because buildings open only a few months tend to be empty and lose money, the mature locations give investors a sense of the basic economics underpinning the entire business. Neumann and Minson used to woo investors by talking about how WeWork had amazing mature margins—more than 30 percent, sometimes more than 40 percent for some buildings—giving them a giant cushion if a recession ever happened.

But numbers presented to investors showed that those margins had hovered around 20 percent since 2017, the oldest numbers included in presentations. The difference seemed to be that WeWork was being more honest in how it counted this figure— including costs that always mattered but had been excluded in the past, investors and former employees who looked at the figures believed. It was a major chasm. By this measure, WeWork's special co-working sauce wasn't special at all. It was roughly even with the long-established competitor IWG, formerly Regus, which managed to be profitable overall, rather than losing 100 percent of its revenue.

IWG's Mark Dixon, who had stewed about WeWork for years, appeared to be right after all: they did have the same business. He just ran his profitably.

As the weeks of october ticked by, jpmorgan was struggling to round up interest. The bank thought it might be able to put together about $5 billion from a group of investors, including private equity investors like Starwood Capital Group, which had long been intrigued by WeWork but was wary of its high valuations. The bank's offer would be composed of debt with very steep interest rates—as high as 15 percent per year. Such extraordinary payments could sink WeWork, particularly if a recession happened and WeWork still had to pay all its leases, too. Minson, always a fan of JPMorgan, spent many days at the bank's headquarters working through the terms with them. He was a big booster of the deal despite the high interest rates, because he wanted to avoid more SoftBank involvement.

Regardless, it became clear to WeWork's advisers that SoftBank was going to have the upper hand. The company had previously committed to giving WeWork another $1.5 billion in May of the following year—a relic of the old deal when SoftBank was once planning to buy most of WeWork. Now, SoftBank told the company's advisers, it would withhold that $1.5 billion payment if JP-Morgan was chosen to lead the new financing round. It was effectively a death blow to JPMorgan's efforts: the bank had been counting on SoftBank's cash to supplement the additional funds it would raise.

Leading the effort for SoftBank was Marcelo Claure, whom Son had deputized to fix WeWork. Claure, a Guatemalan-born entrepreneur who owned stakes in two soccer teams, was ready for the assignment. At six feet, six inches tall, he was a bundle of energy.

He festooned his Instagram with photos showing him training for marathons, mountain biking, and scuba diving—often flanked by his wife and six children. After building up a successful telecom business that was bought by SoftBank, he rose to become the COO of SoftBank and the chairman of SoftBank-backed Sprint.

He had been tangentially involved in WeWork before—in one meeting with Son and Neumann, he was seen watching soccer on his iPad while others pondered details of a multibillion-dollar investment—but now he dived in deep. He would need to negotiate not just with the board's special financing committee but also with Neumann, who still had some cards to play. Not only was he still WeWork's chairman, but he had potent voting shares; SoftBank was going to want him to give up his role on the board and his votes.

Claure's offer on behalf of SoftBank was to put $5 billion of new money into WeWork through a series of loans and to speed up its $1.5 billion commitment. In addition, it would buy $3 billion worth of shares from existing investors—roughly half their stake.

SoftBank was valuing WeWork at roughly $8 billion. Down from $47 billion ten months earlier, it was a drop of historic proportions; few companies had imploded so rapidly and so flamboyantly. It was no Enron—which went from $70 billion to zero—but it wasn't orders of magnitude off. For everyone involved, the low valuation of the offer was a gut punch, but options were few, and the reality was the public markets were likely uninterested in We-Work at even $15 billion.

Once again, however, the sticking point in the deal making was Neumann. He wanted more. Despite still owning roughly 30 percent of WeWork—and having taken out hundreds of millions from loans and share sales over the years—he was at risk of losing much of his financial empire. Because of the way he structured the nearly $500 million debt he'd taken out from banks, including JPMorgan, he risked being in default on the loan. The debt required that he serve as CEO of WeWork. Given that he wasn't any longer, the lenders had the ability to seize his WeWork stock if he couldn't repay them.

Neumann knew his personal fortune was in jeopardy. He and his wife had bought eight homes, and Neumann had spent heavily on other investments like buying up commercial property and making angel investments. He didn't have the cash to pay back the money he'd borrowed. He needed a new loan from SoftBank.

He also wanted something else: a giant payment of cash to go away. He wouldn't give up his potent voting shares without it. Rumors swirled inside WeWork that SoftBank and Neumann were talking about a *$100 million* payout. Any sum, they thought, would be ludicrous, given that his greed was a big reason the company was worth so little now. In effect, he would be asking for a lump sum simply to stop hurting his own company.

Claure could have taken a hard tack. He could have pressured Neumann by waiting and seeing what happened once he ran into trouble with JPMorgan over his loan.

But SoftBank had its own pressures. Top executives were scheduled to fly to Saudi Arabia for the kingdom's financial conference, where they were still hoping they could secure large commitments for a second Vision Fund. Company after company in the Vision Fund was suffering embarrassing revelations as the press scrutiny intensified after the WeWork debacle. With it, the chances of Son's pulling off a second Vision Fund were fading. Executives needed a clean and swift resolution to WeWork.

SoftBank blinked. Claure agreed to Neumann's requests. SoftBank would give him a new loan to repay his $500 million in debt, and he could sell roughly $1 billion of his shares alongside employees and other investors. The conglomerate even assented to Neumann's request to forgive his debts to WeWork—the roughly $1.7 million he owed the company for all his personal private jet trips and other expenses from recent months. His surf vacations in the G650ER, the personal errands WeWork staff did for the Neumanns—all were now being paid for by WeWork.

Finally, Claure agreed that SoftBank would pay Neumann money structured as a consulting fee, one that would come in as a few separate payments over time. He'd have a non-compete and couldn't start another co-working company.

The amount: $185 million.

WeWork's board accepted the offer from SoftBank on October 22. JPMorgan was dismissed.

A press release went out just before 10:00 p.m. announcing the SoftBank deal. For many, there was relief: the company wouldn't declare bankruptcy; it had a giant cushion of money to stay afloat. Still, board members quietly expressed disgust to each other at the size and the terms of Neumann's payout. Neumann's avarice and antics had made the company so toxic it couldn't go public. Now he'd be walking away with over $1.1 billion in cash and a new $500 million loan. It was an enormous haul for a now-disgraced former CEO.

ADAM AND REBEKAH NEUMANN LIKED TO CITE TEACHINGS FROM Kabbalah in conversations with friends, family, and strangers alike. They'd discuss how they were "learning the game of life," having "the courage to be the full light" that they could be, and "elevating their own consciousness" and that of others.

Another line came up often and required more explanation: "the bread of shame." According to the Kabbalistic maxim, bread tastes good only if it's earned through hard work. Otherwise it has a bitter taste. "If the person you are looking to share with doesn't want to make an effort and is just looking for a 'handout,' it is a case of Bread of Shame," Michael Berg, the director of the Kabbalah Centre, wrote in a 2016 blog post.

The couple would use the term disdainfully to talk about household employees, WeWork and WeGrow employees, and friends and other advisers who they thought simply wanted something from them. When WeGrow's teachers wanted raises, Rebekah Neumann invoked the term as she pushed back against the request.

Now, though, the Neumanns had their own bread of shame—a

connection made by several employees who heard them talk about it over the years. After building up WeWork, Adam Neumann had crashed it into a mountain. He had wasted billions in investor dollars and become a poster child of a reckless CEO.

Now he was leaving extraordinarily rich. Adam Neumann was getting paid to walk away from the mess he created.

THE CRIES OF REVULSION AND ANGER FROM WITHIN WEWORK came swiftly and loudly.

The valuation was horrifyingly low. Until recently, almost every person hired at WeWork had been given stock options in addition to a salary. But for the vast majority of those employees—more than 90 percent of them—the valuation had fallen so much that their options were underwater, meaning they were effectively worthless. For later employees, options weren't a huge chunk of their net worth. But many rank-and-file employees who had been around for three or four years were sitting on hundreds of thousands of dollars in paper wealth that had vanished.

Pouring acid into the wound was Neumann's payout. While most of the staff got years of promises of riches and now had nothing, Neumann was getting a $185 million payout to *not* be CEO of his company anymore, on top of the $1 billion in stock he could sell. Some had planned their whole lives around their paper riches. Now they had nothing. It was one of the biggest CEO golden parachutes in corporate history—given to a CEO who had just presided over a company that lost more than four-fifths of its paper valuation. WeWork investors, too, were disturbed by the move. But unlike the $1.7 million in forgiven debt for plane expenses, which was borne by WeWork, the $185 million was purely SoftBank's money.

Claure entered WeWork in the middle of this storm. With Neumann out, he was now WeWork's executive chairman and would be guiding the company through its next rocky period.

On October 23, the day after SoftBank announced its bailout

deal, he arrived at WeWork's headquarters—his new place of business. He'd soon settle in and get his own office, but to start off, he called a town hall meeting for the staff.

Bodies filed into a large room at headquarters and found a lineup of top executives onstage that captured the awkwardness of the moment. In addition to Claure, Artie Minson and Sebastian Gunningham—WeWork's new co-CEOs—sat on chairs onstage off to the side. Minson sat quietly, looking vacant, his face filled with disbelief. During the long meeting, neither co-CEO spoke.

Instead, it was Miguel McKelvey, the last standing member of the WeWork founding team, who spoke on behalf of the company's old guard. Despite the plunge in value, despite the now pariah status of the co-founder he'd tied himself to nine years earlier, he was a fount of positivity, expressing his gratitude to employees, to advisers, to the WeWork world, and to SoftBank.

"So I think all of us, I think that we're all going to learn to both appreciate Marcelo and the rest of the SoftBank team who is joining and supporting us," McKelvey said on a stage with hundreds of employees in front of him and thousands more watching him on video or listening in. "And every one of you should understand this investment as a belief in you, as a belief that the people that are investing in us as a company are putting their money behind all of you."

McKelvey closed out his remarks and his endless streams of thank-yous. Then the six-foot-eight Oregonian clasped his new boss, Claure, with a big hug.

A FEW DAYS LATER, AS THE DUST BEGAN TO SETTLE, EMPLOYEES AT an experimental WeWork retail store in the Flatiron district of Manhattan noticed that one item was really selling strangely well. The store was a mix of WeWork gift shop—offering swag like sweatshirts and mugs—and a hip coffee shop where guests paid by the minute. One after another, customers were buying white T-shirts sporting the words "Made by We" repeated in a rainbow of colors.

It was the same shirt Neumann wore to Global Summit—the one that was featured in countless acerbic stories in the media about him and WeWork's demise. The occasion was Halloween. Adam Neumann was a costume.

As Adam Neumann look-alikes popped up at parties accompanied by props like a sack of money or a giant SoftBank check, WeWork staff braced for another blow. Executives had spent the weeks after the SoftBank bailout racing to implement something they code-named Project Huxley, a reference to Aldous Huxley, author of the classic dystopian novel *Brave New World*.

Beginning on November 21, one after another wave of employees was called into a conference room on the second floor of headquarters. Inside, Sebastian Gunningham and Artie Minson were seated in the back. An HR leader then started reading from a script. The employees were being laid off. They needed to leave immediately.

It wasn't a surprise. Managers told employees for weeks that the cuts were coming, and some employees even asked to be put on the layoff list, as they called it. Rumors flew constantly that the layoffs were coming within days, and work effectively ceased in many departments: employees stopped showing up for days at a time; the more adventurous ones stayed away for weeks. And for those who were pushed out, the severance package was generous—months of salary and health-care benefits.

But the significance wasn't lost on the current and former workers. While the failed IPO showed that the market didn't buy WeWork's story, this was the effect: thousands of people would be out of work. Designers, salespeople, employees from the well-paid tech team. It was all part of WeWork's reverse metamorphosis, from butterfly to caterpillar. WeWork was shifting from a flashy tech company to a real estate company.

A similar if less dramatic realization was sweeping staff at other companies fueled on the same high-octane Silicon Valley hype. Even Uber zealots who believed they were working for a life-changing Amazon of transportation were now forced to look at the stock price and conclude that the public markets saw it less like the new Google or Amazon and more like the car service app company it was, albeit one growing fast. Mattress companies were becoming mattress companies, not mission-driven, tech-fueled future-of-sleep companies. Scooter companies were just offering scooters, not disrupting walking. Billions on paper were being lost across Silicon Valley—a trend driven in large part by the WeWork disaster.

It was a lesson being absorbed by Masayoshi Son as well. Investors weren't taking him up on his second Vision Fund. The $108 billion in commitments he thought he once had proved illusory; no one was signing. The aura of the founder—the idea that visionaries should be blindly followed so long as they had charisma and charm and spoke the right startup lingo—had begun to wear off. Among investors there was more talk of caution—of the risks of giving twenty- or thirtysomething high-energy entrepreneurs full control of hundreds of millions or even billions of investor dollars.

As the 2010s drew to a close, the traditional rules of business, where profits matter, still applied.

ADAM NEUMANN, VIRTUALLY OVERNIGHT, HAD BECOME A PARIAH in Silicon Valley and New York finance—the paragon of the irresponsible CEO. Even many of his longtime close friends and aides were furious with him. Medina Bardhi, his longtime chief of staff who served on his condo board, gained wide attention when she filed an employment complaint against WeWork in the days after the SoftBank bailout. In addition to alleging that Neumann called her maternity leave "vacation," the document was sprinkled with embarrassing revelations about Neumann and his party-heavy lifestyle.

Part of this vitriol was justified anger at a man whose greed and unfettered hunger for greater power helped tank the potential IPO. Some, though, was a projection on the part of people who should have known better. Neumann's vision was intoxicating, but even his disciples could have asked harder questions. They could have looked around them, seen reality, and spoken up.

As for Neumann, the onetime life of the party was now telling others that he was lonely; his friends and aides were abandoning him. In the days after Neumann resigned, Rebekah returned to the building to address the WeGrow staff and families. She pledged to continue to support the school, where students had been in session for just a few weeks of the new school year. "I'm here," she told them. "I'm not going anywhere."

By the end of October, however, the Neumanns had pulled their children out of the school, fearful for their safety.

Adam and Rebekah tried to escape the fray. The Neumann family went surfing in the Caribbean, then flew to the Bay Area to the Guitar House for a few days. Even there, media stories on Neumann's fall from grace kept coming, as did a handful of lawsuits from disgruntled staff, seeking remuneration for all they had lost. One person tasked with serving Neumann with court papers arrived at his home and handed the materials to a person who looked exactly like the former CEO. The man denied he was Neumann. The press attention did not let up. The *New York Post* ridiculed the Neumanns for still flying around on private jets.

As the New Year approached, Adam and Rebekah Neumann were ready for a more drastic change. It was time to move back to where Neumann's story started—the country he had left nearly two decades prior as he went searching for fame and fortune in America. They were headed to Israel.

On December 23, someone at San Francisco International Airport—perhaps working off a tip, perhaps just milling around—caught a glimpse of the couple and snapped some photos that would appear in the *New York Post*. Adam Neumann was in a black hoodie and gray jeans, presiding over a cart overstacked with suitcases, waiting in line at the ticket counter. Rebekah was wearing a jacket with a sun beaming rainbow rays as she corralled their children.

They were flying commercial.

Epilogue

They were careless people . . . they smashed up things and creatures and then retreated back into their money or their vast carelessness or whatever it was that kept them together, and let other people clean up the mess they had made.

—F. SCOTT FITZGERALD, *The Great Gatsby*

ON NOVEMBER 6, SIX WEEKS AFTER ADAM NEUMANN STEPPED aside as CEO, Masayoshi Son stood on a stage in Tokyo, sounding humbled.

"My own investment judgment was really bad," Son said. "I regret it."

He was staring into a sea of Japanese reporters and TV cameras at the Royal Park Hotel for SoftBank's quarterly earnings press conference. It was Son's first time publicly offering a long mea culpa on WeWork.

He flipped through a presentation on a screen behind him. Slides showed stark red lines and arrows pointing down, illustrating the dire state of WeWork. One slide simply had two text bubbles: "Significant decrease in profit" and "WeWork problem." The image in the background was one of stormy seas.

He "overestimated Adam's good side," he said, and "should have known better." He "turned a blind eye" to Neumann's bad side, Son said.

The reckless rocket that was WeWork was already well off course by the time Son came into the picture; Neumann had already dabbled heavily in self-enrichment, and the company was far from focused. But as the dust settled after WeWork's implosion, it became clear that Son was Neumann's enabler-in-chief. He handed Neumann far more money than anyone else—more than $10 billion—and encouraged him to engage in even riskier behavior, all despite objections from his own staff. For that $10 billion, Son could have owned *all* of IWG, the profitable serviced office giant, and still had more than $5 billion to spare. It was enough to buy the Empire State Building many times over. Instead, he bought into Neumann's hype and his own delusions of what WeWork could be.

The fallout kicked off a tough few months for the self-styled Warren Buffett of tech. Son became the butt of jokes in Silicon Valley. Once the press and other investors began looking into the Vision Fund more, it became apparent that the largest investment fund ever raised was full of mini WeWorks. Some were sounder businesses than others, but almost all had the same general business plan urged by Son: spend heavily to buy growth; worry about profits later. Just as with WeWork, heavy spending on revenue growth wasn't leading to profits.

The roster of SoftBank flops continued to grow.

Typifying the Vision Fund portfolio company was Wag—the Uber for dog walking, an app that connected dog walkers with dog owners. Wag was looking for around $75 million of investment in 2018 when SoftBank pushed $300 million on it instead. The theory was that the extra money would let Wag spend its way to be the market leader, dominating the burgeoning market. Not only did the strategy not result in a profitable business; it didn't even work to give Wag an edge. Its rival, Rover, raised more money, and Wag's market share stayed embarrassingly small despite the cash, estimated at less than 20 percent, against Rover. By October, SoftBank decided to cut bait: it put its stake up for sale, selling at a valuation well below where it invested.

Other investments withered, too. Zume shut down its robot-made pizza delivery operation in January 2020. A SoftBank-funded company that aspired to beam the internet from space via satellites went bankrupt. Layoffs swept like a virus across SoftBank companies: the delivery company Rappi, the car-sharing startup Getaround, and more. OYO, the hotel company run by Neumann's "little brother" Ritesh Agarwal, pulled out of two hundred cities and cut two thousand staff.

With the growing pile of embarrassments, the sequel fund was on life support. Investors simply couldn't buy into Son's plans for a repeat of the same playbook. Whatever personal sway he had with Crown Prince Mohammed bin Salman, it wasn't enough. Despite announcing $108 billion in commitments the prior year, little if any of that was binding.

Yet Son's troubles weren't over. An activist investor, Elliott Management, took a big stake in SoftBank and began pressuring SoftBank to sell more of its assets—to spend more money boosting the stock through buybacks rather than pouring money into startups. Another dagger came from COVID-19. The onset of the pandemic sent the ride-hailing market into a tailspin, reversing an early 2020 rally in Uber's shares.

Son, again on his back foot, took to PowerPoint. In May 2020, during a call with investors, he featured a slide of horses stampeding into what he called "the valley of the coronavirus" with some unicorns flying out. Some companies would die, he said. Others would fly out stronger.

Amid the storm, he had to admit the obvious: the dream was dead. SoftBank announced it was shelving its fund-raising plans for Vision Fund 2. It would use only its own money for the fund, until it could show the world some good results. "The performance of Softbank Vision Fund 1 is not that great," Son told investors.

By the summer, as Claure was hunkered down in WeWork's

headquarters wrestling with the fallout of the pandemic on the commercial real estate market, Son was already pivoting—focusing on other ways to make money.

Then, by the fall, the dark clouds over SoftBank started to float away. Yes, Son had lost billions; yes, he'd shown lack of discipline and reckless naïveté. But as was true before WeWork, the reality about SoftBank was that its value was largely tied up in its holdings of Alibaba stock. So long as Alibaba kept doing well, Son's misadventures with other people's money were just that. It wasn't a problem, so long as he didn't dive too deep into SoftBank's own coffers to start recklessly buying startups. SoftBank began pouring money into startups once again, though far less than before—and far more focused on software companies, rather than consumer products that required heavy investment.

Son, always the techno optimist, began to shift his investment strategy to the biggest, most established tech companies—a pivot away from the unproven startups. He wagered complex bets on the rise of Amazon, Microsoft, and Tesla, ones that were so large that traders believed they were skewing the entire market, making the tech stocks rise and fall in more volatile ways. Son was dubbed the "Nasdaq Whale." SoftBank's stock came back in favor. It hit a post-dot-com-era high by the fall.

ELSEWHERE, THE STAIN OF ONE OF THE MORE DRAMATIC IMPLO-sions in business history was quickly washed away. Business went back to normal. Everyone started making money once again.

At Goldman Sachs, two of the key bankers on Goldman's We-Work team, David Ludwig and Kim Posnett, were given promotions. Posnett became the co-head of the bank's global investment banking services unit—the first woman to lead the business. Ludwig went on to lead the bank's global capital markets business. Goldman's CEO, David Solomon, meanwhile, didn't offer much of a mea culpa on WeWork. In January 2020, he told a crowd at the

World Economic Forum in Davos, Switzerland, that "the process worked" with WeWork. Investor feedback "ground it in reality." The bank became a lender to SoftBank-controlled WeWork.

At JPMorgan, Noah Wintroub had walked away from WeWork after a fight with Neumann in the days after the IPO was called off. Five months later, he was given a promotion, named one of eighteen "global chairmen" tasked with bringing new clients to the bank. JPMorgan also got paid for the rescue package that was spurned by the board in favor of SoftBank. The bank told WeWork it was owed roughly $50 million in fees for the effort, though We-Work said it wouldn't pay. Ultimately, the two agreed on a smaller amount. Still, Jamie Dimon's long-held hopes to be a top adviser in Silicon Valley stayed unrealized. Morgan Stanley and Goldman continued to dominate.

The mutual fund managers Henry Ellenbogen of T. Rowe Price and Gavin Baker of Fidelity went out on their own, starting new investment funds. While hobbled giant unicorns like WeWork and Uber didn't perform well, their smaller bets from 2014 and 2016 on less flashy business-focused software companies like Twilio rocketed in value.

In the office business, Mark Dixon of IWG seemed relieved and elated after Neumann's fall from grace. In the weeks after Neumann was ousted in the fall of 2019, Dixon flew to New York City and made the rounds with the press. "I've been scratching my head for a while on it," he told CNBC, noting that he wasn't celebrating WeWork's troubles. This is a business, he added, "where there are no shortcuts."

His fortune continued to rise through the fall and early spring. IWG's stock crept up and up, hitting an all-time high in the new year, just before the global pandemic hit.

MEANWHILE, WEWORK'S STRUGGLES CONTINUED. THE SOFTBANK-led team began sifting through the wreckage of the inefficient empire Neumann built with their money, casting for ways to turn the business around and lob off fat.

An easy spot was WeWork's eclectic collection of companies, which were put on the sales block. It disposed of its stake in Wave-garden; it sold Meetup.com and Conductor. In all, the acquisitions were off-loaded for huge discounts, netting WeWork losses of well over $100 million on the portfolio. One ended up doing decently, albeit after WeWork's Creator Fund sold its stake: Laird Superfood conducted an IPO, which valued it at nearly double the price We-Work paid.

Artie Minson and Sebastian Gunningham didn't last long as co-CEOs. They helped oversee some restructuring—even more cutting and streamlining. In February, Marcelo Claure of SoftBank hired a CEO to replace them. Sandeep Mathrani, who ran a company that was one of the country's largest mall owners, was a veteran of the real estate industry. His job was turning WeWork from a buzzy startup that thought of itself as possessing a unique and disruptive mission into a slimmed-down straightforward commercial real estate subleasing company.

Many of the remaining Neumann lieutenants trickled out. Shiva Rajaraman, the tech head, left soon after the transition. McKelvey, frustrated that Mathrani was discarding some initiatives he thought were important, like the company's original mission statement, left midway through 2020, surprising many colleagues. Jen Berrent, however, stayed on for well over a year. One of her tasks under the new management: dealing with the onslaught of investigations WeWork faced in the aftermath of its fall. The SEC, the U.S. Department of Justice, and the New York attorney general's office all opened inquiries, peppering WeWork with questions on topics ranging from how it described compensation to potential employees to details involving ARK. None of these investigations seemed to keep much momentum, and executives at WeWork believed they were unlikely to result in any disciplinary actions. In the end, it seemed WeWork's implosion wasn't caused by fraudulent deception of investors. It was a large-scale self-delusion, all in plain view.

As WeWork played defense on the legal front, under Mathrani the business strategy began to come more into focus. The marching orders were to keep slimming down and turn profitable. There would be no more Summer Camp, no sprawling events team, no surf pools or divisions that advised Fortune 500 companies on culture. WeWork was in the subleasing business. Claure predicted that WeWork would be generating more cash than it consumed by 2021.

Then came the coronavirus.

When the virus spread around the globe in March, many of WeWork's defining features suddenly became vulnerabilities. We-Work's offices were all about social interaction—they were about high density and about going into the office rather than staying at home. And on the business side, they were flexible, easily canceled often with just days' or weeks' notice.

It was hard to imagine a worse marketing pitch in the midst of a deadly virus.

Tenants canceled their memberships in droves, while WeWork scrambled to offer deals to those who committed to stay. Investors worried about bankruptcy—again—and the price of WeWork's bonds plunged to 30 cents on the dollar, a level that implies many investors think a company will fail. SoftBank revalued its WeWork stake at $2.9 billion in May.

It wasn't a good feeling. Over $10 billion of investment had gone into WeWork by late 2019. Thousands of people lost their jobs. Many more lost the value of their stock options.

WeWork, again, was a toxic asset. The company began breaking leases with landlords en masse, extricating itself from buildings around the globe. There was a 230,000-square-foot lease in Düsseldorf, set to be one of WeWork's largest spaces; a lease in London; two buildings in Chicago; a building in Durham, North Carolina. All were canceled, moves that sometimes cost WeWork millions per location just in penalties.

WeWork muddled through the summer, then fall, then winter. Through attrition, outsourcing, and more rounds of layoffs, We-Work's head count eventually fell by more than 8,000 from its peak of over 14,000 to 5,600 by mid-2020. SoftBank's cash provided an important cushion; some competitors were even more strained. It still had plenty of longer-term commitments. Executives felt the un-certainty caused by COVID-19 might actually be able to play in their favor once everyone went back to the office. There were convincing signs that whenever normalcy returned, flexible space would be in demand. While it surely didn't have the novelty of a "physical social network," real estate arbitrage might yet turn into a viable business.

THE RISE AND FALL OF WEWORK WAS ENABLED BY A COLLISION OF forces: a man characterized by charisma, unbridled optimism, and astute salesmanship met an entire financial system primed to fall under his spell.

Had a frothy venture capital sector not been so obsessed with the search for eccentric and visionary founders, WeWork might still oc-cupy only a smattering of buildings in Brooklyn and lower Manhat-tan. If mutual funds hadn't rushed into startups, WeWork might have never had the funds to start expanding to surf pools. If Saudi Arabia's economy hadn't fallen under the control of a new startup-loving prince desperate to diversify its oil wealth, Masayoshi Son might never have written Neumann a check. If bankers hadn't been so fo-cused on the prestige and fees from leading a big IPO, perhaps sober advice could have prevailed before a major public embarrassment.

When all the forces worked together, people thought as a herd. Optimism supplanted critical thinking. Smart minds were bent so that a real estate company looked like a software company. It was the same effect that allowed mattress companies to look like tech companies. Ride-hailing firms weren't just glorified taxi services, but were meant to compete with established retail giants. When everyone stood to get rich, everything had infinite potential.

Amplifying it all was the cult of the founder, in which Silicon Valley lionized self-assured entrepreneurs defined by big vision and just the right levels of crazy. From a distance, the notion that investors would surrender full control over their money to an inexperienced founder at a company that already was losing hundreds of millions—or even billions—of dollars seems difficult to comprehend. Corporate America had undergone decades of improving hygiene around conflicts of interest and shareholder oversight—a cleanup that regressed dramatically in Silicon Valley in the 2010s amid a boom of founder control. As this recipe of poor corporate governance spread virally, it made a WeWork-style disaster inevitable sooner or later.

Wall Street blanched at a number of similar money-losing companies in early 2020—the mattress maker Casper's IPO went quite poorly—as the herd moved from ride hailing and office space toward software and cloud computing. The newly wealthy CEOs tended to be utilitarian nerds obsessed with online data growth, not rock-star-like figures out to elevate consciousness. Tech investors were making money on tech.

For much of the year after WeWork's collapse, change seemed to be in the air; the affair in Silicon Valley appeared to have been a learning experience.

Or was it?

Through the first half of 2020, the electric car manufacturer Tesla—led by an eccentric, unpredictable founder known for overpromising and exciting investors—surged in value as backers saw near-infinite potential in its future. Little had changed in its business, but it started a climb that made it worth more than two times the valuation of Toyota, despite producing a fraction of the cars. CEO Elon Musk would become the richest person on the planet by the beginning of 2021.

That rise had a ripple effect. In the summer of 2020, Nikola Corporation, a six-year-old electric truck company founded by a charismatic entrepreneur named Trevor Milton, went public and its stock soared. Even though Nikola wasn't yet manufacturing trucks, Milton inspired investors by painting a picture of how its design would remake the whole enormous trucking sector. Public market investors, including novices using the app Robinhood—some first-time stock pickers bored and looking for entertainment during the coronavirus shutdown—rushed into the frenzy. Nikola's valuation eclipsed that of Ford, topping $30 billion.

There were eerie parallels to WeWork and Neumann. Milton sold $94 million of stock as the company prepared to go public. Under his watch, Nikola bought a Jet Ski company. He purchased a private plane. He bought a giant estate where he said he planned an organic farm.

And like Neumann's, his empire unraveled—quickly. In September, a short seller released a report challenging Milton's visionary statements as misleading or inaccurate. A video of a prototype truck running on a highway was staged, the report said; the truck was drifting after being let loose downhill. By the end of September, Milton was out as CEO and Nikola's shares had plunged, yet he still left a rich man. It was like WeWork on fast-forward.

People, it seemed, could not resist continuing to dream big.

Society is easily wooed by a charismatic leader with a big vision. It's hard to resist an optimist who promises a lucrative future—a messiah for profits lying just over the next horizon.

BY LATE 2020, IT WAS CLEAR THERE WAS A BIGGER SHIFT IN THE financial markets going on. Perhaps it was the economic rescue actions that came after the virus first hit, perhaps it was the Federal Reserve lowering interest rates and printing trillions in new money, or perhaps it was the growth of stock trading at home by bored millennials wielding the Robinhood app. The U.S. economy was still struggling, yet stocks were surging to all-time highs.

Startups—not just software companies, but money-losing consumer-friendly brands—were back in vogue, and the post-

WeWork chill was quickly forgotten. DoorDash and Airbnb—once worried that WeWork's fallout would spread their way—had extraordinarily successful IPOs, landing on the public markets with valuations that left many of their early investors struggling to understand what was going on. DoorDash was valued by the stock market at $56 billion, nearly double the value of the owner of Pizza Hut, Taco Bell, and KFC. It was a huge windfall for SoftBank, a big DoorDash investor. SoftBank's Vision Fund finally had a success story, having turned $680 million in investment into over $10 billion worth of DoorDash stock. Airbnb CEO Brian Chesky was speechless on a Bloomberg TV appearance when he was informed of Airbnb's expected opening share price. At around $90 billion, Airbnb was worth more than Hilton, Marriott, and Hyatt combined, up from $26 billion a few months earlier. Bankers and institutional investors blamed amateur traders for driving the frenzy.

Suddenly, it was clear the script had flipped—again. The private market for startups was now more conservative than the public markets, where vision and hype were now magnets for traders on Robinhood. Not only were companies with losses suddenly welcome, but numerous electric car and battery companies without any revenue started to fetch multibillion-dollar valuations—all by promising a heady future. The pendulum swung back to founders. Chesky and his co-founders increased their grip by getting twenty votes per share, up from ten—the move that Adam Neumann attempted. DoorDash's founders got twenty votes per share. The founder of the software company C3.ai got fifty.

The stock markets were finally buying what Silicon Valley was selling. Now it was the public market investors holding the bag.

By February, the market was on fire. One startup after another was going public through a less rigorous public listing process than an IPO, using a once-esoteric vehicle called a special-purpose acquisition company (SPAC), where a publicly traded shell company that has no assets beyond its cash merges with a startup, bringing it public in a faster process. Billions piled into the sector by the week.

It was like the startup sector was hit by another Vision Fund, but spread across dozens of SPACs. Valuations surged upward as, once again, far too much money was chasing too few good businesses.

Even long-struggling startups suddenly found light at the end of the tunnel, with new investors willing to hand them money to bring them public. With the market searing and hungry for vision-heavy startups, losses were once again an afterthought. Even companies without any revenue were being valued in the billions.

In a case of history repeating itself, WeWork began flirting with the latest trend—this new spigot of money. It was an alluring prospect: a faster way to go public, with far less fuss and scrutiny than the IPO process. In late March, as this book was going to press, WeWork struck a deal to merge with a SPAC and list publicly within months. The valuation—around $8 billion—was a far cry from its peak. Still, the stars were finally aligning. With the end of COVID on the horizon, WeWork was gearing up to go public once again.

As for adam neumann, he didn't end up the immediate billionaire he'd imagined. He quietly arrived in Israel at the end of 2019. At least there, no one was serving him court papers from a small civil suit. As Neumann's mother, Avivit Neumann-Orbach, told an Israeli publication after he arrived, "People embrace him here and it does him good."

He and Rebekah rented a beachfront villa on the outskirts of Tel Aviv and mostly stayed out of public view. They brought along members of their household staff, including several teachers for their children. They had plenty from Neumann's earlier cash withdrawals, including his portion of the nearly $500 million sold by We Holdings over the years and the $500 million line of credit that SoftBank refinanced. He also had his $185 million exit package to live off, though SoftBank hadn't yet paid the full amount. And by March, he was awaiting another nearly $1 billion set to come from SoftBank, due at the end of the month.

Days before the money was supposed to roll into Neumann's bank account—as well as those of former employees and other investors—SoftBank reneged. Citing multiple provisions in the deal documents that it thought gave it an out—a China financing deal hadn't happened, and WeWork was dealing with investigations from regulators—SoftBank simply refused to pay up. COVID-19 was sweeping the globe. WeWork's finances were looking dire. Masayoshi Son didn't want to spend another $3 billion on WeWork, even if he'd agreed to do it. As he'd told Marcelo Claure in an email later unearthed in a court fight, "Don't do the tender." Claure emailed that it showed Son was realizing he needed more discipline. SoftBank said it was well within its legal rights, given the contract they signed with Neumann and WeWork.

The hundreds of early WeWork employees who'd been counting on the stock sale—who'd seen this as their only consolation for the dashed dreams of the company they'd worked at for years—were furious. So, too, were the early investors. It was a bait and switch: the $3 billion share purchase was a key way SoftBank had sold them on the bailout. Benchmark had already sold enough stock earlier to earn a healthy profit on the company, but even at WeWork's depressed $8 billion valuation it had roughly $600 million tied up in WeWork. Still, it was Neumann who had the most to lose, at least in dollars. With SoftBank withholding Neumann's $970 million cash-out, Bloomberg in April dropped him off its list of the world's billionaires.

Lawsuits followed. Bruce Dunlevie—mostly retired—led one on behalf of old investors, while Neumann filed a separate suit against SoftBank. It wasn't until early 2021 that the sides opted to settle. Eager to get its relationship with WeWork cleaned up in advance of the SPAC deal, SoftBank agreed to buy half the stock it once committed to, paying $1.5 billion to the shareholders, including nearly $500 million to Neumann. Yet again, Neumann negotiated more for himself, getting some valuable perks unavailable to early employees and investors. SoftBank extended its loan to

Neumann—which had a roughly $430 million balance—for five years, and it agreed to pay him $50 million in cash, essentially the remaining balance on his $185 million exit package from fall 2019, which SoftBank had stopped paying amid the legal fight.

The Neumanns didn't last long in Israel. By spring 2020, the family had returned to the United States, heading to the Hamptons to wait out the pandemic with plenty of space and nearby surf spots. They tried to pare down their property portfolio, listing the Guitar House, the second home north of the city, and the Gramercy home. (Just as WeWork was imploding, the Neumanns were given a potential fix to the 5G antenna by their building: they could buy out the phone companies' lease on the antenna. It was too late, because they spent little time there afterward.) Neumann sold his interest in all the San Jose properties to a developer.

He spent his days surfing in Montauk. His squad was mostly gone, but he wasn't completely alone. He was still paying someone to tug him out to the waves on the back of a Jet Ski.

More than anything, he was restless. He was eager to beat Son in the lawsuit and eager to get back to work—to do something new. Just as he could never sit still in a chair for more than a few minutes, he simply couldn't stand to be out of the spotlight for so long.

It was a quality shared by Rebekah Neumann. Her devotion to WeGrow hadn't waned, and she bought the assets of the school—primarily the curriculum—from WeWork in mid-2020, renaming it SOLFL. Pronounced "soulful," it was a phrase she long used: "student of life for life."

Adam Neumann couldn't get away from his past either. He told friends and associates he wanted to build something focused on residential real estate. His focus would be the future of living, he said—investing in startups in the space and owning his own buildings. There's a huge opportunity to create a widely known brand of apartments aimed at young renters—something the fractured residential rental market lacks, he told others. He mused about raising hundreds of millions of dollars from others—of taking over start-ups. After trying to invest in numerous startups, he zeroed in on one struggling apartment services company, Hello Alfred, an on-demand concierge for apartment dwellers. He led a new round of funding and pulled a few still-loyal former aides into the company.

One way or another, Neumann was determined to be seen again—to sell a vision of explosive growth to the investment world.

He was eager and full of energy. He was yearning to get back in the game.

ACKNOWLEDGMENTS

W E ARE DEEPLY GRATEFUL TO A SMALL VILLAGE OF FRIENDS, family, colleagues, mentors, and others who helped us guide this book into existence.

Foremost, *The Wall Street Journal* has been a fantastic professional home for both of us, and this book would not be possible without the paper and the stellar, driven journalists who work there.

Our experience covering WeWork for the *Journal*—both the company's rise and its spectacular unraveling—was foundational for this book. By every measure, it was an extraordinary group effort. Editors throughout the paper recognized the story for its significance, while reporters around the *Journal* empire were essential teammates in unearthing new, important details as the company was imploding.

Thank you to everyone at the *Journal* who touched the story, a lengthy list. Liz Hoffman and Dave Benoit in particular were crucial partners, helping us all spoil our weekends as we ferreted out new breaks in the saga via group text. Jason Dean, Scott Austin, and Liz Wollman were central shepherds of the story from San Francisco, recognizing WeWork as an outlier in a field of startups on wayward paths. As WeWork teetered, Charles Forelle, Dana Cimilluca, Nate Becker, and Marie Beaudette were relentless in pushing the story forward from New York. Ryan Knutson, Kate

Linebaugh, and the whole crew at the *Journal* podcast did a fantastic job expanding the reach of the WeWork tale. Preeta Das was a deft logistics manager–editor–reporter, and Jamie Heller was a fierce supporter, seeing the story's import well before it dominated the headlines. We're indebted to Matthew Rose, whose zeal for the tale made the stories fly higher. And we are extremely grateful to Matt Murray—for everything.

John Helyar, whose *Barbarians at the Gate* was a template for our work, was a steady voice of encouragement, inspiration, and smart critique. Thanks to Ted Mann for his words of counsel, countenance, and criticism. Thanks to Tripp Mickle for talking us through a new craft we all knew nothing about. Thanks to Bradley Hope for all his counsel on the publishing world and investigative reporting.

Our text builds on strong works of others that chronicled Silicon Valley's unicorn party. Thanks for the kind suggestions from Mike Isaac, whose *Super Pumped* shared many similar themes on the rise and ouster of Uber's CEO. Reeves Wiedeman was a generous and decorous competitor, and his *Billion Dollar Loser,* also on We-Work, is well worth a read. Thanks to all our colleagues at other outlets whose work on WeWork helped inform this book, including Ellen Huet, Gillian Tan, Cory Weinberg, Meghan Morris, Steve Bertoni, Charles Duhigg, and Moe Tkacik.

Thanks to all the Israeli journalists who helped us make sense of Adam Neumann's home country, including Ruti Levy and Itay Ilnai.

Thanks to our marvelous friends and family who took time to read our drafts and offer suggestions: Michele Host, Tamara Mann Tweel, Andrew Grossman, Ian Lovett, Owen Washburn, Konrad Putzier, Richard Brown, Dilshanie Perera, John Raskin, Robbie Whelan, Eric Hounshell, Lindsay Ryan, Dustin Volz, Pat Heaney, Caroline Walker, Dana Mattioli, Justin Scheck, Bradley Hope, Dana Cimilucca, Nate Becker, Erik Holm, Phred Dvorak, Chris Varmus, and many others.

And thanks to many more colleagues at *The Wall Street Journal* whose guidance on this story, craft of reporting, and friendship has helped inform our work, including Jenny Strasburg, Steve Grocer, Cara Lombardo, Corrie Driebusch, and Miriam Gottfried.

Eric Lupfer at Fletcher & Co. was an extraordinary ally through-out the process, helping to guide, coach, critique, edit, and humor as we felt our way through the book-writing game.

Our team at Crown has been amazing. Paul Whitlatch and Katie Berry have slogged through endless drafts of our book, and with each pass, we've been awed by how they've elevated our prose and pushed us to think about the bigger picture of this story. Thanks to Dan Novack for his deft and exuberant legal counsel.

We would not have made it to the finish line without Sean Lavery—our fact-checker and a true superhero. We can't begin to thank him for the unending hours he spent poring over our drafts and asking our sources to—once again—recount the stories in this book. His patience and stamina are unmatched.

FROM ELIOT, A SPECIAL THANKS TO TK, LINDSEY, AND SCOTT FOR putting up with me in an unexpected, monthslong quarantine in Brooklyn, where a large chunk of this book was written. Thanks to Natasha Josefowitz for early inspiration of the craft, and deft editing of draft chapters. I'm highly appreciative of all my friends and fam-ily who listened to me carp about revenue multiples, real estate square footage, and venture funding as I pondered the mystery of WeWork over the years. And thanks to my friends and others who have made my time in San Francisco so meaningful. From a stint in a one-bedroom in Oakland's Temescal neighborhood in 2016 through the present in San Francisco's Mission, the Bay Area has taught me much about journalism, non–New York life, and dis-counted consumer products subsidized by venture capital.

. . .

FROM MAUREEN, THANKS TO MY GIANT FAMILY—FARRELLS, Kolbes, Burkes, and particularly my siblings, Patty, Ed, and David—for your friendship and guidance. I wish my dad, Vincent, could read this book; he would have been a key editor and my PR machine. Yet, as a journalist, I try to channel his reverence for the press and the First Amendment each day. I find myself seeking to channel the ability of my mother, Peggy, to create bonds and deep friendships with people she's met five minutes ago and those she's known for a lifetime. I'm grateful every day for her guidance.

A special thanks to my in-laws, Ruth and Larry Kolbe. I would never, ever have written this book without their extreme kindness in allowing us to stay in their house in Cape Cod—our Innisfree—during the pandemic.

But I'm most thankful for their son and my husband, Jason. Since the providentially fated (at least for us) 2003 NYC blackout, my life has been infinitely brighter with you in it. I am endlessly grateful for your year of lots of solo parenting, without which this book would not have come together. To my daughters—Cece and Annabel—thank you for your patience this year as I've written this book. You have made life and quarantine more joyful and entertaining than I could ever have imagined.

NOTES

PROLOGUE: THE SUMMIT

3   **a kaleidoscopic array of spotlights:** Video of Adam Neumann's speech, Jan. 8, 2019.

CHAPTER 1: THE HUSTLER

13   **His reason for the move:** Sadeh, "Everyone Worked Their Ass Off."

14   **collapsible high heel:** Adam Neumann Commencement Address, Baruch College, June 5, 2017.

15   **At a trade show in Manhattan's:** Interview with Daniel Rozengurtel, March 2019.

15   **bewildered department store salespeople:** Interview with Susan Lazar for a *Wall Street Journal* article, July 2017.

15   **Neumann was born:** Itay Ilnai and Yaniv Halili, "The First Man," *Yedioth Ahronoth,* Nov. 6, 2019.

15   **by his own account, was "shitty":** "Speech of Adam Neumann in Summer Camp 2018," YouTube, Aug. 20, 2018, www.youtube.com/watch?v=Hpq4Mq-vWlo.

16   **The kibbutz, Nir Am:** Interview with Micah Ben Hillel, March 2020.

16   **Neumann, then eleven:** Shuki Sadeh, "Everyone Worked Their Ass Off, and He's Living the Good Life," *Marker,* Sept. 27, 2019.

16   **But Neumann eventually endeared himself:** Interview with Elad Shelly, Feb. 2020.

16   **idealistic dreams of the kibbutz:** Interview with Hillel, March 2020.

17   **windsurfing expeditions on the Sea of Galilee:** Interview with Ramon, Sept. 2020.

18   **Wearing a white tank top:** Clip of *Erev Tov Im Guy Pines,* Summer 2001.

18   **In 2006, Neumann wrote:** Adam Neumann to Ranee Kamens, Aug. 14, 2006.

19   **"My birthday is the 19th":** Email from Renee Kamens to Adam Neumann, Nov. 27, 2006.

CHAPTER 2: GREENHORNS

20   **Miguel McKelvey was headed:** "Miguel McKelvey Is Reimagining the Work-place," *The Rich Roll Podcast,* July 7, 2019.

20   **He's breaking all social norms:** Ibid.

21   **McKelvey, too, was raised on a tiny:** "WeWork: Miguel McKelvey," *How I Built This with Guy Raz,* NPR, Sept. 3, 2018.

22   **Sunshine Suites:** Aaron Gell, "Was WeWork's Business a Copy/Paste Job?," *Marker,* Oct. 14, 2019, marker.medium.com/was-weworks-business-a-copy-paste -job-b52d2c45099f.

23   **"an endless faith in his ability":** Katherine Clarke, "Neumann on Tap," *Real Deal,* Jan. 1, 2013.

24   **"high-speed internet access":** "155 Water Street Building to Be a 'Green' Office," *Dumbo NYC,* May 14, 2008, dumbonyc.com/blog/2008/05/14/155 water-greendesk/.

25   **Neumann wanted to pitch:** "WeWork: Miguel McKelvey," *How I Built This with Guy Raz.*

26   **Neumann, McKelvey, and Haklay would be paid:** *Gil Haklay v. Enviro Desk LLC,* New York County Supreme Court, No. 651620/2011, Purchase and Security Agreement, filed as Exhibit B, July 29, 2011.

26   **Neumann, meanwhile, asked McKelvey:** "Miguel McKelvey Is Reimagin-ing the Workplace."

CHAPTER 3: FAMOUS ENERGY

27   **Finkelstein told Neumann:** "Build a Purpose Driven Business, Education, and Life with WeWork Co-founder Rebekah Neumann," *The School of Greatness* (podcast), Nov. 6, 2018.

28   **"You, my friend, are full of shit":** Adam Neumann Commencement Ad-dress, Baruch College, June 5, 2017.

28   **"I just knew he was going to be the man":** "Build a Purpose Driven Busi-ness, Education, and Life with WeWork Co-founder Rebekah Neumann."

28   **"Her mother Evelyn has amazing":** Margaret Abrams, "How Gwyneth Pal-trow's Cousin Co-Founded WeWork," *Observer,* August 3, 2016.

28   **"the perfect childhood":** "Speech of Adam Neumann in Summer Camp 2018," YouTube, posted Aug. 20, 2018, www.youtube.com/watch?v=Hpq4Mq-vWlo.

28   **Evelyn's father co-founded one of the largest:** Moe Tkacik, "Her Search for Enlightenment Fueled WeWork's Collapse," *Bustle,* March 2, 2020.

28   **Rebekah's father, Bobby, added to their fortune:** Ibid.

29   **"There was no being a dilettante":** "Build a Purpose Driven Business, Education, and Life with WeWork Co-founder Rebekah Neumann."

29   **She started seventh grade at Horace Mann:** Ibid.

29   **she briefly flirted with a banking job:** Ibid.

30   **the Kabbalah Centre:** Ibid.

CHAPTER 4: PHYSICAL FACEBOOK

32   **His success in Dumbo:** "WeWork: Miguel McKelvey," *How I Built This with
Guy Raz,* NPR, Sept. 3, 2018.

33   **blurted out, "We Work":** "Miguel McKelvey Is Reimagining the Workplace,"
The Rich Roll Podcast, July 7, 2019.

34   **"With Kabbalah, it's not about** *I—me—mine***":** Yehuda Berg, *Living Kabbalah: A Practical System for Making the Power Work for You* (New York: Kabbalah
Centre International, 2008), 6.

37   **Schreiber didn't negotiate:** Eliot Brown, "WeWork: A $20 Billion Startup
Fueled by Silicon Valley Pixie Dust," *Wall Street Journal,* Oct. 19, 2017.

37   **had to personally sign for the lease:** *We Work 154 Grand LLC v. BSD 26
Maeem LLC,* New York County Supreme Court, No. 651781/2014, Lease and
Guarantee, document 82, filed Dec. 9, 2014.

CHAPTER 5: MANUFACTURING COMMUNITY

38   **Lisa Skye awoke:** Interview with Lisa Skye, Feb. 2020.

38   **They cleaned the brick walls:** "WeWork: Miguel McKelvey," *How I Built This
with Guy Raz,* NPR, Sept. 3, 2018.

39   **her sales strategies also extended:** Interview with Skye, Feb. 2020.

40   **Abe Safdie had worked:** Interview with Abe Safdie, April 2020.

41   **Meanwhile, Neumann was the deal maker:** Interview with Skye, Feb. 2020.

42   **Hungry for expansion:** Interview with David Zar, Jan. 2020.

43   **Danny Orenstein, the company's first head of development:** Interview
with Danny Orenstein, March 2020.

44   **One night he was talking:** Ibid.

47   **Companies like Google were gobbling:** Emily Glazer, "Google Web Grows
in City," *Wall Street Journal,* Feb. 29, 2012.

48   **WeWork added "innovation":** WeWork website, Feb. 11, 2012, accessed via
Internet Archive, web.archive.org/web/20120211172334/http://wework.com/.

CHAPTER 6: THE CULT OF THE FOUNDER

51   **Michael Eisenberg was leaving an event:** Evan Axelrod, "Executive Profile:
Michael Eisenberg, Partner at Aleph VC and Investor in WeWork," *Commentator,*
Nov. 12, 2017.

52   **The modern venture capital industry:** David Hsu and Martin Kenney, "Organizing Venture Capital: The Rise and Demise of American Research & Development Corporation, 1946–1973," *Industrial and Corporate Change,* Aug. 2005.

53   **One early investor in Apple:** Spencer Ante, *Creative Capital: Georges Doriot and the Birth of Venture Capital* (Boston: Harvard Business Press, 2008), 236.

53   **By the 1990s, VC firms:** "US Venture Capital: Index and Selected Benchmarks," Cambridge Associates, June 30, 2020.

54   **introduced Pierre Omidyar to the:** Randall Stross, *eBoys: The First Inside Account of Venture Capitalists at Work* (New York: Crown Business, 2000), Kindle ed., chap. 2.

54   **Two years later, eBay had become:** Ibid., chap. 16.

55   **In 2011, VC firms raised:** Venture Monitor, *Pitchbook,* Third Quarter 2020.

57   **an early backer of Palm:** Stross, *eBoys,* chap. 2.

58   **"it goes up from here":** Ibid., chap. 16.

60   **"Let's give him some money":** Eliot Brown, "WeWork: A $20 Billion Startup Fueled by Silicon Valley Pixie Dust," *Wall Street Journal,* Oct. 19, 2017.

61   **McKelvey approached Neumann:** Reeves Wiedeman, *Billion Dollar Loser: The Epic Rise and Spectacular Fall of Adam Neumann and WeWork* (New York: Little, Brown, 2020), 80.

CHAPTER 7: ACTIVATE THE SPACE

64   **"activate the space":** Eliot Brown, "WeWork: A $20 Billion Startup Fueled by Silicon Valley Pixie Dust," *Wall Street Journal,* Oct. 19, 2017.

65   **mayors like Rahm Emanuel:** Interview with Adam Neumann for a potential *Wall Street Journal* article, Aug. 2013.

66   **"By 2020":** Ibid.

66   **The stats he tossed around:** "Intuit 2020 Report: Twenty Trends That Will Shape the Next Decade," *Intuit,* 2010. Neumann's PR representative in 2013 offered this report in support of Neumann's "40 percent of the entire workforce" statistic.

69   **The firm liked WeWork's progress:** Interview with John Cadeddu for a *Wall Street Journal* story, Sept. 2019.

CHAPTER 8: ME OVER WE

71   **The company lent nearly:** Loan and pledge option agreement between WeWork Companies Inc. and We Holdings LLC, May 30, 2013.

73   **five-thousand-square-foot loft:** Wendy Goodman, "Space of the Week: A Transformation in Tribeca," *New York,* Nov. 7, 2013, nymag.com/homedesign /features/laser-rosenberg-2014-1/.

73   **They paid $10.5 million:** Property report for 41 West Eleventh Street, New York, Property Shark.

73   **plotted a lengthy renovation:** Ernst Architect PLLC, "41 West 11th St: Proposed Horizontal and Vertical Expansion," Presented to NYC Landmarks Preservation Commission, Dec. 30, 2014.

75   **the free-flowing booze:** "Summer Camp 2013/WeWork," YouTube, posted Sept. 27, 2013, www.youtube.com/watch?v=RZJ4_Qp8CNw.

75   **When Ra Ra Riot played:** Interview with Erin Griffith, Sept. 2020.

76   **Neumann got up on the band:** "Summer Camp 2013/WeWork."

CHAPTER 9: MUTUAL FUND FOMO

77   **The bank led a $150 million investment:** Alex Konrad, "Inside the Phenomenal Rise of WeWork," *Forbes,* Nov. 5, 2014.

78   **Airbnb would soon nab a *$10 billion* valuation:** Mike Spector, Douglas MacMillan, and Evelyn Rusli, "TPG-Led Group Closes $450 Million Investment in Airbnb," *Wall Street Journal,* April 18, 2014.

78   **"space as a service":** "WeWork Pitch Deck," Oct. 2014, accessed via Scribd upload from Nitasha Tiku, www.scribd.com/doc/284094314/WeWork-Pitch-Deck.

79   **Henry Ellenbogen, had recently invested:** Lindsay Gellman and Eliot Brown, "WeWork: Now a $5 Billion Co-working Startup," *Wall Street Journal,* Dec. 15, 2014.

79   **"compare it to a brand or tech company":** Ibid.

79   **Since the 1920s, mutual funds:** James McWhinney, "A Brief History of the Mutual Fund," Investopedia, Feb. 6, 2018.

80   **compared his portfolio managers to violin:** Joseph Nocera, *A Piece of the Action: How the Middle Class Joined the Money Class* (New York: Simon & Schuster, 1994).

80   **But by the 1990s, mutual fund managers:** Terry Savage, "Any Way You Look at It, Indexing Wins," *Barron's,* April 14, 1999.

80   **In 1997, the number of U.S.-listed:** Maureen Farrell, "America's Roster of Public Companies Is Shrinking Before Our Eyes," *Wall Street Journal,* Jan. 6, 2017.

80   **he oversaw a 2009 investment in Twitter:** Mary Pilon, "A Gumshoe Investor on Tech," *Wall Street Journal,* April 23, 2011.

80   **returned more than ten times:** Leslie Picker, "The Man Who Taught Mutual Funds How to Invest in Startups," Bloomberg News, July 8, 2015.

80   **it was twenty times:** Lauren R. Rublin, "Henry Ellenbogen's Bet on the Future Pays Off Today," *Barron's,* August 19, 2017.

81   **it was already valued at $104 billion:** Shayndi Raice, Anupreeta Das, and John Letzing, "Facebook Prices IPO at Record Value," *Wall Street Journal,* May 17, 2012.

81   **Amazon, for example, was valued:** Farrell, "America's Roster of Public Companies Is Shrinking Before Our Eyes."

81   **mutual funds had $8 billion:** Kwon, Lowry, and Qian, "Mutual Fund Investments in Private Firms."

82   **raised around $38 billion a year:** "The State of US Venture Capital in 15 Charts," Pitchbook, Oct. 29, 2018.

83   **"What matters the most in venture capital":** Corrie Driebusch, "Getting Shares of Fast-Growing Young Firms Is a Snap for Fidelity Manager," *Wall Street Journal,* March 3, 2017.

84   **he'd be a ski instructor:** Ibid.

85   **to go from $73 million of revenue:** Financial Update, 2015–2018 Plan, WeWork.

85   **WeWork announced the deal on June 24:** "WeWork Announces $400 Million Funding Round," WeWork newsroom, June 24, 2015.

85   **valued WeWork at $10 billion:** Eliot Brown, "WeWork's Valuation Soars to $10 Billion," *Wall Street Journal,* June 24, 2015.

86   **worth around $3 billion on paper:** Eliot Brown, "WeWork: A $20 Billion Startup Fueled by Silicon Valley Pixie Dust," *Wall Street Journal,* Oct. 19, 2017.

87   **sold $120 million between:** "WeWork Companies Inc. Valuation of a Minority Common Stock Interest," Alvarez & Marsal, prepared for WeWork, March 21, 2017.

88   **Mark Zuckerberg had secured his control:** Andrew E. Kramer, "A Russian Magnate's Facebook Bet Pays Off Big," *New York Times,* May 15, 2012.

CHAPTER 10: BUBBLING OVER

91   **At sixteen, he had dropped out:** Matthew Lynn, "Hot Dog Man Is the Top Dog in Offices. Profile: Mark Dixon," *Sunday Times,* Sept. 19, 1999.

91   **a constant stream of giant parties:** David Shaw, "The FIG Life: One Big Party After Another," *Los Angeles Times,* Dec. 1, 1971.

91   **one had fourteen hundred invitees:** Maxine Cheshire, "Hollywood Hype and Cocaine Claims," *Washington Post,* Sept. 21, 1979.

91   **plunged into bankruptcy:** Michael Hiltzik, "Records Show Dispute Before Fegen Collapse," *Los Angeles Times,* Dec. 1, 1982.

91   **Fegen later became a magician:** Fantastic Fig, www.fantasticfig.com.

92   **nearly doubled in size and revenue annually:** "Regus PLC: Supplemental Listing Particulars," Regus PLC, filed on the London Stock Exchange, Oct. 7, 2001.

92   **had a particular hunger:** Interview with Frank Cottle, May 2020.

92   ***Fast Company* declared Regus:** Chuck Salter, "Office of the Future," *Fast Company,* March 31, 2000.

92   **ranked the tenth-richest:** Philip Beresford, "Rankings 2-10—Rich List 2001," with Stephen Boyd, *Sunday Times,* April 22, 2001.

93   **truly enormous in size:** Annual Report and Accounts 2015, Regus.

94   **more than *fifty times* its revenue:** "WeWork Companies Inc. Valuation of a Minority Common Stock Interest," Alvarez & Marsal, prepared for WeWork, March 21, 2017.

96   **Asked on an investor call:** Regus PLC Q1 2015 Sales and Revenue call, April 30, 2015.

96   **people piled into an overbuilding frenzy:** Andrew Odlyzko, "Collective Hallucinations and Inefficient Markets: The British Railway Mania of the 1840s," Jan. 15, 2010, accessed via SSRN: ssrn.com/abstract=1537338.

97   **showed subjects two cards:** Solomon Asch, "Opinions and Social Pressure," *Scientific American,* Nov. 1955.

98   **startup entrepreneur named Ben Yu:** Eliot Brown, "How to Live in San Francisco Without Spending Any Money," *Wall Street Journal,* April 29, 2018.

98   **there were more than ninety by year end:** Scott Austin, Chris Canipe, and Sarah Slobin, "The Billion Dollar Startup Club," *Wall Street Journal,* Feb. 18, 2015.

100   **the glasses seller Warby Parker:** "The World's 50 Most Innovative Companies 2015," *Fast Company,* Feb. 9, 2015.

100   **the beauty products shipper Birchbox:** "The World's 50 Most Innovative Companies 2013," *Fast Company,* Feb. 11, 2013.

100   **"heat-mapping technology":** Steven Bertoni, "WeWork's $20 Billion Office Party: The Crazy Bet That Could Change How the World Does Business," *Forbes,* Oct. 2, 2017.

101   **"cultural search engine":** Geraldine Fabrikant and Alex Kuczynski, "The Media Business: Hearst Is Seen Joining Project of Tina Brown," *New York Times,* Jan. 28, 1999.

101   **The fast casual grilled cheese chain The Melt:** Brad Stone, "Tech Veteran Departs Silicon Valley's Grilled Cheese Play," Bloomberg News, Sept. 2, 2016.

101   **more of a marketing company:** Eliot Brown, "Casper Has Big Dreams, but Wall Street Is Waking Up to Losses as Its IPO Nears," *Wall Street Journal,* Jan. 24, 2020.

102   **he was impressed with the vibe:** Interview with Brandon Shorenstein, Feb. 2020.

103   **Neumann said that he personally:** Ibid.

103   **He was busy, but it rang again:** Ibid.

104   **He wouldn't do more deals with them:** Ibid.

CHAPTER 11: CATNIP FOR MILLENNIALS

105   **large financial loss with Bernie Madoff:** Kevin McCoy, "Madoff Victims Speak Out—in Writing," *USA Today,* Dec. 8, 2014.

108   **The office culture was different:** Interview with Carl Pierre, May 2020.

111   **with the pursuit of utopianism:** "Don't Be Evil: Fred Turner on Utopias, Frontiers, and Brogrammers," *Logic,* Dec. 1, 2017.

111   **Facebook preached its societal good:** George Packer, "Change the World," *New Yorker,* May 20, 2013.

111   **would lead the disaffected youth:** Tamar Weinberg, "SXSW: Mark Zuckerberg Keynote," *Techipedia,* March 10, 2008.

114   **sometimes he'd walk around sweaty:** Eliot Brown, "How Adam Neumann's Over-the-Top Style Built WeWork. 'This Is Not the Way Everybody Behaves,'" *Wall Street Journal,* Sept. 18, 2019.

115   **In a meeting with a *Wall Street Journal* reporter:** This account was of an interview conducted on background in 2016. We have decided to include the details here for multiple reasons. Some of what Neumann said was untrue, and in addition, the episode came up unprompted in numerous interviews with former WeWork employees in the reporting for this book. It caused unease for multiple people involved with internal discussions about the matter at the time.

116   **each taking at least $1 million:** Email with subject line "URGENT: WeWork Board Approval re Share Repurchases," sent by Jen Berrent to WeWork board members, Jan. 13, 2015.

CHAPTER 12: BANKING BROS

118   **Snap, was worth around $16 billion:** Douglas MacMillan, "Snapchat Raises Another $500 Million from Investors," *Wall Street Journal,* May 29, 2015.

118   **Uber was worth $51 billion:** Telis Demos and Douglas MacMillan, "Uber Valued at More Than $50 Billion," *Wall Street Journal,* July 31, 2015.

118   **such as paying for software:** Kevin Dugan and Priya Anand, "Quid Pro IPO? Software Tech IPO Practice Raises Disclosure Questions," *The Information,* Jan. 23, 2020.

119   **The bank paid at least $15 million a year:** "JPMorgan Chase's Naming-Rights Deal with Warriors Likely Most Lucrative in NBA," *Sports Business Daily,* Jan. 28, 2016.

119   **it would be called the Chase Center:** J. K. Dineen, "Warriors Arena to Be Named Chase Center—Bank Buys Naming Rights," *San Francisco Chronicle,* Jan. 27, 2016.

119   **Wintroub was promoted:** Daniel Roberts and Leigh Gallagher, "Introducing the Newest Class of Fortune's 40 Under 40," *Fortune,* Sept. 24, 2015.

120   **after attending Colgate University:** Aleta Mayne, "4 Bytes with Noah Wintroub '98," *Colgate Scene,* Winter 2016.

121   **pin-striped suits, suspenders, and Hermès ties:** William D. Cohan, "Remembering the Can-Do Charm (and Fierce Temper) of Wall St. Legend Jimmy Lee," *Vanity Fair,* June 17, 2015.

121   **When Rupert Murdoch or Henry Kravis:** Dana Cimilluca and Emily Glazer, "Jimmy Lee, Famed J. P. Morgan Deal Maker, Dies," *Wall Street Journal,* June 17, 2015.

122   **Lee said he had no more than fifteen minutes:** "The 'Epitome of a Banker,' Jimmy Lee Always Put Family First," WeWork website, June 22, 2015.

122   **origins involving Alexander Hamilton:** "History of Our Firm," JPMorgan Chase website.

122   **access to more than $500 million in debt:** Preliminary offering memorandum, senior notes, WeWork Companies, April 24, 2018.

123   **Lee, then sixty-two, died:** Dana Cimilluca and Emily Glazer, "Jimmy Lee, Famed J.P. Morgan Deal Maker, Dies," *Wall Street Journal,* June 17, 2015.

123   **After attending his memorial service:** "'Epitome of a Banker,' Jimmy Lee Always Put Family First."

CHAPTER 13: TAKING OVER THE WORLD

125   **"probably one of the best at raising money":** "WeWork Uncorked/Miguel McKelvey in Conversation/RetailSpaces Napa," YouTube, posted Dec. 21, 2015, www.youtube.com/watch?v=GqaulrSFc84.

126   **WeWork was ranked ahead of Spotify:** Scott Austin, Chris Canipe, and Sarah Slobin, "The Billion Dollar Startup Club," *Wall Street Journal,* Feb. 18, 2015.

126   **launched ride hailing in the country:** Jake Spring, "Funding Lifts Uber China Unit's Valuation to $8 Billion but Profits Absent," Reuters, Jan. 14, 2016.

127   **One pinprick came in October 2015:** John Carreyrou, "Hot Startup Theranos Has Struggled with Its Blood-Test Technology," *Wall Street Journal,* Oct. 16, 2015.

127   **the cloud storage startup Box:** Telis Demos and Corrie Driebusch, "Square's $9-a-Share Price Deals Blow to IPO Market," *Wall Street Journal,* Nov. 19, 2015.

128   **"late-stage investors, desperately afraid":** Bill Gurley, "Investors Beware: Today's $100M+ Late-Stage Private Rounds Are Very Different from an IPO," *Above the Crowd,* Feb. 25, 2015.

128   **In 2014, WeWork took in:** "WeWork Companies Inc. Valuation of a Minority Common Stock Interest," Alvarez & Marsal, prepared for WeWork, March 21, 2017.

128   **it expected an operating profit:** "WeWork Five-Year Forecast," Oct. 2014, accessed via Scribd upload from Nitasha Tiku, www.scribd.com/document/284094978/Wework-Five-Year-Forecast-October-2014.

130   **called himself Neumann's "fluffer":** Cory Weinberg, "Neumann's Downfall Upends WeWork's Tight Leadership Circle," *Information,* Sept. 25, 2019.

130   **"vice chairman—and also head DJ":** Adam Neumann in speech to staff, WeWork Global Summit, Los Angeles, Jan. 8, 2019.

133   **pulled out a fire extinguisher:** Maureen Farrell and Eliot Brown, "The Money Men Who Enabled Adam Neumann and the WeWork Debacle," *Wall Street Journal,* Dec. 14, 2019.

CHAPTER 14: FRIENDS IN HIGH PLACES

137   **Startup India, the brainchild:** Sean McLain, "Startup India: Entrepreneurs Draw Up Wish List for Modi Meet," *Wall Street Journal,* Jan. 15, 2016.

139   **Modi vest:** Michael Safi, "How India's 'Modi Jacket' Craze Tears at Fabric of History," *Guardian India,* Dec. 29, 2018.

139   **introduced by a local CEO:** "Launching of Startup India Movement," You-Tube, streamed live on January 16, 2016, https://www.youtube.com/watch?v=X8T4XnjuyoQ (Neumann introduced at 52:40).

140   **"We're in nineteen cities":** Ibid.

140   **"the beginning of the big bang":** Surabhi Agarwal, "Softbank's Masayoshi Son Unfazed by Talk of a Funding Crunch or Bloated Valuations," *Economic Times,* Jan. 18, 2016.

141   **world's richest man in 2000:** "Conversation with Masayoshi Son," *The Charlie Rose Show,* March 10, 2014.

141   **His father had cirrhosis:** Atsuo Inoue, *Aiming High: A Biography of Masayoshi Son* (YouTeacher, 2013), chap. 31.

141   **He barely had a drink:** Interview with Hong Lu, April 2020.

141   **called him "Rojin-kiraah":** Yuri Kageyama, " 'Japan's Bill Gates' Strikes It Rich in Cyberspace," Associated Press, May 29, 1996.

141   **were often referred to as Zainichi:** Inoue, *Aiming High,* chap. 16.

141   **His father, Mitsunori, made:** Ibid., preface.

141   **bootlegging hard liquor and building:** Ibid.

141   **Son to Yasumoto to obscure:** Ibid., chap. 16.

141   **large enough to fit a Ping-Pong table:** Interview with Lu, April 2020.

141   **short high school exchange program:** Inoue, *Aiming High,* chap. 1.

142   **joined his future wife, Masami Ohno:** Ibid.

142   **he'd brainstorm one idea:** Ibid., chap. 5.

142   **Aided by cash from his father:** Interview with Lu, April 2020.

142   **To convince him, Son called:** Ibid.

142   **putting arcade games like *Space Invaders:*** Brendan I. Koerner, "Fat Pipe Dream," *Wired,* Aug. 1, 2003.

142   **bought their own arcade, Silver Ball:** Interview with Lu, April 2020.

143   **Son was big on the idea:** Interview with Forrest Mozer, March 2020.

143   **Son flew regularly to Japan:** Interview with Lu, April 2020.

143   **sold the patent for the translator:** Alan M. Webber, "Japanese-Style Entrepreneurship: An Interview with Softbank's CEO, Masayoshi Son," *Harvard Business Review,* Jan.–Feb. 1992.

143   **Mozer only found out that Son:** Interview with Mozer, March 2020.

143   **His father was sick:** Interview with Lu, April 202.

144   **flew to Seattle to conduct the interview:** Inoue, *Aiming High,* chap. 26.

144   **more than 100,000 people:** Paul Andrews, "Comdex Forecast: Cloudy; Recession, Price Slashing Take Their Toll as Annual Computer 'Party' Begins," *Seattle Times,* Nov. 15, 1992.

144   **a conference founded back in 1979:** "Vegas Comdex Canceled," *Las Vegas Sun,* March 28, 2005.

144   **Son approached Adelson:** Interview with Jason Chudnofsky, April 2020.

145   **I can make the business better:** Ibid.

145   **he took SoftBank public:** Norihiko Shirouzu, "Softbank to Pay $800 Million for Comdex Computer Show," *Wall Street Journal,* Feb. 14, 1995.

145   **looking to sell Comdex:** Interview with Chudnofsky, April 2020.

145   **SoftBank agreed to pay:** Shirouzu, "Softbank to Pay $800 Million for Comdex Computer Show."

145   **would end up in bankruptcy:** Dean Takahashi, "Comdex Computer Trade Show Organizers File for Chapter 11," *San Jose Mercury News,* Feb. 4, 2003.

146   **SoftBank spent nearly $2 billion:** Andrew Pollack, "PC Supplier to Be Sold for $1.5 Billion," *New York Times,* Aug. 16, 1996.

146   **He created what was then:** Neil Weinberg, "Master of the Internet," *Forbes,* July 5, 1999.

146   **shockingly large number of companies:** Bruce Gilley, Chester Dawson, and Dan Biers, "Internet Warrior on the Defensive," *Far Eastern Economic Review,* Nov. 16, 2000.

146   **He told *Forbes* in 1999:** Weinberg, "Master of the Internet."

146   **SoftBank's shares peaked:** Gilley, Dawson, and Biers, "Internet Warrior on the Defensive."

147   **Webvan—discontinued operations:** Joelle Tessler, "Webvan Cashes Out on Bold Experiment," *San Jose Mercury News,* July 10, 2001.

147   **in 1995, Son pushed Yahoo's founders:** Daisuke Wakabayashi and Anton Troianovski, "Japan's Masayoshi Son Picks a Fight with U.S. Phone Giants," *Wall Street Journal,* Nov. 23, 2012.

147   **SoftBank led a $20 million investment:** Henny Sender and Connie Ling, "Softbank to Invest $20 Million in Hong Kong's Alibaba.com," *Wall Street Journal,* Jan. 18, 2000.

147   **"We didn't talk about revenues":** Ibid.

148   **threatened to set himself on fire:** Phred Dvorak "A Web Maverick Sparks Revolution in Wiring Japan," *Wall Street Journal,* Oct. 17, 2003.

148   **$15 billion to buy Vodafone's business:** Jathon Sapsford, "Vodafone Sells Japanese Unit to Softbank for $15 Billion," *Wall Street Journal,* March 17, 2006.

148   **By negotiating directly with Steve Jobs:** Takashi Sugimoto, "Masayoshi Son Talks About How Steve Jobs Inspired SoftBank's ARM Deal," *Nikkei Asia,* Sept. 24, 2016.

148   **$21.6 billion deal in late 2012:** Wakabayashi and Troianovski, "Japan's Masayoshi Son Picks a Fight with U.S. Phone Giants."

148   **spending $117 million for a nine-acre estate:** Katherine Clarke, "The Estate That Wants to Be Silicon Valley's Priciest Home," *Wall Street Journal,* Oct. 18, 2018.

148   **three-hundred-year growth plan:** "SoftBank Next 30-Year Vision," SoftBank corporate website, June 25, 2010.

148   **Humans and robots would grow symbiotic:** Ibid.

149   **"The saddest thing in people's life":** Ibid.

149   **the U.S. government blocked him:** Ryan Knutson and Dana Mattioli, "Sprint Abandons Pursuit of T-Mobile, Replaces CEO," *Wall Street Journal,* Aug. 5, 2014.

CHAPTER 15: IT'S TRICKY

151   **Around 1:30 a.m., Neumann told Minson:** Interview with Artie Minson for a *Wall Street Journal* article, July 2017.

152   **WeWork paid $13.8 million:** Preliminary offering memorandum, senior notes, WeWork Companies, April 24, 2018.

152   **One such person was Jamie Hodari:** Interview with Jamie Hodari, April 2020.

153   **At the start of 2015, WeWork projected:** FY 2015 Financial Results, internal WeWork presentation, 2016.

154   **Airbnb's Brian Chesky would later push:** Jeffrey Dastin and Heather Somerville, "Behind Airbnb's Bet on Show Business to Hook Travelers," Reuters, April 24, 2019.

156   **WeWork fired 7 percent of its staff:** Ellen Huet, "WeWork Is Cutting About 7% of Staff," Bloomberg News, June 3, 2016.

156   **Neumann called out for a surprise guest:** Eliot Brown, "How Adam Neumann's Over-the-Top Style Built WeWork. 'This Is Not the Way Everybody Behaves,'" *Wall Street Journal,* Sept. 18, 2019.

CHAPTER 16: ONE BILLION DOLLARS PER MINUTE

157   **estimated at around $17 billion:** Katia Savchuk, "Jeff Bezos, Mark Zuckerberg Are Biggest Gainers by Far on Forbes List of 100 Richest in Tech," *Forbes,* Aug. 10, 2016.

157   **He'd trade the number one spot:** Dan Alexander, "Here Are the 10 People Who Gained the Most Money in 2016," *Forbes,* Dec. 30, 2016.

159   **"Life's too short to think small":** Sarah McBride, Selina Wang, and Peter Elstrom, "Masayoshi Son, SoftBank, and the $100 Billion Blitz on Sand Hill Road," *Bloomberg Businessweek,* Sept. 27, 2018.

159   **The Qataris were noncommittal:** Arash Massoudi, Kana Inagaki, and Leo Lewis, "SoftBank: Inside the 'Wild West' $100Bn Fund Shaking Up the Tech World," *Financial Times,* June 20, 2018.

160   **tended to be made by consensus:** Margherita Stancati and Summer Said, "Saudi Prince Shakes Royal Family with Crackdown," *Wall Street Journal,* Nov. 10, 2017.

160   **shrewd businessman, doing deals:** Bradley Hope and Justin Scheck, *Blood and Oil: Mohammed bin Salman's Ruthless Quest for Global Power* (New York: Hachette Book Group, 2020), chap. 2.

161   **favor the New York Stock Exchange:** Summer Said and Ben Dummett, "Saudi Arabia Favors New York for Aramco IPO," *Wall Street Journal,* Feb. 21, 2017.

161   **"Undoubtedly, it will be the largest fund":** John Micklethwait et al., "Saudi Arabia Plans $2 Trillion Megafund for Post-oil Era: Deputy Crown Prince," Bloomberg News, April 1, 2016.

162   **largest international investment:** Douglas MacMillan, "Uber Raises $3.5 Billion from Saudi Fund," *Wall Street Journal,* June 1, 2016.

163   **former Deutsche Bank colleagues:** Hope and Scheck, *Blood and Oil,* chap. 7.

163   **thirteen separate planes:** Arash Massoudi, Kana Inagaki, and Simeon Kerr, "The $100Bn Marriage: How SoftBank's Son Courted a Saudi Prince," *Financial Times,* Oct. 19, 2016.

163   **kingdom a $1 *trillion* gift:** Masayoshi Son, interview on *The David Rubenstein Show,* Bloomberg Television, Oct. 1, 2017.

164   **"$45 billion in forty-five minutes":** Ibid.

165   **apologized for arriving late:** Jason Kothari, *Irrationally Passionate* (India: HarperCollins, 2000), p. 179.

165   **he'd called Bhavish Aggarwal:** Ibid.

165   **they'd get "unlimited money":** Ibid., p. 180.

CHAPTER 17: NEUMANN & SON

166   **Jack Ma to celebrities like Kanye West:** Eric Chemi and Mark Fahey, "One Good Way for CEOs to Give Their Stocks a Boost: Visit Trump Tower," CNBC, Jan. 11, 2017.

166   **an old business counterpart, Sheldon Adelson:** Takashi Sugimoto, "Masa and Donald: Why Son Dabbles in Politics," *Nikkei Asia,* March 22, 2017.

167   **"I'm so sorry, but I only have 12 minutes":** Steven Bertoni, "WeWork's $20 Billion Office Party: The Crazy Bet That Could Change How the World Does Business," *Forbes,* Oct. 2, 2017.

168   **He suggested Neumann join him in his car:** Ibid.

168   **in the lobby of Trump Tower:** "President-Elect Trump and SoftBank Founder Remarks at Trump Tower," C-SPAN, Dec. 6, 2016.

169   **But Arora left SoftBank in mid-2016:** Bradley Hope and Jenny Strasburg, "SoftBank's Rajeev Misra Used Campaign of Sabotage to Hobble Internal Rivals," *Wall Street Journal,* Feb. 26, 2020.

CHAPTER 18: CRAZY TRAIN

171   **effects of innovation and rapid obsolescence:** Interview with Lovka, Aug. 2020.

172   **The contractor, Logistics Plus:** "Impossible Is Nothing," Logistics Plus, March 3, 2017, www.logisticsplus.com/impossible-is-nothing.

172   **WeWork paid roughly $50,000:** Maureen Farrell and Eliot Brown, "The Money Men Who Enabled Adam Neumann and the WeWork Debacle," *Wall Street Journal,* Dec. 14, 2019.

173   **a valuation of around $12 billion:** Scott Austin et al., "The Startup Stock Tracker," *Wall Street Journal,* March 3, 2016.

174   **The largest chunk, $3.1 billion:** Steven Bertoni, "WeWork's $20 Billion Office Party: The Crazy Bet That Could Change How the World Does Business," *Forbes,* Oct. 2, 2017.

175   **the cash-out marked:** Eliot Brown, Maureen Farrell, and Anupreeta Das, "WeWork Co-founder Has Cashed Out at Least $700 Million via Sales, Loans," *Wall Street Journal,* July 18, 2019.

175   **when she arrived for the signing:** Jen Berrent, "Welcome Home to WeWork," WeWork website, June 18, 2018.

176   **causing Uber to sell its operations:** Alyssa Abkowitz and Rick Carew, "Uber Sells China Operations to Didi Chuxing," *Wall Street Journal,* Aug. 1, 2016.

176   **$6 billion more into the company:** Mayumi Negishi, "SoftBank Considers $6 Billion Investment in China Ride-Hailing Firm Didi," *Wall Street Journal,* May 12, 2017.

176   **"In a fight, who wins?":** Bertoni, "WeWork's $20 Billion Office Party."

CHAPTER 19: REVENUE, MULTIPLE, VALUATION

180   **the entire San Francisco public school system:** San Francisco Board of Education, "SF Board of Education Approves Budget for 2016–17," press release, June 29, 2016.

180   **It was twelve *Washington Post*s:** Paul Farhi, "Washington Post Closes Sale to Amazon Founder Jeff Bezos," *Washington Post,* Oct. 1, 2013.

181   **struggled to answer the simple question:** "Optimizing Space Itself with WeWork's Adam Neumann/Disrupt NY 2017," YouTube, posted May 15, 2017, www.youtube.com/watch?v=-EKOV71m-PY.

181   **"much more based on our energy":** Steven Bertoni, "WeWork's $20 Billion Office Party: The Crazy Bet That Could Change How the World Does Business," *Forbes,* Oct. 24, 2017.

182   **"If you had positioned this":** Eliot Brown, "WeWork: A $20 Billion Startup Fueled by Silicon Valley Pixie Dust," *Wall Street Journal,* Oct. 19, 2017.

184   **$156 million for the company:** We Co., Form S-1 Registration Statement, SEC, Aug. 14, 2019.

184   **It was due to have just $11 million:** "Flatiron School LLC Profit and Loss Statement," included as part of Application for Provisional Approval to the Higher Education Licensure submitted to the District of Columbia, WeWork, Nov. 6, 2017.

184   **surf pool next to the office space:** "Expedia Campus Re-design," slide in a presentation to WeWork Co.'s board of directors, third quarter 2016.

184   **project's mastermind was Rebekah Neumann:** Irene Plagianos, "WeWork Is Launching a Grade School for Budding Entrepreneurs," Bloomberg News, Nov. 6, 2017.

185   **Meanwhile, Mark Zuckerberg negotiated:** Shayndi Raice, Spencer E. Ante, and Emily Glazer, "In Facebook Deal, Board Was All But out of Picture," *Wall Street Journal,* April 18, 2012.

186   **required huge structural reinforcements:** Maureen Farrell and Eliot Brown, "The Money Men Who Enabled Adam Neumann and the WeWork Debacle," *Wall Street Journal,* Dec. 14, 2019.

188   **it offered big promotions like 20 percent:** Brown, "WeWork: A $20 Billion Startup Fueled by Silicon Valley Pixie Dust."

188   **A shorter-lived promotion offered:** Ellen Huet, "WeWork Is Ratcheting Up Broker Commissions to Lure New Tenants," Bloomberg News, Aug. 23, 2018.

188   **Hodari took an Uber around 4:00 a.m.:** Interview with Hodari, April 2020.

188   **"When I push the button":** Ibid.

189   **Hodari's staff started receiving:** Ibid.

189   **WeWork in 2017 recorded:** We Co., Form S-1.

190   **conducted a study in late 2017:** Ann Cosgrove, "Are Our Members Friends?," Fundamental Research Team, WeWork, published internally, Dec. 2017.

CHAPTER 20: COMMUNITY-ADJUSTED PROFIT

192   **Regis High School:** "Awe-Inspiring Salute to Regis High School's Storied History at the Regis Centennial Gala," Regis High School website, Oct. 28, 2014, www.regis.org/article.cfm?id=3045.

193   **"the finest CFO in America":** Time Warner Cable, "Time Warner Cable CFO Arthur Minson to Depart Company," press release, June 1, 2015.

195   **had raised $1.15 billion:** Douglas MacMillan, "Uber Raises $1.15 Billion from First Leveraged Loan," *Wall Street Journal,* July 7, 2016.

196   **WeWork was "profitable":** Eliot Brown, "WeWork's Valuation Soars to $10 Billion," *Wall Street Journal,* June 24, 2015.

196   **"We don't need to raise any more money":** Ellen Huet and Shawn Wen, "The Universe Does Not Allow for Waste," *Foundering* (podcast), episode 3, Bloomberg News, July 16, 2020.

196   **"hover around" breakeven:** Matthew Lynley, "WeWork's Adam Neumann on How to Hit $1B in Revenue with a Careful Balance," *TechCrunch,* May 15, 2017.

196   **"community-adjusted EBITDA":** Eliot Brown, "A Look at WeWork's Books: Revenue Is Doubling but Losses Are Mounting," *Wall Street Journal,* April 25, 2018.

197   **erased a huge array:** Ibid.

198   **WeWork's revenue doubled:** Ibid.

198   **"rage-inducing Silicon Alley pile":** Thornton McEnery, "WeWork's First-Ever Bond Offering Is a Master Class in Financial Masturbation," *Dealbreaker,* April 25, 2018.

200   **$702 million of bonds to investors:** Brown, "Look at WeWork's Books."

200   **WeWork eventually spent $32 million:** We Co., Form S-1 Registration Statement, SEC, Aug. 14, 2019.

CHAPTER 21: ADAM'S ARK

201   **had indeed been on the cover of *Forbes:*** Steven Bertoni, "WeWork's $20 Billion Office Party: The Crazy Bet That Could Change How the World Does Business," *Forbes,* Oct. 24, 2017.

203   **WeWork the tenant would be:** "WeWork Property Investors LP: Offering of Limited Partnership Interests," WeWork Property Investors, Nov. 2017.

204   **Blackstone, the world's largest real estate fund manager:** Konrad Putzier, "Blackstone Now Owns More Than $100B in Real Estate," *Real Deal,* April 21, 2016.

204   **The biggest ask would be to Saudi Arabia:** Internal fund-raising presentation, slide titled "Saudi Arabia (PIF and SAMA)," WeWork, April 2018.

205   **"We don't need more capital":** Internal fund-raising presentation, slide titled "Fundraising War Room," WeWork, April 2018.

205   **to co-develop 2 World Trade Center:** Internal fund-raising presentation, slide titled "Ark Sub Fund Update," WeWork, April 2018.

CHAPTER 22: THE $3 TRILLION TRIANGLE

207   **As he saw it, his instincts and his gut:** Eliot Brown, Dana Mattioli, and Maureen Farrell, "SoftBank Explores Taking Majority Stake in WeWork," *Wall Street Journal,* Oct. 9, 2018.

208   **"We are unicorn hunters":** Mitsuru Obe and Akane Okutsu, "'We Are Unicorn Hunters,' Says Masayoshi Son," *Nikkei Asia,* June 20, 2018.

208   **Money went to startups like Plenty:** Phred Dvorak and Mayumi Negishi, "How SoftBank, World's Biggest Tech Investor, Throws Around Its Cash," *Wall Street Journal,* Feb. 26, 2018.

209   **"WeWork will be analyzing":** "Corrected Transcript: SoftBank Group Corp. Q1 2018 Earnings Call," FactSet, Aug. 6, 2018.

211   **Now a father-figure type was goading:** Eric Platt and Andrew Edgecliffe-Johnson, "WeWork: How the Ultimate Unicorn Lost Its Billions," *Financial Times,* Feb. 19, 2020.

213   **he wanted $70 billion:** WeWork presentation to SoftBank Group, slide titled "Proposed Investment Structures," July 2, 2018.

213   **had raised about $12 billion:** Rani Molla and Johana Bhuiyan, "How Uber's Funding and Valuation Stack Up Against Competitors Like Didi and Lyft," *Recode,* May 25, 2017.

214   **now expected faster growth for years to come:** WeWork presentation to SoftBank Group, slide titled "Delivering on Our Strategy Will Allow Us to Beat Our $101Bn Growth Goal," July 2, 2018.

215   **he extended the growth curve:** WeWork presentation to SoftBank Group, slide titled "Our 2028 Goals," July 23, 2018.

215   **the entire value of the U.S. stock market:** Vito J. Racanelli, "The U.S. Stock Market Is Now Worth $30 Trillion," *Barron's,* Jan. 18, 2018.

215   **called for $10 billion from Saudi Arabia:** WeWork presentation to SoftBank Group, slide titled "ARK Capital Raise Update: Over $20 B in Discussion," July 23, 2018.

215   **ARK's growth plans depended on $593 billion:** WeWork presentation to SoftBank Group, slide titled "Ark Capital Requirements and Desk Contribution," June 8, 2018.

216   **Another showed how the two companies:** WeWork presentation to SoftBank Group, slide titled "ARK and WeWork Will Contribute to One Another's Success," July 23, 2018.

CHAPTER 23: SUMMER CAMP

217   **about six thousand members:** Mark Sullivan, "At WeWork Summer Camp, 8,000 People Come Together with a Purpose," WeWork website, Aug. 21, 2018.

219   **lined the tent-covered fields:** Ibid.

220   **quoting some anonymous staff members:** Thomas Hobbs, "The Cult of WeWork," *Property Week,* Aug. 30, 2018.

220   **One community manager proposed:** Mark Sullivan, "Surrounded by Colleagues, WeWork Staffer Pops the Question," WeWork website, Sept. 27, 2018.

220   **grocery list given to aides:** Reeves Wiedeman, *Billion Dollar Loser: The Epic Rise and Spectacular Fall of Adam Neumann and WeWork* (New York: Little, Brown, 2020), 222.

220   **two bartenders, a "signature Range Rover":** Ibid.

221   **"I am not here to get peed on":** Reeves Wiedeman, "The I in We," *New York,* June 10, 2019.

221   **WeWork was banning:** Sara Ashley O'Brien, "WeWork Is Banning Meat," CNN Money, July 13, 2018.

221   **bewildered group of senior executives:** Eliot Brown, "How Adam Neumann's Over-the-Top Style Built WeWork. 'This Is Not the Way Everybody Behaves,'" *Wall Street Journal,* Sept. 18, 2019.

221   **one of numerous episodes:** Ibid.

222   **"Just so you guys know":** "Speech of Adam Neumann in Summer Camp 2018," YouTube, posted Aug. 20, 2018, www.youtube.com/watch?v=Hpq4Mq -vWlo.

222   **"With our members around the world":** Ibid.

CHAPTER 24: SHOES OFF, SOULS INSIDE

224 **whispered a word or mantra:** Interviews with Joshua Shanklin, March–Aug. 2020.

225 **found the whole experience off-putting:** Ibid.

225 **could find no single New York school:** Eliot Brown, "Surfing, Schools, and Jets: WeWork's Bets Follow CEO Adam Neumann's Passions," *Wall Street Journal,* March 5, 2019.

226 **cost up to $42,000:** Ibid.

227 **"It was pretty much a mess":** Interviews with Shanklin, March–Aug. 2020.

228 **"more of a universe or village":** Hadley Keller, "Bjarke Ingels Group Creates a Miniature, Indoor Natural Ecosystem for WeWork's WeGrow School," *Architectural Digest,* Oct. 29, 2018.

228 **Adam Braun as the school's chief operating officer:** Rebekah Neumann, "Welcoming Adam Braun to WeGrow," WeWork website, May 16, 2018.

228 **"would all sound so beautiful":** Interviews with Shanklin, March–Aug. 2020.

CHAPTER 25: FLYING HIGH

234 **Stuffed inside was a stash:** Eliot Brown, "How Adam Neumann's Over-the-Top Style Built WeWork. 'This Is Not the Way Everybody Behaves,'" *Wall Street Journal,* Sept. 18, 2019.

235 **The $56 million jet could travel:** Bombardier Global 6000 range, VistaJet, www.vistajet.com/en-us/private-jets/global-6000/.

235 **VistaJet's list rates on the Bombardier:** Interview with Matteo Ati for *Wall Street Journal* story, July 2017.

235 **public companies with jets underperformed:** David Yermack, "Flights of Fancy: Corporate Jets, CEO Perquisites, and Inferior Shareholder Returns," *Journal of Financial Economics,* July 2006.

236 **one round-trip flight Neumann took to Mexico City:** Cory Weinberg and Jessica E. Lessin, "'The Crew Was Not Tipped': The Fallout from WeWork's Excesses," *Information,* Oct. 3, 2019.

236 **white shell was accentuated with thin blue:** "Gulfstream 650ER," internal document presented to board of directors, WeWork, 2018.

237 **unnamed "assets" that cost $63.4 million:** Preliminary offering memorandum, senior notes, WeWork Companies, April 24, 2018.

239 **"We are here in order to change the world":** Inbal Orpaz, "By Harnessing Israeliness, WeWork Joins the Ranks of Uber, Airbnb," *Haaretz,* July 30, 2017.

241 **WeWork had surpassed JPMorgan:** Keiko Morris and Eliot Brown, "WeWork Surpasses JPMorgan as Biggest Occupier of Manhattan Office Space," *Wall Street Journal,* Sept. 18, 2018.

243 **"president of the world":** Brown, "How Adam Neumann's Over-the-Top Style Built WeWork."

243   **world was moving more toward "we":** U.S. Conference of Mayors Winter Meeting, C-SPAN, Jan. 26, 2018.

244   **he aspired to live forever:** Brown, "How Adam Neumann's Over-the-Top Style Built WeWork."

244   **The company even called him the co-founder:** "Our Team and the Power of Imagination," Life Biosciences, June 4, 2019, accessed via Internet Archive, web.archive.org/web/20190604085317/http://lifebiosciences.com/team/.

244   **"That might be forever":** "Build a Purpose Driven Business, Education, and Life with WeWork Co-founder Rebekah Neumann," *The School of Greatness* (podcast), Nov. 6, 2018.

245   **Jeff Skilling was cast as the archetypal:** Rakesh Khurana, "The Curse of the Superstar CEO," *Harvard Business Review,* Sept. 2002.

246   **"will have an infinite time horizon":** Brian Chesky, "Open Letter to the Airbnb Community About Building a 21st Century Company," Airbnb website, Jan. 25, 2018.

247   **two separate Four Seasons hotels:** Itay Hod, "Saudi Crown Prince Mohammed bin Salman Buys Out Four Seasons Hotel for Hollywood Visit," *The Wrap,* April 2, 2018; Cornell Barnard, "Crown Prince of Saudi Arabia Buys Out Four Seasons in East Palo Alto for Visit," ABC7 Bay Area, April 2, 2018.

247   **Lucid Motors, an electric car company:** Kirsten Korosec, "Lucid Motors Secures $1 Billion from Saudi Wealth Fund to Launch the Air," *TechCrunch,* Sept. 17, 2018.

248   **small role in the Trump White House's:** Gabriel Sherman, "You Don't Bring Bad News to the Cult Leader: Inside the Fall of WeWork," *Vanity Fair,* Nov. 21, 2019.

249   **Who could offer such counsel?:** Ibid.

CHAPTER 26: BOTH MARK AND SHERYL

250   **"I am both Mark and Sheryl":** Scott Austin and Eliot Brown, "Meet the New Co-CEOs of WeWork," *Wall Street Journal,* Sept. 24, 2019.

252   **"To nepotism!":** Maureen Farrell and Eliot Brown, "The Money Men Who Enabled Adam Neumann and the WeWork Debacle," *Wall Street Journal,* Dec. 14, 2019.

253   **the children of three directors:** Ibid.

253   **For years, WeWork relied heavily:** Eliot Brown, "WeWork's Long List of Potential Conflicts Adds to Questions Ahead of IPO," *Wall Street Journal,* Sept. 6, 2019.

253   **he railed against perceived "B-players":** Eliot Brown, "How Adam Neumann's Over-the-Top Style Built WeWork. 'This Is Not the Way Everybody Behaves,'" *Wall Street Journal,* Sept. 18, 2019.

255   **"We usually do better with women executives":** "An Inspirational Fireside Chat with WeWork CEO Adam Neumann," New York Stock Exchange, video posted to NYSE Facebook page, June 14, 2017, www.facebook.com/NYSE/videos/10155161160361023/.

256   **She scored low in performance reviews:** *Ruby Anaya v. WeWork Companies Inc.,* New York County Supreme Court, No. 159414/2018, memorandum of law in support of defendant's motion to dismiss the complaint, Oct. 31, 2018.

256   **she filed a lawsuit alleging:** Ibid., Summons + Complaint, Oct. 11, 2018.

257   **email the whole company:** Gaby Del Valle, "A WeWork Employee Says She Was Fired After Reporting Sexual Assault. The Company Says Her Claims Are Meritless," *Vox,* Oct. 12, 2018.

258   **A lawsuit brought in the spring:** *Lisa Bridges v. WeWork Companies Inc. et al.,* New York County Supreme Court, No. 156140/2019, Summons + Complaint, June 20, 2019.

258   **an employment complaint she filed:** *Medina Bardhi v. The We Company,* class and collective administrative charge of discrimination relation and gender pay disparity, filed with Equal Employment Opportunity Commission New York District Office, Oct. 31, 2019.

259   **the board of the Presidio:** "Presidio Trust Public Board Meeting, 09.27.18," Transcript of board meeting provided by Presidio Trust.

CHAPTER 27: BROKEN FORTITUDE

260   **"my good friend":** "Adam Neumann: Co Founder of WeWork Delivers Incredible Speech at UJA Federation," YouTube, posted Dec. 26, 2018, www.youtube.com/watch?v=-4vTTmUByfk.

263   **wouldn't show up at meetings:** Maureen Farrell and Eliot Brown, "The Money Men Who Enabled Adam Neumann and the WeWork Debacle," *Wall Street Journal,* Dec. 14, 2019.

265   **Neumann negotiated to the point:** Eric Platt and Andrew Edgecliffe-Johnson, "WeWork: How the Ultimate Unicorn Lost Its Billions," *Financial Times,* Feb. 20, 2020.

266   **when both expressed uneasiness:** Farrell and Brown, "Money Men Who Enabled Adam Neumann and the WeWork Debacle."

267   **"WeWork is the next Alibaba":** Minoru Satake, "SoftBank's Son Says We-Work Is His 'Next Alibaba,'" *Nikkei Asia,* Aug. 11, 2018.

268   **major outage of SoftBank's own mobile network:** Mayumi Negishi, "Cell Service in Japan Goes Down for Hours, Clouding Year's Biggest IPO," *Wall Street Journal,* Dec. 6, 2018.

268   **reported in *The Wall Street Journal*:** Eliot Brown, Dana Mattioli, and Maureen Farrell, "SoftBank Explores Taking Majority Stake in WeWork," *Wall Street Journal,* Oct. 9, 2019.

268   **SoftBank raised $24 billion:** Mayumi Negishi and Suryatapa Bhattacharya, "SoftBank Unit's Debut Is One of Japan's Worst, After $24 Billion IPO," *Wall Street Journal,* Dec. 19, 2018.

269   **Neumann broke his finger:** Katrina Brooker, "WeWork Rebrands to the We Company," *Fast Company,* Jan. 8, 2019.

269   **on Christmas Eve:** Farrell and Brown, "Money Men Who Enabled Adam Neumann and the WeWork Debacle."

270   **invest an additional $2 billion:** Ibid.

CHAPTER 28: DISECONOMIES OF SCALE

274   **"Our balance sheet has north of $6 billion":** Deirdre Bosa, "Watch CNBC's Full Interview with Ashton Kutcher and WeWork CEO Adam Neumann," CNBC, Jan. 14, 2019.

274   **"This is a business where scale matters":** Ellen Huet, "WeWork, with $900 Million in Sales, Finds Cheaper Ways to Expand," Bloomberg News, Feb. 26, 2018.

276   **sometimes have warehouse sales:** Maureen Farrell and Eliot Brown, "The Money Men Who Enabled Adam Neumann and the WeWork Debacle," *Wall Street Journal,* Dec. 14, 2019.

278   **had fewer than three thousand employees:** Form 10-K, Snap Inc., Feb. 6, 2019.

278   **long lines at a coffee station:** Katrina Brooker, "The Most Powerful Person in Silicon Valley," *Fast Company,* Jan. 14, 2019.

279   **nearly $450 million for a 50 percent stake:** *Parkmerced Investors LLC v. WeWork Companies LLC,* New York County Supreme Court, No. 652094/2020, Term Sheet, filed as Exhibit 1, Sept. 4, 2020.

280   **"transformative companies driving the future of work":** "Job Description: Business Development Associate," WeWork job posting for Creator Fund employee, posted on LinkedIn, early 2019.

280   **usually for less than $5 million:** Internal WeWork documents detailing Creator Fund investments, WeWork, 2020.

280   **to lead a $32 million investment:** Laird Superfood, Form S-1 Registration Statement, SEC, Aug. 31, 2020.

280   **he later told *Fast Company*:** Katrina Brooker, "WeWork Rebrands to the We Company," *Fast Company,* Jan. 8, 2019.

281   **$38 million to Kutcher's venture capital fund:** Internal WeWork documents detailing Creator Fund investments, WeWork, 2020.

281   **two years of rent-free space:** Reeves Wiedeman, *Billion Dollar Loser: The Epic Rise and Spectacular Fall of Adam Neumann and WeWork* (New York: Little, Brown, 2020), 254.

281   **"I realized it was a technology company":** Bosa, "Watch CNBC's Full Interview with Ashton Kutcher and WeWork CEO Adam Neumann."

CHAPTER 29: GUITAR HOUSE

283   **a room shaped like a guitar:** Anna Marie Erwert, "$25M Estate, Formerly Bill Graham's, Is Marin's Greenest—and Most Expensive—Mansion," *SFGate,* March 21, 2017.

286   **They embarked on a renovation:** Pound Ridge Planning Board, Sept. 27, 2018, poundridge.granicus.com/MediaPlayer.php?view_id=1&clip_id=164.

287   **three key employees to sit:** *78 Irving Plaza Condominium v. The Tax Commission of the City of New York,* New York County Supreme Court, No. 265013/2018, Tax Certiorari Petition, Oct. 24, 2018.

287   **her older brother, then twenty-three:** "Build a Purpose Driven Business, Education, and Life with WeWork Co-founder Rebekah Neumann," *The School of Greatness* (podcast), Nov. 6, 2018.

288   **number of phobias:** Ibid.

289   **The time without her "Festina Lente":** Interviews with Joshua Shanklin, March–Aug. 2020.

289   **Rebekah Neumann boasted to an interviewer:** Ariel Levy, feature on Rebekah and Adam Neumann, *Porter,* Fall 2016.

290   **They imagined a $7 billion development:** WeWork presentation to Soft-Bank Group, slide titled "San Jose Development Opportunity," July 23, 2018.

290   **He told Bloomberg:** Ellen Huet, "WeWork Wants to Become Its Own Landlord with Latest Spending Spree," *Bloomberg Businessweek,* May 15, 2019.

291   **"WeWork is me":** Troy Wolverton, "WeWork Is Setting Up a $2.9 Billion Fund to Buy Buildings That It Will Lease to Itself," *Business Insider,* May 15, 2019.

CHAPTER 30: THE PLUNGE BEFORE THE PLUNGE

294   **at the 239-foot *Titania:*** "Titania," my-titania.com/.

294   **valued the company at $24 billion:** Maureen Farrell and Corrie Driebusch, "Lyft Shares Surge in Public Debut," *Wall Street Journal,* March 29, 2019.

295   **He summoned a WeWork staffer:** Maureen Farrell et al., "The Fall of WeWork: How a Startup Darling Came Unglued," *Wall Street Journal,* Oct. 24, 2019.

295   **"I do not have an exact date":** Neumann email to WeWork employees, April 29, 2019.

296   **valuation could be as high as $120 billion:** Liz Hoffman, Greg Bensinger, and Maureen Farrell, "Uber Proposals Value Company at $120 Billion in a Possible IPO," *Wall Street Journal,* Oct. 16, 2018.

297   **For Uber, he worked shifts:** Maureen Farrell and Liz Hoffman, "Morgan Stanley Banker Is Also an Uber Driver," *Wall Street Journal,* Oct. 18, 2018.

298   **played him some of his music:** Reeves Wiedeman, *Billion Dollar Loser: The Epic Rise and Spectacular Fall of Adam Neumann and WeWork* (New York: Little, Brown, 2020), 266.

298   **handed Neumann a picture-filled book:** IPO pitch presentation to WeWork, Goldman Sachs, May 2020.

299   **valued between $61 billion and $96 billion:** Ibid.

299   **"his personal banker":** Maureen Farrell and Eliot Brown, "The Money Men Who Enabled Adam Neumann and the WeWork Debacle," *Wall Street Journal,* Dec. 14, 2019.

300   **"You have the full resources":** Dimon to Neumann and IPO team, Spring 2019.

300   **helping the exercise-bike startup:** Matt Turner, "A Bunch of Cycling Enthusiasts Just Helped Peloton Cycle Raise $325 Million—Betting It Could Be 'the Apple of Fitness,'" *Business Insider,* May 24, 2017.

300   **Lyft's stock plunged below its IPO price:** Corrie Driebusch, "Lyft Shares Falter on Second Trading Day," *Wall Street Journal,* April 1, 2019.

300   **"superpowers" of "scale" and "technology":** IPO pitch presentation to WeWork, JPMorgan Chase, May 2020.

300   **JPMorgan's range: $46 billion to $63 billion:** Eric Platt, Andrew Edgecliffe-Johnson, James Fontanella-Khan, and Laura Noonan, "WeWork Turmoil Puts Spotlight on JPMorgan Chase and Goldman Sachs," *Financial Times,* September 24, 2019.

301   **got to work on a deal:** Maureen Farrell, "WeWork to Raise Billions Selling Debt Ahead of IPO," *Wall Street Journal,* July 7, 2019.

302   **charge $200 million in up-front fees:** "Project Poseidon: GS Response," Goldman Sachs presentation to WeWork, May 2020.

303   **to help WeWork borrow $6 billion:** Gillian Tan, "WeWork Seeks $6 Billion Financing, Contingent on IPO Success," Bloomberg News, Aug. 1, 2019.

303   **JPMorgan, and other banks that joined it:** Michelle Sierra, "WeWork Loan Modified to Reduce Lender Risk Ahead of IPO," Reuters, Sept. 13, 2019.

CHAPTER 31: TO THE ENERGY OF WE

306   **"We are a global physical platform":** Internally circulated draft Form S-1, WeWork, May 2020.

306   **constant stream of WeWork employees:** Maureen Farrell et al., "The Fall of WeWork: How a Startup Darling Came Unglued," *Wall Street Journal,* Oct. 24, 2019.

308   **"Step into the World of We":** We Co., Form S-1 Registration Statement, SEC, Aug. 14, 2019.

309   **"To the energy of We":** Ibid.

309   **profit margins of more than 30 or even 40 percent:** "Optimizing Space Itself with WeWork's Adam Neumann/Disrupt NY 2017," YouTube, posted May 15, 2017, www.youtube.com/watch?v=-EKOV71m-PY.

311   **summoned the heads of the NYSE and the Nasdaq:** Farrell et al., "Fall of WeWork."

312   **the $48 price investors paid *four years* earlier:** Uber Technologies, Form S-1 Registration Statement, SEC, April 11, 2019.

312   **a record for a U.S. startup:** Eliot Brown, "Uber Wants to Be the Uber of Everything—but Can It Make a Profit?," *Wall Street Journal,* May 4, 2019.

CHAPTER 32: TWENTY TO ONE

314   **had no voting rights at all:** Maureen Farrell, "In Snap IPO, New Investors to Get Zero Votes, While Founders Keep Control," *Wall Street Journal,* Jan. 16, 2017.

315   **the company's investments in his:** Eliot Brown, "Surfing, Schools, and Jets: WeWork's Bets Follow CEO Adam Neumann's Passions," *Wall Street Journal,* March 5, 2019.

315   **generate huge tax savings for Neumann:** Eric Platt, James Fontanella-Khan, and Miles Kruppa, "WeWork Revamp Creates Tax Benefit for Company Insiders," *Financial Times,* Aug. 8, 2019.

316   **he had drawn down $380 million:** We Co., Form S-1 Registration Statement, SEC, Aug. 14, 2019.

316   **Neumann owned 83 percent of We Holdings:** "Flatiron School LLC Profit and Loss Statement," included as part of Application for Provisional Approval to the Higher Education Licensure submitted to the District of Columbia, We-Work, Nov. 6, 2017.

316   **long list of relatives:** Ellen Huet and Gillian Tan, "WeWork Was a Family Affair, Until Things Got Complicated," *Bloomberg Businessweek,* Sept. 28, 2019.

317   **Neumann had taken out more than $700 million:** Eliot Brown, Maureen Farrell, and Anupreeta Das, "WeWork Co-founder Has Cashed Out at Least $700 Million via Sales, Loans," *Wall Street Journal,* July 18, 2019.

318   **Peloton had twenty votes per share:** Jessica Bursztynsky, "'We Weren't Greedy'—Peloton CEO Says IPO 'Left Something on the Table on Pricing,'" CNBC, Sept. 26, 2019.

CHAPTER 33: WEWTF: THE S-1 SH*T SHOW

325   **Cramer would later say:** "Why Jim Cramer Isn't Sold on WeWork," TheStreet, August 14, 2019.

326   **"the news item that caused me":** Matt Levine, "Money Stuff: We Looks Out for Our Selves," Bloomberg, Aug. 19, 2019.

326   **penned a piece on WeWork titled "WeWTF":** Scott Galloway, "WeWTF," *No Mercy No Malice* (blog), Aug. 16, 2019, profgalloway.com/wewtf.

326   *Stratechery* **that laid out what a bull case:** Ben Thompson, "The WeWork IPO," *Stratechery* (blog), Aug. 20, 2019.

327   **his "nadir" of 2019:** Ben Thompson, "The 2019 Stratechery Year in Review," *Stratechery* (blog), Dec. 18, 2019.

327   **"When the best investors all agree":** Victoria Turk, "How WeWork Became the Most Hyped Startup in the World," *Wired UK,* June 6, 2018.

328   **going to be less than $30 billion:** Maureen Farrell and Eliot Brown, "WeWork Weighs Slashing Valuation by More Than Half amid IPO Skepticism," *Wall Street Journal,* Sept. 5, 2019.

CHAPTER 34: A SETTING SON

330   **commitments totaling $108 billion:** Saheli Roy Choudhury, "SoftBank Launches New $108 Billion Fund to Invest in A.I.," CNBC, July 25, 2019.

331   **were significantly lagging behind expectations:** Parmy Olson, "SoftBank Chip-Design Unit Yet to Conquer Internet of Things," *Wall Street Journal,* July 8, 2019.

331   **Saudi Arabia's PIF was noncommittal:** Phred Dvorak, Liz Hoffman, and Mayumi Negishi, "Does SoftBank Really Have $108 Billion for Its Vision Fund 2?," *Wall Street Journal,* Aug. 6, 2019.

331   **Vision Fund's profits were up 66 percent:** Mayumi Negishi, "SoftBank's Vision Fund 2 Plans to Begin Investing as Soon as Next Month," *Wall Street Journal,* Aug. 7, 2019.

332   **sprinted north over Lake Ontario:** Flight path for N1872, FlightAirMap website, accessed Aug. 26, 2019.

334   **SoftBank had just invested in Greensill's business:** Duncan Mavin, "SoftBank Invests $800 Million in Supply Chain Finance Firm Greensill," *Wall Street Journal,* May 13, 2019.

CHAPTER 35: PARANOIA

336   **story published after his departure:** Kirsten Grind, Sarah Krouse, and Jim Oberman, "Star Fidelity Manager Gavin Baker Fired over Sexual Harassment Allegations," *Wall Street Journal,* Oct. 12, 2017.

336   **T. Rowe Price—had become so embittered:** Maureen Farrell and Eliot Brown, "The Money Men Who Enabled Adam Neumann and the WeWork Debacle," *Wall Street Journal,* Dec. 14, 2019.

339   **brokered the meeting:** Ibid.

339   **Neumann announced that Frances Frei:** Ibid.

343   **The *Journal*'s piece:** Eliot Brown, "How Adam Neumann's Over-the-Top Style Built WeWork. 'This Is Not the Way Everybody Behaves,'" *Wall Street Journal,* Sept. 18, 2019.

344   **Neumann had to shoot the video:** Farrell and Brown, "Money Men Who Enabled Adam Neumann and the WeWork Debacle."

CHAPTER 36: THE FALL OF ADAM

348   **who had devoted much of her summer:** Maureen Farrell and Eliot Brown, "The Money Men Who Enabled Adam Neumann and the WeWork Debacle," *Wall Street Journal,* Dec. 14, 2019.

349   **WeWork's troubled IPO was off:** Maureen Farrell, "WeWork Parent Postpones IPO," *Wall Street Journal,* Sept. 17, 2019.

351   **"played the private market game":** Eliot Brown, "How Adam Neumann's Over-the-Top Style Built WeWork. 'This Is Not the Way Everybody Behaves,'" *Wall Street Journal,* Sept. 18, 2019.

352   **Masayoshi Son was hosting a three-day summit:** Farrell and Brown, "Money Men Who Enabled Adam Neumann and the WeWork Debacle."

352   **"Adam Neumann was flying high":** Brown, "How Adam Neumann's Over-the-Top Style Built WeWork."

353   **isn't viewed as permissively:** Ellen Huet and Shawn Wen, "IPO—Just Kidding," *Foundering* (podcast), episode 6, Bloomberg News, July 23, 2020.

354   **Schwartz, who had recently praised:** Maureen Farrell et al., "Some WeWork Board Members Seek to Remove Adam Neumann as CEO," *Wall Street Journal,* Sept. 22, 2019.

355   **pushed to remove CEO Travis Kalanick:** Mike Isaac, "Inside Travis Kalanick's Resignation as Uber's CEO," *New York Times,* June 21, 2017.

356   **An onlooker snapped a photo:** Reeves Wiedeman, *Billion Dollar Loser: The Epic Rise and Spectacular Fall of Adam Neumann and WeWork* (New York: Little, Brown, 2020), 302.

356   ***Journal* published its story:** Farrell et al., "Some WeWork Board Members Seek to Remove Adam Neumann as CEO."

357   **trekked to midtown to see Jamie Dimon:** Maureen Farrell et al., "The Fall of WeWork: How a Startup Darling Came Unglued," *Wall Street Journal,* Oct. 24, 2019.

358   **meet his three closest investors:** Ibid.

359   **filed into the carriage house:** Farrell et al., "Fall of WeWork."

360   **posted stories on Neumann's ouster:** Eliot Brown et al., "WeWork's Adam Neumann Steps Down as CEO," *Wall Street Journal,* Sept. 24, 2019; David Gelles et al., "WeWork C.E.O. Adam Neumann Steps Down Under Pressure," *New York Times,* Sept. 24, 2019.

360   **At 1:45 p.m., the official press release:** WeWork, "WeWork's Board of Directors Announces Leadership Changes," press release, Sept. 24, 2019.

CHAPTER 37: DENEUMANNIZATION

362   **the pink couches in Rebekah Neumann's office:** Maureen Farrell et al., "The Fall of WeWork: How a Startup Darling Came Unglued," *Wall Street Journal,* Oct. 24, 2019.

363   **The jet would be put up for sale:** Meghan Morris, "WeWork Is Selling the Company's $60 Million Luxurious Private Jet That Adam Neumann and His Family Personalized and Used to Fly All over the World," *Business Insider,* Sept. 26, 2019.

365   **a $14 billion drop in Juul's valuation:** Jennifer Maloney, "Altria Cuts Value of Juul Stake by $4.5 Billion," *Wall Street Journal,* Oct. 31, 2019.

367   **$108 billion in tentative commitments:** SoftBank Group, "Launch of SoftBank Vision Fund 2," press release, July 26, 2019.

368   **snorkeling with him in the Red Sea:** Liz Hoffman and Bradley Hope, "Rajeev Misra Built SoftBank's Huge Tech Fund. Now He Has to Save It," *Wall Street Journal,* Oct. 30, 2019.

CHAPTER 38: BREAD OF SHAME

370   *couldn't even afford layoffs:* Maureen Farrell et al., "The Fall of WeWork: How a Startup Darling Came Unglued," *Wall Street Journal,* Oct. 24, 2019.

370   **got a call from Mark Schwartz:** Maureen Farrell and Eliot Brown, "The Money Men Who Enabled Adam Neumann and the WeWork Debacle," *Wall Street Journal,* Dec. 14, 2019.

371   **"I've stayed silent too long":** Ibid.

371   **became clear to the board:** Maureen Farrell, Liz Hoffman, and Eliot Brown, "SoftBank Seeking to Take Control of WeWork Through Financing Package," *Wall Street Journal,* Oct. 13, 2019.

372   **another 580,000 desks yet to be opened:** "Investor Presentation," WeWork, Oct. 11, 2019, www.wework.com/ideas/wp-content/uploads/2019/11/Investor-Presentation%E2%80%94October-2019.pdf.

372   **numbers presented to investors showed:** Ibid., 21.

372   **roughly even with the long-established competitor IWG:** "Annual Report and Accounts 2018," IWG PLC, March 6, 2019, 26.

373   **Starwood Capital Group:** Liz Hoffman and Maureen Farrell, "WeWork's Valuation Falls to $8 Billion Under SoftBank Rescue Offer," *Wall Street Journal,* Oct. 21, 2019.

373   **very steep interest rates:** Davide Scigliuzzo et al., "WeWork Bonds Tank as Firm Seeks JPMorgan Junk-Debt Lifeline," Bloomberg News, Oct. 4, 2019.

374   **SoftBank was valuing WeWork:** Ibid.

375   **Claure agreed to Neumann's requests:** Maureen Farrell and Eliot Brown, "SoftBank to Boost Stake in WeWork in Deal That Cuts Most Ties with Neumann," *Wall Street Journal,* Oct. 22, 2019.

375   **request to forgive his debts to WeWork:** Farrell and Brown, "Money Men Who Enabled Adam Neumann and the WeWork Debacle."

376   **"If the person you are looking":** Michael Berg, "Transformative Sharing Versus Bread of Shame," Kabbalah Centre website, July 29, 2016.

377   **their options were underwater:** Eliot Brown, "WeWork Employee Options Underwater as Ex-CEO Reaps," *Wall Street Journal,* Oct. 23, 2019.

378   **sat on chairs onstage off to the side:** Farrell et al., "Fall of WeWork."

379   **would be out of work:** Sarah E. Needleman and Eliot Brown, "WeWork to Cut Around 17% of Workforce," *Wall Street Journal,* Nov. 21, 2019.

380   **filed an employment complaint:** David Yaffe-Bellany, "WeWork's Ousted C.E.O. Adam Neumann Is Accused of Pregnancy Discrimination," *New York Times,* Oct. 31, 2019.

381   **still flying around on private jets:** Jennifer Gould, "Ex-WeWork CEO Adam Neumann Flees NYC to Escape 'Negative Energy': Pals," *New York Post,* Dec. 17, 2019.

381   **They were flying commercial:** Jessica Bennett, "Ousted WeWork CEO Adam Neumann Travels to Israel," *New York Post,* Dec. 27, 2019.

EPILOGUE

383   **"My own investment judgment":** Phred Dvorak and Megumi Fujikawa, "SoftBank Founder Calls His Judgment 'Really Bad' After $4.7 Billion WeWork Hit," *Wall Street Journal,* Nov. 6, 2019.

384   **estimated at less than 20 percent, against Rover:** Tomio Geron, "Since Receiving SoftBank's $300 Million Check, Wag Has Gained Little Ground," *WSJ Pro: Venture Capital,* April 25, 2019.

385   **Layoffs swept like a virus:** Josh Constine, "Layoffs Hit Flexport, Another SoftBank-Backed Startup Worth $3.2B," *TechCrunch,* Feb. 4, 2020.

385   **OYO, the hotel company:** Vindu Goel, Karan Deep Singh, and Erin Griffith, "Oyo Scales Back as SoftBank-Funded Companies Retreat," *New York Times,* Jan. 13, 2020.

385   **An activist investor, Elliott Management:** Jenny Strasburg and Bradley Hope, "Elliott Management Builds More Than $2.5 Billion Stake in SoftBank," *Wall Street Journal,* Feb. 6, 2020.

385   **"the valley of the coronavirus":** "Earnings Results Briefing for FY2019," SoftBank Group, May 20, 2020, group.softbank/en/news/webcast/20200518_01.

385   **It would use only its own money:** Sanchita Dash, "SoftBank Vision Fund 2 Fails to Raise New Funds," *Business Insider,* May 18, 2020.

386   **He wagered complex bets:** Kana Inagaki et al., "SoftBank Unmasked as 'Nasdaq Whale' That Stoked Tech Rally," *Financial Times,* Sept. 4, 2020.

386   **David Ludwig and Kim Posnett, were given promotions:** Elaine Chen, Ed Hammond, and Crystal Tse, "Goldman's Next Generation Takes Shape With New Promotions," Bloomberg, September 21, 2020.

386   **he told a crowd:** Greg Roumeliotis, "Goldman CEO Says Process on Canceled WeWork IPO 'Worked,'" Reuters, Jan. 21, 2020.

387   **named one of eighteen "global chairmen":** "JPMorgan Names New Global Leaders at Investment Bank—Sources," Reuters, Feb. 18, 2020.

387   **The bank told WeWork:** Dakin Campbell, "JPMorgan Will Still Rake in About $50 Million After WeWork Snubbed the $5 Billion Bailout It Pulled Together," *Business Insider,* Oct. 22, 2019.

387   **made the rounds with the press:** "IWG CEO on WeWork and the Commercial Real Estate Market," CNBC, Oct. 1, 2019.

388   **attorney general's office all opened inquiries:** Greg Roumeliotis, Joshua Franklin, and Koh Gui Qing, "Exclusive: New York State Attorney General Investigating WeWork—Sources," Reuters, Nov. 18, 2019.

389   **$2.9 billion in May:** Vlad Savov, "WeWork's Valuation Has Dropped to $2.9 Billion, SoftBank Says," Bloomberg News, May 17, 2020.

390   **to 5,600 by mid-2020:** Arash Massoudi, Kana Inagaki, and Eric Platt, "WeWork on Track for Profits and Positive Cash Flow in 2021, Says Chairman," *Financial Times,* July 12, 2020.

392   **Milton sold $94 million of stock:** Ben Foldy, Mike Colias, and Nora Naughton, "Long Before Nikola Trucks, Trevor Milton Sold Investors on Startups That Faded," *Wall Street Journal,* Oct. 1, 2020.

394   **"People embrace him here":** Diana Bahur Nir, "A Mother Knows: Adam Neumann's Mom Opens Up," *CTech,* March 20, 2020.

395   **an email later unearthed:** *In Re WeWork Litigation,* Delaware Court of Chancery, plaintiffs' motion to compel defendants to produce documents improperly withheld as privileged, C.A. No. 2020-0258-AGB, Oct. 28, 2020.

395   **Bloomberg in April dropped him off:** Tom Metcalf, "Adam Neumann Ousted from Billionaire Ranks on SoftBank Reversal," Bloomberg, April 2, 2020.

INDEX

Abdulaziz bin Saud, 160
Abu Dhabi, 159, 164, 177, 331, 367–368
Adelson, Sheldon, 144–145, 166
Agarwal, Ritesh, 210, 352, 385
Aggarwal, Bhavish, 165
Airbnb
  CEO of, 56
  comparison to, 6, 66, 86, 102,
    126
  IPO of, 393
  Kutcher and, 281
  lack of profitability of, 5
  meetings with, 284–285
  as mission driven, 110, 246
  as private company, 154
  tangential initiatives and, 185
  valuation of, 78, 118
  venture capitalists and, 55
  WeWork compared to, 131
Ajami, Ibrahim, 350
alcohol consumption. *See also under*
  Neumann, Adam
  at Summer Camp, 75, 219
  at WeWork, 4, 40, 65, 108, 109
Alesso, 219
Alibaba, 129, 132, 140, 147, 149, 158, 163,
  210, 214, 386
Allbirds, 98
al-Rumayyan, Yasir, 162, 177, 247, 266,
  339, 352
Altria, 365

Amazon
  as client, 6, 190, 214, 259
  expansion of, 238–239
  founder exceptionalism and, 185
  Goldman Sachs and, 124
  IPO of, 154
  media treatment of, 100
  mutual funds and, 81
  recruiting Gunningham from, 237, 251
  Son and, 386
  Uber and, 99
  Uber comparison and, 313
  venture capitalists and, 52, 55
Anaya, Ruby, 256–258
Apollo, 158
Apple, 52, 53, 54, 55, 117, 154, 201, 214,
  247, 284
Aramco, 161–162, 331
ARK, 204–206, 211, 214, 215–216, 251, 388
Arm Holdings, 331
Arora, Nikesh, 149, 164–165, 169
artificial intelligence (AI), 209, 278
Asch, Solomon, 97
Asci, Jimmy, 322–323, 340
AT&T, 148
autonomous driving robot division, 241
Awake, 45

Bahar, Roni, 106, 108, 116, 152, 190, 247,
  248, 290

bake-off, 296, 297–301
Baker, Gavin, 79–80, 83–84, 129, 336, 387
Bank of America, 259, 350
Bank of Italy building, 290
Bardhi, Medina, 258, 287, 380
Bastille, 219
Beanie Babies, 96
Bear Stearns, 117, 346
Ben-Avraham, Samuel, 42, 44, 174
Benchmark. *See also* Dunlevie, Bruce; Eisenberg, Michael
   DAG Ventures and, 69
   investment from, 56–62, 63, 68, 72, 74
   management structure and, 87–88
   Minson and, 192
   Neumann and, 51
   Neumann's ouster and, 354–355
   potential payout for, 263
   stock sales by, 174
   VC boom and, 53–54
Benioff, Marc, 339
Benzino, Arik, 253, 277, 342
Berg, Michael, 376
Berg, Yehuda, 262
Berrent, Jen
   after Neumann's departure, 388
   ARK and, 205
   at board meetings, 263
   concerns voiced by, 282
   conflict with, 317–318, 320–321
   Gross and, 130
   IPO and, 295
   management structure and, 87
   Middle East deal and, 246–247
   Neumann's ouster and, 356, 357, 360
   Neumann's trust in, 155
   Saudi Arabia and, 178
   SEC and, 322
   SoftBank deal and, 169–170, 174, 175–176, 264–265, 267, 269
   Son and, 210
   trademarks and, 325–326
   triangle strategy of, 212
   Wall Street Journal profile and, 343
   WeWork IPO and, 340, 346–348
   WeWork narrative and, 306
Besmertnik, Seth, 239–240, 289
Beyond Meat, 101

Bezos, Jeff, 55, 157, 180, 185, 238
BGIS, 241
"Billionaire" (McCoy), 201
Birchbox, 100
Blackstone Group, 158, 204
Blade, 307
Blankfein, Lloyd, 260, 298
Bogle, Jack, 80
Bombardier Global Express, 235
bond markets, 194, 196, 198, 199–200
Bosa, Deirdre, 274
Boston Properties, 67, 86, 186
Box, 127
Boyd, Andy, 84, 85
Braun, Adam, 228, 229
bread of shame, 376
Brin, Sergey, 247, 250
Brown, Tina, 101
Bryant, Kobe, 98
bubbles, 96–97
Burr, Aaron, 122
Bush, George W., 249
Business Insider conference, 170
Buttigieg, Pete, 243
Buy.com, 146

C3.ai, 393
Carreyrou, John, 127
Carter, Graydon, 46
Case Design, 106–108
Casper, 5, 101, 391
CBRE, 240
Centricus, 163
Chainsmokers, 108, 219
Chariot Club, 133
Chase, 120–121
Chase Center, 119
Chesky, Brian, 56, 154, 246, 284–285, 393
China, 126, 129–133, 138
Chopra, Deepak, 217–218
Christie, Chris, 288
Chromeo, 219
Chudnofsky, Jason, 145
Citigroup, 350
Claure, Marcelo, 373–374, 375–376, 377–378, 385–386, 388, 389, 395
Clinton, Hillary, 166

Clutter, 98
Cohen, Steve, 5–6
collective psychology, 97
Comdex, 144–145, 166
Comella, Maria, 288
community manager position, 38
community-adjusted EBITDA, 196–199,
     310, 321–322, 372
Compass, 98, 182, 209
Conductor, 239–240, 278, 289, 306, 388
conformity, 97
Cook, Tim, 148, 247, 284
Cottle, Frank, 92
Coursey, Court, 350
COVID-19, 385, 389–390, 394, 395
Cramer, Jim, 324–325
Creator Awards, 114, 253, 273–274, 279,
     281
Creator Fund, 280
Credit Suisse, 316, 350
Cressman, Hunter, 224
cult of the founder, 56, 391, 393
Cunningham, Stacey, 311–312
Cuomo, Andrew, 288
Cushman & Wakefield, 212, 240
CVS, 299

DAG Ventures, 69
Dalberg-Acton, John, 88
Damon, Matt, 18
Danoff, Will, 84–85
Dawson, Rosario, 45
Dealbreaker, 198
Dean, Howard, 183
Dees, Dan, 333
Del Rosario, Dom, 289, 293
DeMatteis, Jared, 170
Deutsche Bank, 162–163
Didi Chuxing, 176
Dillabough, Gary, 290
Diller, Barry, 184
Dimon, Jamie
     financial crisis of 2007–2008 and, 117
     Lee and, 121–122
     media treatment of, 245
     Mohammed bin Salman and, 162
     Neumann and, 123
     Neumann's ouster and, 349, 357–358

post-WeWork status of, 387
Silicon Valley and, 118, 119
WeWork IPO and, 299–300, 301, 303,
     304, 314–315, 318–319, 338, 339, 340
Wintroub and, 120
Dixon, Mark, 90–96, 240, 275, 373, 387
Doherty, Pete, 45
DoorDash, 209, 393
dot-com boom and bust, 54, 92, 93, 120,
     140, 146–147
Doughbies, 99
Dropbox, 339
Dunlevie, Bruce
     Benchmark's investment and, 57–61
     Berrent and, 317
     on board of directors, 72, 73
     closing deal with Softbank and,
          263–264
     concerns voiced by, 126
     lawsuit from, 395
     management structure and, 87–88
     nepotism and, 253
     Neumann's ouster and, 354–355, 356,
          358
     Omidyar and, 54
     Porat and, 284
     push to go public from, 291–292
     SoftBank deal and, 174, 185
     WeWork's financial crisis and, 370

E*Trade, 146
eBay, 54, 58
EBITDA. See community-adjusted
     EBITDA
Egg Baby, 21
Eisenberg, Michael, 51–52, 56–57, 74,
     121, 126, 192, 318, 355, 358, 360
Ellenbogen, Henry, 79–81, 83, 387
Elliott Management, 385
Ellison, Larry, 144, 145
Emanuel, Rahm, 65
Enron, 204, 245
Erdoes, Mary Callahan, 193, 319, 346,
     347, 348–349, 355
Erickson, Mandie, 45
Eridge Park, 217–219
Evercore, 161–162
Expedia, 184

Facebook
  acquisitions of, 48, 185
  as client, 6, 190, 259
  comparison to, 47, 59, 66, 299
  growth of, 54
  IPO of, 81, 297
  JPMorgan and, 118, 122
  media treatment of, 100
  as mission driven, 110
  Mohammed bin Salman and, 247
  network effect and, 95
  Parker and, 46
  profitability of, 208
  Sandberg and, 192, 250
  success of, 98
  terrorism and, 111
  valuation of, 117
  venture capitalists and, 52
  Zuckerberg's control of, 55, 88
Fair, 367
Fano, Dave, 106–108, 155, 184, 251, 277
Fasone, Joseph, 39
Fast Company, 92, 100
Fastow, Andy, 204
Fegen, Paul, 91
Fidelity, 5, 79–80, 83–85, 87, 98, 116, 124,
  129, 336–337, 387
Filo, David, 147
Finkelstein, Andy, 27, 32–33
firings, demand for, 253–254, 256
Fisher, Ron, 267, 354
Fitzgerald, F. Scott, 383
FitzPatrick, Mark, 193, 198
Flatiron School, 184, 220, 247
Forbes, 100–101, 123, 146, 201
Ford factory, 103–104
Forest City Ratner, 67
Fortune, 100
founder, cult of the, 56, 391, 393
"founder-friendly" venture capitalists, 56
Founders Fund, 56
Frankfort, Lew, 263–264, 354, 370
freelancers, 66–67
Frei, Frances, 339
Friedman, Adena, 311–312

G20, 162
GAAP, 321–322

Galloway, Scott, 326
Gama Aviation, 236
Gates, Bill, 143–144, 145, 157
General Electric, 118, 245, 259, 299
GeoCities, 146
Getaround, 385
GIC, 331
Global Summit, 3–5, 7–9, 194, 257, 273,
  281
"glocal" (term), 131
Golden State Warriors, 119
Goldman Sachs
  China and, 126, 129, 131, 132
  interest in WeWork from, 69, 119,
    123–124
  Minson and, 195
  Neumann and, 6, 260
  post-WeWork status of, 386–387
  Silicon Valley and, 118
  SoftBank Group and, 167
  Son and, 333
  status of, 387
  Wall Street Journal profile and, 343
  WeWork IPO and, 296, 298–299,
    301–304, 310, 313, 340, 342, 347,
    349
Gomel, Rich, 251
Google, 47, 52, 55, 81, 117, 239, 247, 250,
  284, 297
Gothamist, 25
Goto, Yoshimitsu, 268–269
Graham, Bill, 283
Great Recession, 35
Green Desk, 23–26, 33–34
Greensill, Lex, 333–334
Greensill Capital, 334
Grimes, Michael, 297–298, 350
Gross, Michael
  al-Rumayyan and, 266
  "Billionaire" (McCoy) and, 201
  bondholders and, 263
  China and, 129–130, 133
  firing of, 363
  Ford factory and, 103, 104
  management structure and, 252
  nepotism and, 105
  Neumann's building investments and,
    202
  promotional video and, 344–345

role of, 251
SoftBank Group and, 167, 174
stock sales by, 116
We Entertainment and, 279
WeWork IPO and, 297, 303–304, 338
Groupon, 54, 118
Grove, Andy, 144, 145
Guitar House, 283, 288–289, 396
Gulfstream, 234–235, 236–237
Gunningham, Sebastian, 237, 251, 359, 360, 362, 363, 369, 378, 379, 388
Gurley, Bill, 128, 354
Guttman, Jack, 22–24, 25–26
Guttman, Josh, 22–24, 25–26
Guy Pines show, 18

Hadley, Stephen, 249
Haklay, Gil, 20, 21, 24, 26
Hallisay, Brian, 29
Hambrecht & Quist, 120
Hamilton, Alexander, 122
Hamilton, Laird, 6, 269, 279–280
Harry's, 101
Harvard University, 6
Hays, Laurie, 356
health insurance, 64
Hello Alfred, 397
herd mentality, 97
Hill, Chris, 89, 105, 116, 252–253, 363
Hobbs, Thomas, 219–220
Hodari, Jamie, 152, 188–189
Holmes, Elizabeth, 100
Hony Capital, 131, 132, 138, 173
Horowitz, Andreessen, 56
Howes, Lewis, 245
HQ Global Workplaces, 93
HSBC, 162
Huffington, Arianna, 352

ice plunge, 238
index funds, 80
India, 137–139, 149, 164
Industrious, 152, 188–189
Ingels, Bjarke, 184–185, 186, 228, 290
InMobi, 164
Instagram, 48, 55, 58, 185

investment banks, 296
iPhone, 54, 148
IPOs. See also under WeWork
  of Airbnb, 393
  of Amazon, 154
  for Aramco, 161–162
  decreased valuations at, 127
  of Facebook, 81, 297
  of Google, 297
  JPMorgan and, 118
  of Lyft, 294, 298, 300
  SoftBank Group and, 266, 267–268
  of Uber, 296–297, 298
  valuations and, 295–297
  venture capitalists and, 81
Iran, 160
irrational choices, 97
Isaacson, Walter, 245–246
Israel Defense Forces, 17
ITC Bangalore, 137
IWG, 240–241, 309, 373, 387

Jefferies, 69
Jobs, Steve, 55, 110, 148, 245–246
Johnson, Edward, II, 80
JPMorgan Chase. See also Dimon, Jamie; Wintroub, Noah
  comparison to, 241
  dismissal of, 376
  interest in WeWork from, 6
  investment from, 77, 87, 122–123, 129, 131
  loan from, 193, 199
  Neumann's ouster and, 357
  personal loans from, 315
  post-WeWork status of, 387
  private conference of, 283
  Silicon Valley and, 117–119
  valuation from, 78, 213
  Wall Street Journal profile and, 343
  WeWork IPO and, 296–297, 299–301, 302–304, 310, 313, 318–320, 328, 339, 340, 342, 346
  WeWork's financial crisis and, 371, 373
"Juicy" (Notorious B.I.G.), 113
Just Kids (Smith), 45
Juul, 365

Kabbalah Centre, 30, 34, 42, 45, 262, 376
Kalanick, Travis, 86, 88, 126, 176, 241, 355
Kamens, Ranee, 19
Karan, Donna, 31
Karp, Alex, 56
Kazakhstan, 331–332
Khashoggi, Jamal, 248–249, 331
kibbutz structure, changes in, 16–17
Kiedis, Anthony, 5
Kimmel, Adam, 255–256, 276
Kingston Technology, 146
Kitu Lite coffee, 280
Knight, Bobby, 229
Kozmo.com, 96–97, 146
Kravis, Henry, 121
Krawlers, 13, 14–15, 18–19, 21
Kushner, Jared, 247–248
Kutcher, Ashton, 4–5, 30–31, 65, 273–274, 279–281

Laird Superfood, 280, 388
Langman, Steven
    on board of directors, 72, 73
    conflict with Neumann and, 339
    conflicts of interest and, 203
    investment from, 61
    as mentor, 42
    nepotism and, 253
    Neumann's building investments and, 202
    Neumann's ouster and, 354, 355, 358
    push to go public from, 291–292
    SoftBank Group and, 169
    WeWork IPO and, 320
    WeWork's fall and, 369
Lapidus, Mark, 75, 105, 116, 253
lead left, 296
Lee, Christian, 277
Lee, Jimmy, 121–123, 124
Legend, John, 352
Legend Holdings, 131
Lennon, Sean, 45
Leto, Jared, 98
Levine, Matt, 326
Life Biosciences, 244
Lime, 185
Linga, Srujan, 303–304

LinkedIn, 118, 122, 208, 297
Linkin Park, 98
Liu, Lucy, 30, 31
Livingston, Ron, 33
LJM, 204
Lobo, Francis, 137–138
Logistics Plus, 172
Lord & Taylor, 185–186
Lorde, 219
Lovka, 171–172
Low, Joey, 70
Lu, Hong, 142, 143
Lucid Motors, 247
Ludwig, David, 124, 195, 310, 349, 386
Luxe, 98
Lyft
    drop in stock price of, 312–313
    IPO of, 294, 298, 300
    losses of, 154, 275
    Neumann's interest in, 241
    valuation of, 126

Ma, Jack, 132, 140, 147, 166, 210
Madoff, Bernie, 105
Madonna, 30, 279
Maldives, 293, 295
Marcus, Robert, 193
marijuana, 107, 234, 286, 343, 347–348, 352–353
Marriott, 205
maternity leave, 258, 380
Mathrani, Sandeep, 388, 389
mature location economics, 309
May, Theresa, 244
McCoy, Travie, 201
McDaniels, Darryl, 156
McKelvey, Miguel
    after Neumann's departure, 388
    Anaya and, 256, 257–258
    background of, 21–22
    Benchmark and, 58, 60–62
    at Business Insider conference, 170
    Claure and, 378
    division of labor and, 41
    early days of WeWork and, 42–43
    expansion of WeWork and, 43
    Green Desk and, 22–26
    meeting Neumann, 20

Minson and, 193
nepotism and, 253
on Neumann, 125
Neumann's destructive acts and, 89
Neumann's ouster and, 359
Reid-Dodick and, 254
role of, 251
start of WeWork and, 32–37
stock sales and, 174–175
at Summer Camp, 76, 220, 222
trademarks and, 323
veganism of, 221
WeWork IPO and, 308, 310–311
WeWork opening and, 38–39
meat, ban on, 221, 226
medical marijuana. *See* marijuana
Meetup.com, 183–184, 278, 306, 363, 388
Melt, The, 101
#MeToo movement, 255
Microsoft, 6, 52, 190, 386
Millman, Michael, 310, 340
Milton, Trevor, 391–392
Minson, Artie
    after Neumann's departure, 388
    ARK and, 205
    background of, 192–193
    bank projections and, 297
    at board meetings, 263
    bond markets and, 194–196, 199
    bondholders and, 263
    cell phone antenna issue and, 287–288
    Claure and, 378
    as co-CEO, 362
    community-adjusted EBITDA and,
        196–198
    concerns voiced by, 282
    expansion of WeWork and, 274–275
    Flatiron School and, 184
    hiring of, 106
    IPO and, 294–295
    layoffs and, 379
    Neumann's ouster and, 349, 356, 359,
        360–361
    role of, 251
    SEC and, 322
    SoftBank deal and, 169–170, 175
    Softbank deal and, 264, 267
    SoftBank deal and, 269
    Son and, 210

status of at WeWork, 192–194
surfing and, 151
trademarks and, 325
Wall Street Journal profile and, 343
WeWork IPO and, 297, 299, 302–303,
    309–310, 313, 346–348
WeWork narrative and, 306
WeWork valuations and, 173
WeWork's financial crisis and, 369–370,
    371–372, 373
Miranda, Lin-Manuel, 219
Misra, Rajeev, 159, 162–163, 266, 267,
    350, 367–368
MissionU, 228
mobile industry, 148, 149, 157
Modi, Narendra, 137, 138–139, 149
Moelis, 162
Mohammed bin Salman (MBS), 159–164,
    165, 247–249, 265–266, 368, 385
Montessori tradition, 226–227, 229
Moore, Demi, 30, 31
Morgan Stanley, 118, 119, 120, 161–162,
    296, 297–298, 331, 350, 387
Morgans Hotel Group, 130
MoviePass, 240
Mozer, Forrest, 142–143
MTV, 25
Mubadala, 177, 266, 331, 350, 367–368
Murdoch, Rupert, 121
Musk, Elon, 111–112, 391
mutual funds, 78–89, 99–100, 128–129,
    173

Napster, 46
Nasdaq, 311
Negro, Federico, 106
Neom, 162
nepotism, 252–253
Netflix, 124
Neumann, Adam
    after fall, 394
    aggrandized sense of self and, 244–245
    alcohol consumption and, 46, 65, 89,
        103, 107, 131, 132–133, 138, 156, 187,
        220, 236, 240
    in Amagansett, 306–307
    Anaya and, 257
    ARK and, 204–206

Neumann, Adam (*cont'd*):
   attempted budget cuts by, 277
   background of, 13–19
   Baker and, 83–85
   bank projections and, 297
   in Bay Area, 283–284, 288–289
   Benchmark and, 58, 60–62
   birthday party in Maldives for, 293–294
   bond markets and, 198–200
   bread of shame and, 376–377
   charitable donations from, 86
   Chesky and, 284–285
   China and, 126–127, 129–133
   compensation package for, 261–262,
      265, 292
   corporate clients and, 190
   cost-cutting measures and, 155–156
   divesting and, 396
   division of labor and, 41
   in Dumbo, 22
   Dunlevie and, 58–59
   early relationship between Rebekah
      and, 27–28, 30–31
   Eisenberg and, 51–52, 56–57
   engagement ideal and, 40
   erratic behavior of, 89, 285–286, 338,
      342, 347–348
   expansion of WeWork and, 6, 43,
      63–64, 105–106, 180–181, 186–188
   fallout of collapse and, 380–381
   Fano and, 106–107
   fear of, 254–255
   Fidelity and, 336–337
   finances and, 42–43
   firings demanded by, 253–254, 256
   Forbes on, 100–101
   fund-raising addiction of, 125–126
   at Global Summit, 3–4, 7–9, 273
   Goldman Sachs and, 69, 123–124
   Green Desk and, 22–26
   Greensill and, 333–334
   growing concerns about, 128–129
   Gurley and, 128
   as Halloween costume, 379
   in India, 137–139, 149
   investment in buildings by, 73–74, 115,
      201–203
   Isaacson and, 245–246
   in Israel, 394

   jet purchase and, 237
   JPMorgan Chase and, 77, 120–121,
      122–123
   lawsuit from, 395
   lifestyle of, 72–73, 113–116
   loans to, 71–73, 315–316
   management style of, 250–252
   McKelvey and, 20, 21–22
   meetings with politicians and, 243–244
   Meetup.com and, 183–184
   Middle East and, 246–247
   military service of, 17–18
   Minson and, 193–194
   Musk and, 111–112
   net worth of, 6, 86, 201
   new office for, 238
   ouster of, 349, 353–361
   Parker and, 46–47
   payout to, 375–377
   planes and air travel and, 234–238
   political ambitions of, 242–243
   portrayal of WeWork as tech company
      by, 78
   promotional video by, 344–345,
      347–348
   real estate purchases of, 286–287,
      289–291
   recruitment by, 38
   sales pitch of, 64–67, 102
   Saudi Arabia's investment and, 177–179
   SEC and, 321–322
   Shanklin and, 227, 232–233
   Shorenstein and, 102–104
   SoftBank deal and, 267, 269–270,
      273–274, 284, 285
   SoftBank Group investment and, 7, 9,
      180
   Son and, 167–168, 169–170, 171–172,
      174–176, 203–204, 210–211,
      212–216, 261–262, 263–264, 265,
      285, 332–335
   staff on, 220
   start of WeWork and, 32–37
   stock options for staff and, 63
   stock sales and, 86–87, 115–116,
      174–175
   Summer Camp and, 218, 221–222
   surfing and, 150–152, 293–294
   T. Rowe Price and, 173

trademarks and, 323, 325–326, 341
triangle strategy of, 211–216, 239
at United Jewish Appeal benefit,
    260–261
Wall Street Journal profile of, 343,
    346–347, 352
Wavegarden and, 150
We Entertainment and, 279
WeGrow and, 232
WeWork culture and, 108–109
WeWork IPO and, 155, 195, 296–304,
    309–310, 311, 313, 314–315, 318–321,
    324–325, 327, 328–329, 336–339,
    340–341, 351–352
WeWork narrative and, 182–183, 306
WeWork opening and, 38
WeWork's financial crisis and, 374–376
Neumann, Adi (sister), 13–14, 15, 18, 253
Neumann, Doron (father), 139
Neumann, Rebekah (née Paltrow)
    aggrandized sense of self and, 244–245
    in Amagansett, 306–307
    background of, 28–30
    in Bay Area, 283, 288–289
    branding efforts by, 44–46, 105
    bread of shame and, 376–377
    cell phone antenna issue and, 287–288
    Chopra and, 217
    comments on women's role by, 220
    early relationship with, 27–28, 30–31
    fallout of collapse and, 381
    film industry and, 45–46
    at Global Summit, 5
    investment possibilities due to, 34
    in Israel, 394
    loan from, 42
    May and, 244
    Miranda and, 219
    Musk and, 112
    nepotism and, 252–253
    Neumann's ouster and, 359
    new office for, 238
    phobias of, 287–288
    real estate purchases of, 286–287, 289
    role of, 221, 222
    sales pitch and, 65
    successor committee and, 320, 340,
        341
    surfing and, 150

WeGrow and, 8, 184–185, 224–227,
    228–230, 231–232, 259, 396
WeWork IPO and, 307–309, 324, 326,
    327
WeWork mission and, 111
WeWork opening and, 41–42
Neumann-Orbach, Avivit (mother),
    15–16, 394
New York
    Neumann's move to, 18
    peripheral ventures and, 279
    startup culture and, 48
New York, 73
Nextdoor, 98
Nikola Corporation, 391–392
Nir Am (kibbutz), 16–17
NYSE, 311

Obama administration, 157, 160, 166
Obama O's, 56
Occupy Wall Street, 40
Odriozola, Josema, 150
Office Space, 33
Ohno, Masami, 142
O'Keefe-Sally, Kyle, 38
Ola Cabs, 165
Omidyar, Pierre, 54
Opendoor, 209
Oracle, 52
Orenstein, Danny, 43, 44
Oscar Health, 98
Oseary, Guy, 279
OYO Hotels, 164, 210–211, 367, 385

P. Diddy, 5
pachinko parlors, 141
Page, Larry, 250
Palantir, 56
Palm, 57
Paltrow, Bobby, 114–115
Paltrow, Gwyneth, 27, 28, 29, 31, 307
Paltrow, Rebekah. *See* Neumann,
    Rebekah (née Paltrow)
Pandora, 118
paperless policy, 221
Parekh, Vikas, 172–173
Parker, Sean, 46–47

Parkmerced, 279
Paul, Weiss, Rifkind, Wharton &
    Garrison, 265, 292, 323, 355
PC Magazine, 143, 146
PC Week, 143–144
Peloton, 246, 300, 318
Pencils of Promise, 228
Pets.com, 198
Philz, 98
Pichai, Sundar, 247, 250
Pierre, Carl, 108–109
Pinterest, 55
Pitt, Brad, 29
PizzaExpress, 131
Plenty, 208–209
Porat, Ruth, 284
Posnett, Kim, 123–124, 298, 349, 386
Powered by We division, 282
Presidio, 259
Project Fortitude, 213, 222–223, 261–265,
    282. See also SoftBank Group; Son,
    Masayoshi (Masa)
Project Huxley, 379
Public Investment Fund (PIF; Saudi
    Arabia), 162, 177, 247, 265–266, 331,
    339

Qatar, 159

Ra Ra Riot, 75
railroad investment, 96
Rajaraman, Shiva, 236, 240, 388
Ramon, Roy, 19
Rappi, 385
Raquette Lake, 74–75
Red Hot Chili Peppers, 5
Regus, 90, 92–96, 100, 131, 188, 189,
    240, 275, 309
Reid-Dodick, John, 254
rent holidays, 197
revenue growth, 82
Rhône Group, 61, 202–203, 204
Richards, Hunter, 45, 46, 47
Rise by We, 184
Robinhood, 392
Robinson, Luke, 138, 253
Roots, The, 219

Rosenberg, Laser, 73
Rover, 384
Rozengurtel, Daniel, 15
Rudin Management, 67, 70
Run-DMC, 156

S-1 (IPO prospectus), 305–306, 307–309,
    313, 316–317, 320, 324–329, 333, 340,
    341
Safdie, Abe, 40–41
Salesforce, 190, 299, 339
Salesforce Tower, 186, 283–284
Salman bin Abdulaziz Al Saud, 160
Sama, Alok, 149, 164
San Jose real estate purchases, 289–291,
    396
Sandberg, Sheryl, 250
Sanderson, Steve, 106
Sarona complex, Tel Aviv, 115
Saudi Arabia. See also Public Investment
    Fund (PIF; Saudi Arabia)
    ARK and, 204–205, 215
    Kushner and, 247–248
    Mohammed bin Salman and, 159–162
    Neumann and, 177–178
    SoftBank deal and, 265–266
    Son and, 163–164, 165
    WeWork IPO and, 339, 350
    WeWork's fall and, 368
Schimmel, Marc, 42, 44, 137, 138, 174
Schmidt, Eric, 250, 350
Schreiber, Joel, 36–37, 42
Schumer, Bob, 243, 355
Schumer, Chuck, 243
Schwartz, Mark, 167, 170, 253, 264, 353,
    354, 360, 370–371
Securities and Exchange Commission
    (SEC), 197, 297, 321–322, 324, 327,
    388
Selina, 286
Series B funding, 68, 71
Series C funding, 77
Series D funding, 79
sexual harassment complaints, 256–257
Shachar, Zvika, 105
Shanklin, Joshua, 224–225, 226–228, 229,
    232–233
Shapack, Jeff, 74, 103

sharing economy, 78, 79
Sharp, 143
Shkreli, Martin, 279
Shleifer, Scott, 130
Shorenstein, Brandon, 102–104
Shorenstein Properties, 102
Silver Ball Gardens, 142
Silverstein Properties, 205
Singularity, 164
Skadden, Arps, Slate, Meagher & Flom, 340
Skilling, Jeff, 245
Skye, Lisa, 38–39, 41
Skyler, Jen, 137, 257
Slack, 126, 363, 364–365
smartphone apps, 54
Smith, Jaden, 5
Smith, Patti, 45
Snap Inc., 118, 314, 355
Snapchat, 55, 86, 88, 118, 126, 154, 278, 297
Snapdeal, 164
Sobieski, Leelee, 255
Social Network, The, 46, 48
SoftBank Group. See also Son, Masayoshi (Masa); Vision Fund
  acquisitions of, 146
  Alibaba and, 140, 147
  ambitions for, 148–149
  B. Schumer and, 243
  closing deal with, 261–267
  collapse of deal with, 269–270, 273–274, 284, 285
  Comdex and, 145
  DoorDash and, 393
  dot-com bust and, 146–147
  due diligence team of, 172–173
  failures of, 384–386
  fall in stock price of, 268–269
  formation of, 143
  founder of, 139
  increased ownership stake of, 216
  India and, 164–165
  investments of, 158
  lawsuit against, 395
  mobile industry and, 157
  Mohammed bin Salman and, 248–249
  Mozer and, 143
  Neumann and, 6

Neumann's misuse of funds from, 279–281
  Neumann's ouster and, 356
  pivot of, 366–367
  refusal of to pay on deal, 394–395
  reliance on, 210
  Saudi Arabia's investment and, 163–164, 165, 177–179
  WeWork and, 7, 9, 169, 172–176, 180, 183
  on WeWork board, 185
  WeWork's financial crisis and, 371, 373–376, 377–378
software distribution, 143
SOLFL, 396
Solomon, David, 260, 298, 302, 386–387
Son, Masayoshi (Masa). See also SoftBank Group; Vision Fund
  acquisitions of, 146
  Alibaba and, 147
  ambitions of, 148–149, 157–158
  apology from, 383–384
  background of, 140–144
  collapse of deal with, 269–270, 282, 285
  Comdex and, 144–145
  dot-com bust and, 146–147
  fall in stock price and, 268–269
  in India, 139–140
  India and, 164–165
  jet purchase and, 237
  Lyft and, 241
  mobile industry and, 148, 149
  Mohammed bin Salman and, 162–164, 165
  Neumann and, 6, 203–204, 210–211, 212–216, 261–262, 263–264, 265, 332–335
  partnership with, 222
  Saudi Arabia and, 205, 265–266
  second Vision Fund and, 330–331
  Trump and, 166, 168–169
  venture capitalism and, 158–159
  Wall Street Journal profile and, 352–353
  WeWork and, 167–168, 169–170, 171–172, 174–176, 185
  WeWork IPO and, 328, 331–335
  WeWork's fall and, 366–368, 380
  WeWork's financial crisis and, 371

Son, Mitsunori, 141, 142
Sound Ventures, 281
sovereign wealth funds, 159, 162, 205,
    215. *See also* Public Investment Fund
    (PIF; Saudi Arabia)
SPAC, 393–394
Spaces, 96
SpaceX, 111
Spiegel, Evan, 88, 314
Spiffy Baby, 15
Spotify, 126, 281
Sprint, 140, 148, 149, 157, 166
Square, 55, 127
St. Lucia, 219
Starbucks, 202
startup bubble, 97–100, 127–128
startup culture, 48
Startup India, 137, 138
Starwood Capital, 182, 373
Steinhaus, Joel, 287
Stern, Ilan, 297, 332, 334, 355, 356–357
Sternlicht, Barry, 182
stock options, 63, 78
Stone, Oliver, 68
straightlining, 197
STX Entertainment, 131
subprime mortgage crisis, 25, 54
Summer Camp, 4, 7, 74–75, 108, 193,
    217–223
Sundaram, Ram, 303–304
Sunshine Suites, 22, 24
surfing, 150–153, 269, 293–294
SurveyMonkey, 339
Sweetgreen, 98, 240

T. Rowe Price, 5, 79–80, 86–87, 129,
    173, 336–337, 387
Tahari, Elie, 115
Talassazan, Abraham, 35–36, 37
Talk, 101
tech startups, 47–48
TechCrunch, 100, 181, 196
Templo, Stella, 287
Tencent, 129
terrorism, social media and, 111
Tesla, 111, 386, 391
text-to-speech device, 142–143
TGIM, 109

Theranos, 86, 100, 127
Thiel, Peter, 56
Thompson, Ben, 326–327
Tiger, Ariel, 105
Tiger Global, 130
Timberlake, Justin, 46
Time Warner Cable, 193
Titania, 294
T-Mobile, 148, 149, 157, 166
Tomorrow Ventures, 350
trademarks, 323, 325–326, 341
triangle strategy, 211–216, 239, 306
Trudeau, Justin, 243–244
Trump, Donald, 166, 168–169, 248
tulips, investment in, 96
Twilio, 387
Twitter, 54, 80–81, 111, 118, 211, 335

Uber
    Benchmark and, 58, 88, 128, 355
    in China, 176
    as client, 106
    comparison to, 6, 7, 66, 78, 86, 102,
        126
    COVID-19 and, 385
    debt markets and, 195
    deflation of, 379–380
    drop in stock price of, 312–313
    fund-raising of, 213
    IPO of, 296–297, 298
    Kutcher and, 281
    lack of profitability of, 5
    losses of, 154, 275
    Saudi Arabia's investment in, 162,
        180
    SoftBank Group and, 241
    valuation of, 79, 85, 99, 118, 365
    venture capitalists and, 55, 98
    Vision Fund and, 266, 331
    WeWork compared to, 131
UBS, 315, 350
unicorn startups, 77, 98, 128, 208, 366
Uniqlo, 157
United Arab Emirates, 159, 178
United Jewish Appeal, 260–261
Universal Studios, 4
Unrein, Larry, 77
UrWork, 131

U.S. Conference of Mayors, 243
utopianism, pursuit of, 110–111

Van Der Beek, James, 30, 31
Vanguard, 80
Varma, Munish, 350
venture capitalists, 48, 52–56, 80–82, 98,
    99–100, 154, 158, 281. *See also*
    individual investors
Verizon, 148
Vision 2030, 161
Vision Fund
    pivot of, 367–368
    promotion of, 352
    Saudi Arabia's investment in, 205, 247,
    249
    second, 330–331, 335, 375, 380, 385
    Son's dispersals from, 207–209
    WeWork and, 172–173, 177, 179, 213,
    265–266
VistaJet, 235, 236
Vodafone, 148

Wag, 367, 384
Wall Street, 68
Wall Street Journal
    Neumann's ouster and, 356
    profile of Neumann in, 343, 346–347,
    352
Walters, Andrew, 363–364
Warby Parker, 98, 100
Washington Mutual, 117
Washio, 99
Wavegarden, 150, 152–153, 156, 184, 242,
    388
We Company
    announcement of, 8
    name change to, 262, 273, 282
We Entertainment, 279
Webvan, 146, 147
Weekend, 219
WeGrow, 212, 224–233, 259, 282,
    288–289, 290, 376, 396
Wei, Cheng, 176
Weinberg, Peter, 370
Welch, Jack, 245
WeLive, 112–113, 212, 242, 284, 290, 363

Wellington, 5
West, Kanye, 166
WeWork
    acquisitions of, 239–241
    after Neumann's departure, 362–368,
    387–390
    autonomous driving robot division of,
    241
    Baker and, 83–85
    Benchmark and, 60–62, 63
    board compensation package and, 292
    board of directors of, 72, 73, 87–88,
    339
    changes to structure of, 87–88
    corporate clients and, 190
    cost-cutting measures at, 155–156
    culture of, 108–110
    delay IPO of, 347–351
    deNeumannization of, 362–368
    duplication at, 277
    early investments in, 42–43, 44
    Eisenberg and, 56–57
    expansion of, 6, 8–9, 42–43, 63–64, 77,
    185–188
    financial crisis of, 369–376
    first Summer Camp of, 74–75
    Global Summit for, 3–5, 7–9, 194, 257,
    273, 281
    Goldman Sachs and, 123–124
    Greensill and, 334
    growth of, 67–68, 105–106, 138,
    241–242, 274–275
    headquarters for, 68
    investments in, 5–6, 56–60, 69–70
    IPO of, 155, 291–292, 294–312,
    314–345
    JPMorgan Chase and, 122
    lack of community in, 190–191
    lack of profitability of, 5, 68, 128,
    153–154, 189, 195–198, 222–223,
    275
    launch party for, 45
    layoffs and, 379
    management structure and, 250–254
    marketing and, 188
    Meetup.com and, 183–184
    opening of, 38–40
    as platform, 66
    profit margins of, 67

WeWork (cont'd):
  profitability of, 85
  push to go public, 126–127, 291–292
  R&D kiosk of, 167
  Regus versus, 93–96
  Saudi Arabia's investment and, 177–179
  sexual harassment complaints and, 256–258
  skepticism of, 337–338
  SoftBank deal and, 269–270, 273–274, 282
  SoftBank Group and, 7, 9, 180, 183, 261–262
  Son and, 167–168, 169–170, 171–172, 383–384
  SPACs and, 394
  staff size of, 156
  start of, 32–37
  startup bubble and, 101–102
  Summer Camp for, 4, 7, 74–75, 108, 193, 217–223
  tangential initiatives and, 183–185, 190
  tech staff of, 277–278
  as unicorn, 77
  as Up-C, 292
  valuation of, 7, 8, 60–61, 69, 77–78, 85, 93–94, 125–126, 127, 132, 173, 174, 181–182, 189, 213, 341–342
  vegetarianism of, 221
  wasteful spending of, 275–277
  Wavegarden and, 152–153
  women at, 255–256, 258
WeWork Labs, 64
WeWork Property Investors (WPI), 202–203
White, Vanna, 91
White Panda, 75
Whole Foods, 202
Wiedeman, Reeves, 220

WilmerHale, 155
Winfrey, Oprah, 247
Wintroub, Noah
  background of, 119–120
  Greensill and, 334
  Minson and, 195
  Neumann and, 120–122, 123–124
  post-WeWork status of, 387
  Son and, 332–333
  WeWork IPO and, 213, 300–301, 302–303, 310, 318–319, 340, 346, 347–348
World Economic Forum, 387
World Trade Center site, 205
Wu Tang Clan, 279

Y Combinator, 56
Yahoo, 147
Yahoo BB, 148
Yanai, Tadashi, 157
Yang, Jerry, 147
Yemen, 160
Yerushalmi, Cheni, 22
Yu, Ben, 98

Zainichi, 141
Zar, David, 42, 43
Zenefits, 98
Zhao, John, 131, 132–133, 253
Ziff Davis, 146
Zimmer, John, 241
Zoom, 299
Zuckerberg, Mark, 46, 55, 88, 111, 157, 185, 247, 250
Zuckerman, Mort, 67, 73
Zume Pizza, 209, 385
Zynga, 118

ABOUT THE AUTHORS

ELIOT BROWN covers startups and venture capital for *The Wall Street Journal*. He joined the *Journal* in 2010, covering commercial real estate from New York. He previously worked at *The New York Observer* and is a graduate of Macalester College in St. Paul. He lives in San Francisco.

MAUREEN FARRELL has been a reporter at *The Wall Street Journal* since 2013. She is a graduate of Duke University and the Columbia University Graduate School of Journalism. She lives in Brooklyn with her husband and two daughters.

ABOUT THE TYPE

This book was set in Bembo, a typeface based on an old-style Roman face that was used for Cardinal Pietro Bembo's tract *De Aetna* in 1495. Bembo was cut by Francesco Griffo (1450–1518) in the early sixteenth century for Italian Renaissance printer and publisher Aldus Manutius (1449–1515). The Lanston Monotype Company of Philadelphia brought the well-proportioned letterforms of Bembo to the United States in the 1930s.